Lecture Notes of the Institute for Computer Sciences, Social Informatics and Telecommunications Engineering 153

More information about this series at http://www.springer.com/series/8197

Jing Tian · Jiwu Jing
Mudhakar Srivatsa (Eds.)

International Conference on Security and Privacy in Communication Networks

10th International ICST Conference, SecureComm 2014
Beijing, China, September 24–26, 2014
Revised Selected Papers, Part II

 Springer

Editors
Jing Tian
Institute of Information Engineering, CAS
Beijing
China

Mudhakar Srivatsa
IBM Thomas J. Watson Research Center
New York, NY
USA

Jiwu Jing
Institute of Information Engineering, CAS
Beijing
China

ISSN 1867-8211   ISSN 1867-822X (electronic)
Lecture Notes of the Institute for Computer Sciences, Social Informatics
and Telecommunications Engineering
ISBN 978-3-319-23801-2   ISBN 978-3-319-23802-9 (eBook)
DOI 10.1007/978-3-319-23802-9

Library of Congress Control Number: 2015948720

Springer Cham Heidelberg New York Dordrecht London

Printed on acid-free paper

Springer International Publishing AG Switzerland is part of Springer Science+Business Media
(www.springer.com)

Preface

This volume contains papers presented at the 10th International Conference on Security and Privacy in Communication Networks, held in Beijing, China, during September 24–26, 2014. The conference was organized by the Institute of Information Engineering, Chinese Academy of Sciences, China.

The main track received 98 submissions, and after a doubly anonymous review process, 27 regular papers and 17 short papers of high quality were selected. The book also includes 22 papers accepted for four workshops (ATCS, SSS, SLSS, and DAPRO) in conjunction with the conference, 6 doctoral symposium papers, and 8 posters. We were helped by 42 Program Committee members for the main track. In this respect, special thanks are due to the TPC members for their handling of the challenging, heavy, and rewarding task of selecting the papers to be included in the proceedings.

This volume highlights and addresses several key challenges in the area of security and privacy in networks. The papers have been grouped into the following topics:

- Security and Privacy in Wired, Wireless, Mobile, Hybrid, Sensor, and Ad Hoc Networks;
- Network Intrusion Detection and Prevention, Firewalls, and Packet Filters;
- Malware, Botnets, and Distributed Denial of Service;
- Communication Privacy and Anonymity;
- Network and Internet Forensics Techniques;
- Public Key Infrastructures, Key Management, and Credential Management;
- Secure Routing, Naming/Addressing, and Network Management;
- Security and Privacy in Pervasive and Ubiquitous Computing, e.g., RFIDs;
- Security and Privacy for Emerging Technologies: VoIP, Peer-to-Peer and Overlay Network Systems;
- Security and Isolation in Data Center Networks;
- Security and Isolation in Software Defined Networking.

The audience of this volume may include professors, researchers, graduate students, and professionals in the areas of network security, cryptology, information privacy and assurance, as well as network and Internet forensics techniques. The book also addresses administrators, programmers, IT managers, or just readers who cannot protect themselves if they do not know the protection techniques of network and privacy.

January 2015

Jiwu Jing
Mudhakar Srivatsa

Organization

SecureComm 2014 was organized by the Institute of Information Engineering, Chinese Academy of Sciences, in cooperation with the European Alliance for Innovation (EAI).

General Chair

Jing Tian   Institute of Information Engineering, CAS, China

Program Chairs

Jiwu Jing   Institute of Information Engineering, CAS, China
Mudhakar Srivatsa   IBM T.J. Watson Research Center, USA

Industry Track Chairs

Yafei Wu   State Information Center, China
Tom Quillin   Intel Corporation, USA

Workshops Chair

Debin Gao   Singapore Management University, Singapore

Publicity Chairs

Shaobin Wang   Intel Corporation, USA
Steve Furnell   Plymouth University, UK

Publications Chair

Wen-Tao Zhu   Institute of Information Engineering, CAS, China

Web Chair

Ji Xiang   Institute of Information Engineering, CAS, China

Local Arrangement Committee

Limin Liu (Chair)   Institute of Information Engineering, CAS, China
Yuhan Wang   Institute of Information Engineering, CAS, China
Rui Wang   Institute of Information Engineering, CAS, China
Qiyuan Guo   State Information Center, China

Program Committee Members

John C.S. Lui	The Chinese University of Hong Kong, China
Danfeng Yao	Virginia Tech, USA
Gabriele Oligeri	University of Trento, Italy
Gildas Avoine	UCL, Belgium
Guofei Gu	Texas A&M University, USA
Peter Gutmann	University of Auckland, New Zealand
Heng Yin	Syracuse University, USA
Urs Hengartner	University of Waterloo, Canada
Aldar C.-F. Chan	Institute for Infocomm Research, Singapore
Mengjun Xie	University of Arkansas at Little Rock, USA
Ying Zhang	Ericsson Research, USA
Pierangela Samarati	University of Milan, Italy
Sencun Zhu	Pennsylvania State University, USA
Angelo Spognardi	Institute of Informatics and Telematics, CNR, Italy
Susanne Wetzel	Stevens Institute of Technology, USA
Nino Verde	University of Roma Tre, Italy
Tam Vu	University of Colorado, USA
Xinyuan Wang	George Mason University, USA
Yi Mu	University of Wollongong, Australia
Peter Reiher	University of California, Los Angeles, USA
Georgios Portokalidis	Stevens Institute of Technology, USA
Kui Ren	University of Buffalo, USA
Roberto Di Pietro	University of Roma Tre, Italy
Sankardas Roy	Kansas State University, USA
Giovanni Russello	University of Auckland, New Zealand
Kasper Bonne Rasmussen	University of California at Irvine, USA
Javier Lopez	University of Malaga, Spain
Jean-Pierre Seifert	Telekom Innovation Laboratories, Germany
Kun Bai	IBM T.J. Watson Research Center, USA
Patrick Lee	The Chinese University of Hong Kong, China
Basel Alomair	University of Washington, USA
Christophe Bidan	Supelec, France
David Chadwick	University of Kent, UK
Claudio Soriente	ETH Zürich, Switzerland
Mohamed Ali Kaafar	NICTA, Australia
Ravishankar Borgaonkar	Telekom Innovation Laboratories, Germany
Lei Hu	Institute of Information Engineering, CAS, China
Kapil Singh	IBM T.J. Watson Research Center, USA
Jinpeng Wei	Florida International University, USA
Jingqiang Lin	Institute of Information Engineering, CAS, China
Shengzhi Zhang	Florida Institute of Technology, USA
Wen-Tao Zhu	Institute of Information Engineering, CAS, China

Steering Committee

Peng Liu (Chair)   Pennsylvania State University, USA
Imrich Chlamtac (Co-chair)   Create-Net, Italy
Guofei Gu (Co-chair)   Texas A&M University, USA
Krishna Moorthy Sivalingam   IIT Madras, India

Sponsoring Institutions

Institute of Information Engineering, CAS, China
Data Assurance and Communication Security Research Center, CAS, China
State Key Laboratory of Information Security, China
Chinese Academy of Sciences, China
National Natural Science Foundation of China, China
Information Security Research & Service Institution of State Information Center, China
Baidu Corporation, China

Contents – Part II

**DAPRO 2014 and SSS 2014 International Workshop on Data Protection
in Mobile and Pervasive Computing (DAPRO) International Workshop
on Secure Smart Systems (SSS)**

International Workshop on System Level Security of Smartphones

Contents – Part I

Network Security

Privacy and Wireless Security

System and Software Security

Crypto

Mobile Security

Posters

Web Security

Doctoral Symposium

A Performance Comparison Study of a Coverage-Preserving Node Scheduling Scheme and Its Enhancement in Sensor Networks

Qun Wang[1,2(✉)], Huanyan Qian[1], Peiyu Ji[2], Yu Xie[1], and Shuhui Yang[3]

[1] Nanjing University of Science and Technology, Nanjing 210094, China
hyqian@mail.njust.edu.cn, xieyuwh@163.com
[2] Jiangsu Police Institute, Nanjing 210031, China
{wqun,jipeiyu}@jspi.edu.cn
[3] Purdue University Calumet, Hammond, IN 46323, USA
yang246@purdue.edu

Abstract. In large wireless sensor networks composed of large numbers of low-powered unreliable sensors, one of the most important issues is saving and balancing the energy consumption of sensors to prolong the life time of the network while maintaining the full sensing coverage. In this paper, we analyze an efficient node scheduling scheme which uses the coverage-based off-duty eligibility rule and backoff-based self-scheduling scheme to perform the job. We give some enhancement to this node scheduling scheme, reducing its overhead without losing much of the capability. In simulation, we make the performance comparison from several aspects of the original coverage-based node scheduling scheme and our enhancement version.

Keywords: Coverage · Node scheduling · Sponsored area · Wireless sensor networks

1 Introduction

Recently there is a huge improvement in the affordable and efficient integrated electronic devices, which leads to the advancing of large wireless sensor networks. Sensor networks [1–3] are usually composed of large numbers of randomly deployed stationary sensors. These sensors are designed to perform information collection task. The data collected will finally be gathered and sent to the users via wireless channel. Sensor networks are the basic platform of a broad range of applications related to national security, surveillance, military, health care, and environmental monitoring. In sensor networks, sensing coverage is the area or discrete points of the target field which could be sensed by a predefined number of sensors [4, 5]. In this paper, we will assume the coverage to be only area coverage. A critical issue of the design of sensor networks is the energy consumption problem, which is how to scheduling the sensor nodes to save their scarce power and prolong the life time of the whole network while maintaining the desired degree of sensing coverage which is an important QoS measurement.

© Institute for Computer Sciences, Social Informatics and Telecommunications Engineering 2015
J. Tian et al. (Eds.): SecureComm 2014, Part II, LNICST 153, pp. 3–9, 2015.
DOI: 10.1007/978-3-319-23802-9_1

In most cases, the density of sensor nodes in a sensor network is much higher than needed [6]. This redundancy can be used to prolong the life time of the network. The whole sensing period of the network can be divided into rounds by making the sensors take turns to work. The non-working nodes are put into sleep mode to save energy, thus the network's life time is prolonged. There are many node scheduling schemes (also called density control) in sensor networks. Node scheduling is, concretely, selecting a set of sensor nodes to work in a round and another random set in another round. In each round, the coverage requirement can be guaranteed. PEAS [7, 8], GAF [9], OGDC [10], et al. are all this kind of algorithms.

In this paper, we analyze one of the efficient node scheduling schemes proposed by Tian and Georganas in [11]. This *coverage-preserving node scheduling scheme* (CPNSS) develops a *coverage-based off-duty eligibility rule* (COER) and a backoff-based self-scheduling scheme. The underlying principle of COER is that, for each sensor, if all its working neighbors can cover its own sensing area together, it is eligible to turn off. We give a variation to COER by replacing the neighbors' position information by directional information, which can efficiently reduce the calculation and also commu-nication overhead. For CPNSS's backoff-based scheduling scheme, which aims at avoiding 'blind spot', we propose a corresponding ID-based self-scheduling scheme to reduce the latency. The simulation results show that these variations can help to reduce overhead largely while introducing some redundancy, which can provide more relia-bility in some demanding applications.

The rest of the paper is organized as follows. In Sect. 2, we give a brief summary of the existing related work. In Sect. 3, we introduce and analyze the CPNSS. Section 4 is the performance comparison study of these schemes by simulation. Section 5 is the conclusion remarks and our future work.

2 Related Work

As mentioned above, there exist several node scheduling schemes in sensor networks. In [12], Slijepcevic *et al.* have proved the problem of finding maximal number of covers (each cover is a set of sensor nodes that can work together to ensure the predefined degree of sensing coverage) in a sensor network to be NP completeness. Therefore, all these schemes are approximate algorithms.

Ye *et al.* [7, 8] developed a distributed density control algorithm named PEAS, which is probing based. In PEAS, a sleeping node wakes up and broadcasts a probing message within a certain range at the end of its sleeping period. This node will turn on to work if no reply is received after a timeout. The node will keep working until it depletes its energy. The probing range can be adjusted to achieve different degree of coverage overlap. But PEAS can't guarantee full coverage, the 100 % coverage of the monitored area. Xu *et al.* [9] introduced GAF. This method divides the monitored area into rectan-gular grids, selects a leader in each grid to be the working node. The maximum distance between any pair of working nodes in adjacent grids is within the transmission range of each other. Again, this method cannot ensure full coverage. Recently, Zhang and Hou's work [10] gets more attention. They introduced a distributed, localized density control algorithm named OGDC which could provide full coverage. In the ideal case, when all the nodes have the same sensing range and transmission range, every three closest nodes in a cover can form an equilateral triangle with the side length $\sqrt{3}rs$, where rs is the sensing range. Thus the overlap of sensing areas of all the nodes is minimized. The working nodes can be activated by a starting node which is randomly generated in a progressively spreading way. Simulation results show that OGDC has better performance than other algorithms in both coverage and energy consumption aspects. But this algorithm is complicated, may require much execution power and time.

In [13], Yan *et al.* proposed an adaptable sensing coverage mechanism which could provide differentiated surveillance service. In their protocol, nodes could dynamically decide their own working schedule to provide not only full coverage, but α degree of coverage, α could be smaller or bigger than 1. A monitored point needs the coverage degree to be 2 means that it needs to be covered by two sensors together all the time. It's a protocol that achieves both energy efficiency and differentiated degree of sensing coverage. It aims at providing varied degree of coverage, but their current algorithm cannot guarantee correctness when $\alpha > 2$. Some other researchers have also done some work in this field, such as [14].

3 Coverage-Preserving Node Scheduling Scheme (CPNSS)

In [11], Tian and Georganas proposed a coverage-preserving node scheduling scheme (CPNSS). There are two parts in CPNSS. One is a coverage-based off-duty eligibility rule (COER), which tells a sensor whether it should turn itself off; the other is a backoff-based self-scheduling step, which provides the exact turn off procedure for a sensor node who is eligible to turn off, to avoid 'blind spot'.

3.1 Coverage-Based off-Duty Eligibility Rule (COER)

In CPNSS, each sensor node can independently decide its status to be 'active' or 'sleep' according to the scheme's coverage-based off-duty eligibility rule.

Here we assume the sensing area of a sensor node to be a disk centered at this node with the diameter r, which is this sensor's sensing range. All the sensors have the identical sensing range. The transmission range of a sensor node is also r. Therefore, a neighbor node B to the sensor node A means that they are in each other's sensing range (A's neighbor set can be defined as $N(A) = \{B \mid d(A, B) \le r, A \ne B\}$, $d(A, B)$ is the distance between them). The main objective of the node scheduling is to turn off the redundant nodes. We can figure out that the 'redundant' node is the sensor node whose all sensing area can be covered by other sensor nodes. The redundant node can then be turned off without hurting the whole coverage. Here comes the concept 'sponsored area'. Sponsored area is the sensing area of one sensor node that can be covered by another sensor node. Such as in Fig. 1(a), the shaded area SB $\to$ A is the sponsored area of sensor node B to A (also is SA $\to$ B). In order to simplify the calculation, another related concept 'sponsored sector' is introduced. In Fig. 1(b), the shaded sector area is the sponsored sector $\Phi B \to A$. Since A and B are in each other's sensing disks, the sector area must be smaller than the original crescent sponsor area. Therefore, this simplicity won't reduce coverage.

It is easy to see that if the sponsored area provided by all (or some) of the nodes in A's neighbor set can cover A's sensing disk, A is safe to turn off. We can calculate the union of all A's sponsored sectors. If the union result is 2Π, then A is said to be eligible to turn off (see Fig. 1(c), the area of disk A is equal to $\cup\Phi Bi \rightarrow A$, Bi is nodes in A's neighbor set). After getting the information about neighbor nodes' distance and direction from itself, node A can use $2\arccos(\frac{d(A,B)}{2\times r})$ to calculate each neighbor's sponsored sector. The authors also give the calculation when sensor nodes have different sensing ranges. We won't give further discussion about it in this paper.

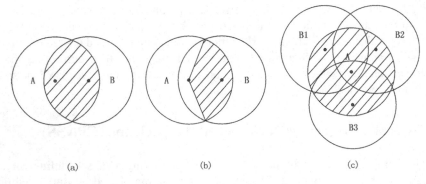

Fig. 1. (a) Sponsored area SB $\rightarrow$ A. (b) Sponsored sector $\Phi B \rightarrow$ A. (c) Node A is eligible to turn off.

3.2   Backoff-Based Self-scheduling Step

The above discussed node scheduling method is localized. Each sensor node broadcasts a *Position Advertisement Message* (PAM) including its ID and position and also receives others' messages to get its neighbor set. Each node then decides its status according to the coverage-based off-duty eligibility rule. It is obvious that a 'blind spot', an area not within any sensor node's sensing range, may occur because two sensor nodes assume each other to cover their overlap area and make decision to turn off at the same time. To avoid 'blind spot', a backoff step is introduced.

The main idea is to insert a random backoff time Td before an eligible node turns itself off. The node should broadcast a *Status Advertisement Message* (SAM) to notify its neighbors that it is off when the time Td expires. If a sensor node receives a SAM during its backoff time, it will recalculate to see whether it is still eligible to turn off without the sponsored area provided by the sender node of the SAM. If not, this sensor node cancels its waiting and decides not to turn off. This scheme may lead to redundant overlap but reduces the possibility of the occurrence of 'blind spot'. If the size of random number selected as backoff time is W, the possibility for two eligible sensor nodes to turn themselves off together is $1/W^2$. Although the possibility may be very small, the 'blind spot' may still exist. To further avoid 'blind spot', another backoff time Tw is introduced. Tw is inserted after Td expires and SAM been sent out. The sensor node will wait another Tw time before really turn itself off. Again, if this node gets some SAMs during the waiting, it recalculates according to the eligibility rule by deleting the senders of SAMs from its neighbor set. Once a node has decided to be on, it won't change its status in this round.

4 Performance Evaluation and Simulation

In this section, we will use simulation to show the performance of the CPNSS and our variation versions to it. In order to simplify the denotation, we will use COER-PO to denote the original coverage-based off-duty eligibility rule using nodes position information, and COER-DI as the new rule using nodes direction information.

4.1 Simulation Environment

We set up the simulation in a 50×50 m^2 network areas. Sensor nodes are randomly distributed in it initially and remain stationary once deployed. To calculate sensing coverage of the whole sensor network, we divide the space into 500×500 unit grids. If the center point of a grid is covered by some sensor node's sensing disk, we assume the whole grid being covered. In the same way, if the required coverage sensing degree is more than 1, say, D, (every point in the target area is supposed to within the sensing area of at least D sensor nodes), then still the center point of each grid is the representative of the whole grid. In the simulation, we will use the middle $(50 - r) \times (50 - r)$ m^2 as the monitored target area to calculate the coverage ratio, in order to ignore the edge effect, for in real case the monitored area will be sufficient larger than the sensor's sensing disk. Since we assume the transmission range of a sensor to be the same with its sensing range r, full coverage of the whole target area implies connectivity of all the sensor nodes. We only need to concentrate on the coverage and energy consumption issues in the simulation.

4.2 Parameters Used and Performance Metrics

In order to evaluate the capability and performance of these schemes, we set several parameters to be tunable in the simulation. They are as follows. (1) The node density. We change the number of deployed nodes (N) from 100 to 1000 to see the effect of node density on the efficiency of the schemes. (2) The sensing range (r). We change the sensing range of the sensor nodes from 6 m to 13 m. (3) Coverage sensing degree (D). Sometimes, more reliability is desired, so D could be more than 1. We vary D's value from 1 to 5 to see the corresponding performance of the schemes.

The performance metrics are: (1) The percentage of coverage, i.e., the ratio of the D degree covered area to the total monitored area. We will use the 500×500 bit map to denote them. (2) The percentage of working sensor nodes to all deployed nodes in one round. Since the fewer working nodes needed, the less energy consumed and the longer the network lives.

4.3   Simulation Results and Comparison

In order to analyze all these schemes' performance, we simulate the following four combinations, COER-PO with backoff-based self-scheduling, COER-PO with ID-based self-scheduling, COER-DI with backoff, and COER-DI with ID. In Fig. 2, we can see that when the required sensing coverage degree is small, all these four algorithms have almost full coverage. With larger D (above 2), the coverage ratio will decrease. The algorithm COER-PO with backoff-based self-scheduling (CPNSS) decreases the fastest and COER-DI with ID the slowest. This is because COER-DI has more coverage redundancy by turning off fewer sensor nodes. ID-based self-scheduling has more redundancy than backoff-based one, but this redundancy increase is less significant than COER-DI to COER-PO.

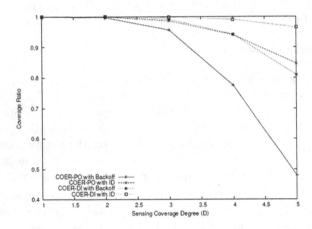

Fig. 2. Coverage ratio with different coverage sensing degree (D) ($r = 10$ m, $N = 500$).

We can see that COER-DI will have more working nodes than COER-PO, but it can reduce the communication overhead and the redundancy is useful when higher sensing coverage degree is required. ID-based self-scheduling scheme will introduce another amount of redundancy compared with backoff-based scheme, but it can save time. Overall, these variation to CPNSS can reduce the overhead by large and without losing too much of performance.

5   Conclusions and Future Work

In this paper, we do some research to one of the efficient node scheduling schemes CPNSS which uses a coverage-based off-duty eligibility rule as well as a backoff-based 'blind spot' avoidance method. In order to reduce overhead, we put forward some enhancement to CPNSS. Instead of position information of sensor nodes, we use directional information, and we remove CPNSS's backoff period to save time. The simulation results show that this variation of CPNSS can provide full coverage, but will introduce more coverage redundancy. Therefore, in some cases where reliability is critical or high coverage sensing degree is demanded, these new schemes are more adaptive. In the future, we will do more research on both improving existing node scheduling schemes and developing new schemes. We can use the two-element tuple (degree, ID), degree is the number of a sensor node's neighbors, to replace the ID in ID-based scheme. This is because the more neighbors a sensor node has, the higher possibility that it can contribute much to the overall coverage if it is turned on. Therefore, we give this node low priority to turn on.

References

1. Akyildiz, I.F., Su, W., Sankarasubramaniam, Y., Cyirci, E.: Wireless sensor networks: a survey. Comput. Netw. **38**, 393–422 (2002)
2. Estrin, D., Govindan, R., Heidemann, J.S., Kumar, S.: Next century challenges: scalable coordination in sensor networks. In: ACM MOBICOM 1999, pp. 263–270 (1999)
3. Kahn, J.M., Katz, R.H., Pister, K.S.J.: Next century challenges: mobile networking for "smart dust". In: ACM MOBICOM 1999, pp. 271–278 (1999)
4. Li, X., Wan, P., Wang, Y., Frieder, O.: Coverage in wireless ad-hoc sensor networks. IEEE Trans. Comput. **52**, 753–763 (2003)
5. Meguerdichian, S., Koushanfar, F., Potkonjak, M., Srivastava, M.B.: Coverage problems in wireless ad-hoc sensor networks. In: INFOCOM 2001, pp. 1380–1387 (2001)
6. Shih, E., Cho, S., Ickes, N., Min, R., Sinha, A., Wang, A., Chandrakasan, A.: Physical layer driven protocol and algorithm design for energy-efficient wireless sensor networks. In: ACM SIGMOBILE, pp. 272–287 (2001)
7. Ye, F., Zhong, G., Lu, S., Zhang, L.: Energy efficient robust sensing coverage in large sensor networks. Technical report, UCLA (2002)
8. Ye, F., Zhong, G., Lu, S., Zhang, L.: Peas: a robust energy conserving protocol for long-lived sensor networks. In: The 23nd International Conference on Distributed Computing Systems (ICDCS), p. 28 (2003)
9. Xu, Y., Heidemann, J., Estrin, D.: Geography-informed energy conservation for ad hoc routing. In: ACM MOBICOM 2001, pp. 70–84 (2001)
10. Zhang, H., Hou, J.C.: Maintaining scheme coverage and connectivity in large sensor networks. Technical report, UIUC (2003)
11. Tian, D., Georganas, N.D.: A coverage-preserving node scheduling scheme for large wireless sensor networks. In: The First ACM International Workshop on Wireless Sensor Networks and Applications, pp. 32–41 (2002)
12. Slijepcevic, S., Potkonjak, M.: Power efficient organization of wireless sensor networks. In: ICC 2001, pp. 472–476 (2001)
13. Yan, T., He, T., Stankovic, J.A.: Differentiated surveillance for sensor networks. In: ACM SenSys 2003, pp. 51–62 (2003)
14. Wang, X., Xing, G., Zhang, Y., Lu, C., Pless, R., Gill, C.: Integrated coverage and connectivity configuration in wireless sensor networks. In: The First International Conference on Embedded Networked Sensor Systems, pp. 28–39. ACM Press (2003)

An Improved Authorization Model in Trust Network

Xianming Gao[1($\boxtimes$)], Xiaozhe Zhang[1], Baosheng Wang[1], and Huiting Shi[2]

[1] School of Computer, National University of Defense Technology, Changsha 410073, China
{gxm9000,xiaozhe,baosheng}@163.com
[2] School of Mechanical Science and Engineering, HUST, Wuhan 430074, China
huiting@163.com

Abstract. Though traditional authorization models can ensure the security of equipment, they don't offer promise both for good quality of service and for strong system robustness. Therefore, this paper presents a semi-distributed authorization model which splits the single decision point into two roles: core-authorization decision point and sub-authorization decision point. In this model, several decision points can provide authorization service for one and the same equipment. The experimental results prove that this model can effectively reduce authorization service time and has some marked advantages on system robustness.

Keywords: Authorization model · Decision point · Centralized/distributed model · Quality of service · System robustness

1 Introduction

At present, the existing mature technologies are usually based on the access control mechanisms provided by third-party to build a safe and reliable network environment [1, 2]. Most access control mechanisms use the centralized authorization models including the sole decision point, to control the access requests from equipment. Unfortunately, the continuous expansion of target network and the increasing amount of equipment, which results in the sharp decrease of quality of service and poor system robustness. Specially, when several equipment concurrently send requests for access, the subsequent requests have to wait to be disposed until the decision point completes the anterior requests, which substantially increases the authorization service time. In order to enhance the quality of service, some research communities proposed the semi-distributed authorization models [3, 4], which have several decision points being only responsible for disposing the access requests in the corresponding area. In the same way, this model can't provide normal authorization service for equipment in some areas, when one or some decision points have a single point of failure.

Therefore, the traditional authorization models cannot meet practical requirements in terms of quality of service and system robustness. So, this paper presents a semi-distributed authorization model, which adopts the hierarchical multi-decision point mode, and spits the decision point of traditional centralized authorization model into one core-authorization decision point and multiple sub-authorization decision points. This model supports for several sub-authorization decision points to dispose the access

© Institute for Computer Sciences, Social Informatics and Telecommunications Engineering 2015
J. Tian et al. (Eds.): SecureComm 2014, Part II, LNICST 153, pp. 10–16, 2015.
DOI: 10.1007/978-3-319-23802-9_2

request of one and the same equipment. So this model still can provide authorization service for equipment, even though some decision points encounter system halted. At last, the experimental results show that authorization service time of proposed model is only 58 % of traditional centralized authorization model when this model deploys five sub-authorization decision points. At the same time, it also can enhance its system robustness by increasing the number of SADPs.

2   Related Works

Many studies have been carried out by industries to ensure the security of equipments. Attempts that solving this problem have resulted in the development of access control mechanism as follows.

For an illustrative purpose, five typical access control mechanisms are presented: Cisco's Network Admission Control (NAC) [5], Microsoft's Network Access Protection (NAP) [6], Juniper's Unified Access Control (UAC) [7], Huawei's Endpoint Admission Defense (EAD) [8], TOPSEC's Trusted Network Architecture (TNA) [9]. We analyze these mechanisms in terms of distributed/centralized, system robustness, authorization service time, and network scale, as shown in Table 1.

Table 1. Comparison of typical access control mechanisms

Technology	Distributed/ centralized	System robustness	Service time	Network scale
NAC	Centralized	Poor	Poor	Medium and small-sized
NAP	Centralized	Poor	Poor	Medium and small-sized
UAC	Centralized	Poor	Poor	Medium and small-sized
EAD	Semi-distributed	Weak good	Weak good	Medium
TNA	Centralized	Poor	Poor	Medium and small-sized

However, these technologies have some lacks in system robustness, quality of service and network scale. Therefore, some research communities propose multiple decision-points model [3, 4], which splits the global authorization strategies into several subsets and issues these subsets to corresponding decision point that only providing authorization service in the defined area.

3   System Overview

The traditional centralized authorization model or semi-distributed authorization model cannot provide normal authorization service, when the failure of network devices or links occurs. Meanwhile, the traditional centralized authorization model also has poor quality of service. Therefore, we propose new authorization model to solve these above problems.

3.1   Design

The decision point in traditional authorization model is a dedicated server, which is equipped to provide authentication service. As illustrated in Fig. 1, our proposed model uses one CADP and multiple SADPs to cooperate the overall functions.

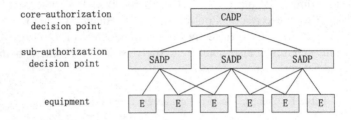

Fig. 1. Proposed authorization model architecture

CADP is the most critical component, which not only provides authorization service, but also is responsible for the planning and distribution of authorization strategies. And SADP only provides authorization service, which can be deployed in network devices rather than in dedicated servers, because SADP is just a special function (or protocol), similar with other routing protocols (such as OSPF, RIP, BGP and so on).

This model splits one decision point into multiple decision points, so how to ensure the consistency of authorization strategies between CADP and SADPs is the primary problem. In startup, CADP stores the global authorization strategies and SADPs don't store any strategy. Only when SADP completes the registration from CADP, CADP will issue the corresponding authorization strategies to this SADP, while CADP sends keeping alive messages to SADPs. If CADP or SADPs can't receive keeping alive messages from others, SADP will clean out authorization strategies, and CADP will cancel the authorization service to make SADP to re-register. On the other hand, the operation of authorization strategies can only be done in CADP, and SADP can get the newest authorization strategies from CADP.

An important feature of this model is that several SADPs can provide authorization service for one and the same equipment, which is the biggest different from other traditional authorization models. Even if an individual SADP has a single of failure, this model is still able to respond to access requests. In this paper, we also define DP trust that refers to the number of decision points providing authorization service for one and the same equipment.

3.2   Data Flow

This authorization service uses client/server authorization mode, which is consistent with traditional authorization system. After SADP completes registration from CADP and obtains authorization strategies, it is able to provide authorization service for network devices. The data flow in this model is as shown in Fig. 2.

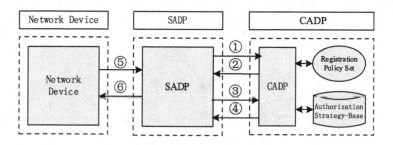

Fig. 2.   Data flow

The processing of authorization service in this model is as follows:

(1) In startup, equipments stay in un-accessed status, and firstly send access requests;
(2) After receiving requests, CADP verifies equipment identity, determines whether to allow this equipment to connect based on its Authorization Strategy-Base. At last, it will return the decision to this equipment.
(3) After the equipment receives response from CADP, it will adopt next action based on this response: if it's positive, the equipment sends registration request to CADP; otherwise, it won't adopt any action.
(4) After receiving the request, CADP verifies equipment identity and decides whether to deploy SADP on this equipment based on Registration Policy Set: If it's positive, CADP will issue corresponding authorization strategies to this equipment; Otherwise, CADP ignores this registration request.
(5) Non-accessed equipment sends access request to the defined SADP.
(6) After receiving request, SADP verifies equipment identity, determines whether to allow this equipment to access to the target network, and returns the decision.

4   Simulation and Analysis

This section validates the superiority of ND-OSDAM based on CERNET topology in terms of authorization service time and system robustness.

4.1   Experimental Environment

In order to verify the real performance, this part uses CERNET topology to set up experimental environment, as shown in Fig. 3. CERNET includes 37 nodes and 46 edges, which further contains 8 core-nodes and 8 backbone edges. Every node (except for core-node) has a three layer of complete ten-ary tree, which make network topology include 3227 nodes and 3236 edges.

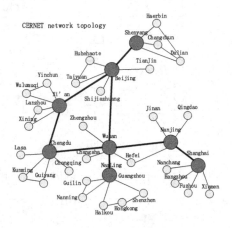

Fig. 3. CERNET topology

Our authorization model, compared with traditional authorization models, can deploy multiple decision points. In order to further analyze the impact of the number of decision point on authorization performance, this paper sets five scenes including different number of SADP, as shown in Table 2. For example, S.2 indicates that two SADPs are deployed respectively in Wuhan and Xi'an.

Table 2. Five scenes

Scene ID	Number of SADP	Location of decision points
S.1	SADP = 1	Wuhan
S.2	SADP = 2	Wuhan, Xi'an
S.3	SADP = 3	Wuhan, Xi'an, Beijing
S.4	SADP = 4	Wuhan, Xi'an, Beijing, Nanjing
S.5	SADP = 5	Wuhan, Xi'an, Beijing, Nanjing, Chengdu

4.2   Authorization Service Time

Authorization service time refers to the time between access request sent by equipment and the equipment having accessed to target network, which is an important indicator to measure the performance of authorization model. To compare the difference between our proposed model and traditional authorization models in terms of authorization service time, this paper uses five scenes in Table 2 to verify that our model has a shorter authorization service time, as shown in Fig. 4.

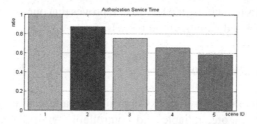

Fig. 4. Authorization service time

Compared with traditional authorization model only having one SADP, our model has a shorter authorization service time. When the number of SADP is two, authorization service time can be reduced by approximate 14 %; when the number is five, authorization service time is only 58 % of traditional authorization model. As the number of SADP increases, authorization service time continually reduces. Thus, our model can greatly reduce the authorization service time, especially, in large-scale network.

4.3 System Robustness

System robustness is an important index to evaluate the feasibility of the authorization system. We adopt the DP trust to measure the system robustness of our model.

Compared with traditional authorization model, our model can support several SADPs to provide authorization service for one and the same equipment, which avoids access requests not to be responded when some SADPs are in invalid. This part calculates the DP trust of every device, as shown in Fig. 5.

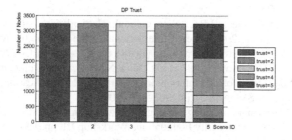

Fig. 5. DP trust

DP trust of each device in traditional centralized authorization model is just one. In our model, DP trust is usually more than one, which is related with the number of SADPs. For example, when it deploys four SADPs, the number of devices is only about 100 of which value of DP trust is one. As the number of SADPs increases, the range of DP trust gradually expands, as well as the value of DP trust continually rises.

DP trust is just one in traditional centralized authorization model. When decision point has a single point of failure, the system cannot provide authorization service for network devices. Even if some SADPs have a single point of failure, our model also offers multiple SADPs to increase the DP trust. It proves that our model has better system robustness than traditional authorization models.

5   Summary and Outlook

Existing mature technologies use access control mechanism to ensure the security of equipment and build a safe, reliable and controllable environment. However, most authorization systems use centralized authorization mode, which does not meet practical requirements in terms of quality of service and system robustness. Thus, this paper presents a new model to solve these problems and to verify the validity of our model.

Acknowledgement. This work is supported by Specialized Research Fund for the Doctoral Program of Higher Education of China (20114307110006) "Research on Technology of Network Quality of Service based on Network Virtualization".

References

1. Liu, A.X., Chen, F., Hwang, J.H., et al.: Designing fast and scalable xacml policy evaluation engines. IEEE Trans. Comput. **60**(12), 1802–1817 (2011)
2. Marouf, S., Shehab, M., Squicciarini, A., et al.: Adaptive reordering and clustering-based framework for efficient XACML policy evaluation. IEEE Trans. Serv. Comput. **4**(4), 300–313 (2011)
3. Kohler, M, Brucker, A.D.: Access control caching strategies: an empirical evaluation. In: Proceedings of the 6th International Workshop on Security Measurements and Metrics, p. 8. ACM (2010)
4. Hilliker, J.: Speculative authorization. In: Second EECE 512 Mini-Conference on Computer Security, p. 9 (2007)
5. Oliveira, L.M.L., Rodrigues, J.J.P.C., Neto, C., et al.: Network admission control solution for 6LoWPAN networks. In: 2013 Seventh International Conference on Innovative Mobile and Internet Services in Ubiquitous Computing (IMIS), pp. 472–477. IEEE (2013)
6. Arkko, J., Eronen, P., Tschofenig, H., et al.: Quick NAP-secure and efficient network access protocol. In: Proceedings of 6th International Workshop on Applications and Services in Wireless Networks (ASWN 2006), pp. 163–170 (2006)
7. La Padula, L.J.: Formal modeling in a generalized framework for access control. In: Proceedings of Computer Security Foundations Workshop III, pp. 100–109. IEEE (1990)
8. Yuyang, Z., Linxian, Z.: The feasibility of endpoint admission defense in the reconstruction of network security. J. Lishui Univ. **2**, 018 (2007)
9. Huangguo, Z., Lu, C., Liqiang, L.: Research on trusted network connection. Chin. J. Comput. **33**(1), 706–717 (2010)
10. CERNET topology: http://www.edu.cn/20010101/21585.shtml

KEMF: Key Management for Federated Sensor Networks

Piers O'Hanlon[1]([✉]), Joss Wright[1], Ian Brown[1], and Tulio de Souza[2]

[1] Oxford Internet Institute, University of Oxford, Oxford, UK
{piers.ohanlon,joss.wright,ian.brown}@oii.ox.ac.uk
[2] Department of Computer Science, University of Oxford, Oxford, UK
tulio.de.Souza@cs.ox.ac.uk

Abstract. We present a lightweight key management protocol that provides secured device registration and communication in federated sensor networks. The protocol is designed for zero configuration and use in small packet low power wireless networks; protocol messages may fit into single packets. We use the Casper security protocol analyser to examine the behaviour and security properties of the protocol model. Within the assumptions of the model, we demonstrate forward secrecy, security against man-in-the-middle attacks, and local network key protection, comparing favourably with related protocols. Our experimental analysis shows that the protocol may feasibly be deployed on current sensor platforms with 256-bit elliptic curve cryptography.

Keywords: Privacy · Security · Sensor networks · Key management · IoT

1 Introduction

There are countless uses for devices that form the fabric of the Internet of Things (IoT) and sensor networks. Wireless sensor networks occur with varying degrees of complexity, the simplest wireless sensor networks have tended to be standalone systems running a single application that defines both the constituent nodes and all other aspects of the network. Increasingly, however, wireless sensor networks are being deployed in a multi-application structure comprising nodes running a common middleware that allows one or more applications to run on the same infrastructure operated by a single provider. The use of middleware, such as Senshare [6], offers a flexible abstraction of the low-level characteristics of the hardware, allowing data from each node to serve a number of applications.

The sharing model can be extended further by allowing *federation* of the infrastructure. A federated network is composed from many devices, which may be sourced from a number of different providers, and allows different entities to deploy nodes into the network and potentially run multiple applications across a common middleware. Federated sensor networking provides an economic benefit, and can lead to longer-term deployments offering a range of sensing options, but also raises privacy concerns for those individuals in the sensing environment [4].

© Institute for Computer Sciences, Social Informatics and Telecommunications Engineering 2015
J. Tian et al. (Eds.): SecureComm 2014, Part II, LNICST 153, pp. 17–24, 2015.
DOI: 10.1007/978-3-319-23802-9_3

We propose a novel protocol, KEMF, for secured device registration and key management for federated sensor and IoT networks. The protocol allows a newly connected device to automatically and securely obtain a network access key from the local gateway to enable secure and private communication. This is facilitated by a pre-arranged agreement between the entity which hosts the gateway and the organisation that provides the devices. However, KEMF does not require the exchange of any device specific secrets before the node enters the network.

We utilise the Casper [8] security protocol analyser to model its behaviour and examine its security properties. We also model another related protocol to provide for a comparison, and to highlight the benefits provided by KEMF.

2   Related Work

Whilst the core security primitives utilised by sensor and IoT networks are drawn from existing techniques and protocols, there are still new mechanisms required. There is a large body of research work in this field [2, 12], though less of it has an emphasis on federated operation. Despite all the research work, the Internet Engineering Task Force (IETF) is has only recently formed the new ACE working group to tackle security issues in IoT and sensor networks.

There are many sensor systems, though there are less that aim to support federated operation with multi-application and multi-party ownership capabilities. One such system is SenShare [6], which is a platform that attempts to address the technical challenges in transforming sensor networks into open access infrastructures capable of supporting multiple applications.

The origins of modern day authentication and key management go back to the late 1970s when the Needham-Schroeder protocol was invented. In 1995 Gavin Lowe developed his advanced security analysis techniques based on Hoare's Communicating Sequential Processes (CSP) [3] and its model checker Failures Divergences Refinement (FDR2) [11], finding an attack [7] on the Needham-Schroeder protocol, and proposing the fixed Needham-Schroeder-Lowe protocol.

There have been many key management schemes developed for use with existing sensor networks [2, 12], but few that aim to tackle the area of federated deployments [5, 10]. MASY [10] is one of the few schemes that is aimed at federated network deployments, but it has its problems as we show in Sect. 4.

3   KEMF Security Protocol

The protocol provides for secure delivery of a network access key, from a local access control gateway, on to a new smart device in a federated network. It is assumed that the device has been distributed with a unique pre-installed asymmetric key, imprinted by its provider. This key is used only to provide for a secured request of its appropriate network access key. The delivery of the actual network access key is secured using a separate locally generated symmetric key. Whilst the protocol does involve communication with the device's provider server

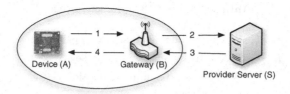

Fig. 1. System Actors and protocol steps

the local network key is not shared with the provider thus not compromising the privacy and security of the local network and allaying pervasive monitoring.

We employ asymmetric cryptography in an atypical fashion by requiring both halves of the keypair to be kept secret, rather than one key being made public and the other kept private. This approach allows the protocol to provide for improved security properties, and in particular forward secrecy. As the public key allows only for encryption of messages, subsequent compromise of the public key by an intruder does not allow compromise of previously sent messages. This approach therefore provides an improvement over the use of a single symmetric key, which could potentially lead to decryption of any previous or future messages. It should also be noted that, whilst we propose that both keys are kept secret, they are still used in the conventional manner whereby the 'public' key is used for encryption and the 'private' key is used for decryption.

Typically sensor and IoT devices are low power and minimally resourced entities. Thus for normal communications it is only feasible to use symmetric encryption, such as the Advanced Encryption Standard (AES). Whilst most modern devices are capable of performing the more onerous computation required for conventional asymmetric cryptography, they can be prohibitively slow even for basic operations. However Elliptic Curve Cryptography (ECC) which was developed by Koblitz and Miller, provides for asymmetric keys with significantly reduced computational requirements, and smaller key sizes. Specifically we employ the Elliptic Curve Integrated Encryption Scheme (ECIES).

We now introduce the details of the KEMF protocol. The three actors in the protocol and their interactions are outlined in Fig. 1, with the key terms defined in Table 1. We begin by defining the roles of the three actors:

Device(A): The sensor device to be registered on, and securely connected to, the network with its imprinted secret asymmetric 'public' key $K^{+}_{S(A)}$.

Gateway(B): The local gateway which provides for local key distribution and liaison with the provider server.

Provider Server(S): The cloud-based server that provides for authentication and authorised use of its devices on registered networks.

Device(A) is imprinted with its secret asymmetric public key, $K^{+}_{S(A)}$, by the provider allowing it to securely communicate with the provider server(S), which shares the corresponding asymmetric private key $K^{-}_{S(A)}$. The protocol

Table 1. KEMF Protocol key terms

$K_{S(A)}^{+}$	S(A)'s 'public' asymmetric imprinted key
$K_{S(A)}^{-}$	S(A)'s 'private' asymmetric key
k_A	A's generated symmetric session key
k_{BS}	Symmetric key agreed between B and S
k_A^{net}	A's local network access symmetric key

Table 2. KEMF Protocol steps and message sizes (in Bytes)

Step	Message	Size
1.	$A \rightarrow B : S, \{A, k_A\}_{K_{S(A)}^{+}}$	48 B
2.	$B \rightarrow S : \{A, \{A, k_A\}_{K_{S(A)}^{+}}\}_{k_{BS}}$	48 B
3.	$S \rightarrow B : \{A, B, k_A, K_{S(A)}^{-}\}_{k_{BS}}$	64 B
4	$B \rightarrow A : \{A, B, k_A^{net}\}_{k_A}$	32 B

assumes that a preconfigured trust relationship exists where the provider server has securely agreed, over a conventional secure channel (e.g. D/TLS), a session key, k_{BS}, with the gateway(B).

The steps of the protocol are outlined in Table 2, which we detail here:

1. The device(A) is switched on within range of a trusted gateway(B). At this stage B's address is unknown to A so it broadcasts out the initial registration message. The registration message is encrypted with A's public key, $K_{S(A)}^{+}$, and contains A's identifier (e.g. EUI-64 address), and its dynamically generated symmetric key k_A.
2. The gateway(B) receives the registration message, and after verifying that it has a pre-established relationship with provider server(S), it forwards the message to S using their agreed symmetric session key k_{BS}.
3. The provider server(S) receives the registration request and after verifying that device(A) belongs to gateway(B) it then decrypts the message and sends A's private key, $K_{S(A)}^{-}$, and generated symmetric key, k_A, to B using k_{BS}.
4. Once gateway(B) receives the message from provider server(S) it encrypts device(A)'s local network access key, k_A^{net}, using A's symmetric key, k_A. In this way B has the option to provide a separate network key to each device.

The protocol may also be broken down into two phases. Firstly the *registration* phase, which involves steps 1–3, only needs to occur once for each device after which B has obtained A's private key, $K_{S(A)}^{-}$, which then allows it to verify subsequent messages from A. Secondly there is the *(re)keying* phase which, after the registration phase has completed, only requires steps 1 and 4, thus freeing the provider server of further work, providing for reduced latency operation, and allowing autonomy for the local gateway to manage keys. To protect against replay attacks in the rekeying phase the device retains all previous keys (k_A^{net}) so to avoid replays of step 4 containing old, potentially compromised, keys. The number of keys retained may be controlled by having the devices periodically utilise step 1 with a new k_A. We have kept the device message sizes within the limits of common low power wireless protocols such as IEEE 802.15.4, without making any compromises on addressing or key sizes. Typically the maximum payload size is around 90 bytes and if one utilises UDP over 6LowPAN then this can go down to 50–60 bytes.

4 Security Analysis

We take a theoretical approach to analysing KEMF by representing the protocol in a security protocol analyser to examine it for potential weaknesses and attacks. Our threat model, which is standard for wireless systems such as IoT and sensor networks, is largely similar to the commonly assumed Dolev-Yao model [1], where the attacker is assumed to have complete control over the communications channel, and may attempt to read any message, remove and change existing messages, or inject new messages. Although not strictly within the Dolev-Yao model we consider some situations with end system compromise.

We assume that the local gateway and provider server are trusted, whilst the sensor devices are potentially susceptible to compromise. Furthermore both the gateway and provider server trust one another, though the provider server has ultimate trust. The trust relationship between the server and gateway means that the server will only provide services for a predefined range of devices, thus limiting damage in the case of gateway compromise. The main threat to the system is for an intruder to obtain A's secret public key, $K_{S(A)}^+$ as the sensor nodes are typically more vulnerable as they are harder to physically secure.

We modelled KEMF using Gavin Lowe's Casper (Compiler for the Analysis of Security Protocols) [8]. Casper is implemented in Haskell and employs the process algebra CSP [3], in conjunction with its model checker FDR2 [11]. Lowe originally utilised CSP and FDR2 to develop a novel method for analysing security protocols, which proved to be remarkably successful in finding attacks upon a number of well known protocols [7,9]. Casper may be used not only model each actor in the protocol but to also explicitly model a malicious agent or *intruder*.

We firstly model the attacker without any knowledge of the device keys and Casper does not find any attacks on KEMF. Secondly we see that the protocol resists some attacks when A's public key, $K_{S(A)}^+$, is compromised. The KEMF protocol can resist a passive attack as an intruder cannot read the contents of the messages from A due to the use of asymmetric cryptography, nor can he read the messages from B due to the protection by A's session key, k_A. This compares well against MASY [10] which cannot resist these attacks.

However an active intruder that has effectively taken control of device(A) and obtained its public key, $K_{S(A)}^+$, may pose as A and obtain A's key to the network. Provided the attack does not occur before a non-compromised registration phase, an intruder node cannot maliciously inject a new key to be used by that or any other node. Furthermore due to the fact that A's public key, $K^+_{S(A)}$ protects the transport of its internally generated key, k_A, any later compromise of $K^+_{S(A)}$ does not allow an intruder to decrypt any previous messages thus affording the node forward secrecy. Once such a key compromise has been detected it can be excluded from the network without affecting the future security of other devices on the network. Finally when both the device's private and public keys are compromised then the system is open to a number of attacks.

We also modelled MASY in Casper to understand its behaviour both with and without key compromise. The MASY protocol utilises an approach where the device is imprinted, by a 'company', with its IP address and symmetric key to provide for secured registration and enrollment on a network. Whilst the MASY provides for a key management solution it suffers from a number of problems. The compromise of the company symmetric key, from such a device, would lead to a general failure of the protocol as an intruder entity could both inject and read any messages from the past or future.

In summary, the KEMF protocol has the following security properties:

Forward Secrecy: The protocol provides for partial forward secrecy of the messages exchanged between the device and the gateway, which holds if either the 'public' asymmetric key, or one of A's existing session keys, is compromised. This is due to the protection of A's session key, k_A, by its public key, $K^+_{S(A)}$, and the use of a suitable KDF for A's session key. However if A's private asymmetric key, $K^-_{S(A)}$, is compromised then forward secrecy fails.

MitM Prevention: A Man in the Middle attack, between A and B, is prevented as the communication from A, via B, to S (or directly to B in a rekeying phase) is encrypted using A's imprinted asymmetric public key, $K^+_{S(A)}$, and communication from B to A is encrypted using A's session key k_A.

Local Network Key Protection: The local network access symmetric key, k^{net}_A, sent from B to A, is protected by A's session key k_A, which in turn is encrypted using A's public asymmetric key $K^+_{S(A)}$.

Replay Attack Protection: With no key compromises there is protection against replay attacks as an adversary cannot maliciously reuse subsections of the protocol due to the retention and non-reuse of old k_A's by A.

5   Experimental Analysis

We analysed the KEMF protocol on an embedded sensor node platform, the iMote2 from MEMSIC Inc, which runs linux-2.6 on a 419 MHz ARMv5. For ECIES, which is a hybrid elliptic curve asymmetric key algorithm, we utilised an implementation, based upon the OpenSSL library, of the SECG standard, using the 'secp256k1' elliptic curve in combination with 128-bit AES in cipher-block chain (CBC) mode, and the SHA512 hash function. The initial message (1), from Table 2, is 48 bytes long, which consists of a 32 byte encrypted payload plus the 16 bytes server ID. With this configuration the iMote2 encrypted the 32 byte payload in an average of 41.5 ms, which means that the protocol is quite feasible on such a platform. The final message (4) sent to the device, to be decrypted by the iMote2, consists of an encrypted payload of the node ID (8 bytes), the gateway ID (8 bytes), and the node's network key (16 bytes). The 32 byte payload is decrypted using the 128-bit AES key, which is far quicker than the ECIES encrypted initiation message, taking an average of 3.9 μs.

Our implementation analysis shows that the protocol is feasible on current sensor platforms using asymmetric ECC based cryptography. The messages sent between the gateway and provider server are also small but are of less concern as they often use link layer technologies with larger MTUs.

6   Conclusions

We have detailed and evaluated KEMF a new device registration and key management protocol for federated networks that provides for low overhead operation. We have utilised the Casper security protocol analyser to show KEMF to be secure within our threat model. It provides for forward secrecy, even if the device's public key is compromised, protection against man in the middle attacks, and local network key security and privacy. It provides for better protection against key compromise than MASY, another similar protocol.

Our experimental analysis has shown that the protocol may feasibly be deployed on a current sensor platform, providing for good performance when using asymmetric elliptic curve cryptography. We also show that the protocol is suited for use in LowPANs where message sizes are very limited.

Acknowledgments. We would like to acknowledge funding from the EPSRC for the FRESNEL (EP/G070687/1), and Being There (EP/L00416X/1) projects.

References

1. Dolev, D., Yao, A.C.: On the security of public key protocols. IEEE Trans. Inf. Theory **29**(2), 198–208 (1983)
2. Simplicio, M.A., Barreto, P.S.L.M., Margi, C.B., Carvalho, T.M.B.: A survey on key management mechanisms for distributed wireless sensor networks. Comput. Netw. **54**(15), 2591–2612 (2010)
3. Hoare, C.: Communicating Sequential Processes. Prentice-Hall, Upper Saddle River (1985)
4. Huygens, C., Joosen, W.: Federated and shared use of sensor networks through security middleware. In: ITNG, pp. 1005–1011 (2009)
5. Khan, S.U., Lavagno, L., Pastrone, C., Spirito, M.: An effective key management scheme for mobile heterogeneous sensor networks. In: i-Society (2011)
6. Leontiadis, I., Efstratiou, C., Mascolo, C., Crowcroft, J.: SenShare: transforming sensor networks into multi-application sensing infrastructures. In: Picco, G.P., Heinzelman, W. (eds.) EWSN 2012. LNCS, vol. 7158, pp. 65–81. Springer, Heidelberg (2012)

7. Lowe, G.: Breaking and fixing the Needham-Schroeder public-key protocol using FDR. In: Margaria, T., Steffen, B. (eds.) TACAS 1996. LNCS, vol. 1055, pp. 147–166. Springer, Heidelberg (1996)
8. Lowe, G.: Casper: a compiler for the analysis of security protocols. In: Computer Security Foundations Workshop, pp. 18–30 (1997)
9. Lowe, G., Roscoe, A.W.: Using CSP to detect errors in the TMN protocol. IEEE Trans. Softw. Eng. **23**, 659–669 (1997)
10. Maerien, J., Michiels, S., Huygens, C., Joosen, W.: MASY: MAnagement of Secret keYs for federated mobile wireless sensor networks. In: IEEE WiMob (2010)
11. Roscoe, A.W.: Model-checking CSP, Chap. 21. Prentice-Hall, Englewood Cliffs (1994)
12. Xiao, Y., Rayi, V.K., et al.: A survey of key management schemes in wireless sensor networks. Comput. Comm. **30**, 2314–2341 (2007)

CPS²: A Contextual Privacy Framework for Social Software

Rula Sayaf[1]([✉]), Dave Clarke[1,2], and Richard Harper[3]

[1] Department of Computer Sciences, IMinds-DistriNet, KU Leuven, Leuven, Belgium
rula.sayaf@cs.kuleuven.be
[2] Department of Computer Sciences, Uppsala University, Uppsala, Sweden
dave.clarke@it.uu.se
[3] Microsoft Research, Cambridge, UK
r.harper@microsoft.com

Abstract. Social software has become one of the most prominent means for communication. Context is essential for managing privacy and guiding communication. In social software, context can be ambiguous due to the overload of data and the mix of various audiences. Such ambiguity may result in privacy issues.

To overcome context and privacy issues, we propose CPS², a conceptual framework for contextual privacy management. The frameworks is based on an analysis of the role of context in communication and privacy management. The analysis identifies the interpretation of data as a key ingredient for privacy management. We present CPS² and how the preservation of interpretation within any context facilitates preserving contextual privacy. We discuss how CPS² can be technically realised, and how it can address context issues and offers fine-granular context control.

Keywords: Context · Privacy · Social software · Data interpretation · Communication · Contextual privacy

1 Introduction

Communication through social software is becoming one of the most prominent ways of daily communication. Social software is an application for the exchange of various types of data to communicate with a large number of users. Such communication is simple as it can be achieved by disclosing data to other users. This simplicity can be associated with privacy issues. Issues specifically occur when data is accessed by an inappropriate audience or put in inappropriate contexts [1]. To mitigate such issues, users should have means to control context to ensure appropriateness and preserve their privacy.

Context is essential for both communication and privacy management [2,3]. Context is the information that characterises situations. Context facilitates the interpretation of data [4]. In communication, context facilitates clarifying and

© Institute for Computer Sciences, Social Informatics and Telecommunications Engineering 2015
J. Tian et al. (Eds.): SecureComm 2014, Part II, LNICST 153, pp. 25–32, 2015.
DOI: 10.1007/978-3-319-23802-9_4

delivering the communicated message [2]. Through communication, the inter-locutors express their identity through the data they disclose. Managing one's identity is the core aspect of privacy as informational self-determination [3,5]. By controlling context, privacy can be managed to manage one's identity. When context is unclear and ambiguous, communication can be disrupted affecting one's identity expression and privacy. Context ambiguity can be seen in social software. Ambiguity is caused by the mixing of different audiences and data from different contexts. As a result, privacy and communication can be affected.

Managing privacy through controlling context is a complex task. Controlling context requires reasoning about the current context and how it may change [6]. Such reasoning is challenging due to the high-dimensionality of context para-meters [4]. Current context-based privacy management approaches address such complexity by simplifying context representation resulting in a limited control over context [7]. To understand the insufficiency of context-based management consider the following scenario that is based on a reported incident of 'prostitutes of Antwerpen' [8]:

Scenario 1. Els is a fashion model, and she posts her photo in a swimming suit on Facebook and makes it public. Els experiences a privacy issue when her photo is disseminated in the context of 'prostitutes of Antwerpen' page, which affects her job applications. In contrast, Els does not face any issue when her photo is disseminated in 'jobs for top models' context.

Current privacy management approaches do not offer sufficient context con-trol to mitigate the violations mentioned in the scenario. Most approaches do not offer the possibility to allow appropriate disseminations and prohibit the inap-propriate ones. They can only either allow all disseminations or prohibit them. In this paper, we address such context control issues by proposing a conceptual framework for contextual privacy management. We analyse the context-privacy relation and argue that the interpretation of data is a key ingredient in con-textual privacy management. We demonstrate that by ensuring the integrity of interpretation, contextual privacy can be managed. The framework is a con-ceptual approach to manage privacy in context without burdening users with reasoning about context and its complexities. The contributions of this paper are the following:

1. Analysing the problems of controlling data and managing privacy in a context-based manner (Sect. 2)
2. Analysing the role of context in privacy management and communication (Sect. 3)
3. Proposing a conceptual framework for Contextual Privacy for Social Software (CPS^2), and presenting how this framework can be technically realised and can address context and privacy issues (Sect. 4).

2　Problem Statement

Communicating while preserving privacy in any context requires a fine-grained control of context [7]. In social software, context identifies situations where various types of data are disclosed and users interact. Context ambiguity is one of the main issues in social software communication. Ambiguity means that it is challenging to accurately identify the current context. Ambiguity obstructs the clarification of the communicative message, and user's assessment of privacy.

Privacy management can be challenging due to context management problems. Privacy is viewed as the means to control the contexts in which data is put [9,10]. According to this view, contextual privacy management requires two types of control: control over the *original* context in which the data was originally disclosed through the software, and control over dissemination contexts by specifying appropriate or inappropriate contexts in which data can be put or not, respectively. Practicing these two types of control is complicated. A user can control the original context by choosing where to disclose data and to whom. However, over time, the original context might change [6] into an inappropriate context. In order to avoid such situations, users should constantly monitor changes. Often, users do not invest much time in managing and monitoring online communication contexts [11], and it is particularly challenging when context is ambiguous. Having control over any dissemination context requires listing possible appropriate or/and inappropriate contexts, depending on the assumed closed- or open-world of contexts. Given the 'theoretically infinite complexity' of social situations, and the infinite set of possible contexts [12,13], it may be infeasible to list all possible contexts [14]. Context issues are often insufficiently addressed by simplistic context representations in privacy management approaches. Such approaches offer limited context control [7] that is insufficient to satisfy privacy and communication requirements in social software.

3   Analysis of Context and Privacy

Context is the information construct that characterises the communication situation [4]. Context is a container of data; it facilitates the inference of the relevant meaning of the communicative message [4]. A data item can have a set of different possible meanings or interpretations, and by identifying the context it is put within, the relevant interpretation can be inferred. An example is the context of the page in which Els's photo is put in Scenario 1. That this context is related to 'prostitutes' can be inferred by the information about the type of page, content, creator, and other meta data. When Els's photo is put in this context, the most relevant meaning of the photo is a 'prostitute_photo'.

In online communication, privacy management can be a means of identity management [5]. The data owner[1] discloses a data item to communicate about it with the selected audience. Through communication, the owner expresses a specific identity and manages it by specifying who the audience are and what data they could access in a specific context [15]. To make the privacy decision of to whom disclose an item, the owner estimates how others would perceive and interpret this item [5]. Thus, the interpretation of data and context are of central roles in the process of privacy management.

---

[1] We do not imply the legal ownership.

The importance of context and the interpretation of data can be mainly observed in two communication types: cooperative and adversarial. These types are the extreme ends of the communication spectrum, and are characterised by variant degrees of trust, context involvement, and privacy concerns [16]. In *cooperative communication*, the interlocutors trust each other [17] and act jointly to understand and interpret the communicated message. Cooperative communication can be achieved by following the Gricean maxims, which concern providing a sufficient amount of information that is true, relevant, and unambiguous to make context explicit [18]. Gricean maxims facilitate clarifying the context to make possible interpreting the communicated message. However, in ambiguous contexts, it is challenging to abide by those maxims. In contrast, in an *adversarial communication*, at least one of the interlocutors—the adversary—can violate Grecian maxims to mislead others into misinterpreting the message and disrupt the communication. Adversarial communication is associated with low trust and high privacy concerns [16]. In both communication types, context ambiguity hinders the correct interpretation of data affecting the identity expression and privacy of the interlocutors.

Based on the above-mentioned argument, we define contextual privacy management as the process of managing data disclosure or dissemination while maintaining the appropriate interpretation of this data, in order to manage the one's desired identity in a specific context. To achieve that, context clarity is essential. However, clarity of context requires an effort to make communication cooperative and avoid adversarial communication. To facilitate contextual privacy management and avoid overloading users with context complexities, we propose CPS^2 in the following section.

4 CPS^2: Contextual Privacy for Social Software

The main idea of CPS^2 is to facilitate communication with an increased level of privacy without burdening users with context management. We propose CPS^2 to manage contextual privacy by maintaining the appropriateness of the interpretation of data. CPS^2 avoids simplifying the representation of context or imposing reasoning about context on users to specify privacy management policies. Given the technological advances in context inference [19] and automatic data interpretation [20], CPS^2 does not requires users to reason about context, rather, it requires owners to only specify the appropriate interpretation of their data. The framework is responsible for guarding the appropriate interpretation upon any change of context or dissemination, as explained in the following.

To understand the principle of CPS^2 consider Scenario 1: Els's profession as a fashion model is indicated on her page, thus, the context of her profile page indicates that the 'fashion-related' interpretation is the most relevant interpretation. Upon viewing the photo, the audience would highly likely perceive the interpretation of the photo as such. When the photo is put in the 'prostitutes' context, the relevance of the 'fashion-related' interpretation is low and the relevance of the 'prostitute' interpretation is high, which affects Els's identity.

With CPS², Els can specify the set of appropriate interpretations of the photo as {fashion_show, swim_suits_show, pretty_model}. Accordingly, the dissemination into the 'prostitutes' context should be prohibited because it results in an interpretation that is not in the set Els has specified, while the dissemination into the 'jobs for top models' context should be allowed.

4.1 Realisation of CPS²

The realisation of CPS² implies a system with three main functions: context inference, interpretation inference, and contextual privacy management. CPS² assumes the existence of an underlying context inference and interpretation inference layers that need not be managed by users, but by the social software provider, for instance. The realisation would comprise the following layers:

1. Context inference layer: responsible for inferring or labelling the context of the current situation within the social software realm. The input to this layer is the social software data: users and their attributes, data items, relations, ads, and the structure of its pages and modules. When data is added to a situation, this layer adapts and infers the new context.
2. Interpretation inference layer: responsible for inferring the interpretation of data based on the context inferred by the previous layer. The data can be interpreted whether it is textual or visual.
3. CPS² control layer: responsible for facilitating contextual privacy management by means of two possible approaches: access control or accountability and auditing approach. The access control approach comprises a policy language to express the contextual privacy policies and an enforcement mechanism. A policy can be formulated to express the appropriate interpretations of a data item. Upon performing an action—resulting in adding or removing data from a context—the control layer consults the policies of data items in the current context and verifies the appropriateness of the interpretation inferred by the previous layer. The action is executed if no interpretation is inappropriate.

In the accountability and auditing approach, users need not specify policies. Rather, upon a context change, the framework marks the actions that cause a change of the interpretation. The data owner can verify the appropriateness of a new interpretation. If the new interpretation is inappropriate, proper actions can be executed against the responsible entity.

4.2 Addressing Issues of Context and Privacy

CPS² could potentially address the problems mentioned in Sect. 2, as follows:

1. Context ambiguity: the framework addresses this problem not by making the context less ambiguous to users, rather, even when context is ambiguous to some users, the context inference layer could still identify context given all the data in the software. Accordingly, only appropriate actions are allowed.

2. Context simplistic representation: by shifting the burden of reasoning about context to the underlying framework, it is not needed to simplify the representation of context.
3. Control over the original context: by facilitating the management of interpretation, owners can indirectly control context to a relatively high degree without having to monitor the changes of context.
4. Control over any context: the previous argument is valid here. The framework facilitates effortless control over any context by continuously monitoring and maintaining the appropriateness of the interpretation in any context.

Moreover, CPS^2 enhances communication to become cooperative even if context is ambiguous, by allowing only appropriate actions that may not affect the interpretation of data. It also facilitates avoiding adversarial communication by preserving data interpretation. CPS^2 facilitates control over data flow in both private or public spaces.

5   Related Work

Many works have incorporated context in privacy management. On the conceptual level, Nissenbaum proposes contextual integrity [21] for privacy management. She presents a list of norms: contexts, actors, attributes, and transmission principles, that must be managed to preserve privacy. Our framework differs from this theory by not requiring an exhaustive specification of the possible contexts or the other ingredients of the theory. The complexity of contextual integrity results in models that adopt simplistic context representation to overcome the complexity. An example is the formal model of Barth *et al.* [22] where context is represented by roles of users.

Another contextual privacy management work is Fong's access control model. In his work, relationships are viewed as contexts [23]. In contrast to CPS^2, Fong's model offers control over the original context but not over dissemination contexts. Generally, the simplification of such models reduces the granularity offered by context and fails in addressing the problems discussed in Sect. 2.

6   Conclusion and Future Work

In CPS^2, we propose maintaining data interpretation to manage contextual privacy and address the complexity of controlling context. The framework facilitates simple management of privacy without reducing the richness context management offers. CPS^2 enhances communication in which interpretation is essential. In other work, we have conducted experiments related to context inference, and we will report them elsewhere. Our future work aims at providing a design to validate the framework and investigate the proper realisation of the framework.

Acknowledgment. This research has been funded by the IWT in the context of the SBO project on Security and Privacy for Online Social Networks (SPION). Thanks are due to Natasa Milic-Frayling and Sören Preibusch at Microsoft Research Cambridge.

References

1. Goldie, J.: Virtual communities and the social dimension of privacy. University of Ottawa Law & Technology Journal **3**(1), 133–167 (2003)
2. Clark, H., Carlson, T.: Context for comprehension. In: Long, J., Baddeley, A. (eds.) pp. 313–330. Lawrence Erlbaum Associates, Inc, Hillsdale (1981)
3. Gürses, S.: Multilateral privacy requirements analysis in online social network services. Ph.D. thesis (2010)
4. Van Dijk, T.A.: Discourse and context. A Sociocognitive Approach. Cambridge University, Cambridge (2008)
5. Palen, L., Dourish, P.: Unpacking "privacy" for a networked world. In: Proceedings of the SIGCHI Conference on Human Factors in Computing Systems pp. 129–136. ACM (2003)
6. Mcculloh, I.: Detecting changes in a dynamic social network. Ph.D. thesis, Carnegie Mellon University (2009)
7. Sayaf, R., Clarke, D.: Access control models for online social networks. Social Network Engineering for Secure Web Data and Services, 32–65 (2012)
8. De Wolf, R.: Over 'spotted', 'hoeren' en 'failed'-pagina's. Electronic article (2013). http://www.knack.be/nieuws/belgie/dader-antwerpse-hoeren-foto-geklist/article-4000230766578.htm, Last checked February 2013
9. Westin, A.: Privacy and Freedom. Atheneum, New York (1970)
10. Petronio, S.: Boundaries of privacy: Dialectics of disclosure. SUNY Press, Albany (2002)
11. Lipford, H.R., Besmer, A., Watson, J.: Understanding privacy settings in facebook with an audience view. In: Proceedings of the 1st Conference on Usability, Psychology, and Security, Berkeley, CA, USA, pp. 2:1 2:8. USENIX Association (2008)
12. Van Dijk, T.A.: Context models in discourse processing. In: The Construction of Mental Representations During Reading, pp. 123–148 (1999)
13. Skantze, G.: Error Handling in Spoken Dialogue Systems-Managing Uncertainty, Grounding and Miscommunication. Doctoral dissertation, KTH. Ph.D. thesis, Department of Speech, Music and Hearing (2007)
14. Lampinen, A., Lehtinen, V., Lehmuskallio, A., Tamminen, S.: We're in it together: interpersonal management of disclosure in social network services. In: Proceedings of the SIGCHI Conference on Human Factors in Computing Systems, pp. 3217–3226, ACM (2011)
15. Wood, A.F., Smith, M.J.: Online Communication: Linking Technology, Identity, & Culture. Routledge, London (2004)
16. Harper, R.H.: Texture: Human Expression in the Age of Communications Overload. MIT Press, Cambridge (2010)
17. Harper, R. (ed.): Trust, Computing and Society. CUP, New York (2014)
18. Grice, H.P.: Logic and conversation. In: Davidson, D., Harman, G. (eds.) The Logic of Grammar, pp. 64–75. Harvard Univ., Cambridge (1975)
19. Cao, H., Hu, D.H., Shen, D., Jiang, D., Sun, J.T., Chen, E., Yang, Q.: Context-aware query classification. In: Proceedings of the 32nd international ACM SIGIR Conference on Research and Development in Information Retrieval, pp. 3–10. ACM (2009)
20. Celikyilmaz, A., Hakkani-Tur, D., Tur, G.: Statistical semantic interpretation modeling for spoken language understanding with enriched semantic features. In: Spoken Language Technology Workshop (SLT), 2012 IEEE, pp. 216–221. IEEE (2012)

21. Nissenbaum, H.: Privacy in context: technology, policy, and the integrity of social life. Stanford Law & Politics, Stanford (2010)
22. Barth, A., Datta, A., Mitchell, J.C., Nissenbaum, H.: Privacy and contextual integrity: framework and applications. In: IEEE S & P'6, pp. 184–198. IEEE Computer Society (2006)
23. Fong, P.W.L.: Relationship-based access control: protection model and policy language. In: Proceedings of the first ACM Conference on Data and Application Security and Privacy. CODASPY 2011, New York, NY, USA, pp. 191–202. ACM (2011)

Are You Really My Friend? Exactly Spatiotemporal Matching Scheme in Privacy-Aware Mobile Social Networks

Ben Niu[1(✉)], Xiuguang Li[1,2], Xiaoyan Zhu[1], Xiaoqing Li[1], and Hui Li[1]

[1] State Key Laboratory of Integrated Services Networks,
Xidian University, Xi'an, China
xd.niuben@gmail.com, lixiuguang00@126.com,
{xyzhu,xqli,lihui}@mail.xidian.edu.cn
[2] Key Laboratory of Information and Network Security,
Engineering University of Chinese Armed Police Force, Langfang, China

Abstract. We propose an exactly spatiotemporal matching scheme for privacy-aware users in MSNs. Based on the carefully designed spatiotemporal profile, our scheme employs a weight-aware pre-matching module to filter out the users with less similarity and some potential adversaries, thus guarantees that no useful information is revealed before determining the best matches. Further, we propose a privacy-preserving exchanging module against Honest-But-Curious users. Finally, the similarity computing module computes the exact matching result to each candidate to determine the best match. Thorough security analysis and evaluation results indicate the effectiveness and efficiency.

Keywords: Mobile social networks · Private matching · Spatiotemporal

1 Introduction

The success of Mobile Social Networks (MSNs) and location-aware mobile devices has resulted in many popular applications. With these applications, mobile users can either communicate with existing friends or make new social interactions, to share news or funny things. In these applications, people always need to release their personal attributes to others, which conflicts with the increasing privacy concerns of mobile users and may lead to serious privacy disclosure.

Early solutions always rely on the trusted third parity [9] to process the matching work between users. However, they may become the single point of failure in the whole system. Although many follow-up works avoid this problem by employing Private Set Intersection [2,4], Secure Multi-party Computation (SMC) [5] or Paillier Cryptosystem [10], they pay much attention to computing the common attributes/interests privately but ignore the heavy computation cost. Sun et al. [8] pointed out the importance of the spatiotemporal information in plenty of social activities, thus proposed the first privacy-preserving spatiotemporal matching scheme to provide more opportunities for mobile users to

© Institute for Computer Sciences, Social Informatics and Telecommunications Engineering 2015
J. Tian et al. (Eds.): SecureComm 2014, Part II, LNICST 153, pp. 33–40, 2015.
DOI: 10.1007/978-3-319-23802-9_5

make new social interactions in MSNs. However, neither of them takes a fully consideration on user's priority on each attribute. Niu *et al.* proposed a series of schemes [6,7] to achieve better matching by employing the similarity-based solutions. Unfortunately, all these schemes need to assume the adversary cannot obtain the processing data from the running protocol.

In this paper, we first present some preliminaries in Sect. 2. Then, based on the carefully constructed *spatiotemporal profile*, our scheme in Sect. 3 uses a weight-aware pre-matching module, which combines a random permutation function with commutation encryption function, to compute a coarse-similarity with other users and filter out the users with smaller similarity as well as some potentially malicious adversaries. We design a reorganized profile exchanging module to guarantee that both the *initiator* and the *responder* in our scheme can only obtain the cells in common as well as the corresponding frequencies. Finally, based on the exchanged *reorganized profile*, our similarity computing module finds out the best match by computing the similarity exactly. We show the security analysis and evaluation results in Sects. 4 and 5, respectively. Finally, the conclusions is drawn in Sect. 6.

2 Preliminaries

2.1 Problem Statement

Our scheme aims to achieve privacy-preserving friend discovery based on spatiotemporal profile private matching, which involves several users and relies on no TTP. Mobile users in our scheme periodically record their own locations (i.e., every 5 minutes), each of which is then assigned into a geographic cell to construct the *spatiotemporal profile* within a predefined grid once the spatiotemporal matching is needed. Let's use a users *Alice* for example, she holds a set of messages $\{\langle timeperiod, c_i, freq_i \rangle\}$, where *timeperiod* represents the time period that is considered in the matching scheme, c_i denotes the index of the geographic cell within the predefined grid and $freq_i$ means the total number of times that a user visits c_i. Since users usually stay in different places with different time period, e.g., *Alice* may stay at home and office with more time but less time in a certain shopping mall, then the $freq_i$ may changes with c_i. Our problem is how to find the best match who has more common cells and with similar visiting frequencies, while guaranteeing that no useful personal information is released.

2.2 Adversary Model

In our work, we mainly consider the Honest-But-Curious model (HBC) as some existing work [5,10], which happens within legitimate users, they will infer private information from running protocol but honestly follow the protocol.

2.3 Motivation and Our Basic Idea

Spatiotemporal matching has been one of the most popular technique employed in current social activities [8] such as friend discovering, social collaboration, etc.

Our work is thus motivated by a set of observations. (1): most of existing schemes [5,7,10] use user's attributes information to process matching, but ignore the spatiotemporal information, which is important and has been thoroughly studied in [8]. (2): although Sun et $al.$ [8] proposed the privacy-preserving spatiotemporal matching scheme for MSNs, their schemes fail to consider an important social fact that mobile users in our real life always spend more time or higher frequencies on some particular locations such as their homes. As the result, cells with different visiting frequencies will be considered as the same, which does not make sense in reality. (3): schemes in [1,6–8] fail to protect legitimate user's information before identifying the identifier of the other party in the matching phase. Therefore, we argue that, if a potential adversary exists, he may add extra attributes as much as possible to match with legitimate user.

Our main idea is to perform spatiotemporal matching, exactly and privately. We design a weight-aware pre-matching module before computing the exactly spatiotemporal matching results between users. Based on our module, the candidates with less similarity and the potential adversaries can be filtered out effectively. Followed, with the help of our similarity computing module, which considers frequencies assigned on all the cells within the $spatiotemporal$ $profile$, the best match can be selected from the others, exactly.

3   Our Proposed Scheme

3.1   System Architecture

Our scheme is a distributed solution, which allows users to process spatiotemporal matching freely without relying on any third party. Users in our scheme communicate with others in vicinity through some short-range communication techniques such as Bluetooth or WiFi. At the beginning, each user reorganizes the own $spatiotemporal$ $profile$ mentioned in Sect. 2.1 into a new $reorganized$ $profile$, which is used for further matching. We set several priority levels for each user, and let users reorganize their $spatiotemporal$ $profiles$ based on $freq_i$. For example, we set three priority levels, which are denoted as $Level_1$, $Level_2$ and $Level_3$. $Level_1$ contains the cells that the user visited with high frequencies, $Level_2$ includes the cells with less frequencies, while $Level_3$ means the cells that the user seldom appeared. Based on $Alice$'s willingness, she can assign all the elements in her $spatiotemporal$ $profile$ into these three levels. Through this way, all the records can be assigned, we further compute the sum of the frequencies ($F^{A_j} = \sum_{r=1}^{m_j} freq_r^{A_j}$) for each priority level. Finally, $Alice$'s $reorganized$ $profile$ RP_A can be constructed. We then present our weight-aware pre-matching, reorganized profile exchanging and similarity computing modules in turn.

3.2   Weight-Aware Pre-matching Module

We suppose that all the entities share a prime q and a hash function $h(\cdot)$ through secure communication channels, which is a wildly used assumption in existing solutions. For any $c_r^{A_j} \in C^{A_j}$, $Alice$ computes $(h(c_r^{A_j}))^{k_A}$ offline and sends to Bob

together with F^{A_j}. *Bob* first transforms the elements in priority level in his *reorganized profile* $(c_t^{B_j})$ into $(\hat{c}_1^{B_j}, \cdots, \hat{c}_t^{B_j}, \cdots, \hat{c}_{n_j}^{B_j})$ offline based on a random permutation function $\prod$, which aims to disorder the elements within the array randomly. Then, he accomplishes some computation work based on the received information as follows. He computes $((h(c_r^{A_j}))^{k_A})^{k_B}$ and performs the random permutation function on them to obtain $\prod(((h(c_1^{A_j}))^{k_A})^{k_B}, \cdots, ((h(c_r^{A_j}))^{k_A})^{k_B}, \cdots, ((h(c_{m_j}^{A_j}))^{k_A})^{k_B})$, namely $(((h(\hat{c}_1^{A_j}))^{k_A})^{k_B}, \cdots, ((h(\hat{c}_r^{A_j}))^{k_A})^{k_B}, \cdots, ((h(\hat{c}_{m_j}^{A_j}))^{k_A})^{k_B})$. Next *Bob* generates a random number r_N, and then computes the hash values to obtain $(h(((h(\hat{c}_1^{A_j}))^{k_A})^{k_B} + r_N), \cdots, h(((h(\hat{c}_r^{A_j}))^{k_A})^{k_B} + r_N), \cdots, h(((h(\hat{c}_{m_j}^{A_j}))^{k_A})^{k_B} + r_N))$. Finally, this message is sent to *Alice* together with $(h(\hat{c}_t^{B_j}))^{k_B}$ and F^{B_j}. *Alice* then computes $((h(\hat{c}_t^{B_j}))^{k_B})^{k_A}$ and sends it back to *Bob*. *Bob* sends the random number r_N to *Alice*. *Alice* computes $(h(((h(\hat{c}_1^{B_j}))^{k_B})^{k_A} + r_N), \cdots, h(((h(\hat{c}_t^{B_j}))^{k_B})^{k_A} + r_N), \cdots, h(((h(\hat{c}_{n_j}^{B_j}))^{k_B})^{k_A} + r_N))$. Next, *Alice* computes the number of common cells in each priority level by

$$k_j = |C^{A_j} \cap C^{B_j}| = |\{h(((h(\hat{c}_1^{A_j}))^{k_A})^{k_B} + r_N), \cdots, h(((h(\hat{c}_{m_j}^{A_j}))^{k_A})^{k_B} + r_N)\}$$
$$\cap \{h(((h(\hat{c}_1^{B_j}))^{k_B})^{k_A} + r_N), \cdots, h(((h(\hat{c}_{n_j}^{B_j}))^{k_B})^{k_A} + r_N)\}|, \quad (1)$$

and *Bob* executes the same procedure by $k_j = |C^{B_j} \cap C^{A_j}|$. Then, we define a weight function on each priority level between *Alice* and *Bob*, it is based on a common sense that the more frequency spent on a particular region in common, the higher similarity will be. Our weight function w_j thus can be computed by

$$w_j = \frac{F^{A_j} + F^{B_j}}{F^{A_1} + F^{A_2} + F^{A_3} + F^{B_1} + F^{B_2} + F^{B_3}}. \quad (2)$$

We compute coarse-similarity of each priority level in pre-matching phase by

$$P_j(C^{A_j}, C^{B_j}) = \frac{|(C^{A_j} \cap C^{B_j})|}{|(C^{A_j} \cup C^{B_j})|} = \frac{|(C^{A_j} \cap C^{B_j})|}{|(C^{A_j}| + |C^{B_j})| - |(C^{A_j} \cap C^{B_j})|}$$
$$= \frac{k_j}{m_j + n_j - k_j}. \quad (3)$$

Based on these formulae, both *Alice* and *Bob* can obtain the weight and coarse-similarity information for each priority level. Finally, the total coarse-similarity can be computed as

$$P(C^A, C^B) = \sum_{j=1}^{3} \{w_j \times P_j(C^{A_j}, C^{B_j})\}$$
$$= \sum_{j=1}^{3} \{\frac{F^{A_j} + F^{B_j}}{F^{A_1} + F^{A_2} + F^{A_3} + F^{B_1} + F^{B_2} + F^{B_3}} \times \frac{k_j}{m_j + n_j - k_j}\}, \quad (4)$$

which indicates a probable similarity between user *Alice* and *Bob*.

3.3   Reorganized Profile Exchanging Module

Since adversaries and users with less similarity can be filtered out in the pre-matching module, our goal here is to launch a privacy-preserving exchanging to exchange the *reorganized profile* with users with high similarity value. Specifically, for each element in *Alice*'s *reorganized profile*, she computes $\langle h(c_r^A)^{k_A}, freq_r^A \rangle$ and sends them to *Bob*. *Bob* computes $\langle h(c_t^B)^{k_B}, freq_t^B \rangle$, and $\langle ((h(c_r^A))^{k_A})^{k_B}, freq_r^A \rangle$, then sends these messages back to *Alice*. Once *Alice* receives these messages, she computes $\langle ((h(c_t^B))^{k_B})^{k_A}, freq_t^B \rangle$ and replies the computation results to *Bob*. This step is accomplished on both sides of *Alice* and *Bob*. Specifically, *Alice* compares each $((h(c_r^A))^{k_A})^{k_B}$ with $((h(c_t^B))^{k_B})^{k_A}$, if they are equal, the value of $min(freq_r^A, freq_t^B)$ is written into $freq_k^C$, and continues if they are not equal. At last, *Alice* outputs the result of $\sum freq_k^C$. While on *Bob* side, he executes the same procedure to obtain the value of $\sum freq_k^C$.

3.4   Similarity Computing Module

Based on the obtained information from the aforementioned modules, user *Alice* and *Bob* can compute the exactly spatiotemporal profile matching results with each other by the following formula.

$$P(C^A, C^B) = \frac{|(C^A \cap C^B)|}{|(C^A \cup C^B)|} = \frac{|(C^A \cap C^B)|}{|(C^A| + |C^B|) - |(C^A \cap C^B)|}$$

$$= \frac{\sum freq_k^C}{\sum freq_r^A + \sum freq_t^B - \sum freq_k^C}. \qquad (5)$$

The obtained $P(C^A, C^B)$ is the exactly matching result between them. According to this number, *Alice* and *Bob* could decide whether to be friends.

4   Security Analysis

Since potential adversaries can be filtered out in the weight-aware pre-matching module, then in the reorganized profile exchanging module, we prove that our scheme is secure under the HBC model.

Theorem 1. *Our scheme is secure if the commutative encryption function is secure.*

Proof. The commutative encryption function and keyed hash function provide end users with a secure channel, it means that only the one who has the secret key can decrypt the message. Suppose user *Alice* is a HBC user, she may illegally construct her reorganized profile in two extreme ways, (1) adding all the possible cells into the first priority level to get more information of *Bob*, (2) putting limited number of cells into each priority level.

For case (1), based on the pre-matching result, users who add all the possible cells into the first priority level will cause smaller matching result and will be filtered out in the weight-aware pre-matching module. Therefore, users with less similarity value cannot be executing the reorganized profile exchanging module with legitimate user. For a special case, if the HBC user has enough abilities to modify the reorganized profile, the Equation in 5 can also outputs a lower similarity value to user to make the decision.

For case (2), this kind of threat happens when *Alice* inputs cells as less as possible, for instance, she just inputs one cell with a higher corresponding frequency to perform our matching algorithm, if she fortunately has one intersection with *Bob*, she could infer that *Bob* goes to this cell (it always refers to a area such as a bar) frequently. But if she input two or more cells and the corresponding frequencies, even she has a intersection with *Bob*, she cannot conclude which cell that *Bob* has been to. So we can see that if the HBC user inputs only one cell with the corresponding frequency, he can learn other's secret information. However, this is a very special case and there are many practical ways to tackle this problem, such as setting a rule to limit the minimum number of input, which meets our real life.

Since all the data are transmitted between entities, and some cryptographic tools such as Public Key Infrastructures (PKI) can be easily adopted onto our scheme, the common cells and the corresponding frequencies can only be seen by the legitimate users with proper keys.

5   Performance Evaluations

5.1   Evaluation Setup

To further study the feasibility of our scheme, we implement aforementioned schemes on a Thinkpad laptop (the cryptography library is Crypto++) with 1.82 GHz CPU, 4 GB RAM to simulate the performance.

5.2   Evaluation Results

In Fig. 1, we first test the offline computation cost when m is changing from 20 to 200. Figure 1 indicates that our scheme has better performance than others [3, 7–9]. The computation cost in [3] is high since there are too many exp_1s employed in their schemes.

Figure 1 compares the online computation cost of all the protocols in the log 10 scale for varying m. We can see the efficiency of our scheme over others. For users in our scheme, they need to perform $2m$ exp_1s and m hs on the *initiator* side and same compute cost on the *responder* side. The online cost of the protocols in [3] are much higher since they utilize several exp_1s in their processes.

In Fig. 1, scheme in [8] shows a better performance on the communication cost than our scheme since we just considering two users in the experiment. Now considering a real situation that there are s users in the vicinity around the *initiator*, the scheme in [8] need to transmits $(6m + 4) \times s$ bits in all, on the contrary, our scheme may just need to transmits $4m \times s + 4m$ bits since our scheme filter out the adversaries and users with less similarity.

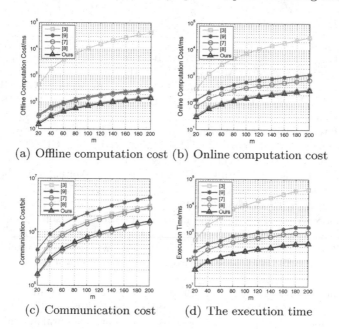

(a) Offline computation cost (b) Online computation cost

(c) Communication cost   (d) The execution time

Fig. 1. Impact of the number of common cells m

Figure 1 provides the total execution time of all the algorithms. Comparing with [3,7,9], our scheme performs better. When we look into our protocol, to get the common cells securely, an *initiator* needs more time to complete the computation. However, it is obvious that our proposed protocol can be finished within about 600 ms in all simulated sceneries.

6   Conclusions

This paper proposed an exactly spatiotemporal matching scheme for privacy-aware users in Mobile Social Networks. Based on the newly constructed spatiotemporal profile, we designed a weight-aware pre-matching module in malicious environment to effectively filter out users with less similarity and the malicious adversaries before determining the best matches. Followed, with executing our reorganized profile exchanging module and the similarity computing module, the best match can be determined exactly against Honest-But-Curious users. Security analysis and evaluation results are also provided.

Acknowledgement. This work was supported by National NSFC under Grant 61003300, Fundamental Research Funds for the Central Universities under Grant K5051201041, and China 111 Project under Grant B08038. The work of Dr. Hui Li was supported by the National Project 2012ZX03002003-002, 863 Project 2012AA013102, IRT1078 and NSFC 61170251.

References

1. Agrawal, R., Evfimievski, A., Srikant, R.: Information sharing across private databases. In: Proceedings of ACM SIGMOD (2003)
2. De Cristofaro, E., Tsudik, G.: Practical private set intersection protocols with linear complexity. In: Sion, R. (ed.) FC 2010. LNCS, vol. 6052, pp. 143–159. Springer, Heidelberg (2010)
3. De Cristofaro, E., Kim, J., Tsudik, G.: Linear-Complexity Private Set Intersection Protocols Secure in Malicious Model. In: Abe, M. (ed.) ASIACRYPT 2010. LNCS, vol. 6477, pp. 213–231. Springer, Heidelberg (2010)
4. Freedman, M.J., Nissim, K., Pinkas, B.: Efficient Private Matching and Set Intersection. In: Cachin, C., Camenisch, J.L. (eds.) EUROCRYPT 2004. LNCS, vol. 3027, pp. 1–19. Springer, Heidelberg (2004)
5. Li, M., Cao, N., Yu, S., Lou, W.: Findu: Privacy-preserving personal profile matching in mobile social networks. In: Proceedings of IEEE INFOCOM (2011)
6. Niu, B., Zhu, X., Liu, J., Li, Z., Li, H.: Weight-aware private matching scheme for proximity-based mobile social networks. In: Proceedings of IEEE GLOBECOM (2013)
7. Niu, B., Zhu, X., Zhang, T., Chi, H., Li, H.: P-match: Priority-aware friend discovery for proximity-based mobile social networks. In: Proceedings of IEEE MASS (2013)
8. Sun, J., Zhang, R., Zhang, Y.: Privacy-preserving spatiotemporal matching. In: Proceedings of IEEE INFOCOM (2013)
9. Wang, Y., ting Zhang, T., zong Li, H., ping He, L., Peng, J.: Efficient privacy preserving matchmaking for mobile social networking against malicious users. In: Proceedings of IEEE TRUSTCOM (2012)
10. Zhang, R., Zhang, Y., Sun, J., Yan, G.: Fine-grained private matching for proximity-based mobile social networking. In: Proceedings of IEEE INFOCOM (2012)

RFID Authentication Protocol Resistant
to the Man-in-the-Middle Attack

Li Zhai[1,2]([⊠]) and ChuanKun Wu[1]

[1] State Key Laboratory of Information Security,
Institute of Information Engineering, Chinese Academy of Sciences,
Beijing 100093, China
{zhaili,ckwu}@iie.ac.cn
[2] University of Chinese Academy of Sciences,
Beijing 100190, China

Abstract. HB+ family protocols that based on LPN problem are effective and well suited for the Internet of Things. However, the HB+ family protocols have vulnerability on the man-in-the-middle attack. In this paper, we propose a new privacy preserving RFID authentication protocol based on the multiplication on Z_{2^k-1}. By analyzing the differential property on Z_{2^k-1}, we show that the protocol is resistant to the man-in-the-middle attack. Moreover, the performance analysis shows the protocol meets the demands of the large-scale RFID systems.

Keywords: RFID · Man-in-the-middle attack · Privacy · Internet of Things

1 Introduction

Radio Frequency Identification (RFID) is a technology that allows RFID readers automatically identification of RFID tags, and it is widely used in many applications. But low-cost RFID tags, in particular, have limited computational capabilities that render them unable to perform complicated cryptography operations.

Privacy preserving protocols based on symmetric key are faced a paradox. On one side, a tag must encrypt its identity with its secret key so that only authorized readers can extract the identity. On the other side, a tag cannot easily identify itself to reader. If the reader does not know any identity of the tag, it cannot determine which key is used to decrypt the protocol message [10]. Therefore, most symmetric-key protocols are using exhaustive search to determine the key.

Molnar and Wagner proposed a tree based RFID authentication protocols [14]. By using their method, a tag can be identified in $O(\log N)$ time. Their method is a tradeoff between the identification efficiency and privacy. Avoine et al. [3] discovered the tree based protocols have vulnerability on compromising attack. Song and Mitchell [16] proposed a constant-time identification protocols. However, their protocol have vulnerability on impersonation and tracking

This work was supported by China national 863 project under No. 2013AA014002.

J. Tian et al. (Eds.): SecureComm 2014, Part II, LNICST 153, pp. 41–47, 2015.
DOI: 10.1007/978-3-319-23802-9_6

attack [6]. Alomair et al. [1] proposed another constant-time identification protocols. Their protocol needs pre-computation and a large database. Moreover, the protocol has vulnerability on denial of service and tracking attack.

Juels and Weis [11] proposed HB+, the first RFID lightweight authentication protocol based on the learning parity problem. HB+ protocol is provable security under LPN problem, but it has security flaw on the man-in-the-middle attack. As Gilbert et al. showed in [8], the security of HB+ is compromised if the adversary is given the ability to modify messages transmitting between the reader and the tag. Karz et al. [12] gave a simpler proof of security for HB+, and proved security for parallel executions. Beinger et al. proposed HB++ [5] protocol.

However, all these protocols were proven to be insecure in the GRS model. They were successfully cryptanalyzed by Gilbert et al. in [7]. In fact, it has been shown in [7] that the secure authentication protocols based on the LPN problem are hard to find. Gilbert et al. proposed the HB# and Random-HB# [9] on the eurocrypt'08. Their protocol enhanced the security on the man-in-the-middle attack. But later, Ouafi et al. present a man-in-the-middle attack against HB# and Random-HB# [15]. Recently, more HB-like protocols are proposed, but they were all broken. Bosley et al. [4] proposed HBN protocol, but they were successfully cryptanalyzed by Avoine et al. [2].

Our Contribution. We proposed a new RFID authentication protocol which is secure under the man-in-the-middle attack. Our protocol does not rely on any cryptography ciphers, it is constructing directly from the multiplication on Z_{2^k-1}. We developed a new pseudorandom function based on the multiplication on Z_{2^k-1}. Due to the nonlinearity of our pseudorandom function, our protocol is secure on the GRS model. And we gives the multiplicative differential property of the Z_{2^k-1}. Based on these results, it shows that our protocol is resistant to the man-in-the-middle attack. Finally, we give the performance analysis of our protocols.

2   Our Protocol

In this section, we introduce our privacy preserving authentication protocol. In Table 1, we give the symbol definition used in this paper.

Initialization. Every tag T_i in the system is initialized with a secret key (x_i, y_i), which x_i and y_i are randomly drawn from G. The N secret keys of the tags are stored in a database. The reader uses a secure connection communicating with the database.

Protocol. Our scheme is a n-round challenge response protocol. Figure 1 illustrates a round of our protocol. Each authentication consists of n rounds, where n is a security parameter. The protocol works as follows:

1. The reader first draw a random element a from G and sends it to the tag.
2. Upon the tag receipt a, it draw a random element b from G, and compute $z = f(a * x) \oplus f(b * y)$, sends (b, z) to reader.

Table 1. Symbol definition

Symbols	Descriptions
k	Security parameter, k is an integer and $2^k - 1$ is prime
r	Security parameter, the number of rounds in our protocol
N	The number of tags on the system
G	Multiplicative group on the $Z_{2^k-1}^*$
$*$	Multiplication on the $Z_{2^k-1}^*$
a, b, x, y	Elements on the group G
$\oplus$	Exclusive or operator
$[x]_i$	The i-th bit of the x binary representation (least significant bit first)
$f(x)$	$f(x) = \bigoplus_{i=1}^{k} [x]_i$

3. The reader receipt (b, z). Then reader exhaustive search the key pair (x_i, y_i), and compute $z' = f(a_i * x) \oplus f(b_i * y)$. If $z' = z$, put (x_i, y_i) into the candidates key set; otherwise exclude (x_i, y_i) immediately.

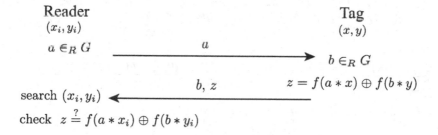

Reader
(x_i, y_i)

$a \in_R G$

$\xrightarrow{\quad a \quad}$

search (x_i, y_i)

check $z \overset{?}{=} f(a * x_i) \oplus f(b * y_i)$

$\xleftarrow{\quad b, z \quad}$

Tag
(x, y)

$b \in_R G$

$z = f(a * x) \oplus f(b * y)$

Fig. 1. The basic authentication step of our protocol.

By repeating for n rounds, if reader found a key passed the verification on all rounds, the reader authenticates the tag successfully. The output of the function $f(a * x)$ is balance. Thus a naive adversary can guess the correct bit of one round is $1/2$, so the probability of the adversary can be authenticated by reader is 2^{-n}.

3 Security Analysis

3.1 Differential Property of the Function $f(X * a)$

In this section, we will show the differential property of the function $f(X*a)$. The resistance of the man-in-the-middle attacks is generally relied on the differential probability of pseudorandom function. If the differential probability of a function is $1/2$, that function is perfectly resistance to the differential attack.

Definition 1 (δ-differential probability of the function $f(X*a)$). *Let $q = 2^k - 1$ be a prime, a, δ be two constant on Z_q^*. Let X be a random variable, X is uniformly distributed over Z_q^*. Let $*$ denote the multiplication operator on the Z_q^*. The δ-differential probability $p(a, \delta)$ of the function $f(X*a)$ is defined as*

$$p(a, \delta) \stackrel{def}{=} \Pr[X \in_R Z_q^* : f((X+\delta)*a \bmod q) \oplus f(X*a \bmod q) = 0]$$

Definition 2. *Let us define a mapping $\phi(a)$ from Z_{2^k-1} to a vector, where $\phi(a) = m_{a_k} m_{a_{k-1}} \dots m_{a_1} v$. Let $\phi(a, i)$ be the i-th element of $\phi(a)$, a be a constant on Z_{2^k-1}, a_i be the i-th bit of a's binary representation. The definition of m_0, m_1, v are as follows:*

$$m_0 = \begin{pmatrix} 1 & 0 & \frac{1}{2} & 0 \\ 0 & 1 & 0 & \frac{1}{2} \\ 0 & 0 & 0 & \frac{1}{2} \\ 0 & 0 & \frac{1}{2} & 0 \end{pmatrix}, m_1 = \begin{pmatrix} \frac{1}{2} & 0 & 0 & 0 \\ 0 & \frac{1}{2} & 0 & 0 \\ 0 & \frac{1}{2} & 0 & 1 \\ \frac{1}{2} & 0 & 1 & 0 \end{pmatrix}, v = \begin{pmatrix} 1 \\ 0 \\ 0 \\ 0 \end{pmatrix}$$

The following theorem gives the differential probability of our pseudorandom function. The computational complexity of Theorem 1 is $O(k)$.

Theorem 1 (Differential probability on the Z_{2^k-1}). *Let X be a random variable distributed uniformly over Z_q, where $q = 2^k - 1$. Let a be a constant value on Z_q. Then the differential probability $p(a, \delta)$ is*

$$p(a, \delta)$$
$$= \frac{2^k \phi(a, f(a) + 1) + 2^k \phi(a+1, 4 - f(a+1)) + \theta(0, a) + \theta(q, a) + \theta(q - a, a) - 3}{q - 1}$$

where $\theta(x, a) = f(x + a \bmod 2^k) \oplus f(x \bmod 2^k)$.

3.2   Man-in-the-Middle Attack of Our Protocol

We assumed a man-in-the-middle adversary has the following abilities: he can fully control the messages between reader and tag; he can modify or replay the message, and look up the protocol result that is succeeded or failed. Without loss of generality, we consider the adversary modifying the message a:

1. Reader sends message a to tag.
2. Adversary intercept the message, changing a to $a' = a + \delta$, and sends a' to tag.
3. Upon tag receipt the message a' from the adversary, tag generate b uniformly at random, and compute $z' = f(a' * x) \oplus f(b * y)$, tag sends (b, z') to reader.
4. Upon receipt (b, z'), reader calculate $z = f(a * x) \oplus f(b * y)$. If $z = z'$ then reader accept the tag, otherwise reader reject the tag.
5. Adversary view the output of the reader and deduce the secret key.

The above attacking method is the famous GRS attack [8,13]. It successfully crack many HB-family protocols. Now we shows that our protocol can resistant GRS attack. According to the assumption, adversary can get the protocol result. If reader accepted tag, then adversary can conclude that $z = z'$, if reader rejected tag then $z = z' \oplus 1$. We can calculate the probability of reader accepting tag while adversary intercepting the messages:

$$\begin{aligned}
&\Pr[\text{Reader Accept Tag}] \\
&= \Pr[z = z'] \\
&= \Pr[f(a * x) \oplus f(b * y) = f(a' * x) \oplus f(b * y)] \\
&= \Pr[f(a * x) \oplus f(a' * x) = 0] \\
&= \Pr[f(a * x) \oplus f((a \mid \delta) * x) = 0]
\end{aligned} \tag{1}$$

We can see the probability (1) is the differential probability defined in Definition 1. If the x and δ are fixed, the probability (1) is fixed. Thus every tag on the systems has a unique differential probability. Adversary can attack our protocol by utilizing the uniqueness of differential probability. Adversary repeats the above process to get many samples of $f(a*x) \oplus f((a+\delta)*x)$. Then he can use the maximize like hood method to approximate the differential probability (1).

For convenience, we denote the probability (1) as $2^{-1} \pm 2^{-m}$, which m is a positive value about k. By using the Theorem 1, given x, δ, we can calculate m. If we choose the key length to 127-bit ($2^{127} - 1$ is a prime), then m is approximating to 40. According to the Chernoff bound, if the probability of adversary succeeded is η, then adversary needs at least n samples to approximate the differential probability, where $n \geq 2^{2m} \ln \frac{1}{\sqrt{\eta}}$. Then adversary needs $O(2^{80})$ samples to get a distinguish attack against our protocol. On the practical environment, adversary cannot get a large amount of samples, and therefore our protocol is secure against these attack.

4   Performance Analysis

In this section, we give the performance analysis of our protocol. We can proof that a reader can exclude a wrong tag within 2 rounds on average. Thus a reader identify a tag needs to run $2N$ times sub-protocol on average, where N is the number of tags on the system. The Algorithm 1 shows the identification process. n is the number of rounds of the protocol. The algorithm's input $(b_1, z_1), \ldots, (b_n, z_n)$ is an array of the tag's output.

Assuming the tag's output z_i is uniformly distributed. If the reader chooses the right key, the verification processes will success in all rounds. If the reader choose the wrong key, the probability of a wrong key passing the verification on i-round is $1/2$. Then the probability of a wrong key just rejected on i-round is (i.e., passed the first $i - 1$ rounds, and rejected on i-th round):

$$p_i = \frac{1}{2^{i-1}} * \frac{1}{2} = \frac{1}{2^i}$$

Algorithm 1. SearchKey $((b_1, z_1), \ldots, (b_n, z_n))$

---
for $j = 1$ to N **do**
  for $i = 1$ to n **do**
    if $z_i \neq f(a_i * x_j) \oplus f(b_i * y_j)$ **then**
      reject key (x_j, y_j) and **break**
    end if
  end for
  if $i = n$ **then**
    accept key (x_j, y_j) and **return** ID_j
  end if
end for
return ID_{error}

The random variable X_i denoted the number of rounds of a wrong key excluded by reader. The random variable X denoted the number of all wrong keys excluded by reader. According to linearity of expectation, $E(X)$ is:

$$E(X) = \sum_{i=1}^{N} E(X_i) = N \sum_{i=1}^{\infty} i * p_i = 2N$$

Protocol Parameter. The basic requirement of the key length is 80-bit, otherwise the adversary can break the protocol by brute force. According to the analysis on Sect. 3.2, we choose the key length of our protocol to be 127-bit.

Computational Cost. Our protocol is based on the multiplication on the Z_{2^k-1}. We implement our pseudorandom function(127-bit) in a personal computer having Intel 2.6 GHz G1610 Celeron Dual Core processor, 4 GB RAM and Linux Debian - 64-bit operating system. By running our pseudorandom function 10^8 times, it cost 350 ms. Our protocol needs to run 2N times PRF to identify a tag on average, where N is the number of tags on the system. On a system have 10^8 tags, we needs 700 ms to identify one tag.

5   Conclusion

In this paper, we construct a new privacy preserving authentication RFID protocol that does not rely on the traditional cryptography ciphers. Our protocol is consist of multiple sub protocols, this structure can be used to speed up the process of searching key on server-side. Furthermore, we give an analysis on differential property of the multiplicative group of the Z_{2^k-1}. According to our analysis, the protocol is secure on the man-in-the-middle attack.

References

1. Alomair, B., Clark, A., Cuellar, J., Poovendran, R.: Scalable RFID systems: a privacy-preserving protocol with constant-time identification. IEEE Trans. Parallel Distrib. Syst. **23**(8), 1536–1550 (2012)

2. Avoine, G., Carpent, X.: Yet another ultralightweight authentication protocol that is broken. In: Hoepman, J.-H., Verbauwhede, I. (eds.) RFIDSec 2012. LNCS, vol. 7739, pp. 20–30. Springer, Heidelberg (2013)
3. Molnar, D., Soppera, A., Wagner, D.: A scalable, delegatable pseudonym protocol enabling ownership transfer of RFID tags. In: Preneel, B., Tavares, S. (eds.) SAC 2005. LNCS, vol. 3897, pp. 276–290. Springer, Heidelberg (2006)
4. Bosley, C., Haralambiev, K., Nicolosi, A.: HBN: an HB-like protocol secure against man-in-the-middle attacks. IACR Cryptology ePrint Arch. **2011**, 350 (2011)
5. Bringer, J., Chabanne, H., Dottax, E.: Hb++: a lightweight authentication protocol secure against some attacks. In: Second International Workshop on Security, Privacy and Trust in Pervasive and Ubiquitous Computing. SecPerU 2006, pp. 28–33. IEEE (2006)
6. Erguler, I., Anarim, E.: Scalability and security conflict for RFID authentication protocols. Wireless Pers. Commun. **59**(1), 43–56 (2011)
7. Gilbert, H., Robshaw, M., Seurin, Y.: Good variants of HB+ are hard to find. In: Tsudik, G. (ed.) FC 2008. LNCS, vol. 5143, pp. 156–170. Springer, Heidelberg (2008)
8. Gilbert, H., Robshaw, M., Sibert, H.: Active attack against HB+: a provably secure lightweight authentication protocol. Electron. Lett. **41**(21), 1169–1170 (2005)
9. Gilbert, H., Robshaw, M., Seurin, Y.: HB#: Increasing the security and efficiency of HB+. In: Smart, N.P. (ed.) EUROCRYPT 2008. LNCS, vol. 4965, pp. 361–378. Springer, Heidelberg (2008)
10. Juels, A.: RFID security and privacy: a research survey. IEEE J. Sel. Areas Commun. **24**(2), 381–394 (2006)
11. Juels, A., Weis, S.A.: Authenticating pervasive devices with human protocols. In: Shoup, V. (ed.) CRYPTO 2005. LNCS, vol. 3621, pp. 293–308. Springer, Heidelberg (2005)
12. Katz, J., Shin, J.S., Smith, A.: Parallel and concurrent security of the HB and HB+ protocols. J. Cryptol. **23**(3), 402–421 (2010)
13. Lyubashevsky, V., Masny, D.: Man-in-the-middle secure authentication schemes from LPN and weak PRFs. In: Canetti, R., Garay, J.A. (eds.) CRYPTO 2013, Part II. LNCS, vol. 8043, pp. 308–325. Springer, Heidelberg (2013)
14. Molnar, D., Wagner, D.: Privacy and security in library RFID: issues, practices, and architectures. In: Proceedings of the 11th ACM Conference on Computer and Communications Security, p. 219 (2004)
15. Ouafi, K., Overbeck, R., Vaudenay, S.: On the security of HB# against a man-in-the-middle attack. In: Pieprzyk, J. (ed.) asiacrypt 2008. LNCS, vol. 5350, pp. 108–124. Springer, Heidelberg (2008)
16. Song, B., Mitchell, C.J.: Scalable RFID security protocols supporting tag ownership transfer. Comput. Commun. **34**(4), 556–566 (2011)

Intrusion Detection

METIS: A Two-Tier Intrusion Detection System for Advanced Metering Infrastructures

Vincenzo Gulisano[✉], Magnus Almgren, and Marina Papatriantafilou

Chalmers University of Technology, Gothenburg, Sweden
{vinmas,almgren,ptrianta}@chalmers.se

Abstract. In the shift from traditional to cyber-physical electric grids, motivated by the needs for improved energy efficiency, Advanced Metering Infrastructures have a key role. However, together with the enabled possibilities, they imply an increased threat surface on the systems. Challenging aspects such as scalable traffic analysis, timely detection of malicious activity and intuitive ways of specifying detection mechanisms for possible adversary goals are among the core problems in this domain.

Aiming at addressing the above, we present *METIS*, a *two-tier streaming-based intrusion detection framework*. *METIS* relies on probabilistic models for detection and is designed to detect challenging attacks in which adversaries aim at being unnoticed. Thanks to its two-tier architecture, it eases the modeling of possible adversary goals and allows for a fully distributed and parallel traffic analysis through the data streaming processing paradigm. At the same time, it allows for complementary intrusion detection systems to be integrated in the framework.

We demonstrate *METIS'* use and functionality through an *energy exfiltration* use-case, in which an adversary aims at stealing energy information from AMI users. Based on a prototype implementation using the Storm Stream Processing Engine and a very large dataset from a real-world AMI, we show that *METIS* is not only able to detect such attacks, but that it can also handle large volumes of data even when run on commodity hardware.

Keywords: Advanced Metering Infrastructures · Intrusion Detection Systems · Data streaming

1 Introduction

The shift from traditional to cyber-physical grids relies on the deployment of Advanced Metering Infrastructures (AMIs) in which communication-enabled meters share data with the utility's head-end and are remotely controlled. In this context, the strict coupling between threats' cyber and physical dimensions

Some preliminary results of METIS that do not overlap with the contribution of this work have been presented in a poster paper at the fifth International Conference on Future Energy Systems (ACM e-Energy), 2014.

© Institute for Computer Sciences, Social Informatics and Telecommunications Engineering 2015
J. Tian et al. (Eds.): SecureComm 2014, Part II, LNICST 153, pp. 51–68, 2015.
DOI: 10.1007/978-3-319-23802-9_7

(that can possibly result in human losses or physical damage [4]) demands for appropriate defense mechanisms. As Stuxnet [7] taught us, malicious activity designed to hide its malicious behavior can be carried out during years before being detected.

Despite the limited number of real attacks documented so far, a considerable number of possible attack vectors has been uncovered [17]. Specification-based Intrusion Detection Systems (IDSs) [1,18], the main defense mechanism proposed so far for this domain, detect malicious activity by means of deviations from defined behavior. Such IDSs usually require a considerable amount of manual labor by a security expert in order to tune them to specific installations [1]. At the same time, they do not provide a comprehensive protection against all possible adversary goals. As an example, they might distinguish messages that comply with a given protocol from messages that do not, but might fail in distinguishing whether a message that does not violate the protocol is sent by an intact or a compromised device.

Challenges. Kush et al. [14] claim traditional IDSs cannot be used effectively in these environments without major modifications and they mention nine challenges, four of which are taken into account in this paper: *scalability, adaptiveness, network topology* and *resource-constrained end devices*. As discussed in [1], AMIs consist of several independent networks whose overall traffic cannot be observed by a centralized IDS. Hence, the IDS should process data in a distributed fashion in order to embrace the different networks composing the AMI. Furthermore, the processing capacity of a centralized IDS would be rapidly exhausted by the big, fluctuating volume of data generated by AMIs' devices. To this end, the IDS should also process data in a parallel fashion in order to cope with the volumes of data and detect malicious activity timely. It should be noted that existing privacy regulations play an important role when it comes to the information accessed to spot malicious activity. As discussed in [19], fine-grain consumption readings reveal detailed information about household activities and could be used to blackmail public figures [8]. For this reason, while being interested in detecting malicious activity, the utility maintaining the AMI might not have access to underlying information owned by energy suppliers. Hence, the IDS should be able to detect malicious activity while relying on partial evidence (i.e., while accessing a limited set of traffic features). Finally, the IDS should avoid expensive per-site customization by providing an efficient way to specify how to detect malicious activities.

Contributions. We present *METIS*[1], an Intrusion Detection framework that addresses these challenges by employing a two-tier architecture and the data streaming processing paradigm [23]. *METIS* has been designed giving particular attention to the detection of malicious activity carried out by adversaries that want to go unnoticed. The challenge in the detection of such malicious activity

---

[1] Named after the mythology figure standing for good counsel, advice, planning, cunning, craftiness, and wisdom.

lies in that suspicious traffic proper of a given adversary goal can be caused by both legitimate and malicious factors. We provide the following contributions:

1. A two-tier architecture that provides a scalable traffic analysis that can be effective while (possibly) relying on a limited set of traffic features. Its two-tier architecture eases the system expert interaction (who can model the traffic features affected by an adversary goal by means of *Bayesian Networks*) and allows for complementary detection mechanisms such as specification-based and signature-based ones to be integrated in the framework.
2. A prototype implementation programmed using Storm [24], a state of the art Stream Processing Enginge used mainstream applications (such as twitter).
3. One of the first evaluations based on data extracted from a real-world AMI and focusing on *energy exfiltration* attacks in which the adversary aims at stealing energy consumption information from AMI users. The evaluation studies both the detection capabilities of the framework and its applicability while relying on commodity hardware. To the best of our knowledge, detection of such attacks has not been addressed before.

The paper is structured as follows. We introduce some preliminary concepts in Sect. 2. In Sect. 3 we overview the *METIS'* architecture while we discuss its implementation in Sect. 4. An example showing how the framework is applied to the energy exfiltration use-case is presented in Sect. 5. We present our evaluation in Sect. 6, survey related work in Sect. 7 and conclude in Sect. 8.

2   Preliminaries

2.1   Advanced Metering Infrastructure Model

We consider a common AMI model, composed of two types of devices: *Smart Meters* (SMs), in charge of measuring energy consumption and exchanging event messages such power outage alarms or firmware updates, and *Meter Concentrator Units* (MCUs), in charge of collecting such information and forwarding it to the utility head-end. Different network topologies exist in real-world AMIs (e.g., point-to-point, hierarchical or mesh ones). In order to encompass all possible networks and represent AMIs that can evolve over time, we consider a generic network, in which SMs are not statically assigned to specific MCUs.

Among the messages that are exchanged by the AMI's devices, two are of particular interest with respect to the use-case that will be introduced in the following: Energy Consumption Request (ECReq) messages, sent by MCUs, and Energy Consumption Response (ECResp) messages, sent by SMs. Such messages are used to retrieve energy consumption and can be exchanged several times per day.

2.2   Intrusion Detection in Advanced Metering Infrastructures

AMIs are characterized by their slow evolution and limited heterogeneity. That is, they are composed by a limited set of device types and their evolution is dictated by small (and often planned) steps (e.g., deployment of a new meter, replacement of a broken meter, and so on). Given a time frame that ranges from days to months, such evolution is "slow" and thus enables for detection techniques, such as anomaly-based ones, building on machine learning mechanisms. Nevertheless, the same evolving nature demands for a continuous learning that evolves together with the AMI (thus addressing the *adaptiveness* and *network topology* challenges discussed in [14]).

As introduced in Sect. 1, distributed and parallel network traffic analysis should be employed in order to embrace the different networks that compose AMIs while coping with the large and fluctuating volume of data produced by their devices. The distinct deployment options for an IDS in this domain can be characterized in a spectrum. At one extreme, the analysis could be performed by the utility head-end system. In this case, the devices should be instructed to report their communication exchanges to the head-end (at least, the ones that are required to detect a given attack). On the other extreme, the computation could be performed by the AMI's devices themselves, as investigated recently in [20]. This option would also be limited by the computational resources of the devices. Intermediate solutions could rely on a dedicated sensing infrastructure that runs the analysis together with the utility head-end system, as discussed in [10]. To our advantage, relying on the data streaming processing paradigm simplifies the deployment of an AMI defense framework to the requirement of providing a set of nodes (sensing devices or servers) that embraces the possible existing networks of the AMI. We refer the reader to [11] for a detailed discussion about how data streaming applications can be deployed at arbitrary number of nodes (thus addressing the *scalability* challenge discussed in [14]).

2.3 Adversary Model

Several types of attacks can be launched against AMIs. On one hand, attacks such as Denial of Service (DoS) or Distributed Denial of Service (DDoS) are meant to be noticed (i.e., they impose a challenge in their mitigation rather than detection). On the other hand, more subtle attacks can be carried out by adversaries that want to go unnoticed. This second type of attacks (imposing a challenge in their detection) are the main target of *METIS*. Such adversaries could be interested in installing a malicious firmware that, while leaving the device's communication unaffected, would allow them to use the AMI as a communication medium [10]. At the same time, a malicious firmware could also be installed to lower bills by reducing the consumption readings reported by the meters (causing an *energy theft* attack [16]).

Energy Exfiltration use-case. In this scenario, the adversary aims at stealing energy consumption information from AMI users. As discussed in [19], fine-grained consumption readings collected over a sufficiently large period reveal detailed information about household activities and could be used to blackmail public figures [8]. Given our AMI model, such malicious activity can be carried out after successfully logging into an MCU or by deploying a (malicious)

MCU replica and collecting energy consumption readings over a certain number of days. The subtle nature of this attack lies in that suspicious exchanges of ECReq and ECResp messages can be caused not only by the adversary, but also by legitimate factors (e.g., noisy communication between devices, unreachable devices, and so on).

2.4   Data Streaming

A stream is defined as an unbounded sequence of tuples $t_0, t_1, \ldots$ sharing the same schema composed by attributes $\langle A_1, \ldots, A_n \rangle$. Data streaming *continuous queries* are defined as graphs of operators. Nodes represent operators that consume and produce tuples, while edges specify how tuples flow among operators. Operators are distinguished into *stateless* (e.g., *Filter*, *Map*) or *stateful* (e.g., *Aggregate*, *EquiJoin*, *Join*), depending on whether they keep any evolving state while processing tuples. Due to the unbounded nature of streams, stateful operations are computed over *sliding windows* (simply windows in the remainder), defined by parameters *size* and *advance*. In this context, we focus on time-based windows. As an example, a window with size and advance equal to 20 and 5 time units, respectively, will cover periods $[0, 20)$, $[5, 25)$, $[10, 30)$ and so on.

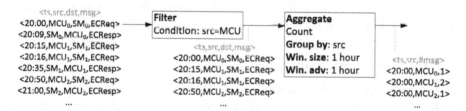

Fig. 1. Sample query that computes the number of messages forwarded by each MCU during the last hour. The figure includes the abstract schema and a set of sample tuples for each stream.

In order to embrace a wide spectrum of real-world installations, the generic schema we take into account for the streams generated by the AMI's devices is composed by attributes $\langle ts, src, dst, msg \rangle$, specifying the timestamp ts at which message msg is forwarded by source src to destination dst. In the remainder, we use the terms tuple and message interchangeably when referring to the devices' communication. Figure 1 presents a sample query that computes the number of messages forwarded by each MCU during the last hour for a given set of input tuples (also shown in the figure).

2.5   Bayesian Networks

Bayesian Networks (BNs) provide a probabilistic graphical model in which a set of random variables (and their dependencies) are represented by means of a Directed Acyclic Graph. Given two random variables A and B, a directed edge from A to B specifies that the latter is conditioned by the former [9]. The conditional probability $P(B = b_j | A = a_i)$ represents the probability of observing b_j given that a_i has already been observed. Figure 2 presents a sample Bayesian Network in relation with our AMI model.

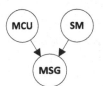
Sample Bayesian Network composed by three variables: MCU, SM and MSG. This Bayesian Network specifies that the probability of observing a given message MSG depends both on the MCU and the SM exchanging it.

Fig. 2. Sample Bayesian Network.

3   *METIS* - Overview

This section overviews *METIS'* architecture and presents how adversary goals can be specified by the system expert. Multiple adversary goals can be specified at the same time. For the ease of the exposition, we provide examples that focus on our energy exfiltration use-case.

3.1   Architecture Overview

Millions of messages are generated on a daily basis by the AMI's devices. Such messages carry heterogeneous information related to energy consumption, energy quality and power outages, among others. If we put ourselves in the role of the system expert, it might be hard to specify how evidence of a given adversary goal could be detected while processing such traffic as a whole. The work required by the system expert can be simplified by splitting it into two narrower tasks: (i) specify how an adversary goal could affect the interaction of certain types of devices (possibly belonging to different networks) and (ii) specify the pattern of suspicious interactions that could be observed over a certain period of time.

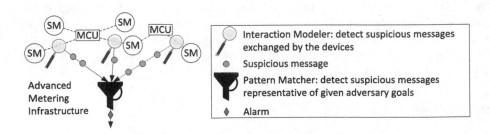

Fig. 3. Overview of *METIS* two-tier architecture.

This decomposition would also ease the deployment of a scalable distributed and parallel traffic analysis. The interaction of the devices could be studied close to the devices themselves (i.e., embracing the different networks of an AMI and monitoring the potentially huge amounts of traffic in parallel). Based on these observations, we designed *METIS* to analyze the AMI traffic by means of two tiers: the *Interaction Modeler* and the *Pattern Matcher* (as presented in Fig. 3). Among its benefits, this two-tier architecture allows for other IDS to be *plugged* into the framework (e.g., by replacing the provided *Interaction Modeler* with a specification-based IDS such as [1]).

Interaction Modeler. This tier analyzes the messages received and sent by each device and relies on anomaly-based detection to distinguish the ones that are expected from the *suspicious* ones.

The anomaly-based technique employed by the *Interaction Modeler* distinguishes between expected and *suspicious* messages based on the probability of observing them. It should be noticed that such probability evolves over time and is potentially influenced by several factors. As an example, the probability of observing an ECReq message could depend on the MCU forwarding it, on the SM receiving it, on the quality of the communication between these two devices, and so on.

If we tackle this aspect from the system expert point of view, it is desirable to have an intuitive way of specifying with traffic features should be taken into account for a given adversary goal. To our advantage, Bayesian Networks (BNs) provide an effective and graphical way of representing such features and their inter-dependencies. At the same time, BNs can also be automatically translated into data streaming queries, as we discuss in Sect. 4.2.

Since *METIS* relies on the data streaming processing paradigm, probabilities are maintained over a window of size IM_{WS} and advance IM_{WA} (specified by the system expert), thus coping with the evolving nature of AMIs. IM_{WS} represents the period of time during which traffic should be observed in order to have representative probabilities. IM_{WA} specifies the amount of information that should be discarded each time the window slides. As an example, if parameters IM_{WS} and IM_{WA} are set to 12 months and 1 months, respectively, probabilities based on the traffic observed during the last year would be produced every month.

Pattern Matcher. The anomaly-based detection mechanism employed by the *Interaction Modeler*, based on the probability with which messages are expected, can result in legitimate messages being considered as *suspicious*. As an example, this could happen when lossy communication between a pair of devices leads to a low expectation associated to a certain legitimate message. For this reason, the *Pattern Matcher* consumes the *suspicious* messages forwarded by the *Interaction Modeler* in order to distinguish the ones that are isolated from the ones representative of a given adversary goal, raising an *alarm* in the second case.

The system expert is required to specify how *suspicious* messages should be processed by means of four parameters. An *alarm* is raised if a threshold T of *suspicious* messages sharing the same values for the set of attributes GB are observed given a window of size PM_{WS} and advance PM_{WA}.

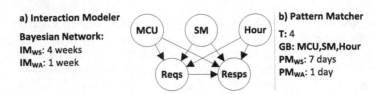

Fig. 4. Input provided by the system expert for *METIS' Interaction Modeler* and *Pattern Matcher*

3.2   Energy Exfiltration Use-Case

Interaction Modeler. Given our adversary model for the energy exfiltration use-case, the malicious traffic would result in an unusual exchange of ECReq and ECResp messages between a pair of MCUs and SMs. Hence, the system expert could define a BN composed by two variables: Reqs (the number of ECReq messages observed in the window) and Resps (the number of ECResp messages observed in the window), with Reqs being a conditional variable for Resps. In our model, SMs are not statically connected to MCUs. Moreover, energy consumption readings can be retrieved multiple times at different hours during each day (the hour actually depends on the MCU). For this reason, more variables could be added to the BN, as shown in Fig. 4a. Since SMs do not change the MCU to which they connect on a daily basis, a window of four weeks ($IM_{WS} = 4$ weeks) updated every week ($IM_{WA} = 1$ week) could be long enough to detect unexpected exchanges of ECReq and ECResp messages.

Pattern Matcher. As discussed in Sect. 2.3, the adversary is willing to collect energy consumption readings over a certain number of days in order to infer detailed information about the victim's household activities. In this example (Fig. 4b), the system expert specifies that an *alarm* should be raised if at least four suspicious messages ($T = 4$) are observed for the same MCU, SM and hour ($GB = MCU, SM, Hour$) given a window of size seven days ($PM_{WS} = 7$ days) and advance one day ($PM_{WA} = 1$ day).

4   Detecting Anomalies by Means of Continuous Queries

As discussed in Sect. 3.1, one of the motivations of *METIS* is to ease the system expert's interaction with the framework. For this reason, *METIS* decouples the semantics of the analysis from its actual implementation and deployment. That is, it requires the expert to specify how to detect a given adversary goal by means of a BN and a set of parameters, while it is responsible for compiling such information into a data streaming query. In the following sections we overview the processing carried out by the query, also discussing how the BN is learnt by means of data streaming operators.

4.1   Continuous Query - Overview

Both the traffic analysis of the *Interaction Modeler* and the *Pattern Matcher*
are carried out by a single data streaming query compiled by *METIS*. For the
ease of the exposition, we present this query by means of four modules: the *Data
Preparer*, the *BN Learner*, the *Probabilistic Filter* and the *Pattern Matcher*
(as presented in Fig. 5). The first three modules perform the analysis of the
Interaction Modeler while the last module is responsible for the analysis of the
Pattern Matcher.

The *Data Preparer* pre-processes the information required to learn the given
BN. It relies on a Filter operator to discard messages that are not relevant for
the BN and on an Aggregate operator to aggregate the information based on
the BN's variables. The tuples forwarded by the *Data Preparer* are consumed
by the *BN Learner*, in charge of maintaining the probabilities over the window
of size IM_{WS} and advance IM_{WA}. The exact number of operators that compose
the *BN Learner* depends on the number of variables specified by the BN, as
we discuss in the following section. The tuples produced by the *BN Learner*
associate the messages observed during the given window to a certain probability. This information is processed, together with the information produced
by the *Data Preparer*, by the *Probabilistic Filter*. As discussed in Sect. 2.2, the
evolving nature of AMIs demands for continuous learning. For this reason, the
Probabilistic Filter compares each tuple produced by the *Data Preparer* with its
associated probability learned over the latest completed window. As an example, if parameters IM_{WS} and IM_{WA} are set to 10 and 5 time units, respectively,
the window will cover periods $P_1 = [0, 10)$, $P_2 = [5, 15)$, $P_3 = [10, 20)$, and so
on. Messages observed in period $[10, 15)$ would be matched with the probabilities learned during period P_1, messages observed in period $[15, 20)$ would be
matched with the probabilities learned during period P_2, and so on. A tuple
produced by the *Data Preparer* is forwarded by the *Probabilistic Filter* based
on a probabilistic trial. As an example, if the probability learned for a certain
message is 0.9, such a message will be forwarded with a probability equal to
0.1. Tuples forwarded by the *Probabilistic Filter* represent the tuples considered
as *suspicious* by the *Interaction Modeler*. As discussed in Sect. 3.1, an *alarm* is
raised if at least T *suspicious* messages sharing the same values for the set of
attributes GB are observed given a window of size PM_{WS} and advance PM_{WA}.
The *Pattern Matcher* relies on an Aggregate operator to count how many *suspicious* messages sharing the same values for the set of attributes GB are received
given a window of size PM_{WS} and advance PM_{WA}. A Filter operator is used

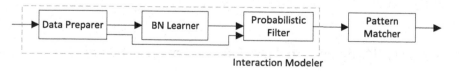

Fig. 5. Overview of the query created by *METIS*.

to filter only the tuples produced by the Aggregate operator whose counter is greater than or equal to T. We provide an example of the continuous query associated to the energy exfiltration use-case in Sect. 5.

4.2   Learning BNs by Means of Data Streaming Operators

The number of operators composing the *BN Learner* depends on the variables defined for the BN. As we discuss in the following, the ability to automatically convert a BN to a query boils down to the ability of computing the probabilities of its variables by means of data streaming operators.

Given two discrete variables X such that $supp(X) \in \{x_0, x_1, \ldots, x_m\}$ and Y such that $supp(Y) \in \{y_0, y_1, \ldots, y_n\}$ and a sequence S of observations $o_1, o_2, \ldots$ such that $o_s = \langle x_i, y_j \rangle$ and all observations belong to the same window, the conditional probability can be computed as

$$P(Y = y_j | X = x_i) = \frac{|\{o_s \in S | o_s = \langle x_i, y_j \rangle\}|}{|\{o_s \in S | o_s = \langle x_i, . \rangle\}|}$$

In order to compute such a value, we need to count the number of occurrences of each pair $\langle x_i, y_j \rangle$ and each value x_i. In terms of data streaming operators, these numbers can be maintained by two Aggregate operators. The first Aggregate operator would count the occurrences of each pair $\langle x_i, y_j \rangle$. Similarly, the second Aggregate operator would count the occurrences of each value x_i. Subsequently, values referring to the same x_i value could be matched by an EquiJoin operator and the resulting division computed by a Map operator.

Figure 6 presents a sample execution of the operators for a given sequence of tuples. In the example, variable X assumes values $\{x_0, x_1\}$ while variable Y assume values $\{y_0, y_1\}$. In the example, the windows' size and advance parameters are both set to 10 time units.

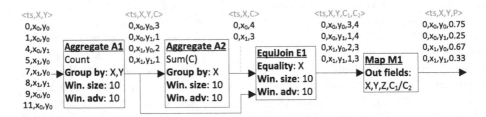

Fig. 6. Continuous query used to compute $P(Y|X)$. The figure includes the abstract schema and a set of sample tuples for each stream.

5   Energy Exfiltration Use-Case - Sample Execution

In this section, we provide a sample execution of the continuous query compiled by *METIS*, given the BN and the parameters presented in Sect. 3.2. The query

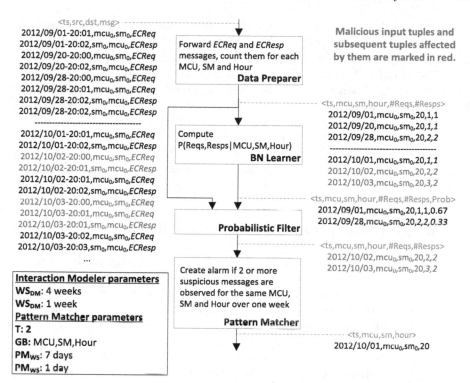

Fig. 7. Sample execution of the query compiled for the energy exfiltration use-case. The figure includes the abstract schema and a set of sample tuples for each stream (Color figure online).

is presented in Fig. 7. For the ease of the exposition, we focus on the messages exchanged between a single pair of MCUs and SMs, $\langle mcu_0, sm_0 \rangle$.

The *Data Preparer* module relies on its Filter operator to forward only ECReq and ECResp messages. These messages are then consumed by the Aggregate operator, in charge of counting how many ECReq and ECResp messages are exchanged between each MCU and SM and for each hour. In the example, malicious messages (injected by the adversary) are marked in red. As shown in the figure, an exchange of a single ECReq and a single ECResp message is observed twice while an exchange of two ECReq and two ECResp messages is observed only once during the month of September. Similarly, exchanges of one ECReq and one ECResp messages, two ECReq and two ECResp messages, and three ECReq and two ECResp messages are observed once during the month of October. The last two tuples produced by the Aggregate operator are marked in red since they are influenced by the malicious input messages.

The probability of observing each combination is computed by the *BN Learner* module. The probability of observing an exchange of one ECReq and one ECResp messages is 67% while the probability of observing an exchange of two ECReq and two ECResp messages is 33%. The probabilities computed by the *BN Learner* and the tuples produced by the *Data Preparer* are matched by the *Probabilistic Filter*. As discussed in Sect. 4.1, each tuple produced by the *Data Preparer* is matched with its associated probability observed in the latest completed window. In the example, tuples produced during the month of October will be matched with the probabilities observed for the month of September. Tuples $\langle 2012/09/01, mcu_0, sm_0, 20, 1, 1 \rangle$, $\langle 2012/09/02, mcu_0, sm_0, 20, 2, 2 \rangle$ and $\langle 2012/09/03, mcu_0, sm_0, 20, 3, 2 \rangle$ have a probability of 0.33, 0.67 and 1, respectively, of being considered as suspicious. In the example, tuples $\langle 2012/09/02, mcu_0, sm_0, 20, 2, 2 \rangle$ and $\langle 2012/09/02, mcu_0, Sm_0, 20, 3, 2 \rangle$ are considered as suspicious and forwarded. Since the threshold T is set to two, an alarm is raised by the *Pattern Matcher*.

6 Energy Exfiltration Use-Case - Evaluation

In this section we evaluate *METIS* with respect to our energy exfiltration use-case and show that (i) it is able to detect malicious activity and that (ii) it can be leveraged by relying on commodity hardware. We first present the evaluation setup, discussing the real world AMI from which data is extracted and the attack injection methodology for the energy exfiltration attacks. We continue by presenting the detection accuracy for a given configuration of the *Interaction Modeler* and the *Pattern Matcher*, also discussing how different configurations affect their detection capabilities. Subsequently, we evaluate the processing capacity of *METIS* (in terms of throughput and latency) when executed by a server that could be deployed at the utility head-end.

6.1 Testbed and Dataset Description

METIS has been implemented on top of Storm, version 0.9.1. The continuous query (*topology* in Storm's terminology) is composed by fourteen operators. The real-world AMI used in our evaluation is composed by 300,000 SMs that communicate with 7,600 MCUs via IEEE 802.15.4 and ZigBee. The network covers a metropolitan area of 450 km^2 with roughly 600,000 inhabitants. The utility extracted data for a subset of 100 MCUs that communicate with approximately 6,500 SMs and made it available for us. The input data covers a period of six months ranging from September 2012 to February 2013. To the best of our knowledge, this dataset is free from energy exfiltration attacks. SMs are not statically linked to MCUs. At the same time, SMs appear and disappear (e.g., because of new installations or decommissioning). MCUs are in charge of collecting energy consumption readings at different hours, usually two or three times per day (the hours at which the collection happens is specific for each MCU). Due to the wireless communication, it is common for MCUs and SMs to lose messages that are thus forwarded multiple times. Each MCU has a maximum of three attempts per hour to retrieve the energy consumption of a given SM. The information kept by the utility does not contain the exact number of messages exchanged for a given MCU, SM and day. Nevertheless, we are able to compute the probabilities with which a message is lost (and hence sent again) based on the logs stored by the MCUs. The ECReq and ECResp messages for each MCU, SM and day are simulated based on such probabilities.

In order to inject adversary traffic, we randomly pick a MCU-SM pair and, during a period that goes from seven to ten days, we inject ECReq and ECResp messages. In total, we inject 50 energy exfiltration attacks, resulting in 995 malicious messages. Note that these messages are subject to the same probability of being lost as any legitimate message. Furthermore, in order to simulate the behavior of a subtle adversary, malicious messages are exchanged at the same hour at which the MCU is actually retrieving energy consumption readings (as it would be trivial to detect an energy exfiltration attack if messages are exchanged when the MCU is not supposed to communicate).

6.2   Detection Accuracy

In this experiment, the BN is the one presented in Sect. 3.2. The *Interaction Modeler*'s parameters IM_{WS} and IM_{WA} are set to four weeks and one week, respectively. The *Pattern Matcher*'s window parameters PM_{WS} and PM_{WA} are set to seven days and one day, respectively. The *Pattern Matcher* is instructed to raise an alarm if at least a threshold T of five suspicious messages sharing the same values for the set of attributes MCU, SM and Hour is observed. A summary of the results is presented in Table 1.

Table 1. Summary of the *Interaction Modeler*'s and the *Pattern Matcher*'s detection results.

AMI data		
	Number of attacks	50
	Number of malicious messages	995
	Overall number of messages	4, 146, 327
	Messages per day (average)	23, 743
	Suspicious messages per day (average)	450
Interaction Modeler	Malicious messages considered as suspicious	857
	Malicious messages not considered as suspicious	138
Pattern Matcher	Number of alarms	488
	Alarms, True Positive	245
	Alarms, False Positive	243
	Detected Attacks	45

During the six months covered by the data, more than 4.2 million messages are exchanged between the 100 MCUs and the 6, 500 SMs taken into account (more than 23, 000 messages on average on a daily basis). Nevertheless, a small number of approximately 450 messages are considered suspicious on average by the *Interaction Modeler* on a daily basis. 857 out of the 995 malicious messages are considered as suspicious. In total, 488 alarms are raised by the *Pattern Matcher*, 245 of which are related to real attacks (45 attacks are actually detected).

We say an alarm raised by the *Pattern Matcher* is a true positive (resp., false positive), if the period of time covered by its window of size PM_{WS} and advance PM_{WA} actually includes days in which malicious activity has been injected for the given MCU, SM and Hour. It should be noticed that since the window slides every day (PM_{WA} is set to one day), multiple alarms can be raised during consecutive days for one or more suspicious messages referring to a given MCU, SM and Hour. The number of false positives (243) raised during the six months period results in one or two false positives per day, on average. This number of false positives is reasonable for the system expert to use the framework (a reasonable threshold is set to no more than ten false positives per day in [15]). We further analyzed the cause of these alarms and interestingly, most of these false positive alarms are due to new smart meters that appear in the traffic. As this evaluation is based on a real deployment, we can draw the conclusion that the number of devices in this environment is not stable (meaning any assumption of the former would cause false alarms).

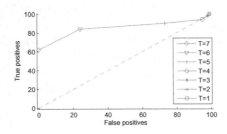

Fig. 8. True Positive and False Positive rates for varying thresholds T.

6.3   Parameters Sensitivity

For a given configuration of the *Pattern Matcher*'s parameters PM_{WS}, PM_{WA} and GB, the number of attacks detected by the former depends on the threshold T (i.e., it depends on the number of days during which suspicious messages should be observed in order to raise an alarm). In this section, we present how the true positive and false positive detection rates are affected by varying the values of the threshold T. Since the *Pattern Matcher*'s Aggregate window size (PM_{WS}) is set to seven days, the experiments are run for $T = 1, \ldots, 7$. As presented in Fig. 8, the minimum true positive rate is achieved when parameter T is equal to seven. In this case, no false positive alarms are raised by the *Pattern Matcher*. It can be noticed that the true positive rate increases to more than 80 % when $T \leq 6$, while it grows to more than 90 % when $T \leq 4$.

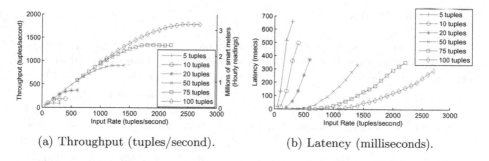

(a) Throughput (tuples/second).   (b) Latency (milliseconds).

Fig. 9. Throughput and latency for increasing input rates and batch sizes.

6.4 Processing Capacity

As shown above, *METIS* is able to detect the majority of the energy exfiltration attacks we injected. In this section, we show it can also cope with the large volume of events produced in a typical AMI. For that reason, we evaluate the processing capacity of *METIS* when running on a server that could be deployed at the utility's head-end, an Intel-based workstation with two sockets of 8-core Xeon E5-2650 processors and 64 GB DDR3 memory.

Among the different parameters that could influence the processing capacity of the query, the *batch* size plays a fundamental role in this context. While processing messages, a trade-off exists between the rate at which such messages can be processed and the latency imposed by the processing itself. In high-throughput systems, it is common to group tuples together in batches (of thousands or tens of thousands of tuples) in order to achieve higher throughput. Nevertheless, this is not an option in our scenario. Each pair of devices exchanges a small number of messages per hour (in the order of tens). If the analysis relies on big batches (e.g., thousands of messages), devices might not be able to log incoming and outgoing messages for the resulting large periods of time and possible attacks would thus not be detected.

Figure 9a presents the processing throughput for different batch sizes, from 5 to 100 tuples. As expected, increasing the batch size results in higher processing throughput. For a batch size of 100 tuples, the server is able to process approximately 2,000 messages per second. Based on our data, each pair of MCU and SM exchanges one ECReq and one ECResp message each time energy consumption is retrieved. If the 2,000 messages processed every second refer to the exchange of 1,000 pairs of MCUs and SMs, the processing capacity of our prototype would enable the monitoring of more than three millions pairs of MCU and SM every hour. Figure 9b presents the corresponding latency (in milliseconds) for the different batch sizes. While a common pattern is observed for all batch sizes (the latency starts increasing when the throughput gets closer to its maximum), it can be noticed that the highest measured latency is of approximately 0.7 seconds. This means that the latency in the detection of an attack would depend on the frequency with which energy consumption readings are retrieved rather than the (negligible) processing time introduced by *METIS*' analysis.

7   Related Work

Despite their recent deployment, a considerable number of potential attacks against AMIs has already been discussed in literature where some have even been seen in the wild [13]. The attacks range from energy theft [16], stealing of users' information [2], up to physical damage of the infrastructure [4].

As outlined in [14], traditional IDSs cannot be used effectively in these environments without major modifications. However, even though there exists a large literature on intrusion detection in general, very few systems have been developed specifically for AMIs. Several papers motivate the need for security in smart grids (where [5] is such an example); others go one step further and discuss detection mechanisms but often concentrating on other parts of the smart grid (such as attack detection in SCADA networks [3], or for process control [12]). Berthier et al. [2] discuss requirements with an outline of a possible intrusion detection architecture suitable for AMIs. To the best of our knowledge, specification-based IDSs are the main defense mechanism proposed so far for AMIs [1,18].

One advantage with our approach is that several detection mechanisms can be used as a sensor in the first tier (the *Interaction Modeler*), meaning that the previously suggested specification-based approaches for AMIs could also be integrated into our framework. However, in this paper we instead suggested Bayesian inference in the first tier. Using Bayesian networks to model attacks merges the best properties of the signature-based approach with the learning characteristics of anomaly detection [26]. A specification-based IDS would require manual labor to tune the system to a specific installation, where a Bayesian attack model would be (relatively) easy to create for the system expert with the added benefit that we automatically can parallelize it in METIS by relying on the data streaming paradigm. Specification-based systems work best in very stable environments; in AMIs it is expected that the traffic will be more dynamic and less deterministic in the future with demand-side networks, as described in [14].

Using several tiers of sensors and analysis engines to improve the detection has been used in traditional IDSs such as [21,25]. Our motivation for having different tiers is that they allow for the implementation of the *Interaction Modeler* to be isolated from the overall event processing. As mentioned above, this approach makes the design and implementation of the attack models easier. The second tier manages the scalability of the approach to allow for the analysis of the underlying traffic in real time.

As discussed in [2,10], the coexistence of distinct networks within the same AMI demands for distributed traffic analysis, either by relying on the devices themselves (as recently investigated in [20]) or by relying on dedicated sensing infrastructures. To this end, the data streaming processing paradigm [23] is an optimal candidate for AMIs traffic analysis, as explored in [6,22,27]. The latter is the closer to our approach, but their evaluation is not based on data from realistic AMIs.[2]

---

[2] They use the KDD Cup 99 dataset, with known problems (http://www.kdnuggets. com/news/2007/n18/4i.html) as well as lacking realistic AMI attacks.

8   Conclusions

This work proposed *METIS*, a two-tier defense framework that eases the modeling of possible adversary goals and allows for a scalable traffic analysis by employing the data streaming processing paradigm. In the paper, besides describing and analyzing its design and implementation, we showed how it is possible for a system expert to model the detection of energy exfiltration attacks, a challenging adversarial goal. Moreover, through the evaluation of the use-case based on big volumes of data extracted from a real world AMI, we showed that *METIS'* analysis can achieve high detection rates, with low false alarm numbers, even when relying on commodity hardware.

It is worth pointing out that the possibility for distributed deployment of *METIS* enables for the detection of a variety of scenarios, including those whose detection is only possible through distributed evidence. The latter opens a path for new research in detecting and mitigating adversarial actions in AMIs, where for scalability and privacy purposes it can be imperative to detect unwanted situations close to the data sources, without the need to store the original data.

Acknowledgments. This work has been partially supported by the European Commission Seventh Framework Programme (FP7/2007–2013) through the SysSec Project, under grant agreement 257007, through the FP7-SEC-285477-CRISALIS project and through the collaboration framework of Chalmers Energy Area of Advance.

References

1. Berthier, R., Sanders, W.H.: Specification-based intrusion detection for advanced metering infrastructures. In: IEEE 17th Pacific Rim International Symposium on Dependable Computing (PRDC) (2011)
2. Berthier, R., Sanders, W.H., Khurana, H.: Intrusion detection for advanced metering infrastructures: requirements and architectural directions. In: First IEEE International Conference on Smart Grid Communications (SmartGridComm) (2010)
3. Cheung, S., Dutertre, B., Fong, M., Lindqvist, U., Skinner, K., Valdes, A.: Using model-based intrusion detection for SCADA networks. In: Proceedings of the SCADA Security Scientific Symposium (2007)
4. Costache, M., Tudor, V., Almgren, M., Papatriantafilou, M., Saunders, C.: Remote control of smart meters: friend or foe? In: Seventh European Conference on Computer Network Defense (EC2ND) (2011)
5. Ericsson, G.N.: Cyber security and power system communication essential parts of a smart grid infrastructure. IEEE Trans. Power Deliv. **25**(3), 1501–1507 (2010)
6. Faisal, M.A., Aung, Z., Williams, J.R., Sanchez, A.: Securing advanced metering infrastructure using intrusion detection system with data stream mining. In: Chau, M., Wang, G.A., Yue, W.T., Chen, H. (eds.) PAISI 2012. LNCS, vol. 7299, pp. 96–111. Springer, Heidelberg (2012)
7. Falliere, N., Murchu, L.O., Chien, E.: W32. Stuxnet dossier. Technical report, Symantec Corporation (2011)
8. FORWARD Consortium: White book: emerging ICT threats. http://www.ict-forward.eu/media/publications/forward-whitebook.pdf
9. Friedman, N., Geiger, D., Goldszmidt, M.: Bayesian network classifiers. Mach. Learn. **29**, 131–163 (1997)

10. Grochocki, D., Huh, J.H., Berthier, R., Bobba, R., Sanders, W.H., Cárdenas, A.A., Jetcheva, J.G.: AMI threats, intrusion detection requirements and deployment recommendations. In: IEEE Third International Conference on Smart Grid Communications (SmartGridComm) (2012)
11. Gulisano, V., Jimenez-Peris, R., Patino-Martinez, M., Soriente, C., Valduriez, P.: Streamcloud: An elastic and scalable data streaming system. IEEE Trans. Parallel Distrib. Syst. **23**(12), 2351–2365 (2012)
12. Hadiosmanovic, D., Bolzoni, D., Hartel, P., Etalle, S.: MELISSA: towards automated detection of undesirable user actions in critical infrastructures. In: Seventh European Conference on Computer Network Defense (EC2ND) (2011)
13. KrebsonSecurity: FBI: Smart Meter Hacks Likely to Spread, April 2012. http://krebsonsecurity.com/2012/04/fbi-smart-meter-hacks-likely-to-spread/
14. Kush, N., Foo, E., Ahmed, E., Ahmed, I., Clark, A.: Gap analysis of intrusion detection in smart grids. In: Proceedings of the 2nd International Cyber Resilience Conference (2011)
15. Lippmann, R., Haines, J.W., Fried, D.J., Korba, J., Das, K.: The 1999 DARPA off-line intrusion detection evaluation. Comput. Netw. **34**(4), 579–595 (2000). Elsevier
16. McLaughlin, S., Podkuiko, D., McDaniel, P.: Energy theft in the advanced metering infrastructure. In: Rome, E., Bloomfield, R. (eds.) CRITIS 2009. LNCS, vol. 6027, pp. 176–187. Springer, Heidelberg (2010)
17. McLaughlin, S., Podkuiko, D., Miadzvezhanka, S., Delozier, A., McDaniel, P.: Multi-vendor penetration testing in the advanced metering infrastructure. In: Proceedings of the 26th Annual Computer Security Applications Conference (2010)
18. Mitchell, R., Chen, I.-R.: Behavior-rule based intrusion detection systems for safety critical smart grid applications. IEEE Trans. Smart Grid **4**(3), 1254–1263 (2013)
19. Molina-Markham, A., Shenoy, P., Fu, K., Cecchet, E., Irwin, D.: Private memoirs of a smart meter. In: Proceedings of the 2nd ACM Workshop on Embedded Sensing Systems for Energy-Efficiency in Building (2010)
20. Raciti, M., Nadjm-Tehrani, S.: Embedded cyber-physical anomaly detection in smart meters. In: Hämmerli, B.M., Kalstad Svendsen, N., Lopez, J. (eds.) CRITIS 2012. LNCS, vol. 7722, pp. 34–45. Springer, Heidelberg (2013)
21. Razak, S.A., Furnell, S.M., Clarke, N., Brooke, P.J.: A two-tier intrusion detection system for mobile ad hoc networks – a friend approach. In: Mehrotra, S., Zeng, D.D., Chen, H., Thuraisingham, B., Wang, F.-Y. (eds.) ISI 2006. LNCS, vol. 3975, pp. 590–595. Springer, Heidelberg (2006)
22. Simmhan, Y., Cao, B., Giakkoupis, M., Prasanna, V.K.: Adaptive rate stream processing for smart grid applications on clouds. In: Proceedings of the 2nd International Workshop on Scientific Cloud Computing (2011)
23. Stonebraker, M., Çetintemel, U., Zdonik, S.: The 8 requirements of real-time stream processing. ACM SIGMOD Rec. **34**(4), 42–47 (2005)
24. Storm project. http://storm.incubator.apache.org/. Accessed 10 March 2014
25. Tombini, E., Debar, H., Mé, L., Ducassé, M.: A serial combination of anomaly and misuse IDSes applied to HTTP traffic. In: 20th Annual Computer Security Applications Conference (2004)
26. Valdes, A., Skinner, K.: Adaptive, model-based monitoring for cyber attack detection. In: Debar, H., Mé, L., Wu, S.F. (eds.) RAID 2000. LNCS, vol. 1907, p. 80. Springer, Heidelberg (2000)
27. Zinn, D., Hart, Q., McPhillips, T., Ludascher, B., Simmhan, Y., Giakkoupis, M., Prasanna, V.K.: Towards reliable, performant workflows for streaming-applications on cloud platforms. In: Proceedings of the 11th IEEE/ACM International Symposium on Cluster, Cloud and Grid Computing (2011)

Online Detection of Concurrent Prefix Hijacks

Shen Su[1(✉)], Beichuan Zhang[2], and Binxing Fang[1]

[1] Harbin Institute of Technology, Harbin, China
johnsuhit@gmail.com, bxfang@pact518.hit.edu.cn
[2] The University of Arizona, Tucson, USA
bzhang@cs.arizona.edu

Abstract. Prefix hijacking is a major security threat to the global Internet routing system. Concurrent prefix hijack detection has been proven to be an effective method to defend routing security. However, the existing concurrent prefix hijack detection scheme considers no prefix ownership changes, and online concurrent prefix hijack detection endures seriously false positive. In this paper, we study the possible characters to filter out false positive events generated online by machine learning, and apply such characters in the online detection. Our result shows that our refined online concurrent prefix hijack detection can detect all offline detected events with no false positive. We also confirm that (1) neighboring ASes seldom hijack each other's prefixes; (2) large ISPs seldom suffer from prefix hijacks or conduct hijacks.

Keywords: Prefix hijack · False positive · Online detection

1 Introduction

Internet is composed of tens of thousands of ASes (Autonomous Systems), which uses BGP (Border Gateway Protocol) to exchange the routing information towards prefixes. Because BGP doesn't consider security, no authentication is required when exchanging routing information. As a result, an AS is able to announce any prefix without authentication (called prefix hijacks), and broadcast it to the rest of the world. Nowadays, prefix hijacking has been the most popular cyber attacks, and widely applied in man in the middle (MITM), phishing scams, and DDOS attacks towards SpamHaus and cloudflare. The traffic to victim prefixes are redirected to attacking networks by such attacks. Attackers may blackhole the victim prefix, impersonate the victim prefix to communicate other entities, or conduct MITM attacks.

To enable authentication, existing proposals [5,6,9,10] require to change BGP, i.e. they require to change existing network configurations and operations which are hard to deploy. Other proposals devote to detect prefix hijacking [3,7,8,11]. Such works collect routing messages and compare them with prefix ownership. The prefix ownership is known as priori [2,7] or inferred from collected routing information [4,8]. However, an up-to-date and complete priori prefix ownership need collaborative works, which is hard to deploy. Approaches

© Institute for Computer Sciences, Social Informatics and Telecommunications Engineering 2015
J. Tian et al. (Eds.): SecureComm 2014, Part II, LNICST 153, pp. 69–83, 2015.
DOI: 10.1007/978-3-319-23802-9_8

based on ownership inference also suffer seriously from false positive alarms because prefix hijacks and some legitimate operational practises have similar behaviors. Our previous work [1] develops a off-line scheme that detects concurrent prefix hijacks which greatly reduce the risk of false positive alarms. In this paper, we propose an improvement on their detection algorithm in online scenarios.

Our previous concurrent prefix hijack detecting scheme relies on the lifetime of prefix announcement to infer prefix ownership. When an AS is observed announcing a prefix for more than one day, it is inferred as an owner. However, in online environment, lifetime cannot reveal prefix ownership changes immediately, e.g. when an AS is a new owner of a prefix, its announcements' lifetime is short, and our previous scheme would treat its announcements as prefix hijacks. Consequently, our previous scheme endures more false positive in online environment.

Towards minimizing the false positive generated online, we analyse the potential characters of false positive alarms. Our idea is based on the assumption that offenders always tend to hijack prefixes effectively at little cost. In cases that the prefix owner can easily detect the routing announcement of the offender, or can easily tackle with the hijack, the prefix hijack is probably a false positive. In practise, we focus on the offender, the offending target (i.e. prefix owner), and the distance between them. As a offender, a transit provider takes risks to hurt its business interest once its customers realize the hijack; large ISPs (Internet service provider) invest more resource into the network security than stub ASes, hijacks towards their prefixes turn out to be bad ideas; hijacking neighboring ASes's prefixes can also be detected and tackled with easily. We look into the offline detection and false positive generated online. Our analysis shows that the prefix hijacks between neighboring ASes and large ISPs seldom occur, but a non-trivial number of false positives fall into the above two cases. Applying the two characters in the online detection, our result shows that we manage to filter out all false positive events. At the same time, our online detection detect the same set of prefix hijack events as the offline scheme.

In the rest of this paper, we discuss related works in Sect. 2. In Sect. 3 we introduce concurrent prefix hijacks detecting scheme and its limitations. In Sect. 4 we introduce our online detection scheme. In Sect. 5, we evaluate our scheme by experimental results and conclude in Sect. 6.

2   Related Works

A number of solutions have been proposed to eliminate the problem of false routing announcements. Such works can be categorized into two broad categories: prevention [5, 6, 9, 10] and detection [3, 7, 8, 11].

The prevention techniques attempt to prevent ASes from announcing false routes. Many prevention proposals [6, 9] are difficult to deploy, because they require extensive cryptographic key distribution infrastructure, and/or a trusted central database. PGBGP and QBGP monitor the origin AS for each prefix according to BGP updates, and a router avoids using new routes if the old route is still available. PGBGP focuses on minimizing few false negatives, however it ends up with many false positives which causes an increase in the time to adopt legitimate new routes. Instead, concurrent prefix hijack detection may have false negatives but zero false positives allows traffic source networks to automate their responses to prefix hijack events.

The detection techniques attempt to identify prefix hijack events through monitoring the routing system, including control plane and data plane information. Such techniques can be categorized as: (a) Traceroute based solutions and (b) Control-plane based solutions. These detection solutions require no change to BGP protocol and thus are more deployable. However it is important to note that existing detection systems are geared towards protecting individual prefix owners, i.e. safeguarding the allocated prefix block of a network against any on-going prefix hijacks. Whereas the traffic source networks needs to protect their entire routing table from any on-going prefix hijacking attacks in order to safeguard all of their data traffic. Therefore each existing detection system poses its own practical limitations in safeguarding an entire routing table for traffic source network, thereby making them ineffective.

Traceroute based solutions protect their prefixes by periodically probing data paths to the protected prefixes, such as iSPY [11] and Lightweight Probing [12]. Such solutions are good to be used when the quantity of prefixes to be protected is small. However, for traffic source networks, the protection list is too long to utilize such traceroute based solutions.

Control-plane-based solutions [8], monitor the entire routing table passively according to BGP data. However, due to limited vantage point locations and legitimate reasons for anomalous updates [4], the results include too many false positives as well as false negatives. Certain control-plane-based solutions, such as PHAS [7] and MyASN [2], use information prefix ownership information to filter out false positives, but then their effectiveness is limited by the number of participating prefix owners. Furthermore, certain solutions, such as [4], combine anomaly detection of control plane information with data-plane fingerprints to perform joint analysis, but the detection accuracy is still limited by the vantage points locations of both data sources. With the high false positives produced by existing control-plane-based solutions, traffic source network could suffer from erroneously dropping correct route updates and thus impacting Internet connectivity. In contrast to existing control plane based systems, concurrent prefix hijack detection correlates suspicious routing announcements along the time dimension and thus minimizes false positives, enabling automated response to prefix hijack attacks without requiring human intervention from traffic source networks.

3   Offline Detection Scheme and Its Limitation

In this section, we first briefly introduce our original detection scheme, then discuss its limitations and possible problems we may encounter when we apply it online.

3.1   Offline Prefix Hijack Detecting Scheme

Our previous concurrent prefix hijack detecting scheme relies on BGP routing data to infer prefix ownership. The inference is based on prefix's announcement lifetime. Usually the owner AS of a prefix is expected to announce the prefix persistently for a long duration. In our scheme, we associate every prefix with a stable set and a related set containing ASes that probably can legitimately announce the prefix. **Stable Sets** captures ASes that are likely owners of a prefix. In practise, any AS announcing a prefix cumulatively for one day or more within a year is included in the prefix's stable set. **Related Sets** captures ASes that are not the owner of the prefix but can legitimately announce it in operation. We have found the following four cases useful for our detection algorithm.

First, an AS in a prefix's stable set also belongs to related set of all its sub-prefixes.

Second, for all ASes in a prefix's stable set, their direct provider ASes also belong to this prefix's related set. For this purpose we use a simple heuristic to identify stable provider-customer inter-AS links. We start with a list of well-known tier-1 ASes, and given an AS path, the link from a tier-1 AS to a non-tier1 AS is provider-customer, and any link after that is also provider-customer due to the commonly deployed No-Valley policy. This can be considered as a subroutine in most of the existing AS relationship inference algorithms, and thus the accuracy in inferring provider-customer relationship should be similar, although we do not need to infer peer-peer or sibling-sibling relationship, which is the challenging part of general AS relationship inference.

Third, ASes participating in an Internet Exchange Point (IXP) can legitimately announce the IXP's prefixes, and similarly the IXP AS can also legitimately announce the prefixes of its participating ASes.

Fourth, ASes belonging to the same organization are related and can legitimately announce each others prefixes. We simply infer such relation from the domain name of the contact emails listed in the WHOIS [13] database.

Any AS not belonging to a prefix's stable set or related set but originating the prefix is deemed to be an offending AS, attempting to potentially hijack the prefix. In such case, we also say that the AS is offending the prefix's stable set, which represents the owner of the prefix. For an offending AS, we defense its offense value as the number of unique ASes that this AS is offending at any given moment. The offense value captures how many other networks are being potentially hijacked simultaneously. Based on the filtered global view of origin changes, we compute offense value for every AS for the entire year.

Algorithm 1 summarizes the above steps. It uses one year of archived BGP tables and updates, available at Route Views Oregon monitors, to construct stable and related sets. Thereafter every BGP routing announcement is checked whether it is suspicious or legitimate by checking origin AS against stable and related set of prefix. Anytime the offense value of an AS exceeds the threshold of 10, it is reported to be a concurrent hijack.

Algorithm 1. Offline prefix hijack detection scheme.

Input:

    StableSets(*p*): stable set of prefix *p*;

    RelatedSets(*p*): related set of prefix *p*;

1: FOR all BGP routing messages
2:    IF AS X announces prefix p at time t
3:       IF AS $X \notin$ *StableSets*(*p*) or *RelatedSets*(*p*)
4:          Update AS X's offense value by *StableSet*(*p*);
5:    ELSIF AS X withdraws prefix p at time t
6:       IF AS $X \notin$ *StableSet*(*p*) or *RelatedSet*(*p*)
7:          Reduce AS X's offense value by *StableSet*(*p*);
8:    Report prefix hijack event: if AS X's offense value $>= 10$

3.2 Limitations

[1] has proved our offline scheme can safely detect prefix hijack events with zero-false positive. However, we still face a few limitations when we apply it in online scenario. And such limitation may impact the detection accuracy.

First of all, to detect prefix hijack events of a year, the offline scheme requires to calculate stable and related sets of each prefix from the BGP routing messages of the entire year. While, in online scenarios, we have no access to the BGP messages which are generated after current time.

Second, the offline detection scheme considers no dynamical factors when inferring stable and related sets. However, prefix ownership, AS topology, and other dynamical factors change over time. So prefix announcement lifetime may mistakenly reflect prefix ownership, especially in online scenarios. Actually, ASes with a short announcement lifetime may legitimately announce a prefix when the above dynamical factors happens. When we observe announcements from such a legitimate announcer, our detecting scheme may report it as a prefix hijack announcement, which is a de facto false positive. For instance, AS A is an owner of prefix p, and we can persistently observe its announcement. So we take the announcement of AS A for granted. At time t, AS B becomes another owner of prefix p. However, we can not infer AS B as an owner until one day after t according to the lifetime. And during that period, we get a false positive.

The above two limitations make us lack the knowledge of whether our detection is suffering from Internet dynamics, i.e. when we observe an announcement originated from an inexperienced AS online, we cannot tell whether this is a prefix hijack or a legitimate announcement because we have no idea of what BGP messages are to be announced.

4 Online Prefix Hijack Detection Scheme

Based on the offline detection scheme, we now design the online detection scheme. Our principle is to minimize the false negative with assurance of no false positive.

To consider dynamical factors, we perform the online detection scheme over a moving observation window $[t - T, t)$ worth of BGP routing messages where

---

Algorithm 2. Online prefix hijack detection scheme.

Input:

        t: current time, $t_0 = t$: time to update Stable and Related sets;

        N: the interval to refresh the observation window;

        T: size of observation window;

 1: Initialize the observation window;

 2: FOR all BGP routing messages in window $(t - T, t)$

 3:    Track duration of prefix-origin AS and AS relation;

 4: Initialize Stable and Related Sets of every prefix;

 5: For all online observed BGP routing messages

 6:    Put this message into the observation window;

 7:    t=time stamp of this BGP message;

 8:    IF AS X announces prefix p at time t

 9:      IF AS $X \notin StableSets(p)$ or $RelatedSets(p)$

10:        Update AS X's offense value by $StableSet(p)$;

11:    ELSIF AS X withdraws prefix p at time t

12:      IF AS $X \notin StableSet(p)$ or $RelatedSet(p)$

13:        Reduce AS X's offense value by $StableSet(p)$;

14:    Report prefix hijack event: if AS X's offense value $>= 10$

15:    IF $t >= t_0 + N$

16:      Update duration of prefix-origin and AS relation;

17:      Update Stable and Related Sets of every prefix;

18:      $t_0 = t$;

---

t is the current time and T is the size of observation window. For the offline detection scheme, one year worth of training data is used to construct the initial stable and related sets for each prefix. Considering the stable and related sets for every prefix can not remain static, we need to dynamically update the stable and related sets with the movement of observation window. The duration of every prefix-origin AS pair and duration of every AS relation pair is updated by tracking the announcement and withdrawal BGP routing messages. With a certain frequency, aforementioned announcement durations are re-evaluated and the stable and related sets of every prefix are updated as shown in Algorithm 2.

Following the offline detection scheme described in Algorithm 1, we check each in-coming BGP routing message online to detect prefix hijack events. Since no future can be observed from the observation window, we require prediction in our online detection. Our idea is to look for characters of prefix hijack events to label false positive out. In the rest of this section, we first discuss the size and recalculating frequency of the observation window. Then we evaluate the seriousness of caused false positive online. Next, we discuss the strategies to filter out such false positives. Finally, we refine the above detection scheme.

4.1   Configuration

We first discuss the size of the observation window. Generally, more considered routing information generates more prefix ownership. However, prefix ownership changes over time, thus our inference may includes outdated prefix ownership. So a bigger observation window in size generates more prefix ownership including more outdated prefix ownership. More prefix ownership helps us to detect more de facto prefix hijacks, while we take more risk with more outdated prefix ownership. Consequently, the size of the observation window is a tradeoff between false positive and false negative.

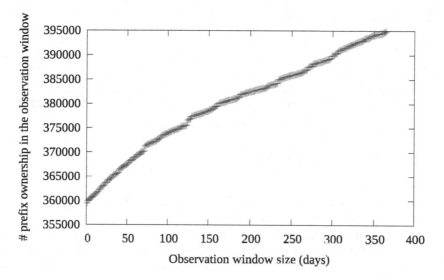

Fig. 1. # prefix ownership over time.

In Fig. 1, we show the total quantity of prefix ownership inferred from the routing information in the observation window during the year of 2011. Considering that the routing table itself is growing in size, we filter out the prefixes which cannot be observed according to the routing data before 2011 (i.e. new prefixes). The x-ray represents the size of the observation window, the y-ray represents corresponding quantity of prefix ownership inferred from the observation window. We notice that even with one-day's routing data, we can infer almost 360,000 (90 % of all) prefixes's ownership. The total quantity goes up to 400,000 linearly with a growth rate around 100 prefixes per day.

We compare the prefix ownership inferred from routing data of each day, and show the cumulated prefix ownership changes over time in Fig. 2. The x-ray represents the observing duration, and the y-ray represents the accumulated quantity of prefixes with a ownership change. We observe a linear growth rate (20–30 prefixes per day), and totally there are less than 10,000 (2.5 % of all) changing ownership prefixes.

To our surprise, neighbor prefix ownership quantity nor prefix ownership changing rates turn out to be a bottle neck factor to the observation window size. With a observation window in size of one day or one year, we have prefix ownership for almost the entire routing table and not too many prefixes

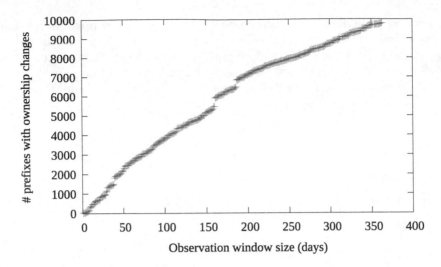

Fig. 2. # prefixes with ownership changing over time.

experiencing ownership changes. Considering our principle (minimizing the false negative with assurance of no false positive) and the tradeoff between false positive and false negative, we decide to set the size as one year. This is because we still need to involve prediction in the detection which is dedicated to filter out false positive alarms. And we want to maximize the value of our detection scheme.

For the frequency to update the stable and related sets, it is a tradeoff between computation cost and outdated information caused detection inaccuracy including both false positive and false negative. A intensive update schedule (update every hour) is unnecessary because there are only around 20–30 prefix ownership changes every day. Our program is written in perl and takes 2–5 minutes to conduct an update on one-year Oregon data. So we decide to update the stable and related sets every day.

4.2   False Positives

Given the outline of the detection scheme, our problem now is to eliminate the false positives generated online. To that end, we begin with depicting the false positive. In Fig. 3, we compare the quantity of prefix hijack instances detected by offline and online detection scheme (following Algorithm 1). We refer to a prefix hijack instance as an offending case when we observe an AS is announcing other ASes' prefix, noted as a triple (T, A, B). T refers to the time when the prefix hijack instance happens, A refers to the offending AS who conducts the prefix hijack instance, and B refers to the origin AS who owns the prefix. Curve "offline" represents the prefix hijack instances observed offline, and Curve "false positive online" represents the online prefix hijack instances which are not observed offline.

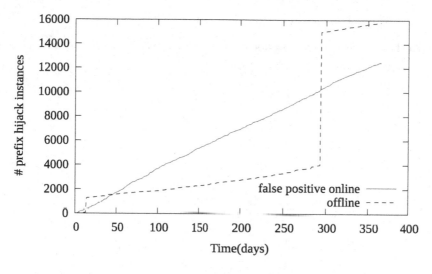

Fig. 3. # prefix hijack instances.

As observed in Fig. 3, online generated false positive are even more than prefix hijack instances detected offline (besides the prefix hijack events happened in Jan and in Oct). So online detected false positive is seriously impacting the accuracy of our online prefix hijack detection. We also notice the linear growth rate of the false positive which is consistent to the linear growth of the prefix ownership changes.

4.3   Increase Threshold

One simple idea comes to us is to increase the threshold. If the offense value of a prefix hijack event is T offline, and T' online. The threshold should be increased by $T' - T$. Following the detection scheme described above, we change the threshold and compare the generated reports with the one generated offline for the year of 2011 on Oregon data [14] (show in Table 1).

In the offline detection, our scheme detects 12 prefix hijack events. When the threshold is 10, we get 12 false positive events. With the threshold going up, the quantity of false positive events gets smaller, but the detection misses more de facto prefix hijack events. When the threshold is 67, we clear all false positive events, but there is only 3 prefix hijack events left in the detection. Consequently, simply increasing threshold can hardly solve the false positive problem. Since the increasement varies among prefix hijack events, if the increasement is small, there are still lots of false positive events; if the increasement is big, the offline detected prefix hijack events are also filtered out.

4.4   Characters of False Positive Instances

Our further strategies to predict false positive is: analysing possible characters which can be used to discriminate false positive instances and de facto prefix

Table 1. Results of online detection with different threshold.

Threshold	# online detected events	# false positive events	# false negative events
10	24	12	0
11	21	10	1
12	19	8	1
13	16	6	2
14	15	5	2
17	12	4	4
19	10	2	4
21	9	1	4
24	8	1	5
28	7	1	6
67	3	0	9

hijack instances (as described in Sect. 4.2). Such characters require to satisfy one of the following conditions: (1) no de facto prefix hijack instance has this character, and some false positive instances have this character; (2) all de facto prefix hijack instances have this character, and some prefix hijack instances don't have this character. For the former, we ignore instances with such characters; for the latter, we ignore without such characters. Since it is a hard job to find a character that all de facto prefix hijack instances have, in this paper, we focus on the characters satisfy the former condition. We analyse characters by first assuming possible characters, then validating with actual BGP data from Oregon in 2011. Totally, we get 12457 false positive instances, and 15786 de facto prefix hijack instances.

Neighboring ASes. Since the information we collect to infer related sets is incomplete, the de facto related set is bigger than the inferred one. Our scheme may takes an AS in the de facto related set as an offender, and cause a false positive. Considering that most ASes in the related set are neighboring ASes of the prefix owner, we assume "the offender and the prefix ownership are neighboring ASes" as a character of the false positive instance.

In practise, among all the false positive instances during 2011, there are 1046 (8.4 % of all) false positive instances which have this character. Among the de facto prefix hijack instances, there are only 43 (0.27 % of all) instances which have this character. Consequently, the character "the offender and the prefix ownership are neighboring ASes" satisfy our requirement to label the false positive instances.

Large ISP. A number of ASes lie in the central of Internet, and provide transit service for a lot of stub ASes. Comparing with stub ASes, such ASes controlled by large ISPs invest much more manpower into their network's routing security. Consequently, prefix hijack towards such ASes are more likely detected and tackled with. In the meanwhile, if a large ISP conduct a prefix hijack to other ASes's prefix, its business interest will be badly harmed once its customer ASes or peering ASes realize the hijack. Thus we assume "the offender or the prefix owner belongs to a large ISP" as a character of the false positive instances.

According to the common understanding that the number of neighboring ASes of an AS can reflect its scale, in this paper, we determine the scale of an AS's belonged ISP based on its quantity of neighboring ASes. In Fig. 4, we show the CDF of offended ASes' (i.e. prefix owners') scale. Curve "false positive" represents false positive instances, and curve "offline" represents de facto prefix hijack instances. We observe that the scales of offended ASes in false positive instances are obviously bigger than the ones in de facto prefix hijack instances. Only 3.2 % of all de facto instances's offended AS are in a scale of more than 100 neighboring ASes. For false positive instances, 17 % of all instances's offended ASes fall into that scale. As a result, we derive a more specific character "the prefix owner's neighboring ASes are more than 100" to label false positive instances.

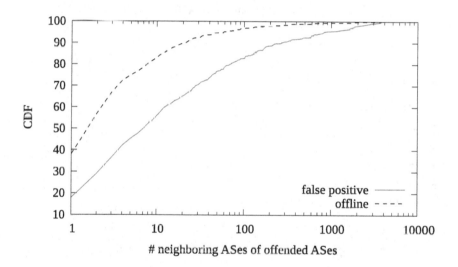

Fig. 4. CDF of offended ASes' scale.

Similarly, in Fig. 5, we show the CDF of offending ASes' scale. As observed, the scales of offending ASes in false positive instances are obviously bigger than that of prefix hijack instances. Only 8.5 % of all de facto instances's offending AS are in a scale of more than 40 neighboring ASes. For false positive instances, 51.2 % of all instances's offending ASes fall into that scale. As a result, we derive a character "the offending AS's neighboring ASes are more than 40" to label false positive instances.

As shown in Algorithm 3, we refine our detection scheme. For each in-coming BGP routing message online, we check if the instance has the two characters before updating the offense value. If it has, we ignore that instance.

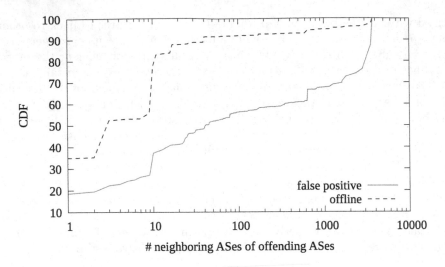

Fig. 5. CDF of offending ASes' scale.

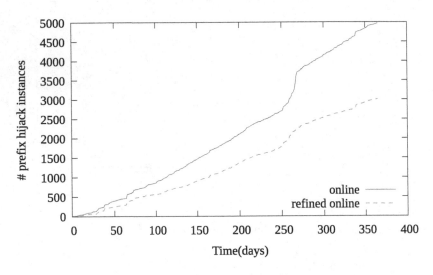

Fig. 6. De facto prefix hijack instances online.

5   Results

In this section, we evaluate our online detection scheme. Since we study the configuration and characters of false positive instances according to the Oregon data in 2011, to prove that our scheme is independent from the data set measured, we use Oregon data in 2012 in this section.

In Fig. 6, we show the CDF of de facto prefix hijack instances detected online. Curve "online" represents de facto prefix hijack instances detected before applying false positive characters, and curve "refined online" represents de facto prefix

Algorithm 3. Online prefix hijack detection scheme.
_____
Input:
    t: current time, $t_0 = t$: time to update Stable and Related sets;
    N: the interval to refresh the observation window;
    T: size of observation window;
  1: Initialize the observation window;
  2: FOR all BGP routing messages in window $(t - T, t)$
  3:    Track duration of prefix-origin AS and AS relation;
  4: Initialize Stable and Related Sets of every prefix;
  5: For all online observed BGP routing messages
  6:    Put this message into the observation window;
  7:    t=time stamp of this BGP message;
  8:    IF AS X announces prefix p at time t
  9:      IF AS X is a neighboring AS of $StableSets(p)$
10:      next;
11:      ESLIF AS X has more than 40 neighboring ASes or an AS in $StableSets(p)$
    has more than 100 neighboring ASes
12:      next;
13:      ESLIF AS $X \notin StableSets(p)$ or $RelatedSets(p)$
14:        Update AS X's offense value by $StableSet(p)$;
15:    ELSIF AS X withdraws prefix p at time t
16:      IF AS X is a neighboring AS of $StableSets(p)$
17:      next;
18:      ESLIF AS X has more than 40 neighboring ASes or an AS in $StableSets(p)$
    has more than 100 neighboring ASes
19:      next;
20:      ESLIF AS $X \notin StableSet(p)$ or $RelatedSet(p)$
21:        Reduce AS X's offense value by $StableSet(p)$;
22:    Report prefix hijack event: if AS X's offense value $>= 10$
23:    IF $t >= t_0 + N$
24:      Update duration of prefix-origin and AS relation;
25:      Update Stable and Related Sets of every prefix;
26:      $t_0 = t$;
_____

hijack instances detected after applying false positive characters. We notice that about 40 % of the prefix hijack instances are filtered out after we refine the detection scheme. However, we also notice that the two curves share a similar shape. Their cliff points are at almost the same set of time points, i.e. both curves capture the same prefix hijack events. Consequently, our refined detection scheme can capture the de facto events at the cost of offense value decrease.

In Fig. 7, we show the CDF of false positive prefix hijack instances detected online. Curve "false positive online" represents false positive instances detected before applying false positive characters, and curve "false positive refined" represents false positive instances detected after applying false positive characters. Our refined scheme labels out 80 % of the false positive instances. Moreover, our refined scheme does not have obviously cliff points which may induce false positive events.

Actually, during the year of 2012, the offline detection scheme detects 11 prefix hijack events. The original online detection scheme detect 46 prefix hijack

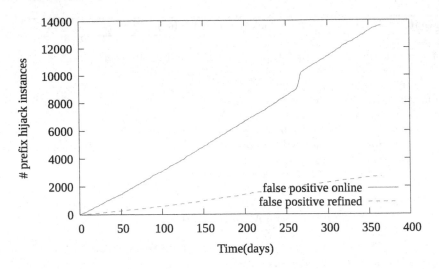

Fig. 7. False positive instances online.

events, in which 35 of them are false positive events. While the refined online detection scheme detects 11 prefix hijack events during 2012, which matches perfectly with the offline detection.

6   Conclusion

In this paper, we propose an online concurrent prefix hijack detection scheme. By analysing characters of false positive instances, we manage to filter out false positive events generated online. In the meanwhile, our detection scheme captures all the prefix hijack events offline.

In the process of studying suitable characters for filtering out false positive instances, we also learn that attackers seldom hijack neighboring ASes' prefixes. Attackers also seldom hijack large ISP's prefix, and vice versa.

Acknowledgement. This research was partially supported by the National Basic Research Program of China (973 Program) under grant No. 2011CB302605, the National High Technolgy Research and Development Program of China (863 Program) under grants No. 2011AA010705 and No. 2012AA012506, China Internet Network Information Center (CNNIC) under grants No. K201211043, the National Key Technology R&D Program of China under grant No. 2012BAH37B00, the National Science Foundation of China (NSF) under grants No. 61173145 and No. 61202457.

References

1. Varun, K., Qing, J., Zhang, B.: Concurrent prefix hijacks: occurrence and impacts. In: IMC (2012)
2. RIPE myASN System. http://www.ris.ripe.net/myasn

3. Chi, Y.-J., Oliveiro, R., Zhang, L.: Cyclops: the AS level connectivity observatory. SIGCOMM Comput. Commun. Rev. **38**(5), 5–16 (2008)
4. Hu, X., Mao, Z. M.: Accurate real-time identification of IP prefix hijacking. In: IEEE Symposium on Security and Privacy (2007)
5. Karlin, J., Forrest, S., Rexford, J.: Pretty Good BGP: improving BGP by cautiously adopting routes. In: ICNP (2006)
6. Kent, S., Lynn, C., Mikkelson, J., Seo, K.: Secure border gateway protocol (S-BGP). IEEE JSAC **18**, 103–116 (2000)
7. Lad, M., Massey, D., Pei, D., Wu, Y., Zhang, B., Zhang, L.: PHAS: a prefix hijack alert system. In: USENIX Security Symposium (2006)
8. Qiu, J., Gao, L., Ranjan, S., Nucci, A.: Detecting bogus BGP route information: going beyond prefix hijacking. In: SecureComm (2007)
9. Subramanian, L., Roth, V., Stoica, I., Shenker, S., Katz, R. H.: Listen and whisper: security mechanisms for BGP. In: NSDI (2004)
10. Zhang, M., Liu, B., Zhang, B.: Safeguarding data delivery by decoupling path propagation and adoption. In: INFO-COM (2010)
11. Zhang, Z., Zhang, Y., Hu, Y. C., Mao, Z. M., Bush, R.: iSPY: detecting IP prefix hijacking on my own. In: SIG-COMM, pp. 327–338 (2008)
12. Zheng, C., Ji, L., Pei, D., Wang, J., Francis, P.: A light-weight distributed scheme for detecting IP prefix hijacks in real-time. In: ACM SIGCOMM (2007)
13. Whois Database. http://www.whois.net/
14. University of Oregon Route Views Archive Project. http://www.routeview.org

Countermeasures for Mitigating ICN Routing Related DDoS Attacks

Eslam G. AbdAllah$^{(\boxtimes)}$, Mohammad Zulkernine, and Hossam S. Hassanein

Queen's University, 99 University Ave, Kingston, ON K7L 3N6, Canada
{eslam,mzulker,hossam}@cs.queensu.ca

Abstract. Information Centric Networking (ICN) is a new communication paradigm for the future Internet that focuses on contents rather than infrastructures or end-points. Distributed Denial of Service (DDoS) attacks that may occur in many scenarios in an ICN, can overwhelm ICN routing and caching resources. In this paper, we focus on routing related DDoS attacks from both publisher and subscriber points of view and how they impact ICNs. We then propose a generic solution independent of a specific ICN architecture. This solution is based on a number of countermeasures: request satisfaction ratio, request rate limit, rating for contents and publishers, and test message. We present the implementation results, which show that the solution mitigates the routing related DDoS attacks and efficiently enhances the ICN performance in the existence of these attacks.

Keywords: Information centric networking · Distributed denial of service · ICN routing.

1 Introduction

The Internet was originally developed in the 1970's as the Internet of hosts. Nowadays, the Internet appears as Internet of things, Internet of services, Internet of people and Internet of media. According to Cisco Visual Networking Index 2013, global IP traffic per month will reach approximately 126 Exabytes by the year 2017 [1]. Information Centric Networking (ICN) is one of the proposed alternatives for these new Internets and requirements. ICN mainly depends on location-independent naming, name-based routing, built-in security and in-network caching [2]. The most popular ICN architectures are Named Data Networking (NDN), Data Oriented Network Architecture (DONA), Network of Information (NetInf), and Publish Subscribe Internet Technology (PURSUIT) [3]. All ICN architectures share several common components: information object, naming, routing, caching, security, and application programming interface.

This paper investigates the routing related Distributed Denial of Service (DDoS) attacks in an ICN in general regardless of a specific ICN architecture. We address seven different scenarios in which the attacker can be a malicious subscriber or a malicious publisher or both.

© Institute for Computer Sciences, Social Informatics and Telecommunications Engineering 2015
J. Tian et al. (Eds.): SecureComm 2014, Part II, LNICST 153, pp. 84–92, 2015.
DOI: 10.1007/978-3-319-23802-9_9

The proposed solution consists of five countermeasures. First, the request satisfaction ratio (RSR) measures the ratio between satisfied and outgoing requests per ICN router interface. RSR depends on a one-to-one relation between the request and the response in an ICN architecture. Second, the request rate limit applies rate limitations for ICN requesters that exceed the request rate thresholds. The ranking for ICN contents (third) and publishers (fourth) mitigates the effects of malicious contents and publications. Fifth, test message is utilized to check the validity of announced routes. To evaluate our solution, we implement the solution on ndnSIM [4]. The ndnSIM is a simulator for Named Data Networking (NDN) architecture and it is an NS-3 based module. The suggested solution is specifically tailored for various unique aspects of the ICN. The in-network caching is one of the major ICN components and not available in non-ICN environments. There are no host addresses; therefore the solution does not depend on any IP-based addressing as in non-ICN environments. The request satisfaction ratio depends on the ICN property that each request has only one response and there is no response without a request. However, in non-ICN environments, a request can receive many data packets. The rating for ICN contents ranks the contents regardless of its source. The other two countermeasures (request rate limit and rating for publisher) depend on the RSR.

2   Attack Scenarios

In this section, we present a comprehensive list of routing related DDoS attack scenarios in the ICN. We used a generic model of an ICN architecture as a reference model. This model consists of ICN routers, distributed storage location, and ICN users. ICN routers contain routing and caching capabilities. The distributed storage locations are used to store the ratings for ICN contents and publishers. ICN users are classified into publishers and subscribers. ICN subscribers can send a subscription message or vote against an invalid content.

An attacker can overwhelm the ICN resources such as bandwidth, routing tables, processing, and storage in the following scenarios:

1. Attacker sends malicious requests for available contents. (subscriber)
   (a) For the same content.
   (b) For different contents.
2. Attacker sends malicious requests for unavailable contents. (subscriber)
3. Attacker sends malicious requests for available and unavailable contents. (subscriber)
4. Attacker announces invalid routes. (publisher)
5. Attacker announces invalid contents. (publisher)
6. Attacker votes against valid contents. (subscriber)
7. Attacker announces invalid contents and another attacker requests for invalid contents and does not vote against these contents. (publisher and subscriber)

An attacker can be a malicious subscriber or a malicious publisher or both as indicated after each scenario listed above. The impacts of these attacks may be amplified if the attackers act in a distributed manner. Scenario 1.a does not need any special countermeasure in an ICN, as there is in-network caching that can respond from an access router connected to subscribers. Scenario 1.b is similar to scenario 7. The main difference is the practical difficulty of scenario 1.b, as an attacker needs to send many different requests for available contents. In scenario 7, a malicious publisher announces invalid contents and a malicious subscriber requests for them dynamically. Scenario 4 causes the same impacts of the request timeout as scenario 2. As a part of our solution depends on user voting against malicious publications, thus scenario 6 is included.

Some existing works address malicious subscriptions [5–7]. They work on a specific ICN architecture and each one of them addresses a specific type of DDoS attack. Gasti et al. [8] present a high level classification of DDoS attacks and their solutions in NDN. Some other papers also classify DDoS attacks and their detection/prevention mechanisms in general [9–11]. The famous countermeasures for DDoS in the Internet architecture are IP trace back, packet filtering, and rate limiting. These techniques cannot be used in the ICN as they depend on IP addresses for the end-points.

3   Countermeasures

The proposed solution consists of five countermeasures for ICN routing. When the subscriber sends a request, an ICN router checks its cache, and if the requested content is not in the cache it forwards the request to the ICN. The ICN tries to get the best available content with the best trusted publisher based on their ranking stored in the distributed storage. The ICN router forwards the response to the subscriber and updates the request satisfaction ratio for this user. The request rate limit, rating for contents, and rating for publishers countermeasures are dependent on the RSR. The subscriber also can vote against an invalid content. The publisher sends an announcement for his/her content route. The RSR, request rate limit, rating for contents, and rating for publishers handle the attack scenarios 1, 2, 3, and 7. The test message addresses the attack scenario 4. The RSR, rating for contents, and rating for publishers handle the attack scenarios 5 and 6. This solution is implemented with a pushback mechanism that allows ICN routers to cooperate for achieving a better performance [5,6]. The countermeasures are as follows:

Request Satisfaction Ratio (RSR): RSR measures the number of the satisfied requests with respect to the number of outgoing requests. The request satisfaction ratio for interface i (RSR_i) is calculated by the following equation:

$$RSR_i = \frac{number\ of\ satisfied\ requests}{number\ of\ outgoing\ requests} \qquad (1)$$

ICN architectures can manage a distributed storage depending on whether the architecture contains a name resolution entity or not. In the architectures with a name resolution entity (e.g., DONA, NetInf), the vote can be directed to the connected name resolution entity. The name resolution entity then updates the other name resolution entities as a normal publication process in these architectures. Each entry in the name resolution entity contains the ratings for the contents and publishers in addition to the normal record. In the architectures without a name resolution entity, there are also two other situations. When the architecture has global locations for publication and subscription like the PUSURIT architecture, the votes can be directed to the connected rendezvous network and the interconnected networks update the ratings for contents and publishers. When there is no centralization of any sort like the NDN architecture, we need a storage capability such as distributed databases, distributed hash table or cloud-based solutions to store the ratings for contents and publishers.

The solution incorporates three messages to the ICN API primitives "publish" and "subscribe" as follows: (1) vote message: subscriber votes against a certain content. It uses the content name as the main parameter, (2) alert message: ICN router sends an alert to a subscriber when a content or publisher rate is more than a certain threshold value, and (3) test message: ICN router sends a test message through a route that does not return any response to check whether this route is malicious or not.

Request Rate Limit: This countermeasure limits the incoming requests based on the traffic rate and the request satisfaction ratio. For a given time interval, if the number of requests from interface i exceeds a certain threshold limit, then the ICN limits the incoming requests from interface i by:

$$Request\ rate\ limit = \frac{RSR_i * L_{max}}{n} \tag{2}$$

where L_{max} is the maximum number of routing table entries and n is the total number of the interfaces.

Rating for Contents: This countermeasure ranks ICN contents, consequently an ICN can select the best trusted available content. The voting weight against content c ($W_{content}$) is calculated by the following equation:

$$W_{content} = \sum_{i=1}^{n} \frac{CV_{Ui}}{number\ of\ U_i\ votes} * RSR_i \tag{3}$$

where U_i is the user who connected to interface i, CV_{U_i} is the U_i votes against content c, and n is the number of votes against this content. The voting ratio against content c ($R_{content}$) is calculated based on the following equation:

$$R_{content} = \frac{number\ of\ votes\ against\ (c)}{number\ of\ downloads\ for\ (c)} \tag{4}$$

From Eqs. (3) and (4), we drive the following equation:

$$Rating\ for\ content\ (c) = W_{content} * R_{content} \tag{5}$$

Rating for Publishers: This countermeasure ranks ICN publishers. As a result, an ICN can select the best trusted publisher. The voting weight against publisher p ($W_{publisher}$) is calculated by the following equation:

$$W_{publisher} = \sum_{i=1}^{n} \frac{PV_{Ui}}{number\ of\ U_i\ votes} * RSR_i \tag{6}$$

where U_i is the user who connected to interface i, PV_{U_i} is the U_i votes against publisher p, and n is the number of votes against this publisher. The voting ratio against publisher p ($R_{publisher}$) is calculated by the following equation:

$$R_{publisher} = \frac{number\ of\ publications\ that\ received\ voting}{number\ of\ publications\ from\ (p)} \tag{7}$$

From Eqs. (6) and (7), we get the following equation:

$$Rating\ for\ publisher\ (p) = W_{publisher} * R_{publisher} \tag{8}$$

Figure 1 presents the flowchart of the proposed solution. The flowchart uses two functions (check request availability and user voting) that are shown in Algorithm 1 and 2, respectively. This solution is implemented in ICN routers. Once the subscriber sends a request, the router checks its availability. If this request passes the availability check, the router forwards it and waits for the response (assuming the requested content is not in the cache). Then the ICN finds the best available content based on our ranking to ICN contents and publishers. An ICN router checks the response in three cases. First, when the content is found, the router updates the RSR for this interface and checks the rating for ICN contents and publishers. If the rating is more than a certain threshold value, it sends an alert message to the subscriber, who decides whether to accept this content or not. If the subscriber receives a content, he/she can vote against it. Second, when there is no content found with the requested name, the router just updates the RSR for this interface. Third, when the request is timed out, the router first checks the behavior of this interface. If the RSR of this interface is under a certain value, then the router directly updates the RSR for this interface. If the RSR is above the threshold value, the router sends a test message to check the announced route. If the router gets a response, then it retransmits the request again. Otherwise, it marks this route as a malicious one and also updates the RSR. All the threshold values can be dynamically set by ICN administrators. In Algorithm 2, the router detects whether this request is legitimate or not by checking the RSR and request rate for an interface.

Algorithm 1 describes the user voting against a false content. Then ICN routers send the voting message with the calculated weight to the storage location.

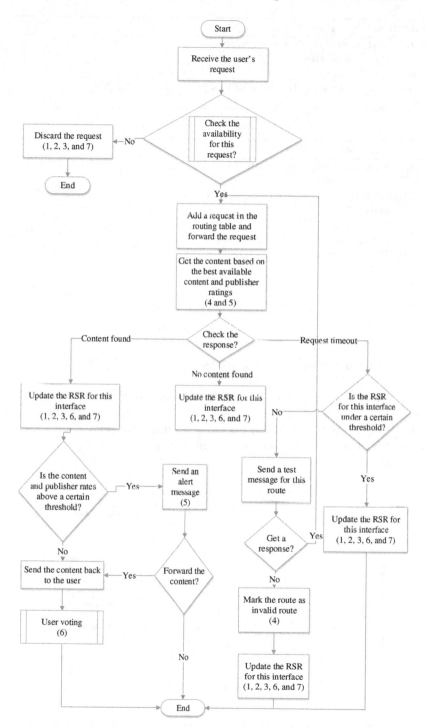

Fig. 1. Solution steps and countermeasures for ICN routing related DDoS attacks scenarios (the numbers inside the boxes indicate the affected scenarios)

Algorithm 1. User voting

Input: Received content upon users request
1: **if** *content* is *invalid* **then**
2:      send vote message
3:      update the rating for the content and publisher by the ICN
4: **end if**

Algorithm 2. Check request availability

Input: Incoming users request via interface i
1: **if** RSR_i is *valid* **then**
2:      **if** request rate $<$ threshold limit **then**
3:          **return** Yes
4:      **else**
5:          **return** No
6:      **end if**
7: **else**
8:      **return** No
9: **end if**

4   Implementation and Results

In this section, we study the impacts of ICN routing related DDoS attacks with
and without the proposed solution. We evaluate the solution using the ndnSIM
as a proof of concept. We build our experiments using the AT&T network which
is Internet-like real network. Our implementation parameters are as follows: no.

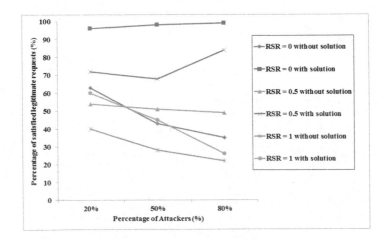

Fig. 2. Percentage of satisfied legitimate requests in the existence of attack scenarios
1, 2, 3, and 7 with and without the proposed solution

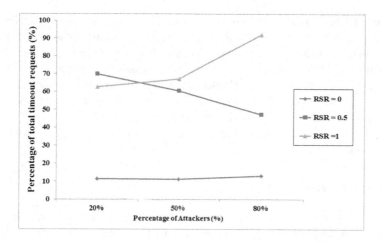

Fig. 3. Ratio of timeout requests with and without the proposed solution in all ICN nodes in the existence of attack scenarios 1, 2, 3, and 7

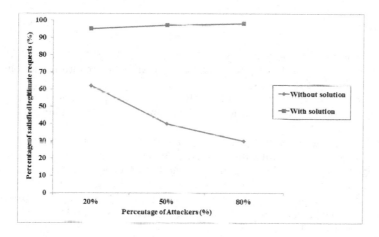

Fig. 4. Percentage of satisfied legitimate requests in the existence of attack scenario 4 with and without the proposed solution

of requests/s for the legitimate user = 100, no. of requests/s for the attacker = 1000, no. of subscribers = 20, no. of publishers = 3, no. of publishers in evaluating the test message = 20, packet size = 1 Kbytes, Pending Interest Table (PIT) size = 1000, cache size = 1000. We used the default values for any other parameters. There are three cases with different RSRs: RSR = 0 for unavailable content requests; RSR = 0.5 for 50 % unavailable content requests and 50 % different available content requests; RSR = 1 for different available content requests. We perform these experiments when the percentage of the attackers to the legitimate users are 20 %, 50 %, and 80 %. As depicted in Fig. 2, the solution mitigates the routing related DDoS attacks and enhances the ICN performance in the three cases. When RSR = 0.5, as the number of attackers increases more than 50 %, the solution achieves better performance. This happens because the solution limits more requests from the attackers. As shown in Fig. 3, the solution also decreases the percentage of timeout requests in the three cases. These experiments cover scenarios 1, 2, 3, and 7. Figure 4 shows that the results of the impact of scenario 4 are close to the impact of scenario 2. The minor difference between the two impacts comes from the extra overhead due to test messages. For attack scenarios 5 and 6, the solution ranks ICN contents and publishers, which makes these attack scenarios difficult and also lessens their impacts on ICN.

5   Conclusion

ICN is one of the proposed architectures for the future Internet. DDoS attacks have significant impacts on ICN resources. In this paper, we present different scenarios of routing related DDoS attacks that may happen in an ICN. We also present our proposed generic solution, which consists of five countermeasures. The solution enhances the ICN performance in all attack cases.

References

1. Cisco visual networking index: forecast and methodology, 2012–2017 (2013)
2. Pan, J., Paul, S., Jain, R.: A survey of the research on future internet architectures. IEEE Commun. Mag. 49(7), 26–36 (2011)
3. Bari, M.F., Chowdhury, S.R., Ahmed, R., Boutaba, R., Mathieu, B.: A survey of naming and routing in information-centric networks. IEEE Commun. Mag. 49(12), 44–53 (2012)
4. Afanasyev, A., Moiseenko, I., Zhang, L.: ndnsim: NDN simulator for NS-3, Technical Report, University of California, Los Angeles (2012)
5. Compagno, A., Conti, M., Gasti, P., Tsudik, G.: Poseidon: Mitigating interest flooding DDoS attacks in named data networking, arXiv preprint:1303.4823 (2013)
6. Afanasyev, A., Mahadevany, P., Moiseenko, I., Uzuny, E., Zhang, L.: Interest flooding attack and countermeasures in named data networking. In: Proceedings of IFIP Networking, Brooklyn, New York, USA (2013)
7. Fotiou, N., Marias, G., F., Polyzos, G., C.: Fighting spam in publish/subscribe networks using information ranking. In: 6th EURO-NF Conference on Next Generation Internet (NGI), pp. 1–6, Paris (2010)
8. Gasti, P., Tsudik, G., Uzun, E., Zhang, L.: DoS and DDoS in named data networking. In: Proceedings of the 22nd International Conference on Computing Communications and Networks. IEEE (2013)
9. Zargar, S., Joshi, J., Tipper, D.: A survey of defense mechanisms against distributed denial of service (DDoS) flooding attacks. IEEE Commun. Surv. Tutorials 15(4), 2046–2069 (2013)
10. You, Y., Zulkernine, M., Haque, A.: A Distributed defense framework for flooding-based DDoS attacks. In: Proceedings of the International Conference on Availability, Reliability and Security, pp. 245–252. IEEE CS Press, Barcelona, Spain (2008)
11. Keromytis, A., Misra, V., Rubenstein, D.: SOS: an architecture for mitigating DDoS attacks. IEEE J. Sel. Areas Commun. 22(1), 176–188 (2004)

A New Anomaly Detection Method Based on IGTE and IGFE

Ziyu Wang[✉], Jiahai Yang, and Fuliang Li

Tsinghua National Laboratory for Information Science and Technology (TNList),
Institute for Network Sciences and Cyberspace,
Tsinghua University, Beijing 100084, China
wangziyu11@mails.tsinghua.edu.cn, yang@cernet.edu.cn,
lifuliang207@126.com

Abstract. Network anomalies have been a serious challenge for the Internet nowadays. In this paper, two new metrics, IGTE (Inter-group Traffic Entropy) and IGFE (Inter-group Flow Entropy), are proposed for network anomaly detection. It is observed that IGTE and IGFE are highly correlated and usually change synchronously when no anomaly occurs. However, once anomalies occur, this highly linear correlation would be destroyed. Based on this observation, we propose a linear regression model built upon IGTE and IGFE, to detect the network anomalies. We use both CERNET2 netflow data and synthetic data to validate the regression model and its corresponding detection method. The results show that the regression-based method works well and outperforms the well known wavelet-based detection method.

Keywords: Anomaly detection · Regression · IGTE · IGFE

1 Introduction

Network anomalies have been a serious challenge for the Internet nowadays. There are basically two classes of detection methods. The first class is called misused detection, also known as signature-based detection [10,12,17,19,25]. The primary advantage of misused detection is its high degree of accuracy. However, the misused detection is incapable of detecting emerging anomalies (zero day attacks), whose features are not known in advance. The second class of detection methods is called anomaly detection [1,5,16,23]. Anomaly detection typically derives a normal model of the network data, then computes an "outlier score" for each data point. The normal model is usually derived from different quantities of the network traffic, such as the number of packets, the number of bytes, the number of flows, etc. Outlier score is a measure about the level of "outlierness" of each data point, based on the deviation distance from the normal model. The concept of outlier score is similar to residual which is commonly used in the field of anomaly detection. In this paper, we will treat these two concepts equivalently without distinction. Once certain outlier score exceeds predefined

© Institute for Computer Sciences, Social Informatics and Telecommunications Engineering 2015
J. Tian et al. (Eds.): SecureComm 2014, Part II, LNICST 153, pp. 93–109, 2015.
DOI: 10.1007/978-3-319-23802-9_10

threshold, an alarm is triggered. Since anomaly detection only cares about the statistical properties of network traffic rather than specific anomaly features, it is capable of detecting zero day attacks. This capability is the strong advantage of anomaly detection over misuse detection. Hence, anomaly detection has been well studied by researchers in recent years [24,27,30,32].

The wavelet analysis is widely applied in anomaly detection [7,9,11,26,28]. Barford et al. [2] first introduce wavelet techniques into the field of network anomaly detection. They first use wavelets filters to decompose single-link traffic into three parts: low-frequency part, mid-frequency part, high-frequency part, and then they use the local variances of mid-frequency part and high-frequency part to generate a V-signal, then apply thresholding to the V-signal to detect anomalies. The basic idea of the wavelet-based detector is to compare local variance with global variance. However, it ignores the fact that the variance of network traffic is usually proportional to the absolute volume of network traffic. High traffic volume usually corresponds to massive active users in the network. Therefore, large local variance is more likely to be a result from normal network behavior rather than anomalies. Unfortunately, the wavelet-based detector ignores this fact and is prone to generate false positives.

Given the shortcomings of wavelet-based detector, we propose a new anomaly detection method based on two new metrics—IGTE and IGFE. These two metrics are basically entropies summarizing the distribution of the traffic volume and the number of IP flows among different groups. We focus on the relation between IGTE and IGFE rather than the variance, which makes this new method unaffected by the absolute network traffic volume. First, we randomly map the network flows which constitute the network traffic into fixed number of groups. The number of bytes and the number of network flows are calculated for each group. Consequently, we obtain two matrices, which are called Randomly Aggregated Traffic Matrix (RATM) and Randomly Aggregated Flow Matrix (RAFM). It is assumed that the distribution of the traffic volume among different groups and the distribution of the number of flows should resemble each other. Then we calculate two types of entropies based on the columns of RATM and RAFM respectively. These two entropies are called Inter-group Traffic Entropy (IGTE) and Inter-group Flow Entropy (IGFE). It is found that IGTE and IGFE are highly correlated under normal condition, and when anomalies occur, this correlation will be destroyed. Based on this observation, we propose a regression-based detection method. Using CERNET2 Netflow data and synthetic data, we validate that our regression-based detector is capable of achieving high detection rate and low false positive rate.

The main contributions of this paper are: (1) putting forward two new metrics—IGTE and IGFE—which are effective for anomaly detection, (2) validating the highly linear correlation between IGTE and IGFE, (3) proposing a new effective regression-based anomaly detection method built upon IGTE and IGFE, (4) analyzing the shortcomings of wavelets-based detection method [2].

The remainder of this paper is organized as follows. Section 2 presents related work in the field of anomaly detection. In Sect. 3, we introduce the procedure of generating RATM and RAFM. In Sect. 4, we illustrate how to derive two new metrics—IGTE and IGFE—from RATM and RAFM, and show the highly linear correlation between them. We explain the principle and rationale of the regression based detector in Sect. 5. In Sect. 6, we compare the regression-based detector and the famous wavelets-based detector by using both CERNET2 Netflow data and synthetic data. We conclude this work in Sect. 7.

2   Related Work

In recent years, lots of researches have been devoted to the field of anomaly detection. Yaacob et al. [29] introduce a new approach through using Auto-Regressive Integrated Moving Average (ARIMA) technique to detect potential attacks in the network. Although they show the capability of ARIMA model of predicting future data, their validation process is rough, and the threshold they choose is heuristic.

Silveira et al. [22] state that when many network flows are multiplexed on a non-saturated link, their volume changes tend to cancel each other out over short timescales, making the average change across flows approximately follows the normal distribution. Based on this observation, they propose the ASTUTE-based anomaly detector. While it is good at detecting anomalies which involve many small IP flows, it fails to detect anomalies caused by a few large IP flows. Besides that, the efficacy of the ASTUTE-based detector highly depends on the stationarity of network traffic. The authors claim that at short timescales (less than a hour), the traffic can be well modeled by stationary processes. However, this conclusion does not always holds for all networks. It performs poorly in those networks in which IP flows are changeable. For example, the CERNET2 Netflow data used in this paper contains many IP flows which emerge and vanish quite suddenly. The ASTUTE-based detector marks almost every point in the data set as anomalous, which is practically impossible in real world. We manually check Netflow data and consult the operators of CERNET2, it turns out that most of the anomalies detected by the ASTUTE-based detector are false positives. Therefore, we do not adopt ASTUTE-based detector as comparison in this paper.

Lakhina et al. [14,15] first apply principal component analysis (PCA) in network-wide anomaly detection. PCA-based detector (also referred to as subspace-based detector) uses the first few principal components to derive normal model from the original link traffic matrix, and then applies thresholding to the residual traffic to detect anomalies. The advantage of the PCA method is its capability of detecting small anomalies distributed over multiple links which are hard to detect in single-link traffic. Since this method is applied to link traffic matrix, it is limited to the network-wide anomaly detection. Besides, there are some inherent weaknesses of PCA based detector. For example, a large anomaly may inadvertently pollute the normal subspace, the effectiveness of PCA is sensitive to the level of aggregation of the traffic measurements, and the false positive rate is sensitive to small differences in the number of principal components in the normal subspace [18,31]. Rubinstein et al. [21] show that the attackers can successfully evade PCA-based detection by only adding moderate amounts of poisoned data. Besides, since all kinds of PCA-based detectors need to operate on the link traffic matrix, it is necessary to collect data from all links in the networks simultaneously. However, it is usually a difficult task for large networks. The lack of scalability limits the application of PCA-based detectors. In this paper, we only focus on anomaly detection for single-link traffic.

3   RATM and RAFM

Before introducing RATM and RAFM, we give the definition of IP flow here for the purpose of illustration. In practice, an IP flow can be defined in multiple ways according to different contexts. In this study, an IP flow is defined as a sequence of packets that share the same five-tuple value (Source IP address, Destination IP address, Source port, Destination port and Protocol type).

We select the five-tuple values of IP flows as key, and hash them into fixed number of groups. The number of groups are selected by the network operators according to the needs. For each group, we calculate the overall traffic volume of the IP flows mapped into it during each time interval, then the RATM is generated. The rows of RATM correspond to different time intervals, the columns correspond to different groups. In detail, the (i, j) entry of RATM corresponds to the traffic volume of group j at time instant i. Similarly, the RAFM is generated by counting the number of IP flows in each group during each time interval. Thus, the (i, j) entry of RAFM corresponds to the number of IP flows in group j at time instant i.

4   Two New Metrics—IGTE and IGFE

Intuitively, for a given group, under normal condition, the more IP flows mapped into the group, the higher traffic volume would be contained in that group. Consequently, the distribution of traffic volume among different groups should resemble to the distribution of number of IP flows. Entropy can be used as a summarization tool for probability distributions from the point of view of information theory [15]. Thus we calculate the entropies for the rows of RATM and RAFM respectively. The entropy for RATM is named Inter Group Traffic Entropy (IGTE), the entropy for RAFM is named Inter Group Flow Entropy (IGFE). The details for calculating IGTE and IGFE are given as follows.

Suppose a $t \times p$ RATM T, where t is the number of time intervals considered, p is the number of groups predefined. For a given row i of T, the definition of IGTE is defined as follows:

$$IGTE_i = -\sum_{j=1}^{p} \left\{ \frac{T(i,j)}{\sum_{j=1}^{p} T(i,j)} \ln \frac{T(i,j)}{\sum_{j=1}^{p} T(i,j)} \right\} \tag{1}$$

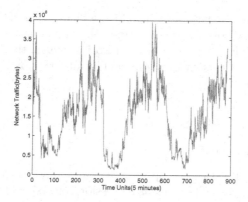

Fig. 1. Network traffic from CERNET2

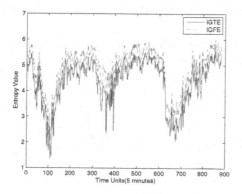

Fig. 2. IGFE series versus IGTE series from CERNET2

where $T(i,j)$ is the (i,j) entry of T, $1 \leq i \leq t$, $1 \leq j \leq p$. Similarly, for a given row i of a RAFM denoted by F, the definition of IGFE is defined as follows:

$$IGFE_i = -\sum_{j=1}^{p} \left\{ \frac{F(i,j)}{\sum_{j=1}^{p} F(i,j)} \ln \frac{F(i,j)}{\sum_{j=1}^{p} F(i,j)} \right\} \qquad (2)$$

where $F(i,j)$ is the (i,j) entry of F, $1 \leq i \leq t$, $1 \leq j \leq p$. Therefore, based on RATM and RAFM, we can obtain an IGTE series and an IGFE series respectively. Note that IGTE and IGFE are essentially entropies. If the distribution of traffic volume and that of the number of flows resemble to each other, IGTE and IGFE should be highly correlated. In order to validate this conjecture, we calculate the IGTE and IGFE series from approximately three-day network traffic obtained from CERNET2 (an academic network in China which will be described in detail later) which is shown in Fig. 1, and plot the IGTE and IGFE series in Fig. 2. It is shown that the curve of IGFE series is extremely similar to the curve of IGTE series, which implies that IGFE and IGTE are highly linearly correlated. To verify this conjecture rigorously, we calculate the correlation coefficient between these two series. The result is 0.976, which means IGTE and IGFE are indeed highly linearly correlated. Note that the three-day network traffic may contain anomalies which are not known a priori. Even so, the linear relationship between IGTE and IGFE is strong enough. This observation lays the foundation of our regression based detector.

5   Detection Methods

5.1   Regression-Based Detection

Based on IGTE and IGFE, we propose a new anomaly detection method using linear regression analysis. The goal of regression analysis is to construct mathematical models which describe relationships that may exist between variables [20]. Usually, we are interested in just one variable, i.e. the response variable, and we want to study how it depends on a set of variables which are called explanatory variables.

Let y denote the response variable, $x_1, x_2, \ldots, x_p$ denote the set of explanatory variables. Denote the samples from y as $Y = (y_1, y_2, \ldots, y_n)^T$, the samples from $x_1, x_2, \ldots, x_p$ as $X_e = \begin{pmatrix} x_{11} & x_{12} & \cdots & x_{1p} \\ x_{21} & x_{22} & \cdots & x_{2p} \\ \vdots & \vdots & \ddots & \vdots \\ x_{n1} & x_{n2} & \cdots & x_{np} \end{pmatrix}$. The goal of regression analysis is to obtain the relationship of dependency between y and $x_1, x_2, \ldots, x_p$.

Regression analysis assumes y and $x_1, x_2, \ldots, x_p$ satisfy the following linear regression equation:

$$y = \beta_0 + \beta_1 x_1 + \ldots + \beta_p x_p + e \tag{3}$$

where $e \sim N(0, \sigma^2)$, $\sigma, \beta_0, \beta_1, \ldots, \beta_p$ are parameters to be determined. From Eq. (3), the corresponding samples should satisfy the following equation:

$$Y = X\beta + E \tag{4}$$

where $X = (1, X_e)$ is defined as the extended matrix of X_e, $\beta = (\beta_0, \beta_1, \ldots, \beta_p)^T$, $E \sim N(0, \sigma^2 I)$.

Define $Q(\beta) = \sum_{i=1}^{n} \{y_i - (\beta_1 x_{i1} + \beta_2 x_{i2} + \ldots + \beta_p x_{ip})\}^2 = ||Y - X\beta||^2$, then $Q(\beta)$ measures the noise of the regression equation. The optimal estimate of β should make $Q(\beta)$ as small as possible. Thus the estimate of β is as follows:

$$\hat{\beta} = (X^T X)^{-1} X^T Y \tag{5}$$

Then the estimate of σ^2 is as follows:

$$s^2 = \frac{1}{n - p - 1} Q(\hat{\beta}) \tag{6}$$

We define the normal model of Y as follows:

$$\hat{Y} = X\hat{\beta} \tag{7}$$

Then the estimate of E is

$$\hat{E} = Y - \hat{Y} \tag{8}$$

Note that $\hat{E}$ is the outlier scores, i.e. residuals, of all data points. Intuitively, if the residual of a given data point is close to 0, the data point would be normal, otherwise, the point would be abnormal.

The procedure of detection is as follows. First, we calculate $\hat{E}$ from the samples as described above. For convenience, we denote $\hat{E}$ as $(\hat{e}_1, \hat{e}_2, \ldots, \hat{e}_n)$. For a given sample point i, where $1 \leq i \leq n$, under normal condition, $\hat{e}_i$ should follows the normal distribution $N(0, s^2)$, based on the assumption of Eq. (3). For a given confidence level $1 - \alpha$, if $|\frac{\hat{e}_i}{s}| > z_{\alpha/2}$, where $z_{\alpha/2}$ is the upper $\alpha/2$ quantile of standard normal distribution $N(0, 1)$, the data point i is marked as an anomaly. The meaning of the confidence level is that when a data point is marked as an anomaly, the probability of being a false alarm is α.

Note that the success of the regression model depends greatly on the linear correlation between the response variable and the set of explanatory variables. Given the discussion in Sect. 4, IGTE and IGFE are highly linearly correlated. Therefore, we choose IGTE as the response variable, IGFE as the explanatory variable in this study. Let y denote IGTE and x denote IGFE. The regression equation built upon them is give below.

$$y = \beta_0 + \beta_1 x + e \tag{9}$$

where $e \sim N(0, \sigma^2)$, σ, β_0 and β_1 are parameters to be determined.

The details of our regression based detector is summarized in Algorithm 1 .

Note that there is an important auxiliary procedure which is not illustrated in Algorithm 1 due to space limitations. After $Y = (IGTE_1, IGTE_2, \ldots, IGTE_t)^T$ and $X = (1, X_e)$ are calculated, i.e. after step 7, it is necessary to test rigorously whether it is appropriate to build regression equation upon them. In other words, we must test whether the dependence of Y on X is strong enough for the correctness of the regression model. There are two kinds of significance tests for this: F test and t test [20]. Only when the data passes both tests, the corresponding regression model can be considered reasonable.

5.2   Rationale Behind Regression-Based Detection Method

Network traffic consists of IP flows. Anomalies usually change the number of IP flows on the link or the traffic volume of certain IP flows. Some anomalies such as port scans, would generate lots of small IP flow in the network. This leads to large increase in the number of IP flow, which makes the IGFE change dramatically. However, the traffic generated by the anomalies is very small compared to the overall traffic volume on the link, which barely changes the IGTE value. Therefore, the linear correlation between IGTE and IGFE is destroyed, and the regression-based detector generates large residual to trigger alarms.

Some anomalies such as DDoS attacks, would increase the number of IP flows and the traffic volume at the same time. However, the magnitude of traffic volume change is much larger than the number of IP flows. Hence, the degree of

---

Algorithm 1. Regression based anomaly detector

Input: $t \times p$ RATM; $t \times p$ RAFM; $z_{\alpha/2}$;

Output: Time intervals containing anomalies;

1: **for all** i such that $1 \leq i \leq t$ **do**

2:     $IGTE_i = -\sum_{j=1}^{p} \left\{ \frac{T(i,j)}{\sum_{j=1}^{p} T(i,j)} \ln \frac{T(i,j)}{\sum_{j=1}^{p} T(i,j)} \right\}$;

3:     $IGFE_i = -\sum_{j=1}^{p} \left\{ \frac{F(i,j)}{\sum_{j=1}^{p} F(i,j)} \ln \frac{F(i,j)}{\sum_{j=1}^{p} F(i,j)} \right\}$;

4: **end for**

5: $Y = (IGTE_1, IGTE_2, \dots, IGTE_t)^T$;

6: $X_e = (IGFE_1, IGFE_2, \dots, IGFE_t)^T$;

7: $X = (1, X_e)$;

8: $\hat{\beta} = (X^T X)^{-1} X^T Y$;

9: $\hat{E} = (\hat{e}_1, \hat{e}_2, \dots, \hat{e}_t)^T = Y - X \times \hat{\beta}$;

10: $Q(\hat{\beta}) = \sum_{i=1}^{n} \{y_i - (\beta_1 x_{i1} + \beta_2 x_{i2} + \dots + \beta_p x_{ip})\}^2$;

11: $s = \sqrt{\frac{1}{n-p-1} Q(\hat{\beta})}$;

12: $\hat{E} = \hat{E}/s$;

13: **for** $i = 1$ to t **do**

14:     **if** $|e_i| > z_{\alpha/2}$ **then**

15:         Output: Time interval i;

16:     **end if**

17: **end for**

---

change of IGTE is much large than IGFE. It results in the breach of the linear relation between IGTE and IGFE, and the anomalies would be detected by the regression-based detector.

There are also some anomalies which would increase the number of IP flows and decrease the traffic volume. Take Low-rate DDoS attacks [13] for example, the attackers would generate millions of attacking IP flows, which will definitely change the IGFE value. On the other hand, the traffic volume generated by the attacking IP flows is very low on average, since these attacks are performed in the form of pulses. At the same time, the traffic volume of the normal IP flows would be reduced dramatically due to the congestion control mechanism in network. Therefore the overall traffic on the link would decrease dramatically, which would cause the change of IGTE value. Though both IGTE and IGFE change, they change in opposite directions, which destroys the linear relationship between them. Hence, these anomalies can be detected by the regression-based detector.

6   Validation

6.1   Dataset

The data used in this paper is Netflow Records collected from the Second Generation of China Education and Research Network (CERNET2). CERNET2 connects 25 PoPs including Peking University, Tsinghua University, Beijing

University of Aeronautics and Astronautics (Beihang University), University of Science and Technology, etc. The Netflow data is collected from a border router connecting CERNET2 backbone and Beihang University Campus Network. The data collection architecture is shown in Fig. 3. The Netflow V9 protocol [4] is used to collect the data passing through the border router (i.e. Netflow exporter), and transfer the Netflow records to a storage server. The sampling rate is set to 1 : 1000. Lots of information for each IP flow within every five minutes are saved, including the five-tuple value, the total number of bytes and packets, the starting time and finishing time, etc. The average traffic volume in five minutes is about 1.525×10^8 bytes. The average traffic volume of each IP flow is about 985 bytes. The average number of IP flows is about 154730. Note that these numbers are calculated from the sampled data. The numbers should be multiplied by 1000 for the un-sampled data.

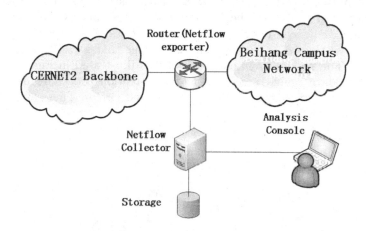

Fig. 3. Data collection architecture

We collected Netflow records from a border router connecting CERNET2 backbone and Beihang University campus network from 21:45 in August 26 to 23:10 in August 29, 2013. The corresponding network traffic is already shown in Fig. 1. We set the number of groups as 1024. Since the Netflow records are stored every five minutes, there are totally 882 time units during the data collection period, then a 882×1024 RATM and a 882×1024 RAFM are generated respectively.

In this paper, we use the CERNET2 data by two different means. One is to directly apply the detection methods on the CERNET2 data. The other one is to manually inject anomalies into the "cleaned" CERNET2 data, and then apply the detection methods on this synthesized data. The advantage of using CERNET2 data directly is that it can compare the performance of different detection methods in real networks. The advantage of using synthetic data is the capability of obtaining the detection rate and false positive rate by controlling the process of injecting anomalies.

6.2   Validation Using Real World Data

From the 882×1024 RATM and RAFM above, an IGTE series and an IGFE series—both of length 882—are obtained. Their curves are already presented in Fig. 2. We choose IGTE as the response variable, denoted by y, and IGFE as the explanatory variable, denoted by x. From Eqs. (5), (6) and (9), we have:

$$y = -0.72631 + 1.09724x + e \qquad (10)$$

where $e \sim N(0, 0.048^2)$. Next, we check the significance of regression Eq. (10). Recall that both F test and t test are used in this work for significance test. We use the famous statistical software R [3] to do the tests. We set the confidence level as $1 - \alpha = 1 - 0.05 = 0.95$. The $p - value$ of F test outputted by R is 0.26×10^{-8}, which is much less than $\alpha = 0.05$. $P - value$ is a commonly used metric in hypothesis testing [6]. If the $p - value$ is less than α, the regression model is accepted as valid. The $p - value$ of F test means that Eq. (10) fits the data quite well. The resulting $p - value$ of t test is 0.11×10^{-9}, which is again much less than $\alpha = 0.05$, which also means that Eq. (10) is appropriate for the data. The residual related to Eq. (10) is illustrated in Fig. 4. We check these residual data points according to the detection procedure described in subsect. 5.1, and mark the abnormal points in red circles. There are totally 53 anomalies detected.

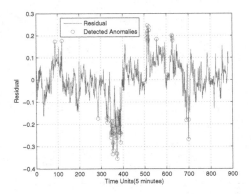

Fig. 4. Anomalies detected by regression-based detector for CERNET2 data (Color figure online)

As a comparison, we apply the wavelets-based detector [2] to the same data set. We set the sliding window length as 12. This window size corresponds to one hour traffic. Thus the output of wavelets-detector, i.e. "deviation scores", does not contain the first 11 points in CERNET2 data. In other words, the output size of wavelets-detector is $882 - 11 = 871$. The results are shown in Fig. 5, the red circles point out the 60 anomalies detected.

Comparing Figs. 4 and 5, we find that only 3 anomalies are detected commonly by both detection methods. Does that mean that our regression-based

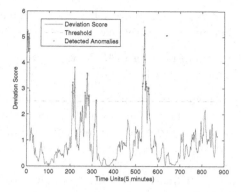

Fig. 5. Anomalies detected by wavelets-based detector for CERNET2 data (Color figure online)

detection method is ineffective? We argue that the wavelets-based detector has its own limits—it ignores the fact that the variance of network traffic is usually proportional to the absolute volume of network traffic (as shown in Fig. 1). Comparing Figs. 1 and 5, it is observed that the anomalies detected by wavelets-based detector coincide with the time intervals in which traffic volume is high. It is known that high traffic volume usually corresponds to massive active users in the network, and the variance of network traffic becomes large accordingly. In other words, large local variance is more likely to be a result from normal network behavior rather than anomalies. Unfortunately, the wavelets-based detector ignore this fact and mark these data points as anomalies arbitrarily. Thus we have reason to believe that most of the alarms triggered by wavelets-based detector are likely to be false alarms. We manually check the Netflow data and also consult the operators who run CERNET2, it turns out that there were no sign of large-scale attacks during the data collecting period, which supports our statement. In the following subsection, we will validate this claim quantitatively and rigorously.

6.3   Validation Using Synthetic Data

To evaluate the performance of different anomaly detection methods rigorously and quantitatively, we manually inject anomalies into the "cleaned" CERNET2 Netflow data. The detail is as follows: first, we abandon those time intervals which are marked by regression-based detector or wavelets-based detector. The remaining 772 time intervals are considered as "clean" traffic. In other words, we assume that these 772 time intervals contain no anomalies. Since the only two detectors applied on the "clean" traffic are regression-based detector and wavelets-based detector, this assumption makes sense. Then, we manually inject certain number of anomalous IP flows every 22 time intervals. Thus the total number of injected anomalies is 35. In the area of anomaly detection, a general assumption is that the anomalies contained in the data are much less than the normal points. Thus the number of injected anomalies we choose is reasonable.

According to the number of anomalous IP flows injected, we evaluate the performance of detection methods in two cases:

- Anomalies involving a small number of IP flows.
- Anomalies involving many small IP flows.

In the first case, we focus on the impact of the traffic volume of injected anomalies. We inject 11 anomalous IP flows and gradually increase their traffic volume. The true positive rate (detection rate) curves and false positive rate curves are shown in Figs. 6 and 7 respectively. The horizontal coordinates represent the proportion of the anomalous traffic volume in the total traffic volume of the link. The vertical coordinates represent the true positive rates and the false positive rates. The definitions of true positive rate and false positive rate in this paper originate from the introductory document about ROC analysis [8]. It is illustrated that as the anomalous traffic volume increases, the detection rate of regression-based detector rises sharply, and the false positive rate falls quickly. When the anomalous traffic volume reaches 42.8 % of the total traffic volume, the regression-based detector can detect all the injected anomalies while generate no false alarms. It means that the regression-based detector is good at detecting anomalies involving a few large IP flows for which the ASTUTE-based detector performs poor [22]. However, for the wavelets-based detector, the detection rate increases very slowly. Even when the anomalous traffic volume reaches 60 %, which means the order of magnitude of anomalous traffic volume reaches around 10^9 bytes, the detection rate is below 5.8 %. This result is unacceptable for practical application. The performance of wavelet-based detector in the point of view of false positive rate is also poor. As the anomalous traffic increases, the false positive rate is hardly decreasing, and converges to around 2.4 %. In contrast, the false positive rate of the regression-based detector falls down quickly. When the anomalous traffic volume reaches 15 %, no false positive is generated.

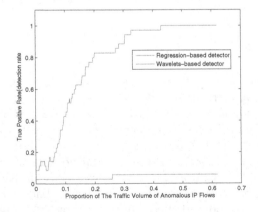

Fig. 6. True positive rate for a small number of anomalous IP flows

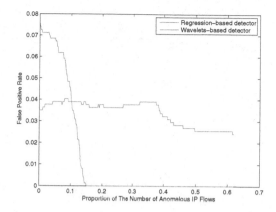

Fig. 7. False positive rate for a small number of anomalous IP flows

In the second case, we focus on the impact of the number of anomalous IP flows. We simulate the scenario of DDoS attacks. We first set the traffic volume of each injected IP flow as 50 bytes. Considering the average traffic volume of each IP flow in CERNET2 is around 985 bytes, the traffic volume per anomalous flow we choose is reasonable and small. Then we gradually increase the number of injected IP flows. The detection rates and false positive rates of the two detectors are shown in Figs. 8 and 9. Note that the horizontal coordinates here represent the proportion of the number of anomalous IP flows in the total number of IP flows in the link. For the regression-based detector, as the number of anomalous flows grows, the detection rate curve rises sharply and the false positive rate curve falls quickly. When the proportion of injected IP flows reaches 41 % of the total number of IP flows, the detect rate reaches 80 %. The false positive rate reaches 0 when the number of anomalous IP flows reaches no more than 4 %. On the other hand, for the wavelets-based detector, the detection rate keeps below 3 % and does not grow with the number of anomalous flows. The false positive rate of the wavelet-based detector keeps around 4 %, which seems acceptable at first. However, when we look deeper into the anomalies marked by the wavelets-based detector, we find that the number of false positives keeps around 34 and the number of true positives keeps close to 1. This observation holds no matter how much the proportion of the number of injected IP flows accounts for. Comparing the amount of false positives and the amount of true positives it detect, the performance is really poor. We also try other values of traffic volume for each injected IP flow, the results are similar.

For both cases, we find that the alarms generated by the wavelets-based detector again coincide with the time intervals with high traffic volume. This observation strongly support our reasoning about the shortcomings of wavelets-based detector—it ignores the fact that large local variances are usually related to the high traffic volume generated by normal users.

In summary, based on the synthetic CERNET2 data, our regression-based detector achieves higher detection rate and lower false positive rate than the

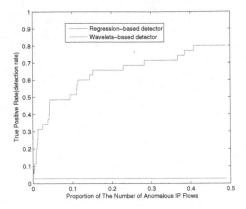

Fig. 8. True positive rate for a large number of anomalous IP flows

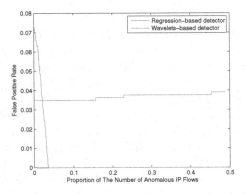

Fig. 9. False positive rate for a large number of anomalous IP flows

wavelets-based detector. Besides, the regression-based detector is good at detecting both anomalies involving a few large IP flows and anomalies involving many small IP flows. Note that we ignore the scenario where anomalies involve many large IP flows on purpose. Because in this case, the volume of the network traffic would change so much that the anomalies can be identified even by the naked eyes. Both the wavelet-based detector and the regression-based detector perform excellently in this case. There is no need to show the experiment results in this case for the sake of brevity.

7   Conclusions and Future Work

In this paper, we propose two new metrics, IGTE and IGFE, for anomaly detection. It is found that IGTE and IGFE are highly linearly correlated. When anomalies occur, this linear correlation will be destroyed. Based on this observation, we propose the regression based detector which is built upon IGTE and IGFE. We validate that the regression based detector can achieve high detection rate and generate very few false positives. We show that the regression-based detector is good at detecting both anomalies involving a few large IP flows and anomalies involving many small IP flows. We compare the regression based detector with the wavelet-based detector, and find that the former outperforms the latter. We analyze the reason for the failure of wavelets-based detector. The wavelets-based detector uses local variance of traffic volume to measure the degree of anomaly. However, large local variance are usually caused by large number of normal users. Thus the wavelets-based detector usually generates too many false positives. We do not deny the possibility that the CERNET2 data used in this paper bias for the regression-based detector while bias against the wavelet-based detector. In the future, we plan to use more data sources to validate the regression-based detector.

Acknowledgments. We are grateful to Lujing Sun for providing us with the Netflow data from CERNET2, and to Kun Wen and Chenxi Li for many helpful discussions. We also thank anonymous reviewers for their constructive comments. This work is supported by the National Basic Research Program of China under Grant No. 2012CB315806, the National Natural Science Foundation of China under Grant No. 61170211, 61202356, 61161140454, Specialized Research Fund for the Doctoral Program of Higher Education under Grant No. 20110002110056, 20130002110058.

References

1. Andryulak, T., Saganowski, L., Choraś, M.: DDoS attacks detection by means of greedy algorithms. In: Choraś, R.S. (ed.) Image Processing and Communications Challenges 4. AISC, vol. 184, pp. 301–308. Springer, Heidelberg (2013)
2. Barford, P., Kline, J., Plonka, D., Ron, A.: A signal analysis of network traffic anomalies. In: Proceedings of the 2nd ACM SIGCOMM Workshop on Internet Measurment, pp. 71–82. ACM (2002)
3. The r project for statistical computing. http://www.r-project.org/
4. Cisco systems netflow services export version 9. http://www.rfc-base.org/rfc-3954.html
5. Brauckhoff, D., Salamatian, K., May, M.: Applying pca for traffic anomaly detection: Problems and solutions. In: INFOCOM 2009, pp. 2866–2870. IEEE (2009)
6. Casella, G., Berger, R.L.: Statistical Inference. Duxbury Press, Belmont (1990)
7. Cong, F., Hautakangas, H., Nieminen, J., Mazhelis, O., Perttunen, M., Riekki, J., Ristaniemi, T.: Applying wavelet packet decomposition and one-class support vector machine on vehicle acceleration traces for road anomaly detection. In: Guo, C., Hou, Z.-G., Zeng, Z. (eds.) ISNN 2013, Part I. LNCS, vol. 7951, pp. 291–299. Springer, Heidelberg (2013)
8. Fawcett, T.: An introduction to ROC analysis. Pattern Recogn. Lett. **27**(8), 861–874 (2006)
9. Guzman, J., Poblete, B.: On-line relevant anomaly detection in the twitter stream: an efficient bursty keyword detection model. In: Proceedings of the ACM SIGKDD Workshop on Outlier Detection and Description, pp. 31–39. ACM (2013)
10. Jamshed, M.A., Lee, J., Moon, S., Yun, I., Kim, D., Lee, S., Yi, Y., Park, K.: Kargus: a highly-scalable software-based intrusion detection system. In: Proceedings of the 2012 ACM Conference on Computer and Communications Security, pp. 317–328. ACM (2012)

11. Jiang, D., Zhang, P., Xu, Z., Yao, C., Qin, W.: A wavelet-based detection approach to traffic anomalies. In: 2011 Seventh International Conference on Computational Intelligence and Security (CIS), pp. 993–997. IEEE (2011)

12. Jiang, H., Zhang, G., Xie, G., Salamatian, K., Mathy, L.: Scalable high-performance parallel design for network intrusion detection systems on many-core processors. In: Proceedings of the Ninth ACM/IEEE Symposium on Architectures for Networking and Communications Systems, pp. 137–146. IEEE Press (2013)

13. Kuzmanovic, A., Knightly, E.W.: Low-rate tcp-targeted denial of service attacks: the shrew vs. the mice and elephants. In: Proceedings of the 2003 Conference on Applications, Technologies, Architectures, and Protocols for Computer Communications, pp. 75–86 (2003)

14. Lakhina, A., Crovella, M., Diot, C.: Diagnosing network-wide traffic anomalies. ACM SIGCOMM Comput. Commun. Rev. **34**, 219–230 (2004). ACM

15. Lakhina, A., Crovella, M., Diot, C.: Mining anomalies using traffic feature distributions. ACM SIGCOMM Comput. Commun. Rev. **35**, 217–228 (2005). ACM

16. Palmieri, F., Fiore, U.: Network anomaly detection through nonlinear analysis. Comput. Secur. **29**(7), 737–755 (2010)

17. Paxson, V.: Bro: a system for detecting network intruders in real-time. Comput. Netw. **31**(23), 2435–2463 (1999)

18. Ringberg, H., Soule, A., Rexford, J., Diot, C.: Sensitivity of PCA for traffic anomaly detection. ACM SIGMETRICS Perform. Eval. Rev. **35**, 109–120 (2007). ACM

19. Roesch, M., et al.: Snort: Lightweight intrusion detection for networks. In: LISA, pp. 229–238 (1999)

20. Ross, S.M.: Introductory statistics. Academic Press (2010)

21. Rubinstein, B.I., Nelson, B., Huang, L., Joseph, A.D., Lau, S.h., Rao, S., Taft, N., Tygar, J.: Antidote: understanding and defending against poisoning of anomaly detectors. In: Proceedings of the 9th ACM SIGCOMM Conference on Internet Measurement Conference, pp. 1–14. ACM (2009)

22. Silveira, F., Diot, C., Taft, N., Govindan, R.: Astute: detecting a different class of traffic anomalies. ACM SIGCOMM Comput. Commun. Rev. **40**(4), 267–278 (2010)

23. Simmross-Wattenberg, F., Asensio-Perez, J.I., Casaseca-de-la Higuera, P., Martin-Fernandez, M., Dimitriadis, I.A., Alberola-López, C.: Anomaly detection in network traffic based on statistical inference and alpha-stable modeling. IEEE Trans. Dependable Secure Comput. **8**(4), 494–509 (2011)

24. Soldo, F., Metwally, A.: Traffic anomaly detection based on the IP size distribution. In: 2012 Proceedings IEEE INFOCOM, pp. 2005–2013 (2012)

25. Vasiliadis, G., Polychronakis, M., Ioannidis, S.: Midea: a multi-parallel intrusion detection architecture. In: Proceedings of the 18th ACM Conference on Computer and Communications Security, pp. 297–308. ACM (2011)

26. Wang, W., Lu, D., Zhou, X., Zhang, B., Mu, J.: Statistical wavelet-based anomaly detection in big data with compressive sensing. EURASIP J. Wireless Commun. Networking **2013**(269), 1–6 (2013)

27. Winter, P., Lampesberger, H., Zeilinger, M., Hermann, E.: On detecting abrupt changes in network entropy time series. In: De Decker, B., Lapon, J., Naessens, V., Uhl, A. (eds.) CMS 2011. LNCS, vol. 7025, pp. 194–205. Springer, Heidelberg (2011)

28. Wu, J., Cui, Z., Shi, Y., Su, D.: Traffic flow anomaly detection based on wavelet denoising and support vector regression. J. Algorithms Comput. Technol. **7**(2), 209–226 (2013)

29. Yaacob, A.H., Tan, I.K., Chien, S.F., Tan, H.K.: Arima based network anomaly detection. In: Second International Conference on Communication Software and Networks. ICCSN 2010, pp. 205–209. IEEE (2010)
30. Zhang, B., Yang, J., Wu, J., Qin, D., Gao, L.: Mcst: Anomaly detection using feature stability for packet-level traffic. In: 2011 13th Asia-Pacific Network Operations and Management Symposium (APNOMS), pp. 1–8. IEEE (2011)
31. Zhang, B., Yang, J., Wu, J., Qin, D., Gao, L.: Pca-subspace method is it good enough for network-wide anomaly detection. In: 2012 IEEE Network Operations and Management Symposium (NOMS), pp. 359–367. IEEE (2012)
32. Zhang, B., Yang, J., Wu, J., Wang, Z.: Mbst: detecting packet-level traffic anomalies by feature stability. Comput. J. 56(10), 1176–1188 (2013)

International Workshop on Applications and Technologies in Cyber Security (ATCS)

Forensic Potentials of Solid State Drives

Zubair Shah[✉], Abdun Naser Mahmood, and Jill Slay

School of Engineering and IT, University of New South Wales, Canberra, Australia
Zubair.Shah@student.afda.edu.au, {A.Mahmood,J.Slay}@adfa.edu.au

Abstract. Extracting useful information from Solid State Drives (SSD) is a challenging but important forensic task. However, there are opposing views [14,15,22] that (1) SSDs destroy the forensics evidences automatically and (2) even after sanitization of SSDs, data can be recovered. This paper investigates this issue and reports experimental findings that identify the reason why certain SSDs seem to destroy forensic evidences while other SSDs do not. The experiments provide insight and analyses of the behaviour of SSDs when certain software components, such as Background Garbage Collector (BGC) and Operating System functions, such as TRIM, are executed on the SSD.

Keywords: Forensics · Solid state drives · SSD

1 Introduction

In recent years, more and more criminal investigations have centered on finding digital evidences extracted from computing devices, such as Computers, Mobile Phones and Notebooks. The evidences of crimes in physical dimensions are in tangible form; however the evidence of cyber-crimes exists electronically.

The investigation process of cyber-crimes often begins from the analysis of the storage media. Every computing device stores its data on the storage media and every activity of the computing device leaves some traces on the storage media. Meta-data of the electronic media can contain more useful information such as date, time, keys and often this meta-data have greater acceptability than paper based evidences [2,3]. However, if an inefficient recovery is performed then these evidences can be altered, therefore, would become erroneous. Consequently, any change in these evidences may impact court proceedings as well [4,5].

The evidence collected in recovery process requires confirmation to assess its reliability and integrity and it is really important to identify any loss and alteration that has happened in the recovery process [6]. If the data collected for the forensic purpose is altered or lost then it is the responsibility of the party submitting the evidence to prove the integrity of the data. If not, the opposing party can raise questions about the integrity of evidences [7]. Avoiding alteration or loss during the recovery process depends on the error free data recovery mechanism. Usually, write blocking along with bit stream copying process is used in the recovery process. This mechanism allows recovery of the data along with completeness, precision and reliability [8].

© Institute for Computer Sciences, Social Informatics and Telecommunications Engineering 2015
J. Tian et al. (Eds.): SecureComm 2014, Part II, LNICST 153, pp. 113–126, 2015.
DOI: 10.1007/978-3-319-23802-9_11

To reduce loss or alteration, it is necessary for the recovery process to thwart overwriting of data on the relevant drive. For example all the processes need to be stopped by shutting down the system before creating forensic image of the disk in order to minimize the chance of alteration or loss of data [9] by processes in memory. Also, hash value is calculated for collected forensic image in order to check the integrity of the forensic data. This hash value can validate if the forensic image is created multiple times or if the forensic image is placed in some place where alteration is possible in the forensic image [9].

Hard Disk Drives are magnetic storage devices that have well known forensic properties. Most computing activities that rely on disk access, including illegal activities, leave traces that can be later identified through forensic investigation. SSD is a newer technology and a superior alternative to HDDs that offers many benefits over HDD [10] such as read/write speed, durability against shock vibration and temperature. However SSD has some limitations such as life time of a cell in terms of writing data on it (10,000-100,000 times) and need of erasing the blocks before rewriting on the same block [11].

Wear leveling [1] technique is used to randomly select the pages for rewriting the data which prohibit the blocks from approaching the critical failure conditions due to overuse. To solve the problem of erasing the pages before writing, BGC [12] and TRIM command [13] are proposed. Background Garbage Collection (BGC) is a mechanism used in current SSD controllers to improve the write speed of data by deleting/zeroing the unused/garbage pages.Similarly TRIM is a command in modern operating system to inform the SSD controller that particular blocks of data are no longer required or not in use and should be wiped internally. BGC and TRIM commands are the two sources that could destroy the evidences which otherwise could be available for the recovery.

From existing literature it is evident that SSDs destroy forensics evidences and there is no chance to recover the deleted data by any means [14]. However, some research also points that existing data sanitization techniques available for HDDs are not useful or not sufficient for SSDs and new techniques are required specifically for SSDs [15]. The term Data sanitization has different meanings such as nulling out, masking data, shuffling records, encryption and censorship etc. In our context data sanitization means nulling out data to prevent its recovery by any means.

The purpose of this paper is to study the forensics potentials of SSDs of different manufacturers and to experimentally verify the availability or unavailability of the data after deleting or formatting the SSDs.

We have experimentally verified that SSDs destroy forensics evidences only if either the firmware of SSDs has BGC functionality enabled or if TRIM command is supported by SSD's firmware and configured properly in operating system and associated software. It has been our finding that in the absence of BGC and TRIM command support, SSDs do preserve data and live acquisition is possible like traditional HDDs. Sometimes, data can also be recovered from an SSD even after it has been formatted.

Rest of the paper is organized as follow, Sect. 2 presents some preliminaries about SSDs and forensics, related study is elaborated in Sects. 3 and 4 presents our methodology, experiments and results. Conclusion is given in Sect. 6.

2 Preliminaries

2.1 Solid State Drive (SSD)

SSD [16] is an emerging technology for storing data persistently, and slowly replacing the leading HDD storage technology. SSDs are quite different from HDD. For example, SSDs don't have electromechanical component and thus are much faster than traditional HDD. SSD stores data in microchips just like USB flash drive. They store data or retrieve files instantly and do not need to wait for moving parts to position on required sector of magnetic platter. However SSD suffer from a problem which does not exist in HDDs. They first need to erase a block before a new data can be written into it [17,18]. This obviously causes problems for successfully retrieving forensic information from the drives.

2.2 SSD and Forensics

With the emergence of SSD technology computer forensics faced newer challenges than traditional HDD. The SSD devices are usually based on flash memory such as battery backed SRAM or DRAM which includes flash backing storage. These types of memories include some key features which complicate forensics analysis [11,19]. For example;

- Flash memory is divided into pages of 2 KB, 4 KB or larger instead of 512 bytes blocks as in HDD.
- Flash memory pages must be erased before performing write operation instead of just writing in a single pass as in HDD.
- Rewriting a block does not necessarily rewrite on the same page because of wear leveling mechanism employed in SSDs.
- Each page of SSD has a number of write and erase cycles typically 10,000 to 100,000.
- Before storing the data on SSD it is often encrypted, erasing the encrypted data is done by deleting the older encryption key and generating a new one and marking those as garbage.

The SSD controllers are considerably more complex in performing the task of reading and writing data on to media as compared to HDD, with the following distinguished features [11,19].

- *Wear Leveling:* It is a mechanism which is used to avoid a block to physically wear out quicker than other blocks by spreading the data eventually. Using wear leveling technique, the firmware of SSD uses all the blocks evenly instead of using few blocks repeatedly and reducing their life. SSDs have Flash Translation Layer (FTL) which is used to perform wear leveling. It maps logical sectors to physical pages. FTL is contained within SSD and are not accessible to end users.

– *Read, Modify, Relocate+Write:* When a partial page is required to modify, the firmware first reads the entire page into a cache built inside SSD, then it modifies blocks being written and writes the new page in a new location. The older page is marked for garbage collection.

These features are very good from forensics point of view because a block being modified might be available in cache or in its previous location if it is still not wiped internally by SSD. However, there are three other issues that complicate forensics evidence gathering because they make the data recovery almost impossible.

1. *Garbage Collector*
   SSD uses garbage collection mechanism to improve its write speed [12]. Write performance is improved by eliminating the need of erasing before writing. The erasing operation is performed in background and during free time when controller is not busy. GC accumulates data blocks which are marked unused by erasing it and reclaim blocks for reuse for later write operations [17,18]. However GC has implications on computer forensics. It operates independently without the need of intervention from the operating system. After about 150 s of power on, GC starts erasing the garbage blocks previously marked by the file system [14,17,18]. Therefore, there is a risk that the GC may delete the content of the media even during performing forensic copy in the lab.

2. *TRIM*
   TRIM is a command in modern operating system to inform the SSDs controller that particular blocks of data are no longer required or not in used and should be wiped internally. In the absence of BGC, TRIM command is an alternate to improve write performance of SSDs. It enables the controller to handles the garbage collection overhead in advance, which could otherwise significantly slow down future writes. In order for the TRIM command to work, the SSDs firmware, operating system and associated software must be properly configured. Usually modern operating systems such as Windows 7 have built-in TRIM command utility that can be configured in BIOS settings. Since this command if configured properly completely purges the data, therefore, the data recovery will becomes impossible.

3. *Encryption and Compression*
   Modern SSD controllers perform compression and encryption on data before saving them on the disk. Compression increases the speed of writing data on SSD and also allows more data to be stored on SSD. The encryption of data before writing to SSD's cells has two advantages. First it improves security and secondly this technique enables controller to erase entire SSD disk. Rather than wiping the entire media, deleting the encryption key leads

to the inability to recover or read the data. So in the forensic analysis even if the data is recovered without knowing or recovering its encryption key, it is usually impossible to read the recovered data and it may cause difficulty in the way of forensic analysis.

3 Related Work

In this Section we discuss the literature on recovery of data from flash based memories. In [20] Luck et al. recommended a three stage approach to retrieve files in general and video files in particular from a mobile phone (Containing NAND Flash Memory). During the first stage, the authors illustrate the method of renewing FAT and distillation of extant files by building version table which includes all available versions of logical sectors. In the first stage the authors have further described a six step approach which contain (i) Building Version Table, (ii) Rebuilding File Allocation Table (FAT) volume, (iii) Analyzing Volume Boot Record (VBR), (iv) Extracting directory, (v) Extracting extant files and (vi) Recovering lost chains and lost files. The main goal of all those six steps is building a data structure or rebuilds a file system that maps the logical data abstracted to physical location.

In the next stage authors' aim was to find again a chain of clusters and files. They described that although the directory entry is overwritten in many cases but cluster chain is still in the phone memory and need to secure all chains that exist in the memory, including all lost and partial fragments of lost chains [20]. The authors have described MPEG-4 3 GP file format and suggested that it is important for the forensic examiner to understand MPEG-4 3 GP file system as it helps in reconstructing deleted videos. In the third stage of their approach they used a technique called "Xtractor". The purpose of Xtractor is to play incomplete video by playback software like Apple QuickTime 7. They showed that as defective sectors can be recognize and replaced with null sectors (0×00) and using Xtractor they could still be played.

Although the research by Luck et al. is very useful for data recovery from NAND flash, however, it is related to the memories of the mobile phones. First memories installed in mobile phones do not apply "garbage collection" and as an end result the deleted files may still be present in memory and could be recovered by the approach suggested by the author. Second the approach is well elaborated and tested for video data (i-e MPEG-4) only. Therefore, the approach has very limited application in the SSDs forensics and data recovery. The only link that could be established is the process of rebuilding the FAT volume by building a version table containing all available versions of logical sectors. But it is still limited to FAT12 or FAT16 in mobile phones where first entry point is VBR rather than Master Boot Record (MBR).

In [15] Freeman et al. tested possible available tools and procedures for securely deleting data from SSDs. They found that all tools except GNU core utility dd left some file information which was recovered, but none of the recovered files were workable.

Authors started their explanation from the fact that SSDs store files in 4 KB page, yet data can only be deleted in 512 KB blocks. The procedure stores pages in disk controller cache as the file is being deleted, the disk controller remove all the pages from the block. Once the pages are removed from the block, the required authentic data is fetched from the cache and reallocated on an available block. The reset block is added to the SSDs free space [21]. Every 32 GB SSDs have 2.2 GB space which is used as cache and it is not visible to operating system. The controller of SSD uses this additional free space to save files, that reduces the need for the deletion of blocks that keeps the drive at best performance [15]. Authors uses 32 GB PQI SATA II 2.5 in. SSD. They have used the drive to connect to secondary SATA port. They formatted SSD as NTFS and for experimental purpose they saved and deleted data of varying size and file type. dd (GNU core utility), Eraser (version 5.8.7), Wipe and SDelete were the tools they have tested for data deletion/sanitization and Scalpel was used for file carving purposes.

The approach and findings of Freeman et al. proposed that there is no (except dd of GNU) available tool that can guarantee completion deletion of data from SSDs. Authors note that "Even after employing eraser tools to delete the data from SSD there is still remnant data in SSDs that could be recovered".

In the article [22] Wei et al. have discovered the inability or difficulty of deleting/purifying data from the SSDs. The authors have conducted a number of experiments with the aim of finding any remnant data after applying (1) built-in ATA or SCSI commands for sanitization and (2) software based sanitization. Authors conducted several experiments and showed results of experiments and the percentage of data they had recovered after applying different techniques. They claimed that none of the existing hard drive-oriented techniques for individual sanitization are effective on SSDs [22]. They showed that the sanitization of the SSD with currently available tools is extremely difficult and the tools available for sanitizing the HDD cannot be used to sanitize the SSD. Using these tools to sanitize the SSD will leave data in the SSDs which can be recovered by sophisticated software.

In [14] Bell et al. reports about "self-corrosion" which is actually caused by "garbage collection" mechanism employed in entrenched controllers of modern SSDs. The authors used only 64 GB P64 Corsair SSD directly connected to the secondary SATA channel on the motherboard. Authors tested the data to see what portion of the sampled bytes were "zero bytes". The experiment shows that almost all the data were zeroed within 300 s.

After a single run of GO program the authors managed a forensic analysis of the SSDs. They were able to recover 1090 files out of 316,666 files, none of which could be used to reconstruct the original file. They conducted various experiments on the same SSD and found that the SSD is able to delete the data automatically even during construction of forensic image.

At the end the authors provided a list of guidance for forensics of SSDs and claimed that the "golden age for forensic recovery and analysis of deleted data and deleted meta-data may now be ending" [14]. From the literature review two opposite and interesting facts are revealed.

- "Even after applying sanitization techniques on SSDs there are still remnant data" [15,22].
- "Golden age for forensic recovery and analysis of deleted data and deleted meta-data may now be ending" [14].

The first view is that even if someone tries to remove the data in any possible way then there is still chance of leftover part of the data. In other words, it is not easy to accurately delete data from SSDs using the conventional techniques [15,22]. The second view is that the SSDs controller removes almost all the data and hardly any data could be recovered, for example, even during a quick format which does not require erasing the data [14]. This has motivated us to conduct further experiments and possibly find support for either view.

4   Proposed Method

As the results and conclusions from [14,15,22] had gone into the opposite directions. So it seems that there is a gap that needs to be filled. This is the main motivation of our research and that's why we aimed to conduct the SSDs forensics analysis further under a number of possible assumptions that these authors might had missed and possibly fill the gap between their results. Our experimental setup and assumptions are different than those employed by [14,15,22].

- First of all, previous research is conducted by attaching the SSD to a secondary channel of the motherboard. No experiment is conducted having SSDs as primary drive and an operating system installed on it. We believe that in reality when SSD is attached as a primary drive this may change its behavior because of the operating system. Since the operating system maintains the primary and secondary drive differently and garbage collector may behave differently as well. Even if the garbage collector deletes the data automatically we are interested to find out when the GC comes into action. Thus we want to conduct experiments both using SSD as primary drive as well as secondary drive.
- In the experiment conducted in [14], the SSD is filled entirely with data and then they have applied quick format. It is possible that if the controller is unable to find free space for incoming data then it activates the garbage collector. In other words it is possible that garbage collector's behavior changes with the amount of available free space or amount of space marked for throwing away (i.e., Garbage Collection)
- As the garbage collector from different manufacturers will behave differently, therefore, we conducted the experiments over SSDs from different vendors.

Table 1. Specifications of the Computers

Category	Description
Dell Laptop	
Manufacturer	Dell Inc
Model	INSPIRON 1545
Operating System	Microsoft Windows 7 Home Premium
RAM	4 GB
Hard Disk Drive	500 GB
Processor	Intel(R) Core(TM)2 Duo CPU T6600 @ 2.20 GHz, 2200 MHz, 2 Core(s), 2 Logical Processor(s)
Dell Desktop	
Manufacturer	Dell Inc
Model	OPTIPLEX 755
Operating System	Microsoft Windows 7 Professional
RAM	4 GB
Hard Disk Drive	250 GB
Processor	Intel(R) Core(TM)2 Quad CPU Q9300 @ 2.5 GHz, 2500 MHz, 2

5   Experiments and Results

We have performed three sets of experiments using three types of SSDs on two types of computers. The specifications of the computers used in the experiments are given in Table 1. The three types of SSDs used in our experiments are given in Table 2. We have selected Microsoft Windows 7 Professional and Microsoft Windows 7 Home Premium as the experimental operating systems. Windows 7 has native support for the TRIM command. For the TRIM to work, it is necessary that the underlying SSD support TRIM command and TRIM must also be enabled on Windows 7. To enable TRIM command on Windows 7 the following three options must be configured.

– Turn off system protection
– Enable AHCI mode in system BIOS
– Enable AHCI mode in window 7 registry.

For the recovery of files, PC Inspector [23] was used. PC Inspector is an open source software specially designed for the recovery of multimedia files from the camera memory or micro SD. It is open source and specifically designed for flash based memories. The drawback of PC Inspector is that it can only recover multimedia files of different formats. Paragon Partition Manager is used for partitioning and initial formatting of the SSDs in order to use it and view it in Windows operating system.

Table 2. Specifications of the SSDs

Category	Description
Crucial m4 64 GB	
Name	Crucial M4 SSD
Model	CT064M4SSD2
Capacity	64 GB
Form factor	2.5
Sequential READ	up to 500 MB/s
Sequential WRITE	up to 95 MB/s
Samsung 470 Series 64 GB	
Name	Samsung 470 Series
Model	MZ-5PA0641
Capacity	64 GB
Form factor	2.5
Sequential READ	up to 250 MB/s
Sequential WRITE	up to 170 MB/s
Kingston SSDNow V 100 64 GB	
Name	Kingston SSDNow V 100 SSD
Model	SV100S2N1646
Capacity	64 GB
Form factor	2.5
Sequential READ	up to 250 MB/s
Sequential WRITE	up to 145 MB/s

5.1 Experiment 1: Connecting SSDs to Dell Laptop Using USB Port

The purpose of this set of experiments is to check if the SSDs can preserve data after a quick format. Through experiments it was found that, data can only be preserved if there is no background garbage collector and the TRIM command is not performed, because these are the two possible causes that could delete the data from the SSD and no data will be recovered. In all other cases the data must be available for the recovery.

Experiment 1.1: Recovery from Crucial M4 SSD: In this experiment we connected the crucial M4 SSD to the USB port of laptop using Kingston USB case. The entire space of the crucial SSD is filled out by pasting a 3.44 MB JPEG image 17627 times. A free space of 272 KB is left over that could not hold any further image of the selected size. After this the SSD is quick formatted and system is restarted after 15 min. When the Five minutes after the system reboot, the recovery software was started to recover the JPEG images. The recovery process completed 100 % in about 32 h and 15 min to complete.

From the recovered data it is observed that 17625 pictures were recovered and the software miss only two pictures out of 17627 pictures. From the result it is clear that the crucial M4 SSD does not have background garbage collector. It is also cleared that TRIM command also does not work under this experimental setup.

Experiment 1.2: Recovery from Samsung 470 Series SSD: The same experiment as conducted in Experiment 1.1 with the crucial SSD is repeated with the Samsung SSD. This experiment took almost the same time as that of Experiment 1.1. The result of this experiment also similar to Experiment 1.1. This SSD also does not have background garbage collector and not even TRIM command worked in our experimental setup.

Experiment 1.3: Recovery from Kingston SSDNow V 100 SSD: The same experiment as conducted in Experiment 1.1 and 1.2 is repeated with the Kingston SSDNow V 100 as well. This experiment took almost the same time as that of Experiment 1.1 and 1.2. Kingston SSDNow V 100 also did not have GC and TRIM enabled, and we were able to recover the same number of files from this SSD.

5.2   Experiment 2: Connecting SSDs to Dell Desktop Using Secondary SATA Port

As it is clear from the previous results that TRIM does not work with the USB port, the purpose of this experiment was to check the support of Windows 7 TRIM command for the SSD connected to SATA secondary port. Windows 7 was installed on a separate hard disk drive which was attached to the primary SATA port of the system. It was evident from previous experiments that Windows 7 cannot send TRIM command on USB port. Here we want to clarify the work of TRIM on SSD attach to secondary SATA port. The necessary preparations for this set of experiments are similar to Experiment 1.

Experiment 2.1: Recovery from Crucial M4 SSD: The Crucial M4 SSD was connected to SATA 1 on the dell desktop computer. As scanning of the large 64 GB SSD for files recovery is much time consuming, therefore, we decided to create two partitions in the SSD. One partition had a capacity of 5.85 GB and the second one had the remaining capacity of 59.6 GB. The 5.85 GB drive was filled by pasting a 3.48 MB JPEG image 1719 times. Only 2.89 MB space was free that could not hold any more image of the selected size. After filling the drive, it was quick formatted and the system was shut down after 15 min of the format operation and then restarted. When the system fully booted the PC Inspector was started for file recovery. The whole recovery process ran for about 3 h and 30 min.

The result of this experiment is similar to Experiment 1.1. It was found that connecting with USB port and connecting with the SATA secondary port does not make any difference. Almost all the files were recovered by the PC Inspector. TRIM command did not work with SATA secondary port as well.

Experiment 2.2: Recovery from Samsung 470 Series SSD: The same experiment as conducted in experiment 2.1 with the crucial SSD was repeated with the Samsung SSD as well. This experiment took almost the same time as that of Experiment 2.1. The result of this experiment was not different from the experiment 2.1. The TRIM command did not worked for this SSD as well while connecting it to SATA secondary port.

Experiment 2.3: Recovery from Kingston SSDNow V 100 SSD: The same experiment as conducted in Experiments 2.1 and 2.2 was repeated with the Kingston SSDNow V 100 as well. This experiment took almost the same time as that of Experiments 2.1 and 2.2.

The result of the Kingston SSD was similar to the other two SSDs. The TRIM command does not work either with the USB port or with the secondary SATA port. All these three SSDs were able to preserve data after quick format. If there is no background garbage collector in the SSD then the TRIM command never activates any garbage collection cycle in the SSDs if they are attached externally to the computer.

5.3   Experiment 3: Connecting SSDs to Dell Desktop Using Primary SATA Port

As it is clear from the previous results that TRIM does not work with the USB port and SATA secondary port. So in this setup the SSD is connected to the SATA primary port and operating system is installed on it. Windows 7 professional was installed on each of the three SSDs. During the installation we made two partitions (for all the three SSDs) were made one was labeled as C having size of 55.7 GB and the other one was labeled as D having a size of 3.90 GB. For each of the three SSDs, operating system was installed on the C partition. TRIM command was enabled by making the necessary changes in the OS and BIOS.

Experiment 3.1: Recovery from Crucial M4 SSD: In this experiment, the 3.90 GB of D drive was filled with 1522 JPEG images of size 2.59 MB. Only 1.31 GB space was left out as free. After filling the drive, it was quick formatted and the system was shut down after 15 min of the format operation and then started again. When the system fully booted PC Inspector was started for file recovery. The whole recovery process ran for about 2 h.

This time the result was completely different from all the previous experiments. The software scanned the entire D partition but could not find even a single byte of data on the SSD. The TRIM command worked perfectly in this scenario of the experiment. We were not able to recover any single image from the drive.

Experiment 3.2: Recovery from Samsung 470 Series SSD: The same experiment as conducted in Experiment 3.1 with the crucial SSD was repeated with the Samsung SSD as well. This experiment took almost the same time as that of Experiment 3.1. Just like crucial SSD the Samsung SSD also erase all the data as the software was unable to recover any data. The Samsung SSD also shows that TRIM command works if the SSD is the primary drive. The experimental results shows that both crucial and Samsung SSDs cannot preserve data when connected on the SATA primary port.

Experiment 3.3: Recovery from Kingston SSDNow V 100 SSD: The same experiment as conducted in Experiments 3.1 and 3.2 was repeated with the Kingston SSDNow V 100 as well. This experiment took almost the same time as that of Experiments 3.1 and 3.2.

Just like Crucial and Samsung SSD, Kingston SSD also erases all the data and the software was unable to recover any data. The Kingston SSD also shows that the TRIM command works if the SSD is the primary drive. The experimental results show that all of the three SSDs, Crucial, Samsung and Kingston cannot preserve data when they are connected on SATA primary port.

6 Discussion and Conclusion

With the growth of emerging technology of SSDs in computers and other similar devices like cellular phones, tablets and netbooks, there are challenges for forensics analysis which are not experienced with traditional HDDs. Existing forensics analysis tools treat SSDs much like traditional hard disks drives. However, the technological difference between SSDs and HDDs requires new forensics tools designed specifically to address SSDs.

The purpose of wear leveling technique is to prevent blocks that contain frequently altering data from going bad faster than those which holds static data. Wear leveling techniques are usually implemented in Flash Translation Layer or in the Controller. It provides an opportunity to recover old data as well as metadata after a file is deleted or changed and new information is rewritten to a new physical location.

We have experimentally verified that SSD behavior differs when it is attached to the secondary SATA ports and the primary SATA ports with the operating system installed on it. TRIM command only works in the latter case. And it is even worse than BGC and has the potentials to destroy forensics evidences instantly after the deletion is performed. It is also important to note that BGC is not implemented in all the SSDs available in market and those having BGC start erasing garbage blocks approximately 150 s after the deletion is performed [14].

The firmware does not clear or zero the SSD automatically. It requires an operating system that supports the TRIM command to erase the data permanently. Therefore, in the absence of BGC and inability of the TRIM command, live acquisition is still possible. If encryption is enabled then the data recovered during live acquisition without encryption key is almost useless for forensics analysis, since it is hard to understand or make sense of encrypted data.

References

1. Lofgren, K.M.J., Norman, R.D., Thelin, G.B., Gupta, A.: Wear leveling techniques for flash EEPROM systems, 8 May 2001 (U.S. Patent 6,230,233)
2. Flusche, K.J.: Computer forensic case study: espionage, Part 1 just finding the file is not enough!. Inf. Syst. Secur. **10**(1), 1–10 (2001)
3. Janes, S.: The role of technology in computer forensic investigations. Inf. Secur. Tech. Rep. **5**(2), 43–50 (2000)
4. Guide, N., Ashcroft, J., Electronic Crime Scene Investigation: A Guide for First Responders Series: NIJ Guide
5. Carrier, B., Spafford, E.H.: Getting physical with the digital investigation process. Int. J. Digital Evid. **2**(2), 1–20 (2003)
6. Boddington, R., Hobbs, V., Mann, G.: Validating digital evidence for legal argument (2008)
7. Berg, E.C.: Legal ramifications of digital imaging in law enforcement. Forensic Science Communications, 2(4) (2000)
8. Kenneally, E.E., Brown, C.L.: Risk sensitive digital evidence collection. Digital Investig. **2**(2), 101–119 (2005)
9. Carrier, B.: File System Forensic Analysis, vol. 3. Addison-Wesley, Boston (2005)
10. Kasavajhala, V.: Solid State Drive vs. Hard Disk Drive Price and Performance Study, Dell Technical White Paper, Dell Power Vault Storage Systems (2011)
11. Hu, X.Y., et al.: Write amplification analysis in flash-based solid state drives. In: Proceedings of SYSTOR 2009, The Israeli Experimental Systems Conference. ACM (2009)
12. Lee, J., et al.: A semi-preemptive garbage collector for solid state drives. In: IEEE International Symposium on Performance Analysis of Systems and Software (ISPASS). IEEE (2011)
13. Seppanen, E., O'Keefe, M.T., Lilja, D.J.: High performance solid state storage under linux. In: IEEE 26th Symposium on Mass Storage Systems and Technologies (MSST). IEEE (2010)
14. Bell, G.B., Boddington, R.: Solid state drives: the beginning of the end for current practice in digital forensic recovery? J. Digital Forensics Secur. Law **5**(3), 1–20 (2010)
15. Freeman, M., Woodward, A.: Secure state deletion: testing the efficacy and integrity of secure deletion tools on Solid State Drives. In: Australian Digital Forensics Conference (2009)
16. Olson, A.R., Langlois, D.J.: Solid state drives data reliability and lifetime. Imation White Paper (2008)
17. Agrawal, N., et al.: Design Tradeoffs for SSD Performance. In: USENIX Annual Technical Conference (2008)

18. Chen, F., Koufaty, D.A., Zhang, X.: Understanding intrinsic characteristics and system implications of flash memory based solid state drives. In: Proceedings of the eleventh international joint conference on Measurement and Modeling of Computer Systems. ACM (2009)
19. Garfinkel, S.L.: Digital forensics research: the next 10 years. Digital Invest. **7**, S64–S73 (2010)
20. Luck, J., Stokes, M.: An integrated approach to recovering deleted files from NAND flash data. Small Scale Digital Device Forensics J. **2**(1), 1941–6164 (2008)
21. Roberts, D., Kgil, T., Mudge, T.: Integrating NAND flash devices onto servers. Commun. ACM **52**(4), 98–103 (2009)
22. Wei, M.Y.C., et al.: Reliably erasing data from flash-based solid state drives. In: Proceeding FAST (2011)
23. Arthur, K.K., Venter, H.S.: An investigation into computer forensic tools. In: Proceeding ISSA (2004)

Cloud Security from Users Point of View: A Pragmatic Study with Thematic Analysis

Saira Syed[(✉)] and Quazi Mamun

School of Computing and Mathematics, Charles Sturt University, Sydney, Australia
ssyed01@postoffice.csu.edu.au, qmamun@csu.edu.au

Abstract. Despite economic pressure for business to cut costs and fervent assurances from cloud service providers, security remains a top barrier to cloud adoption. Interests in cloud computing are high and many organisations say they are planning to move in that direction. However, the reality is that only 20 % of UK organisations are using infrastructure-as-a-service and only 36 % are using software-as-a-service, according to the National Computing Centre (NCC, UK) research. Lack of trust in cloud computing is slowing broader adoption of cloud services. Therefore, it is important to understand the consumers' perspective on cloud security concerns, especially data security issues. This allows the future research to proceed in the right direction to alleviate users' concerns. In this paper, we present an empirical analysis of IT experts and professionals viewpoint related to security issues in clouds. The study is based on the surveys conducted by three different groups in the time period from 2010 to 2013. Qualitative research analysis is used to collect perception of IT experts and professionals by using interviewing technique. The viewpoints of the experts are then analysed and a qualitative and thematic analysis is presented. The study presents most critical threats, possible causes, and fundamental strategies to avoid them.

Keywords: Cloud computing · Data security · Threats · Cause · Strategies

1 Introduction

The advantages of the cloud computing model of a reduced cost of ownership, no capital investment, scalability, self-service, location independence and rapid deployment are widely extolled. What will it take to get businesses to adopt cloud computing *en masse*? The short answer is that it all boils down to trust.

Cloud computing is the latest IT paradigm which promises to bring many benefits to businesses. However, there are some risks and security concerns that must be addressed correctly [1]. Many research studies [2–4] claim that the most significant reason for deterring cloud computing is the fear of losing control over the data.

Traditional models of data protection such as firewalls and intrusion detection systems are insufficient to protect against complex data security issues of cloud computing. Therefore, this area is currently the focus of attention for the researchers' community. Security is one of the most crucial aspects of this new technology.

© Institute for Computer Sciences, Social Informatics and Telecommunications Engineering 2015
J. Tian et al. (Eds.): SecureComm 2014, Part II, LNICST 153, pp. 127–140, 2015.
DOI: 10.1007/978-3-319-23802-9_12

Users, in many cases, are unaware of security threats and may judge security only based on their uninterrupted availability of the respective cloud service. Even if the user understands potential security threats he/she may not be able to restrict the damage in real time or get control of the service.

No matter, how big the company with cloud based services is security incidents are seen in terms of service interruptions to phishing attacks and data leaks. However, it is very important to explore and understand the users' perception in regards to data security and the countermeasures which are currently in place.

This research study presents an empirical analysis of data security issues and their countermeasures from user-centric perspective. The reason for choosing an empirical research method is to discover and interpret facts. Furthermore, this method has been chosen to answer the questions about the topic under investigation. Empirical research can be divided into quantitative method and qualitative method. However this paper is based on qualitative research as this method is appropriate in the early stages of research. In addition qualitative method tends to be applied more easily in real world setting.

The remainder of the paper is organized as follows. Section 2 describes the research themes. In Sect. 3 overview of cloud computing is provided. Section 4 presents synopsis of the literature. In Sect. 5 research methodology is provided. Section 6 presents result followed by discussion in Sect. 7. Finally, in Sect. 8, we conclude the paper and provide the future work.

2   A Basic Overview of Cloud Computing

Cloud computing has been defined by several other researchers, while the most respected one is provided by National Institute of Standards & Technology [5] as a model for enabling convenient, on-demand network access to a shared pool of configurable computing resources that can be rapidly provisioned and released with minimal management effort or service provider interaction. Some researchers argue that cloud computing is not a new term but only recently it has become a fashionable term [6]. This latest IT paradigm provides large number of benefits to the businesses. Research [7] indicates that the benefits of cloud computing mainly include low-cost, availability, innovation power, high expandability, friendly utilizations and environmental protection. In addition, on-demand self-service, elastic and scalable, consumption-based pricing model are some of the advantages identified by Burton Group, a research and consulting firm [8]. The cloud computing technology is based on three service delivery models and three main deployment models which are as follows:

The deployment models are (1) **Private cloud:** a platform dedicated for specific organization, (2) **Public cloud:** a platform available to public users and (3) **Hybrid cloud:** a private cloud that can extend to use resources in public clouds.

The cloud service deliver models are

(1) **Infrastructure-as-a-service (IaaS):** where computational resources, storage and network as internet-based services are available. For example Amazon EC2

(2) **Platform-as-a-service (PaaS):** where platforms, tools and other business services are available that enable customers to develop, deploy and manage their own application. This model may be hosted on top of IaaS model or on cloud infrastructure directly. MS Windows Azure and Google Apps are the well examples of this model.
(3) **Software-as-a-service (SaaS):** where cloud providers deliver applications hosted on the cloud as a service for end user. SaaS may be hosted on top of PaaS, IaaS or directly on cloud infrastructure. For example: SalesForce CRM.

3   Literature on Cloud Security

Research study conducted by Chow et al. [9] claim that there is a lack of control and transparency [10] when the third-party holds the data. In addition, this study argues that current countermeasure do not adequately address third-party's data storage and processing needs. As a result Chow et al. [9] proposes to extend countermeasures by suggesting the use of trusted computing and cryptographic techniques. However this study is limited to their vision only.

Although the issue of third-party can be addressed by employing trusted third-party (TTP) services [10, 11]. A TTP is an entity which facilitates secure interaction between two parties who both trust this third party. As TTP creates secure zone, its best role is played in cryptography [10]. However Wang et al. [12] argue that cloud storage is not just the third-party data warehouse. The cloud data may not only be accessed but also be frequently updated including insertion, deletion, modification by the users. This makes the data security even more challenging in the cloud environment. Complex data security and privacy issues exist in all stages of data life cycle such as from generation to destruction of data. Many research studies explore and identify [4, 9, 12] complex data security issues in cloud computing however these are limited to derive from existing body of literature. Although, extensive literature survey provides complex data security issues however, there is an urgent need to understand the user's point of view in regard to data security in the cloud.

Clearly, very few research studies have employed different approaches to explore and identify the data security by understanding user's perception. Carroll et al. [13] in 2010 conducted semi-structured interview of 15 participants to explore the issues from user's point of view. On the other hand, Tanimoto et al. [14] analyse risks of utilizing cloud computing extracted from a user's viewpoint. However this study is limited to Japan.

3.1   Strategies and Countermeasures

Any kind of security and privacy violation of data in the cloud is critical and can produce dire consequences [3]. In order to overcome this problem large number of research studies have been conducted which present different strategies and countermeasures to address the data security issues. Moreover, an issue of trusting cloud is a paramount concern for most organizations. However, it is not about trusting the cloud providers' intentions, rather cloud computing's capabilities are questionable. This research study

[16] is based on the fact that the challenges of trusting cloud computing don't lie entirely in the technology alone. This study raises the concern that adoption of cloud computing came before the appropriate technologies appeared to tackle the challenges of trust. Other researches therefore conducted the similar studies in regard to trust issues. Regarding the trust issues, this study recommends to use encryption for identity and data privacy. However research study conducted by Vormetric warns that if encryption keys are not sufficiently protected, they are vulnerable to theft by malicious hackers [15]. Recently Sugumaran [28] suggested that a key is generated for set time duration then get expiry after the time duration. Finally the user updates a private key from the authority in a time intervals.

An encryption is considered as an important technique to retain control over the data in the cloud. However, encryption limits data use. In particular, searching and indexing the data becomes problematic. State-of-the-art cryptography offers new tools to solve these problems [9]. In order to understand the cryptography tools and techniques, more research needs to be done [17]. A recent study conducted by Sood [3] has taken a step forward by proposing a frame work that claims to efficiently protect the data from the beginning to the end by classifying data on three cryptographic parameters, i.e., Confidentiality, Availability and Integrity. Other researchers have attempted to propose security frame work in the past which are based on cryptography.

More recently, new research studies are emerging which are pointing to the fact that, data is not fully secured by applying cryptographic techniques. Surianarayanan and Santhanam [18] therefore, argue that security mechanisms should be applied at each level such as network level, system level, virtual machine level and application level. This study presents different policies, procedures and controls to mitigate the risks associated with each level. However, this research is limited to cloud service provider's end. Securing each level in the cloud computing is of critical importance because cloud services do pose as an attractive target to any cyber-criminal. Research study conducted by Khorshed et al. identify the most common attacks which could lead to top threats for the real world cloud implementation [19]. Moreover, this study [19] proposes a proactive threat detection model by adopting three main goals: (i) detect an attack when it happens, (ii) alert related system (system admin, data owner) about the attack type and take combating action, and (iii) analyse the pattern and generate information about the type of attack.

In order to make the cloud environment more secured, researchers are introducing multi-clouds. These research studies [20, 21] claim that multi-clouds can improve reliability, trust, and security as compared to single clouds by distributing them among multiple cloud providers.

Thus, the above mentioned literature review indicates that past research studies have been conducted in all different directions. However, users are reluctant to move their data to cloud [19]. In addition the past studies have failed to establish user's trust on cloud computing. Therefore, it is important to carry out a study on understanding the user's point of view in regard to data security concerns and issues, causes and fundamental strategies to avoid those issues.

4   A Qualitative Empirical Study on Cloud Security

This research study is conducted by a qualitative empirical study using the datasets from the open sources and in-depth literature review. The qualitative patterns from the sources are then examined to conduct a thematic analysis. This study results in presenting data security concerns, possible causes and strategies to avoid the threats.

4.1   Data Sources

The data related to cloud security is collected from open sources. We chose the sources where survey by interview approach was used.

- AccelOps, the leader in integrated Security Information and Event Management (SIEM) [22].
- Pew Research Centre's internet and American Life Project [23].
- Cloud Security Alliance (CSA) [24].

These surveys used standardized open ended questions to collect qualitative and quantitative data to better understand professionals' view on cloud security issues. The detail of the data sources is provided in Table 1. These data sources are selected due to the following reasons.

- These sources are among the cloud technology experts.
- Based on survey by interview.
- Survey results are qualitatively presented.

Table 1. Data Sources

Source	Sampling	Participants	Year
Pew research centre's	Online survey of 895 participants	Internet experts and users	2010
AccelOps	176 online and conference participants	IT security professional	2013
Cloud security alliance	Unspecified number of participants	Industry experts	2013

The interviewees in these surveys were asked several questions about different aspects of cloud computing, such as benefits, characteristics, adopters, inhibitors and security issues. Majority of question were open ended to gain detailed insight into users' perspective.

4.2   Thematic Analysis

This research study is based on thematic analysis as a data analysis method. Thematic analysis is a common method for qualitative analysis of transcripts for identifying, analysing and reporting themes or patterns within data.

This research article analyzed the survey conducted by three independent groups, resulting in an average of 350–450 participants per group. The survey finding provide some important information of how users view the cloud computing and the security in regard to their data.

Each survey was read carefully and thoroughly in order to develop the following themes (Table 2).

Table 2. Major patterns and Related Themes

Themes	Identified patterns
Major data security threats	Not trusting the cloud for data related services. Dissatisfaction with the data storage on the cloud. Negative real life examples in regard to data breach in the cloud. Reluctant to move data in to the cloud
Causes of the threat	Reasons for not trusting the cloud for data services. Possible root cause of data threats Who is responsible for the threat? Any data breach incident? If yes why? Dissatisfaction with the existing data security tools and measures
Strategies to avoid the threats	Necessary steps before moving data in the cloud. Customers' dissatisfaction with service level agreement. Who is responsible for ensuring cloud data security?

From this point, categorising of data is taken place by labelling passage of data according to what they are about. These categories are then rearranged into different themes by finding relationships between them. The occurrence of themes is seen in the following Tables 3, 4 and 5.

Table 3. Threats and their Occurrences

Major data security threats	Occurrences
Data breach	95 %
Data loss	85 %
Data unavailability	72 %
Third-party data control	69 %
Data privacy	45 %

Table 4. Causes and their occurrences

Possible causes of data security threats	Occurrences
Malicious insiders	100 %
Lack of security tools	89 %
Lack of users knowledge about the cloud environment	75 %
Lack of transparency	69 %
Weak set of interfaces	69 %
Insufficient service level agreement	50 %

Table 5. Strategies and their Occurrences

Strategies to avoid the threats	Occurrences
Risk assessment and mitigation plan	75 %
Disaster recovery and backup plan	72 %
Data encryption	85 %
Service level agreement (SLA)	55 %

Clearly, the above mentioned analysis presents the emerging themes and their occurrence in regard to data security in the cloud. Although, some other themes were emerged after the applying thematic analysis on the collected data. However, this study is focused on the themes which are presented above.

5   Identified Data Security Threats, Causes and Avoidance Strategies

At first, this section presents the key data security threats and issues that are explored and investigated from the empirical data gathered from the surveys. We then discuss the causes and the countermeasure of the identified threats and issues.

5.1   Data Security Threats and Issues

Although cloud computing may seem attractive to all the participants in the survey. According to Research firm Gartner public cloud market is expected to reach $206.6 billion in 2016 from $91.4 billion in 2011. However this much growth is only possible after addressing some security issues and challenges mentioned by the interviewees. Among those issues, this research study identifies the major data security issues and threats in the cloud. As storing, accessing and sharing company's data remotely on the internet poses great risk on the company's profile. One of the major security concerns related to cloud computing is the security of data [26]. Based on the survey reports, the main data security issues are as follows;

i. Data Breach

A data breach is an incident in which sensitive, protected or confidential data has potentially been viewed, stolen or used by individual unauthorized to do so. Data breach is the most critical concern in the surveys conducted by CSA [24], AccelOps [22] and Pew Research Centre [23]. Organizations are fearful of having their information compromised. One of the respondents predicts that in 2020 the cloud will be barley in use because of data privacy. Data breaches can be embarrassing and costly. Sensitive data stored within cloud environment must be safeguarded to protect its owners and subject alike. According to [25] confidentiality of data must be ensured be the system as the large businesses like banks would not like to do the transactions through clouds which involves the interaction of another system. The identified list of the top threats published in 2010, data breach was ranked at 5th position however, and in 2013 it is ranked at number 1. Clearly, it indicates that industry professionals and experts consider the data breach as the most serious threat of the cloud environment.

ii. Data loss

Data loss is an error condition in information systems in which information is destroyed by failure or neglect in storage, transmission or processing. It is evident from the AccelOp's survey that 63 % respondents claim data loss as top-of-mind issue for security professional. It has been recognised that data is the lifeblood of a enterprise [30]. As per CSA [24] survey report data loss takes on 2nd position as compared to 5th in 2010. Mat Honan, writer for wired magazine loses all his personal data from Apple, Gmail and Twitter accounts after they have been broken by some attackers. However experts in CSA's survey report argue that in addition to malicious attackers, physical catastrophe, accidental deletion by cloud provider can lead to data loss. The risk of data lost becomes higher due to the mobile devices. As one of the respondents point out in Pew's survey that the mobile phone will be the key instrument everywhere from supermarket to school.

iii. Data Unavailability

In simple terms, availability means that resources and data are accessible and usable at all times. Availability can be affected temporarily or permanently due to many factors. A research study [26] claims that organizations are wary of cloud computing and often worry about availability, which could be jeopardized due to technical as well as non-technical reasons. However, the surveys identify the denial of service (DoS) attack as the most common threat to prevent the users to access their data. A DoS attack involves saturating the target with bogus request to prevent it from responding to legitimate request in a timely manner. As per CSA's survey, DoS attack has many forms such as Distributed denial-of-service and asymmetric application-level DoS attacks. A fear of service outages forces the customers to reconsider before moving the company's critical data to the cloud. "How do you retrieve your prized novel or your business records if the cloud fails?" warns one respondent in the survey conducted by Pew. The CSA's survey reports indicates denial-of-service attack is at 5th position in the latest list of top security threat in cloud computing.

iv. Third-party Data control

It is evident from the AccelOps's survey that over half of the respondents concern over controlling the data that is moved to the third-party in the cloud. As the data is not in the control of the owner when in the cloud, anything can be possible. Entrust your data on to a third party who is providing cloud services is an issue [29]. It is apparent from the survey's findings that there is a lack of transparency from the provider's side on how data flows through their services and who has access to the data. Surprisingly, in other surveys the fear of data control by third-party is not reported. It is believed by the participating professionals that cloud providers should manage the data control risks.

v. Data privacy

Data or information privacy is way of collecting, storing and disseminating the data legally and ethically. It is clearly evident from the surveys that potential cloud consumers are reluctant to move their valuable asset to the cloud due to privacy reasons. One individual predicts that in 2020, everyone will keep the data at in-home storage and will be available via cloud to the personal devices in order to keep the information private. The majority of respondent felt that to further accelerate the cloud adoption; providers need to ensure the data privacy and control to consumers' sensitive data. In order to ensure the integrity of user authentication, companies need to be able to view data access logs and audit trails to verify that only authorized users are accessing the data [25].

5.2 Triggers for Data Security Threats and Issues

The second major finding of the thematic analysis is the possible causes of data security threats which are discussed below.

- Malicious insiders, those who have or had access to the sensitive information. Malicious insiders could steal sensitive information, sell the data to other parties or perform any number of other malicious activities. There are large numbers of incidents reported since 2001 about data breaches as a result of malicious insiders.
- Lack of tools and security measures at consumers end. The increased availability and use of social media, personal Webmail, and other sites can impact the security of the browser, its underlying platform, and cloud service accounts. Traditional antiviruses' solutions and firewalls are not sufficient to protect consumers' end.
- Lack of understanding about cloud service provider's environment. Security is at risk if cloud consumers are unaware of cloud providers' environment such as their hardware, software detail and VMware.
- An Organization rushes to adopt cloud technologies without trusting the providers. Lack of trust is one of the major causes of data security threats. Before selecting a cloud service provider, Organization must assess their capabilities, policies and procedures.

- Lack of transparency between the providers and the consumers. Cloud providers and consumers must maintain strong and transparent relationship between them.
- Reliance on a weak set of interfaces exposes organizations to variety of data security threats. Cloud consumers manage and interact with cloud providers using these sets of interfaces. Thus the security of the cloud services is dependent upon the security of these basic interfaces.
- Privacy rules are designed with the assumption that privacy protections are most reasonable at the ends. Privacy protection mechanisms and procedures are not fully examined before defining the privacy rules. Cloud service providers; therefore assume that both ends are privacy protected.
- Poorly designed service level agreement (SLA). The present SLAs discuss only about the services provided and the waivers given if the services do not meet the agreement. SLA has to discuss the other issues like policies, methods and their implementations.

5.3   Strategies for Avoiding the Data Security Threats

Security administrators need to decide how much time, money, and effort needs to be spent in order to develop the appropriate security policies and controls. Each organization should analyse its specific needs and determine its resource and scheduling requirements and constraints. Computer systems, environments, and organizational policies are different, making each computer security services and strategy unique. However, the principles of good security remain the same, and this document focuses on those principles.

Although a security strategy can save the organization valuable time and provide important reminders of what needs to be done, security is not a one-time activity. It is an integral part of the system lifecycle. The activities described in this document generally require either periodic updating or appropriate revision. These changes are made when configurations and other conditions and circumstances change significantly or when organizational regulations and policies require changes. This is an iterative process. It is never finished and should be revised and tested periodically. Thus, an efficient security technology is cloud computing is required to have proper secured cloud computing and to speedup cloud implementation [28].

Below is the list, in addition to the conventional approaches, of the strategies for avoiding the data security threats that we found during the empirical studies:

- Complete Risk assessment and mitigation strategies at consumers end. Organisations rush to adopt cloud technologies, therefore they avoid making plans for risk assessment and mitigations. This seems to be the first step before moving to the cloud.
- Disaster recovery and backup plan. The cloud providers must include detailed backup and disaster recovery plan. However, cloud consumers take necessary action to ensure all plans are in place.
- An organization should encrypt the data before storing it in the cloud and keep the encryption key secured. This provides confidence to the consumers that they are in control of their sensitive data.

– Consumers should look to prohibit the sharing of account credentials between users and services. Cloud computing is multitenant environment, therefore consumers must ask the providers to keep their credential detail private without sharing with others.
– Security monitoring software should be implemented by the consumers. There are many security monitoring software are available which should be implemented at the consumers end.
– Well prepared service level agreement (SLA). Avoid any jargons in the agreement.

6 Discussion of the Findings

The result presented in this research study indicate that majority of respondents believe that cloud is here to stay. However, most participants pointed that some hurdles must be crossed successfully before this latest IT paradigm gains more adopters as shown in Fig. 1. Among the other factors, the issue of security and controlling the data should be addressed first. To further accelerate adoption, cloud providers need to provide increased clarity, more transparency and better assurance about their security controls. This study is based on three different findings which are as follows;

- Most critical data threats
- Possible causes for the threats
- Fundamental strategies to avoid the threats

The above mentioned findings are analysed from the surveys conducted from 2010 to 2013 from three important groups. In the survey, respondents were asked to highlight their perspective on multiple aspects of cloud computing. However, the current study attempts to discuss three important findings in regard to data in the cloud.

Thus, with the help of the report presented in three different surveys, this study identifies five most critical threats such as data breach, data lost, third-party data control, data unavailability, and data privacy. Although CSA [24] identified nine top threats however these identified concerns and threats seem most critical to the users' community. In addition, six possible causes of these threats are analyzed in this study. Other research studies [5, 6, 10] seem to be consistent with the current findings. In 2012, 9 million records are lost as a consequence of a breach, it appears that data alone is not the only asset; company's reputation is at risk too. Thus, before a business moves its assets into the cloud, it needs to consider all the related issues.

Other major findings in the current study are the possible causes and strategies to avoid the threats. A considerable amount of literature has been published on counter-measures and strategies to protect data in the cloud. However, these research studies do not take in account the users perspectives. This can be seen in the study conducted by Morsy et al. [27] where a detail analysis of cloud security problems is presented. However their findings are from the cloud architecture, stakeholders' and delivery perspective. This study attempts to provide key features that should be covered in a security solution model. On the other hand a study [6] was carried out in Taiwan to understand IT executives and professional perspective on cloud computing. However this analysis is used to underpin the identification of the factors which encourage and prevent the cloud computing adoption.

Clearly, the previous research studies do not take into account the users' perspective about data security in the cloud. Therefore, in our research we did a deep analysis into surveys' participants' responses to identify the most critical data security concerns according to users' perspective. Moreover, this study presents the root causes and key strategies to the identified issues and concerns. As a result, with description and analysis of these data security threats, this study guides the cloud providers, users and researchers' community to take necessary actions to resolve these issues.

This is very important to gain users' trust by addressing their most critical concerns and issues. Therefore, the current research study attempts to fill this gap by analysing users' perspective in regard to dissatisfaction and hesitation for adopting cloud computing. According to [11] understanding and clearly documenting specific users' requirement is imperative in designing a solution targeting at assuring these necessities. The fact is nothing is ever 100 % secured in the real or virtual world. However by avoiding the possible causes, cloud environment can be trusted and secured. According to [10] security is considered a key requirement for cloud computing consolidation as a robust and feasible multipurpose solution.

7   Conclusion and Future Work

The research study is based on qualitative empirical research approach. In this research three different sources are used which are qualitative surveys conducted in the past three years. The current study identifies the major data security threats as per the survey results. A thematic analysis has been applied in order to develop important themes and their occurrences. Security is the crucial aspect in providing trusted environment before moving the data in the cloud. This research study identifies most critical concerns and issues in regard to data in the cloud. The result represents that data breach appears to be the most critical threat to the Organisations. It is then followed by data loss, unavailability, lack of control and privacy at the end. These issues are obstacles for trusting the cloud.

In order to find the users point of view in regard to the above mention threats, possible causes are also identified. This analysis indicates that malicious insiders should be examined and trained thoroughly in order to alleviate the concerns of the users. Furthermore, lack of tools, lack of transparency, weak set of interfaces and insufficient service level agreement contribute in triggering data security threats.

Therefore, this paper presents few fundamental strategies to avoid data security threats and providing trusted cloud adoption. According to the users point of view these strategies include detailed risk assessment, disaster recovery plan, using encryption and securing their keys and final comprehensive service level agreement.

This research study provides a detailed insight in to users' perspective in regards to data security in the cloud. Therefore, research community can increase their focus in this area in order to alleviate the users concerns about cloud computing. This work enhances our current understanding of data security in the cloud from the users' viewpoint however more research is required to understand the threats and their consequences in detail.

In the future, we are planning to conduct the interviews by recruiting selective participants. Current countermeasures will be evaluated and the most concerned areas will be examined and addressed in order to gain users trust on this latest technology of cloud computing.

References

1. Dahbur, K., Mohammad, B., Tarakji, A.B.: A survey of risks, threats and vulnerabilities in cloud computing. In: Proceedings of the 2011 International Conference on Intelligent Semantic Web-Services and Applications - ISWSA 2011, pp. 1–6 (2011)
2. Ii, J.C.R.: Who can you trust in the cloud? A review of security issues within cloud computing. In: Security, pp. 15–19 (2011)
3. Sood, S.K.: A combined approach to ensure data security in cloud computing. J. Netw. Comput. Appl. 35(6), 1831–1838 (2012)
4. Chen, D., Zhao, H.: Data security and privacy protection issues in cloud computing. In: 2012 International Conference on Computer Science and Electronics Engineering, pp. 647–651 (2012)
5. Mell, P., Grance, T.: The NIST Definition of Cloud Computing (Draft). Recommendations of the National Institute of Standards and Technology, p. 145
6. Lin, A., Chen, N.-C.: Cloud computing as an innovation: percepetion, attitude, and adoption. Int. J. Inf. Manage. 32, 533–540 (2012)
7. Linthicum, D.S.: Cloud Computing and SOA Convergence in Your Enterprise. A Step-by-Step Guide. Addition Wesley Professional, Boston (2009)
8. Blum, D., Watson, R., Creese, G., Blakley, B., Haddad, C., Howard, C., Manes, A.T., Passmore, D., Lewis, J.: Cloud computing: transforming IT, pp. 1–51 (2009)
9. Chow, R., Golle, P., Jakobsson, M., Shi, E., Staddon, J., Masuoka, R., Molina, J.: Controlling data in the cloud: outsourcing computation without outsourcing control, pp. 85–90 (2009)
10. Mogre, P.V., Agarwal, G., Patil, P.: Data security and its technique in cloud storage-a review, vol. 1, pp. 1–5 (2012)
11. Zissis, D., Lekkas, D.: Addressing cloud computing security issues. Futur. Gener. Comput. Syst. 28, 583–592 (2012)
12. Wang, C., Member, S., Wang, Q.: toward secure and dependable storage services in cloud computing. 5, 220–232 (2012)
13. Carroll, M., Merwe, A., Van Der Kotzé, P.: Secure cloud computing benefits, risks and controls, vol. 12, pp. 12–14 (2012)
14. Tanimoto, S., Hiramoto, M., Iwashita, M., Sato, H., Kanai, A.: Risk management on the security problem in cloud computing. In: 2011 First ACIS/JNU International Conference on Computer Networks, Systems and Industrial Engineers, pp. 147–152 (2011)
15. Khan, K.M., Malluhi, Q.: Establishing trust in cloud computing (2010)
16. Information, P.B., Public, I.N., Environments, H.C.: Data security in the cloud, pp. 1–4 (2012)
17. Ryan, M.D.: Cloud computing security: the scientific challenge, and a survey of solutions. J. Syst. Softw. (2013)
18. Surianarayanan, S., Santhanam, T.: Security issues and control mechanisms in cloud. In: 2012 International Conference on Cloud Computer Technologies, Applications and Management, pp. 74–76 (2012)
19. Khorshed, M.T., Ali, A.S., Wasimi, S.A.: A survey on gaps, threat remediation challenges and some thoughts for proactive attack detection in cloud computing. Futur. Gener. Comput. Syst. 28, 833–851 (2012)

20. AlZain, M., Pardede, E., Soh, B., Thom, J.: Cloud computing security: from single to multi-clouds. In: 2012 45th Hawaii International Conference on System Science, pp. 5490–5499 (2012)
21. Cachin, C., Haas, R., Vukolic, M.: Dependable storage in the Intercloud: Research Report RZ, 37–83 (2010)
22. Manage, E.: AccelOps Cloud SeCurity Survey 2013. www.accelops.com/cloudsurvey2013 (2013)
23. Anderson, J.Q.: The Future of Cloud Computing, pp. 1–26. www.northbridge.com/2010 (2010)
24. Threats, T., Group, W.: The Notorious Nine Cloud Computing Top Threats in 2013. https://downloads.cloudsecurityalliance.org/.../top_threats/ (2013)
25. Kumar, K., Rao, V., Rao, S., Technology, I.: Cloud computing: an analysis of its challenges & security issues, vol. 1 (2012)
26. Sinha, N., Khreisat, L.: Cloud computing security, data, and performance issues, pp. 1–6 (2014)
27. Al Morsy, M., Grundy, J., Müller, I.: An analysis of the cloud computing security problem (2010)
28. Science, C., Lanka, S.: Data security in cloud computing, pp. 810–813 (2013)
29. Sugumaran, M.: An architecture for data security in cloud computing (2014)
30. Technologies, C.: Data security issues in cloud environment and solutions (2014)

A Secure Real Time Data Processing Framework for Personally Controlled Electronic Health Record (PCEHR) System

Khandakar Rabbi[1(✉)], Mohammed Kaosar[2], Md Rafiqul Islam[1], and Quazi Mamun[1]

[1] School of Computing and Mathematics, Charles Sturt University, Bathurst, Australia
{krabbi,mislam,qmamun}@csu.edu.au
[2] Department of Computer Science, Effat University, Jeddah Saudi Arabia
mkaosar@effatuniversity.edu.sa

Abstract. An era of open information in the healthcare is now underway. This information can be considered as 'Big data', not only for its sheer volume but also for its complexity, diversity, and timeliness of data for any large eHealth System such as Personally Controlled Electronic Health Record (PCEHR). The system enables different person or organization to access, share, and manage their health data. Other challenges incorporated with the PCEHR data can be very excessive to capture, store, process and retrieve the insight knowledge in real time. Various PCEHR frameworks have been proposed in recent literature. However, big data challenges have not been considered in these frameworks. In this paper, we argue the PCEHR data should be considered as big data and the challenges of big data should be addressed when to design the framework of the PCEHR system. In doing so, we propose a PCEHR framework, which deals with real time big data challenges using the state-of-the-art technologies such as Apache Kafka and Apache Storm. At the same time the proposed framework ensures secure data communication using cryptographic techniques. Using a qualitative analysis, we show that the proposed framework addresses the big data challenges.

Keywords: PCEHR · Big data · Apache kafka · Apache storm · Big data security

1 Introduction

On 8 March 2014, the Malaysian Airlines flight MH370 was scheduled from Kuala Lumpur to Beijing and lost contact with the air traffic control about an hour after it took off. Within few weeks of this incident took place, the search text "Malaysian airlines MH370 missing" in Google returned about 160,000,000 results. As the news was updated very frequently, anyone could view the latest news from the result filtering option and could see the news coming from last 24 h. This huge list of result can be categories by 'Visited pages', 'Not yet visited', 'Reading level' and so on. This filter is a good example of so call "Big data Processing" where all data are coming from multiple, heterogeneous and anonymous places and they have a complex relationship which is evolving and growing each second.

© Institute for Computer Sciences, Social Informatics and Telecommunications Engineering 2015
J. Tian et al. (Eds.): SecureComm 2014, Part II, LNICST 153, pp. 141–156, 2015.
DOI: 10.1007/978-3-319-23802-9_13

Big data is one of the current and future research trends [2, 3]. Big data can be characterised by their *volume, velocity,* and *variety* (3V) [1]. Here volume refers to the size of *big data,* where velocity refers to the speed of data, and variety indicates the various sources of data [4]. In some cases there could be an extra feature, depending on the requirements, which can be any of *Value, Variability* or *Virtual* [1]. In general, *big data* is a collection of diversified large data sets which is extremely difficult or nearly impossible to process using the traditional data processing and management techniques [1]. *Big data* is also formidable to capture, cure, analyse and visualise using the existing technologies [1]. Thus, within current technology limitation there are few challenges in *big data* including *Storage, search, sharing, analysis, visualization, capture, security, privacy* and *curation.*

The increasing volume of the data generated in the eHR systems indicates that the healthcare organizations will not be able to complete analysing these real time data [19]. Moreover, about 80 % of overall medical data is unstructured and clinically important [19]. These huge amount of data is retrieved from multiple sources like EMR, lab and imaging systems, physicians prescriptions, medical correspondence, insurance claims even Customer Relationship Management (CRM) systems and finances [19]. Thus, the verity of data is great in numbers. Since each person has medical records therefore the volume and velocity is also large. Figure 1 shows the number of people register in PCEHR from July 2012 to July 2013.

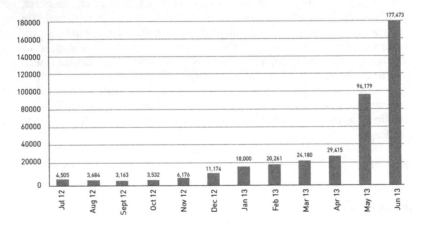

Fig. 1. Number of people registered in the PCEHR [21]

Illustrating Fig. 1, for the volume of the data in PCEHR; it can be considered as *big data.* A figure of Austrian Institute of Technology shows in Fig. 2 which state a collection of components are interconnected for processing for a eHealth platform [20].

Big data application includes healthcare, medical and government services where these data are often shared or released to the third party partners or public to analyse the insight knowledge [5]. Recently, National E-Health Transition Authority Australia, introduces PCEHR (Personally Controlled Electronic Health Record) to manage individuals health record and allow them to authorise other individuals who is eligible to view their electronic health records (eHR) [22]. It helps individual, their doctors and

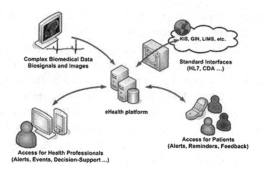

Fig. 2. eHealth platform [20]

other health care providers to view their medical record and provide the best possible medical care [6, 22].

Many different relevant works have been published over the past few years [6–16]. In most of them, authors around the world try to improve the system usability through different surveys. Some of the papers described and improved the system without evaluating the system as a *big data* platform. Thus a very important aspect of research has been missing until now.

Since data generated in PCEHR is a considered as *big data*, some immediate research questions are to be addressed in which not much significant research work has been done, such as:

- How to store and process the big amount of data generated in PCEHR.
- How to handle and analyse the *big data* in real time to make sure there is no health hazard due to delay.
- How to ensure data security and privacy.

In this paper, we address the aforementioned issues of *big data* while proposing the framework for PCEHR system. We use the state-of-the-art technologies like Apache Kafka and Apache Storm for real time data capturing and processing. We use public key cryptographic technique to preserve privacy.

The rest of the paper is organized as follows: Sect. 2 describes the existing framework for eHR system. Section 3 discusses about the background of the related technologies. Section 4 describes the proposed framework. A qualitative analysis has been carried out at Sect. 5, and finally the paper ends with conclusion and future work in Sect. 6.

2   Existing eHealth System Frameworks

In recent years, many eHealth systems have been proposed. To design and develop these systems, researchers put emphasis on different issues such as privacy preserving, secure data transactions, high data availability through cloud and distributed approach, real time decision and storage. Some researchers perform surveys to measure the user acceptance and adoption capabilities. However the proposed systems fail to address the issues of *big data* circumstances. Below is a brief description of different approaches of existing eHealth system.

To ensure the maximum privacy, in [6] a PCEHR model has been proposed where a fully homomorphic encryption technique is proposed. Proposed end to end framework shows several entities like General Practitioners, Specialist doctors, Nurses, Pharmacist, diagnostic Labs, Private clinics, Hospitals, Family & Friends and how they access a global encrypted database server. To ensure maximum protection, an authentication server, an ACL (Access Control List) server and an authorization Server is used. Although it can ensure the privacy of data, the authors in [6] do not evaluate their concept in big data scenario. Hence to evaluate the system under *big data* environment, the challenges and research questions yet to be answered. A design of patient safety reporting system is introduced in [11]. XML parser and code generator is used to communicate with different database system (sources) and generate a report which helps personnel a secure and safety lifestyle. To enable privacy and security authors use data encryption techniques. Challenges in Big data are out of the scope of the paper. Privacy and security issues are also discussed on the paper [13]. A description of current available methods is discussed and some of the issues are mentioned briefly. However, the discussion was only limited to privacy and no further discussion on *big data* was included. In [9], the authors proposed a framework which illustrates a secure process and a recovery process to ensure the privacy. The scope of the paper was only the security and recovery and no *big data* environment is considered.

In [7], a platform call MyPHRMachine describes a way to reduce the impediments to data transfer. Authors claims that the proposed platform is low cost and can substitute by cheap software components. The platform is open sourced and trustable which is a cloud-based system where patients provide access their data to different third parties. It ensures some of the privacy, however the challenges of *big data* is out of the scope of the paper. The scope of paper [12] is to present a technique showing how to collect data from different hospitals. It uses a server client model with different gateways which collects data from multiple sources. This distributed model uses XML files to communicate with a local server and all the clients. Although the scope of the paper was collecting information, the entire picture for continuous (*big data*) data is missing. A simulation model of centralized and distributed data structure is carried out for health care data in [15]. The model uses Monte Carlo method which iteratively evaluate by a set of random numbers as inputs. The model examines on 10,000 patients input data. However, the scenario of continuous and unstructured data was out of the scope of the paper.

In [8], a health management system survey is carried out. No framework is proposed thus a *big data* and its challenges are out of the scope of the paper. An interview study on the benefit of electronic health record system is reported by [16]. A theoretical framework known as DeLone and McLean's Information Systems Success Model (D&M IS Success Model) is used to measure the adaptability of electronics health record system. They examine three health care models including 'RSL Care', 'Uniting Care Ageing South Easter Region' and 'Warrigal Care'. This theoretical framework (D&M IS Success) helps to understand an information system in terms of 'system quality', 'information quality', 'service quality', 'ease of use', 'user satisfaction' and 'net benefit'. However all the three abovementioned health care models doesn't support and implement continuous and unstructured data. Thus *big data* challenges are missing from this study.

Authors in [10], describes a personal health record system of Lombardy, Italy. The system provides a complete, integrated and contextualized patient history which helps patients by real time decision supports. It also supports storage system thus it can increase efficiency and real time emergency care. However security and privacy was missing and the big data challenges are out of the scope of the paper. New York Presbyterian System is described in [14]. The system helps patients to manage their health profile with list of medical reports and available medication they are going through. Patients can see the list of healthcare and care providers, insurer and can enroll them into any of the available system. However, the system allows patients to manage their profile and it uses typical database management system. Thus the concept and challenges in *big data* is out of the scope of the paper.

In the next section we perform some background study of state-of-the-art technologies which is used in our proposed framework in Sect. 4.

3   Technology Required for PCEHR

The previous section illustrates different eHealth systems, and identifies the stipulation of state-of-the art technology incorporation for a large scaled eHealth system such as PCEHR. These technologies would be able to process real time unstructured, continuous data set arriving from multiple heterogeneous sources. A brief description of these technologies are provided below.

3.1   Apache Kafka

Apache kafka is a fast, scalable, durable and distributed publish-subscribe messaging system. It can handle hundred of megabytes of read/write from thousands of clients in real time. When data is too big and continuous; data streams are partitioned and spread over a distributed machines (clusters). Data is persisted on disk and can be replicated within the cluster which prevents data loss. Each cluster is called "Brokers" which can handle terabytes of data without any impact on performance. Kafka can be actively use for real time processing where raw data can be consumed and then several data analysis activities such as aggregated, summarized, or transformed to another format is done for further consumption [17].

3.2   Apache Storm

Apache Storm is a distributed real time computation system. It is scalable, fault-tolerant and guarantees that data will be processed. Storm provides some set of general primitives to do real time computation. It creates topologies deployed in clusters. A topology is a graph of computation which contains processing logic and links among nodes which indicates how data is passed throughout the nodes. There are two types of nodes in storm cluster: 'Master' and 'Worker'. Master nodes run on a daemon which is known as 'Nimbus' which is responsible for distributing the code around the clusters, assigning tasks to different machines, and monitoring the success and failure. Worker nodes runs a daemon called supervisor which listen to the work assigned to the individual machine, start and stop worker processes when necessary based on what Nimbus assigned. Each workers execute a subset of topology (a running topology consists of many worker processed across many machine). The coordination between Nimbus and Supervisor is done through a Zookeeper cluster. A Zookeeper is a state-full cluster which keeps track of session/data into memory or local disk. On the other side both Nimbus and Supervisor is state-less. This means, even if Nimbus and Supervisor is failed, the entire data and session will not be destroyed. Figure 3 shows the component of storm cluster.

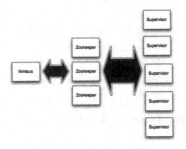

Fig. 3. Component of storm cluster [18]

Storm provides 'spouts' and 'bolts' for doing stream transformations. A spout is a source of stream where a bolt consumes any number of input streams and does some processing. For doing fairly complex computation requires multiple steps and thus multiple bolts. Bolt can do anything like, running a function, searching memory, aggregation even connecting with database. The network of spouts and bolts are a package which is known as a topology. Figure 4 shows a basic topology.

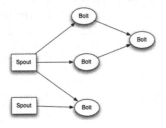

Fig. 4. A simple storm topology [18].

4   Proposed PCEHR Framework

The proposed model of PCEHR is depicted in Fig. 5. The model is divided into four modules consist of 'Patient Care', 'PCEHR Data Receiving', 'PCEHR Data Processing' and 'PCEHR System DB and Access System'. The proposed distributed system is an end to end solution showing how the whole PCEHR system works. This system is deployed into different locations. The first part of the system is 'Patient Care' which is deployed into patients home. This module is also deployed in a smart home or nursing home where sensors and web applications are available to send health data. The next part is 'Data Receiving' section which is deployed in the PCEHR application server. The 'PCEHR Data processing' unit is also deployed in Application Server from where data will store in an encrypted database server. The rest of "Access System" is taken from [6] where operations operate through Authenticated server, ACL server and Authorization server. In the rest of the subsection, we have discussed each part of the entire system separately.

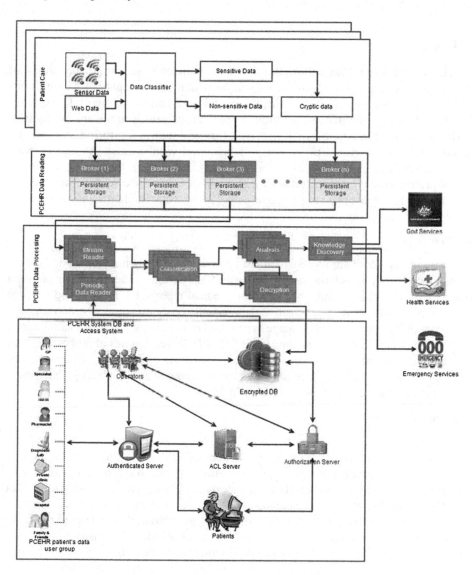

Fig. 5. Proposed architecture of the system.

4.1 Patient Care

This part of the system is deployed into individual's home or hospital or nursing home. Multiple sensors can generate huge data as well as doctors, nurses, pathologies, hospitals, laboratories or even nursing home agents can post complied data into the system. 'Patient Care' module consists of several sub-modules including sensor data, web data, data classifier, sensitive data, non-sensitive data and cryptic data. The next sub-section briefly describes all those sub-modules.

- *Sensor Data*

   This captures real time unstructured data from different sensor devices. A list of sensors can be deployed at patient's location which receives patient's continuous data such as blood pressure, sugar level etc. and post data to the internal processor. The list of sensors includes smart mobile application, sensor hardware or any type of device which can capture real time data for continuous monitoring. An internal processor is an integrated processor which is bind with sensors. As an example, smart phone devices have sensors and integrated processors. Sensor data are raw thus a preliminary processor required it to pre-process for post management activities. In real life, bar code reader, road cameras for vehicle identification are such examples of sensor device.

- *Web Data*

   This captured data are more structured and usually post by individuals or by third party. Doctors, diagnosis lab assistants or nurses posts data of a patient's current physical status. This type of data embeds describing medical reports, lab reports, and medical conditions. It includes several sensitive data including patients name, age, and address. This type of data also includes image type data i.e. scan copy physical/mental/dental reports. Thus, before posting the data to the PCEHR Server, a series of processing such as extraction, normalization, cleansing, transformation, joining is required. After performing the appropriate processing data can be standardize by an acceptable format (XML) which can be posted to 'Data Classifier'.

- *Data Classifier*

   It classifies data as sensitive or non sensitive. The purpose of the proposed framework is to perform proper privacy preserving practices thus this part of the system plays an important role in the entire architecture. Before the classifier works, patients can specify which data can be sensitive for them. If any patient doesn't perform how their data sensitivity classifier works then a default one is used. To protect the unauthorized access of the private data, this part indentifies sensitive data through user's defined rules. As an example, user can specify that s/he have their 'date of birth' is a sensitive data. Thus within a complete data set, 'Data Classifier' validates and tag the 'date of birth' as a sensitive data and send it to the appropriate handler. Other than that, non-sensitive data are sent to the appropriate handler.

- **Sensitive Data**

  Sensitive data can be defined as information that must be protected against unwanted disclosure. It may include personal information, dental record history, mental treatment history or report. In the stage of the system, the proposed framework applies different privacy/security algorithms to make sure data is secure to release. A wide verity of data encryption algorithm is available from the last decades. One of the state-of-the-art-technology in data encryption is homomorphic encryption technique. Since homomorphic encryption algorithm requires longer execution time thus we are not considering this technique in this proposed framework. The proposed system will apply the public key cryptography algorithm to ensure that sensitive data is protected against unauthorized access.

- **Non-sensitive Data**

  This module temporarily holds non-sensitive data. A patient has some of the non-sensitive information such as their family medical history, their life style including smoking, high risk sports, alcohol etc. Typically, non-sensitive information are the dataset a by which a patient can't be individually identified. This data can be post to any system for the purpose of govt. service, research activities. This type of data doesn't require any algorithms to protect from public access. This part of proposed framework holds the non-sensitive data and posts it to the 'PCEHR Data Receiving' module.

- **Cryptic Data**

  A modified data set which hold un-meaningful, non-understandable data. This is the modified sensitive data which can be post publicly. The proposed framework applies public key cryptography technique and stores the modified cipher data in this section. This type of cryptography technique depends on a piece of accessory information usually called 'key'. In this case the sensitive data is encrypted by a public key. The public key is open and anybody can use to encrypt the data. The data can be only decrypted by a private key. This is one of the most popular encrypted techniques which allow encrypting almost everything. Without the knowledge of the key it is near impossible to decrypt the cipher text into readable format.

4.2   PCEHR Data Receiving

A large number of patient's data are sent continuously. The propose framework uses Apache Kafka brokers to handle large data stream. Each broker consists of persistent storage, where data are store before processing. Kafka deploys as many as broker needed depending on the volume of the data. This module guarantees each data is ready for processing and kept in the memory as long as it is not processed.

4.3 PCEHR Data Processing

In this module of the propose framework Apache Storm has been used for real time data processing. One of the great characteristics of Apache Storm is it ensures no data failures. It is responsible of reading the stream data and sends it to classifier. Classifier classifies data and sends it to database. It also sends the encrypted data to decryption module to decrypt it. Both classification module and decryption module send the data to real time analysis module for analysing. After analysis, data is sent to knowledge discovery module. Classification is also responsible for data storage to database. Knowledge Discovery module sends the aggregated knowledge to different external sources like emergency server, health service and govt. service. Next sub section describes the internal sub-modules.

- *Stream Reader*

  This module pulls data from Apache Kafka brokers and sends it to classification module. This module contains both cipher and non sensitive data. 'Stream Reader' represents a simple program which pulls data from broker. This small module helps to maintain a strong, flexible and scalable architecture. In the typical system, data usually posted to web services regardless of how resourceful server is. If the data posting becomes more than expectable, cases were server rejecting data (data lost) or server crash. The proposed system used storm 'Spout' (described in previous section) which make the system flexible and a way to guarantee of data processing, failure prevent system.

- *Periodic Data Reader*

  This module pulls structured data from database. Data summarization, aggregation can help govt. and researchers to utilize the inside knowledge. Periodic data reader read data and sends it to classifier aiming to facilitate govt. or apply other health services to individuals. This is also a data reader module which read data from database. This structured data can be complied with an acceptable format so that data analysis process can be fastened. This part of propose framework uses data compression technique thus the amount of data will not be large enough to handle.

- *Classification*

  Classification classifies encrypted and non-encrypted data. Encrypted data is sent to the 'Decryption' module. Classification module is also responsible for classifying data. Some data may not be important to store and a data compression and summarization algorithm performs to compress a large a dataset into a tiny data set. As an example a patient's normal blood sugar for a range of time which is erased from the system if necessary. It will help reduce the overhead costs and complexity of the entire database server. However, classification also sends non-encrypted data to 'Analysis' module.

- *Decryption*

  This module is responsible to decrypt the sensitive data before analysis. A secret key can be stored to decrypt the data. After decryption, data is sent to 'Analysis' module of the framework. In relation with the previous encryption module, data decryption is necessary prior to analysis. Some of the data is not necessary for analysis. A private key is stored in this section to decrypt the sensitive data. The proposed system used public key cryptography technique since it is low cost, highly available for any type of data and low time complexity.

- *Analysis*

In this module, both sensitive and non-sensitive data is analyzed. Data is properly structured, classified, anatomized (if necessary) before discovering insight knowledge. A wide verity of data analysis is performed in this section depending on the needs which may include 'Frequency Distribution', 'Descriptive statistics', 'Mean comparison', 'Cross-tabulation', 'Correlations', 'Linear regressions' and 'Text analysis'. Analysis can act like a filter which sorts out huge pile of data (*big data*) before reaching to any conclusion. Data analysis can help to sort out further knowledge from data. Thus the analyzed data will be complied into any secure format and delivered to 'Knowledge discovery' section.

- *Knowledge Discovery*

This module runs different machine learning algorithms or data mining algorithms to discover insight knowledge of a given data set. Based on the discovered knowledge, it can post the data to the associated third party service provider which is govt. services, patients health Services or emergency services.

4.4   PCEHR System DB and Access System

This part has been taken from [6] where authors used homomorpic encryption. Regardless of [6], we preferred to use public key cryptography technique. The rest of the model consists of several sub-modules which describe as follows:

- **PCEHR Patient's Data User Group**

It refers to a person or organizations or a group of persons who required to access patients data. They include general practitioner (GP), specialist doctor, pharmacist, health care provider, insurance, nurse, laboratory, hospital administrators, family members, and friends. The users can be categories in different roles with certain restrictions, such as GP might need to access history data whether laboratory doesn't required. They use patient's data to provide them better health services.

- *Authentication Server, Access Control List (ACL) Server and Authorisation Server*

This server ensures that all the activity in PCEHR system is legitimate. Every users of PCEHR system is registered and whenever they require accessing PCEHR, they use their own username and password to login into the system. A large verity of algorithm can be associated with authentication server such as challenge response protocol, Kerberos, public key encryption to ensure high level of authenticity. Access Control List (ACL) server ensures a wide verity level of access list which ensures which users will be accessing which part of the system. It can use different type relationship among subjects, objects and actions. As an example a mental health doctor doesn't have a view access to patient's dental health or an insurance company will not have a write access on patient's data. Thus this allows access to different object with its associated objects. To ensure maximum privacy, authorization server ensures the accessibility of patient's data. If patient provides permission to other users then this authorisation server will retrieve encrypted data which will only be decrypted by patient's private key. This way patient's data remains more secure and accessible only when patient wants to. A patient's profile can be divided into many sub profile including 'Mental profile', 'Sexual Profile', 'Physical Profile'. A patient may not interest to show his/her mental profile to a physical doctor. On the other hand patient may hide all of his/her profiles. Thus, if psychiatrist requires handling patient's mental health, they will ask for patient's permission. When patient provide proper access level permission, psychiatrist will be able to access patient's data though Authorisation server [6].

- *Operators*

  They are usually responsible for operating of PCEHR database system. They must respect the instruction and recommendation (if any) given by PCEHR Jurisdictional Advisory Committee and the PCEHR Independent Advisory Council (2013).

5   Analysis of the Proposed Framework

In this section we present a qualitative analysis to demonstrate how the proposed framework overcomes the *big data* challenges such as storing and processing data, handling and analysing data in real time, preserving privacy and maintaining security. Table 1 shows a comparison of different frameworks. It shows that our proposed model support and overcomes storing and processing, real time handling and analysis and privacy and security challenges. Table 2 shows a comparison of different framework which supports big data platform. From Table 2, it can be illustrated that only our proposed PCEHR system supports *big data* platforms. The following subsections describe how the proposed framework deal with *big data* challenges.

- *Storing and Processing*

  Classification in 'PCEHR Data Processing' is connected with the database server. As we describe previously classification will classify data about which data may need to store in database. For an example a patient's normal blood pressure or normal sugar level may not require to store. In such a case, classification module does not store the data. A data compression and summarization algorithm runs in a regular interval and a modified version of data is stored in database. This helps to increase data storing capability and fastens the search capabilities. Since a smaller version of data is storing regularly thus, data processing capabilities improves.

- ### *Real Time Data Handling*

Real time data handling is done by Apache Storm which is integrated with 'PCEHR Data Processing' module. As describe previously, when data analysis is done, data is sent to the Knowledge discovery module. In this module different complex machine learning algorithms runs. Apache Storm guarantees each data will be handled in real time at least once. So our proposed framework supports real time data handling.

- ### *Privacy and Security*

From the 'Patient Care' to 'Patient's Data User Group' in every point of our proposed framework ensures that patient's privacy is properly preserved. Sensitive data is encrypted before publish into the PCEHR system. This ensures users data privacy. And decryption happens only in the data processing module before sending to 'Knowledge Discovery' section. The storage data are also encrypted. The decrypted key is only kept securely in data processing unit.

Table 1. Comparison of different frameworks

eHealth systems	Storing and processing	Real time handling and analysis	Privacy and security
PCEHR model in [6]	No	No	Yes
Health care in [7]	No	No	Yes
Health care in [8]	No	No	No
Framework in [9]	No	No	Yes
Health record system in [10]	Yes	Yes	No
Patient safety reporting system in [11]	No	No	Yes
Medical data collection system in [12]	Yes	No	No
Electronic health record system in [13]	No	No	Yes
Personal heath record system in [14]	No	No	No
Health care system in [15]	No	No	No
Health record system in [16]	No	No	No
Our proposed model	Yes	Yes	Yes

Table 2. Comparison of different frameworks

eHealth system	Big data system	Database system
PCEHR model in [6]	No	Yes
MyPHRMachine in [7]	No	Yes
Health care in [8]	No	Yes
Framework in [9]	No	Yes
Health record system in [10]	No	Yes
Patient safety reporting system in [11]	No	Yes
Medical data collection System in [12]	No	Yes
Electronic health record system in [13]	No	Yes
Personal heath record system in [14]	No	Yes
Health care system in [15]	No	Yes
Health record system in [16]	No	Yes
Our proposed model	Yes	No

6   Conclusion and Further Works

In this paper we propose a framework for PCEHR system. Previous sections show that the PCEHR data is growing exponentially. Thus it is very important to consider *big data* scenario when developing an eHealth platform. Based on the motivation, this paper shows how structured and un-structured data are capture, classify sensitive and non-sensitive data, publish, process and gain knowledge to facilitate an individual. The qualitative analysis shows that using this model, *big data* challenges can be overcome. Further researches are being carried out by implementing different privacy preserving algorithms, implementing new and/or existing data mining algorithms and implementing knowledge discovery.

References

1. Philip Chen, C.L., Zhang, C.-Y.: Data-intensive applications, challenges, techniques and technologies: a survey on big data. Inf. Sci. **275**, 314–347 (2014)
2. Savitz, E.: Top 10 strategic technology trends for 2013 (2012). http://www.forbes.com/sites/ericsavitz/2012/10/23/gartner-top-10-strategic-technology-trends-for-2013/. Accessed 14 June 2014
3. Savitz, E.: 10 critical tech trends for the next five years (2012). http://www.forbes.com/sites/ericsavitz/2012/10/22/gartner-10-critical-tech-trends-for-the-next-five-years/. Accessed 14 June 2014

4. Laney, D.: 3D data management: controlling data volume, velocity, and variety. Appl. Deliv. Strat. Meta Group **949**, 1–4 (2001). http://blogs.gartner.com/doug-laney/files/2012/01/ad949-3D-Data-Management-Controlling-Data-Volume-Velocity-and-Variety.pdf

5. Zhang, X., Yang, C., Nepal, S., Li, C., Dou, W., Chen, J.: A MapReduce based approach of scalable multidimensional anonymization for big data privacy preservation on cloud. In: IEEE Third International Conference on Cloud and Green Computing, pp. 105–112 (2013)

6. Begum, M., Mamun, Q., Kaosar, M.: A privacy-preserving framework for personally controlled electronic health record (PCEHR) system. In: Australian eHealth Informatics and Security Conference, pp. 1–10 (2013)

7. Van Gorp, P., Comuzzi, M., Jahnen, A., Kaymak, U., Middleton, B.: An open platform for personal health record apps with platform-level privacy protection. Comput. Biol. Med. **51**, 12–23 (2014)

8. Ant Ozok, A., Wu, H., Garrido, M., Pronovost, P.J., Gurses, A.P.: Usability and perceived usefulness of personal health records for preventive health care: a case study focusing on patients' and primary care providers' perspectives. Appl. Ergon. **45**, 613–628 (2013)

9. Huang, L.-C., Chu, H.-C., Lien, C.-Y., Hsiao, C.-H., Kao, T.: Privacy preservation and information security protection for patients' portable electronic health records. Comput. Biol. Med. **39**, 743–750 (2009)

10. Barbarito, F., Pinciroli, F., Barone, A., Pizzo, F., Ranza, R., Mason, J., Mazzola, L., Bonacina, S., Marceglia, S.: Implementing the lifelong personal health record in a regionalised health information system: the case of Lombardy, Italy. Comput. Biol. Med. **59**, 1–11 (2013)

11. Lin, C.-C., Shih, C.-L., Liao, H.-H., Wung, C.H.Y.: Learning from Taiwan patient-safety reporting system. Int. J. Med. Inform. **81**, 834–841 (2012)

12. Jian, W.-S., Wen, H.-C., Scholl, J., Shabbir, S.A., Lee, P., Hsu, C.-Y., Li, Y.-C.: The Taiwanese method for providing patients data from multiple hospital EHR systems. J. Biomed. Inform. **44**, 326–332 (2010)

13. Ghazvini, A., Shukur, Z.: Security challenges and success factors of electronic healthcare system. Procedia Technol. **11**, 212–219 (2013)

14. Gordon, P., Camhi, E., Hesse, R., Odlum, M., Schnall, R., Rodriguez, M., Valdez, E.: Bakkenf, S: Processes and outcomes of developing a continuity of care document for use as a personal health record by people living with HIV/AIDS in New York City. Int. J. Med. Inform. **81**, e63–e73 (2012)

15. Lapsia, V., Lamb, K., Yasnoff, W.A.: Where should electronic records for patients be stored? Int. J. Med. Inform. **81**, 821–827 (2012)

16. Yu, P., Zhang, Y., Gong, Y., Zhang, J.: Unintended adverse consequences of introducing electronic health records in residential aged care homes. Int. J. Med. Inform. **82**, 772–788 (2013)

17. Apache Projects: Apache kafka (2014). http://kafka.apache.org. Accessed 20 May 2014

18. Apache Projects: Apache storm (2014). http://storm.incubator.apache.org/. Accessed 20 May 2014

19. IBM: Harness your data resources in healthcare (2010). http://www-01.ibm.com/software/data/bigdata/industry-healthcare.html. Accessed 20 May 2014

20. Austrian Institute of Technology: eHealth platform (2010). http://www.ait.ac.at/research-services/research-services-safety-security/health-information-systems/ehealth-platform/?L=. Accessed 20 May 2014

21. Department of Health: Australian Government: Personally controlled electronic health record system operator: annual report 2012–2013 (2014). http://www.health.gov.au/internet/main/publishing.nsf/Content/PCEHR-system-operator-annual-report2012-2013. Accessed 20 May 2014
22. Department of Health: Australian Government: The personally controlled eHealth record system (2014). http://www.nehta.gov.au/. Accessed 20 May 2014

Novel Iterative Min-Max Clustering to Minimize Information Loss in Statistical Disclosure Control

Abdun Naser Mahmood[1]([✉]), Md Enamul Kabir[2], and Abdul K. Mustafa[3]

[1] School of Engineering and Information Technology,
University of New South Wales Australian Defence Force Academy,
Canberra 2600, Australia
Abdun.Mahmood@unsw.edu.au
[2] School of Human Movement Studies, University of Queensland,
St Lucia 4072, Australia
e.kabir@uq.edu.au
[3] School of Applied Technology, Humber College, North Campus,
Toronto, Canada
abdul.mustafa@humber.ca

Abstract. In recent years, there has been an alarming increase of online identity theft and attacks using personally identifiable information. The goal of privacy preservation is to de-associate individuals from sensitive or microdata information. Microaggregation techniques seeks to protect microdata in such a way that can be published and mined without providing any private information that can be linked to specific individuals. Microaggregation works by partitioning the microdata into groups of at least k records and then replacing the records in each group with the centroid of the group. An optimal microaggregation method must minimize the information loss resulting from this replacement process. The challenge is how to minimize the information loss during the microaggregation process. This paper presents a new microaggregation technique for Statistical Disclosure Control (SDC). It consists of two stages. In the first stage, the algorithm sorts all the records in the data set in a particular way to ensure that during microaggregation very dissimilar observations are never entered into the same cluster. In the second stage an optimal microaggregation method is used to create k-anonymous clusters while minimizing the information loss. It works by taking the sorted data and simultaneously creating two distant clusters using the two extreme sorted values as seeds for the clusters. The performance of the proposed technique is compared against the most recent microaggregation methods. Experimental results using benchmark datasets show that the proposed algorithm has the lowest information loss compared with a basket of techniques in the literature.

Keywords: Privacy · Microaggregation · Microdata protection · k-anonymity · Disclosure control

© Institute for Computer Sciences, Social Informatics and Telecommunications Engineering 2015
J. Tian et al. (Eds.): SecureComm 2014, Part II, LNICST 153, pp. 157–172, 2015.
DOI: 10.1007/978-3-319-23802-9_14

1   Introduction

In recent years, the phenomenal advance of technological developments in information technology enable government agencies and corporations to accumulate an enormous amount of personal data for analytical purposes. These agencies and organizations often need to release individual records (microdata) for research and other public benefit purposes. This propagation has to be in accordance with laws and regulations to avoid the propagation of confidential information. In other words, microdata should be published in such a way that preserve the privacy of the individuals. Microdata protection in statistical databases has recently become a major societal concern and has been intensively studied in recent years. Microaggregation for Statistical Disclosure Control (SDC) is a family of methods to protect microdata from individual identification. SDC seeks to protect microdata in such a way that can be published and mined without providing any private information that can be linked to specific individuals. SDC is often applied to statistical databases before they are released for public use.

To protect personal data from individual identification, SDC is often applied before the data are released for analysis [2,25]. The purpose of microdata SDC is to alter the original microdata in such a way that the statistical analysis from the original data and the modified data are similar and the disclosure risk of identification is low. As SDC requires suppressing or altering the original data, the quality of data and the analysis results can be damaged. Hence, SDC methods must find a balance between data utility and personal confidentiality.

Various methods for Microaggregation has been proposed in the literature for protecting microdata [3,4,7,8,11,12,20,22]. The basic idea of microaggregation is to partition a dataset into mutually exclusive groups of at least k records prior to publication, and then publish the centroid over each group instead of individual records. The resulting anonymized dataset satisfies k-anonymity [18], requiring each record in a dataset to be identical to at least $(k-1)$ other records in the same dataset. As releasing microdata about individuals poses privacy threat due to the privacy-related attributes, called quasi-identifiers, both k-anonymity and microaggregation only consider the quasi-identifiers. Microaggregation is traditionally restricted to numeric attributes in order to calculate the centroid of records, but also has been extended to handle categorical and ordinal attributes [4,8,19]. In this paper we propose a microaggregated method that is also applicable to numeric attributes.

The effectiveness of a microaggregation method is measured by calculating its information loss. A lower information loss implies that the anonymized dataset is less distorted from the original dataset, and thus provides better data quality for analysis. k- anonymity [17,18,21] provides sufficient protection of personal confidentiality of microdata, while ensuring the quality of the anonymized dataset, an effective microaggregation method should incur as little information loss as possible. In order to be useful in practice, the dataset should keep as much informative as possible. Hence, it is necessary to seriously consider the tradeoff between privacy and information loss. To minimize the information loss due to microaggregation, all records are partitioned into several groups such that each group contains at least k similar records, and then the records in each group are replaced by their corresponding mean such that the values of each variable are the same. Such similar groups are known as clusters. In the context of data mining, clustering is a useful technique that partitions records into groups such that records within a group are similar to each other, while records in different groups are most distinct from one another. Thus, microaggregation can be seen as a clustering problem with constraints on the size of the clusters.

Many microaggregation methods derive from traditional clustering algorithms. For example, Domingo-Ferrer and Mateo-Sanz [3] proposed univariate and multivariate k-Ward algorithms that extend the agglomerative hierarchical clustering method of Ward et al. [23]. Domingo-Ferrer and Torra [6,7] proposed a microaggregation method based on the fuzzy c-means algorithm [1], and Laszlo and Mukherjee [13] extended the standard minimum spanning tree partitioning algorithm for microaggregation [26]. All of these microaggregation methods build all clusters gradually but simultaneously. There are some other methods for microaggregation that have been proposed in the literature that build one/two cluster(s) at a time. Notable examples include Maximum Distance [15], Diameter-based Fixed-Size microaggregation and centroid-based Fixed-size microaggregation [13], Maximum Distance to Average Vector (MDAV) [8], MHM [9] and the Two Fixed Reference Points method [27]. Most recently, Lin et al. [28] proposed a density-based microaggregation method that forms clusters by the descending order of their densities, and then fine-tunes these clusters in reverse order.

The reminder of this paper is organized as follows. We introduce the problem of microaggregation in Sect. 2. Section 3 introduces the basic concept of microaggregation. Section 4 reviews previous microaggregation methods. We present a brief description of our proposed microaggregation method in Sect. 5. Section 6 shows experimental results of the proposed method. Finally, concluding remarks are included in Sect. 7.

2   Problem Statement

The algorithms for microaggregation works by partitioning the microdata into groups, where within groups the records are homogeneous but between groups the records are heterogeneous so that information loss is low. The similar groups are also called clusters. The level of privacy required is controlled by a security parameter k, the minimum number of records in a cluster. In essence, the parameter k specifies the maximum acceptable disclosure risk. Once a value for k has been selected by the data protector, the only job left is to maximize data utility. Maximizing utility can be achieved by microaggregating optimally, i.e. with minimum within-groups variability loss. So the main challenge in microaggregation is how to minimize the information loss during the clustering process. Although plenty of work has been done, to maximize the data utility by forming the clusters, this is not yet sufficient in terms of information loss. So more research needs to be done to form the clusters such that the information loss is as low as possible. This paper analyses the problem with a new multi-dimensional sorting algorithm such that the information loss is minimal.

Observing this challenge, this work presents a new clustering-based method for microaggregation, where a new multi-dimensional sorting algorithm is used in the first stage. In the second stage two distant clusters are made simultaneously in a systematic way. According to the second stage, sort all records in ascending order by using a sorting algorithm in the first stage explained in Sect. 5) so that the first record and the last record are most distant to each other. Form a cluster with the first record and its $(k-1)$ nearest records and another cluster with the last record and its $(k-1)$ nearest records. Sort the remaining records $((n-2k)$, if dataset contains n records) by using the same sorting algorithm and continue to build pair clusters at the same time by using the first and the last record as seeds until some specified records remain. Finally form one/two cluster(s) depending on the remaining records. Thus all clusters produced in this way contain k records except the last cluster that may contain at the most $(2k-1)$ records. Performance of the proposed method is compared against the most recent widely used microaggregation methods. The experimental results show that the proposed microaggregation method outperforms the recent methods in the literature.

3   Background

Microdata protection through microaggregation has been intensively studied in recent years. Many techniques and methods have been proposed to deal with this problem. In this section we describe some fundamental concepts of microaggregation.

When we microaggregate data we should keep in mind two goals: data utility and preserving privacy of individuals. For preserving the data utility we should introduce as little noise as possible into the data and preserving privacy data should be sufficiently modified in such a way that it is difficult for an adversary to reidentify the corresponding individuals. Figure 1 shows an example of microaggregated data where the individuals in each cluster are replaced by the corresponding cluster mean. The figure shows that after aggregating the chosen elements, it is impossible to distinguish them, so that the probability of linking any respondent is inversely proportional to the number of aggregated elements.

Consider a microdata set T with p numeric attributes and n records, where each record is represented as a vector in a p-dimensional space. For a given positive integer $k \leq n$, a microaggregation method partitions T into g clusters, where each cluster contains at least k records (to satisfy k-anonymity), and then replaces the records in each cluster with the centroid of the cluster. Let n_i denote the number of records in the ith cluster, and $x_{ij}, 1 \leq j \leq n_i$, denote the jth record in the ith cluster. Then, $n_i \geq k$ for $i = 1$ to g, and $\sum_{i=1}^{g} n_i = n$. The centroid of the ith cluster, denoted by $\bar{x}_i$ is calculated as the average vector of all the records in the ith cluster.

In the same way, the centroid of T, denoted by $\bar{x}$, is the average vector of all the records in T. Information loss is used to quantify the amount of information

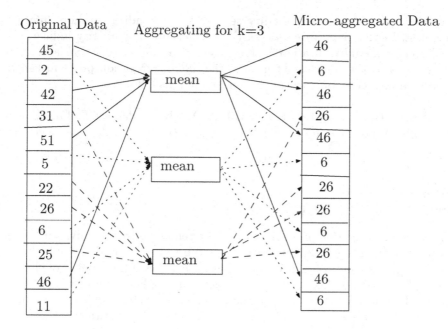

Fig. 1. Example of Microaggregation using mean

of a dataset that is lost after applying a microaggregation method. In this paper we use the most common definition of information loss by Domingo-Ferrer and Mateo-Sanz [3] as follows:

$$IL = \frac{SSE}{SST} \tag{1}$$

where SSE is the within-cluster squared error, calculated by summing the Euclidean distance of each record x_{ij} to the average value $\bar{x}_i$ as follows:

$$SSE = \sum_{i=1}^{g} \sum_{j=1}^{n_i} (x_{ij} - \bar{x}_i)' (x_{ij} - \bar{x}_i) \tag{2}$$

and SST is the sum of squared error within the entire dataset T, calculated by summing the Euclidean distance of each record x_{ij} to the average value $\bar{x}$ as follows:

$$SST = \sum_{i=1}^{g} \sum_{j=1}^{n_i} (x_{ij} - \bar{x})' (x_{ij} - \bar{x}) \tag{3}$$

For a given dataset T, SST is fixed regardless of how T is partitioned. On the other hand, SSE varies of a dataset depending on the partition of the dataset. In essence, SSE measures the similarity of the records in a cluster. The lower the SSE, the higher the within-cluster homogeneity and the higher the SSE, the lower the within cluster homogeneity. If all the records in a cluster are the same, then the SSE is zero indicating no information is lost. On the other hand, if all the records in a cluster are more diverse, SSE is large indicating more information is lost. In this paper, we used SSE as a measure of similarity indicating a record will be included in a particular cluster if it causes least SSE among all other records in the dataset. Therefore, the microaggregation problem can be enumerated as a constraint optimization problem as follows:

Definition 1 (Microaggregation Problem). Given a dataset T of n elements and a positive integer k, find a partitioning $C = \{C_1, C_2, ..., C_c\}$ of T such that

1. $C_i \cap C_j = \Phi$, for all $i \neq j = 1, 2, ..., p$,
2. $\cup_{i=1}^{p} C_i = T$,
3. SSE is minimized,
4. for all $C_i \in T$, $\mid C_i \mid \geq k$ for any $C_i \in C$.

The microaggregation problem stated above can be solved in polynomial time for a univariate dataset [12] but has been shown to be NP hard for multivariate dataset [14]. It is a natural expectation that SSE is low if the number of clusters is large. Thus the number of records in each cluster should be kept close to k. Domingo-Ferrer and Mateo-Sanz [3] showed that no cluster should contain more than $(2k - 1)$ records since such clusters can always be partitioned to further reduce information loss.

4   Previous Microaggregation Methods

Previous microaggregation methods have been roughly divided into two categories, namely fixed-size and data-oriented microaggregation [3,9]. For fixed-size microaggregation, the partition is done by dividing a dataset into clusters that have size k, except perhaps one cluster which has a size between k and $(2k-1)$, depending on the total number of records n and the anonymity parameter k. For the data-oriented microaggregation, the partition is done by allowing all clusters with sizes between k and $(2k-1)$. Intuitively, fixed-size methods reduce the search space, and thus are more computationally efficient than data-oriented methods [28]. However, data-oriented methods can adapt to different values of k and various data distributions and thus may achieve lower information loss than fixed-size methods.

Domingo-Ferrer and Mateo-Sanz [3] proposed a multivariate fixed-size microaggregation method, later called the Maximum Distance (MD) method [15]. The MD method repeatedly locates the two records that are most distant to each other, and forms two clusters with their respective $(k-1)$ nearest records until fewer than $2k$ records remain. If at least k records remain, it then forms a new cluster with all remaining records. Finally when there are fewer than k records not assigned to any cluster yet, this algorithm then individually assigns these records to their closest clusters. This method has a time complexity of $O(n^3)$ and works well for most datasets. Laszlo and Mukherjee [13] modified the last step of the MD method such that each remaining record is added to its own nearest cluster and proposed Diameter-based Fixed-size microaggregation.

This method is however not a fixed size method because it allows more than one cluster to have more than k records.

The MDAV method is the most widely used microaggregation method [15]. MDAV is the same as MD except in the first step. MDAV finds the record r that is furthest from the current centroid of the dataset and the record s that is furthest from r instead of finding the two records that are most distant to each other, as is done in MD. Then form a cluster with r and its $(k-1)$ nearest records and form another cluster with s and its $(k-1)$ nearest records. For the remaining records, repeat this process until fewer than $2k$ records remain. If between k and $(2k-1)$ records remain, MDAV simply forms a new group with all of the remaining records. On the other hand, if the number of the remaining records is below k, it adds all of the remaining records to their nearest clusters. So MDAV is a fixed size method. Lin et al. [28] proposed a modified MDAV, called MDAV-1. The MDAV-1 is similar to MDAV except when the number of the remaining records is between k and $(2k-1)$, a new cluster is formed with the record that is the furthest from the centroid of the remaining records, and its $(k-1)$ nearest records. Any remaining records are then added to their respective nearest clusters. Experimental results indicate that MDAV-1 incurs slightly less information loss than MDAV [28]. Another variant of the MDAV method, called MDAV-generic, is proposed by Domingo-Ferrer and Torra [8], where by the threshold $2k$ is altered to $3k$. If between $2k$ and $(3k-1)$ records remain, then find the record r that is furthest from the centroid of the remaining records and form a cluster with r and its $(k-1)$ nearest records and another cluster with the remaining records. Finally when fewer than $2k$ records remain, this algorithm then forms a new cluster with all the remaining records. Laszlo and Mukherjee [13] proposed another method, called Centroid-based Fixed-size microaggregation that is also based on a centroid but builds only one cluster during each iteration. This algorithm first find a record r that is furthest from the current centroid of the dataset and then find a cluster with r and its $(k-1)$ nearest records. For the remaining records repeat the same process until fewer than k records remain. Finally add each remaining record to its nearest clusters. This method is not a fixed-size method as more than one cluster has more than k records. Solanas et al. [16] proposed a variable-size variant of MDAV, called V-MDAV. V-MDAV first builds a new cluster of k records and then tries to extend this to up to $(2k-1)$ records based on some criteria. V-MDAV adopts a user-defined parameter to control the threshold of adding more records to a cluster. Chang et al. [27] proposed the Two Fixed Reference Points (TFRP) method to accelerate the clustering process of k-anonymization. During the first phase, TFRP selects two extreme points calculated from the dataset. Let N_{min} and N_{max} be the minimum and maximum values over all attributes in the datasets, respectively, then one reference point C_1 has N_{min} as its value for all attributes, and another reference point C_2 has N_{max} as its value for all attributes. A cluster of k records is then formed with the record r that is the furthest from C_1 and the $(k-1)$ nearest records to r. Similarly another cluster of k records is formed with the record s that is the furthest from C_2 and $(k-1)$ nearest records to s.

These two steps are repeated until fewer than k records remain. Finally, these remaining records are assigned to their respective nearest clusters. This method is quite efficient as C_1 and C_2 are fixed throughout the iterations. When all clusters are generated, TFRP applies a enhancement step to determine whether a cluster should be retained or decomposed and added to other clusters.

Lin et al. [28] proposed a density-based algorithm (DBA) for microaggregation. The DBA has two different scenarios. The first state of DBA (DBA-1) repeatedly builds a new cluster using the k-neighborhood of the record with the highest k-density among all records that are not yet assigned to any cluster until fewer than k unassigned records remain. These remaining records are then assigned to their respective nearest clusters. The DBA-1 partitions the dataset into some clusters, where each cluster contains no fewer than k records. The second state of DBA (DBA-2) attempts to fine-tune all clusters by checking whether to decompose a cluster and merge its content with other clusters. Notably, all clusters are checked during the DBA-2 by the reverse of the order that they were added to clusters in the DBA-1. After several clusters are removed and their records are added to their nearest clusters in the DBA-2, some clusters may contain more than $(2k - 1)$ records. At the end of the DBA-2, the MDAV-1 algorithm is applied to each cluster with size above $(2k - 1)$ to reduce the information loss. This state is finally called MDAV-2. Experimental results show that the DBA attains a reasonable dominance over the latest microaggregation methods.

All of the microaggregation methods described above repeatedly choose one/ two records according to various heuristics and form one/two cluster(s) with the chosen records and their respective $(k - 1)$ other records. However there are other microaggregation methods that build all clusters simultaneously and work by initially forming multiple clusters of records in the form of trees, where each tree represent a cluster. The multivariate k-Ward algorithm [3] first finds the two records that are furthest from each other in the dataset and build two clusters from these two records and their respective $(k - 1)$ nearest records. Each of the remaining record then forms its own cluster. These clusters are repeatedly merged until all clusters have at least k records. Finally the algorithm is recursively applied to each cluster containing $2k$ or more records. Domingo-Ferrer et al. [10] proposed a multivariate microaggregation method called μ-Approx. This method first builds a forest and then decomposes the trees in the forest such that all trees have sizes between k and $\max(2k - 1, 3k - 5)$. Finally, for any tree with size greater than $(2k - 1)$, find the node in the tree that is furthest from the centroid of the tree. Form a cluster with this node and its $(k - 1)$ nearest records in the tree and form another cluster with the remaining records in the tree.

Hansen an Mukherjee [12] proposed a microaggregation method for univariate datasets called HM. After that Domingo-Ferrer et al. [9] proposed a multivariate version of the HM method, called MHM. This method first uses various heuristics, such as nearest point next (NPN), maximum distance (MD) or MDAV to order the multivariate records. Steps similar to the HM method are then applied to generate clusters based on this ordering. Domingo-Ferrer *et al.* [7] proposed a microaggregation method based on fuzzy c-means algorithm (FCM) [1]. This method repeatedly runs FCM to adjust the two parameters of FCM (one is the number of clusters c and another is the exponent for the partition matrix m) until each cluster contains at least k records. The value of c is initially large (and m is small) and is gradually reduced (increased) during the repeated FCM runs to reduce the size of each cluster. The same process is then recursively applied to those clusters with $2k$ or more records.

5   The Proposed Approach

This section presents the proposed least information loss clustering algorithm based on minimum and maximum pairs of pairs of instances that minimizes the information loss and satisfies the k-anonymity requirement. It has been observed that the reason many of the existing techniques has high information loss is due to some clusters containing very *different* observations which increases the information of a cluster. Therefore, the initial choice of cluster(s) is often difficult since these observations are not known in advance. The proposed technique solves this problem by creating the lower information loss cluster using the proposed Min-Max technique as explained in Sect. 5.1. Next, this process is incorporated in an iterative pairwise clustering algorithm that takes the minimum or maximum distant instances to create two clusters repeatedly by minimizing information loss and observing k-anonymity. The algorithm is described in Sect. 5.2.

5.1   Min Distance and Max Distance

It has been observed that arbitrarily choosing cluster centroids (e.g., K-Means, MDAV, V-MDAV, MD, etc.) has its disadvantages. In particular, there is a possibility that the clustering process may include an outlier in a cluster in order to obey K-anonymity. However, this has the undesired effect of noticeably increasing the information loss. It has been shown [21] that by simultaneously building clusters whose centroids are farthest from the centroid of the dataset helps to improve the information loss. However, this technique still has drawbacks. For example, in some cases the two farthest points from the centroid of the dataset may fall in the same cluster, at other times they may fall in entirely different clusters, thus limiting the performance of the algorithms in these circumstances. This paper proposes a deterministic technique based on maximum and minimum distance points in the dataset in order to create clusters with lowest information loss in all cases. In order to achieve the lowest information loss, the algorithm iteratively chooses either two most distant points or two closest points in the dataset depending on which clustering would result in the lowest information loss. The Least MinMax distance based algorithm is described in the next section.

Table 1. Least Min-Max distance microaggregation algorithm

Input: a dataset T of n records and a positive integer k
Output: a partitioning $C = C_1, C_2, ..., C_c$ of T, where $c = |C|$
and $|C| \geq k$ for $i = 1$ to c

1. Let $C = \phi$, and $T' = T$;
2. Let Max_1, Max_2, and Min_1, Min_2 such that distance
$D(Max_1, Max_2) \leq D(i, j), \forall i, j \in 1, ..., n$;
3. Form a cluster C_1 containing first record Max_1 adn its $(k-1)$ nearest records in T';
and another cluster C_2 containing Max_2 record and its $(k-1)$ nearest records in T';
Let IL_{Max_1} IL_{max_2} represent the information loss calculated using equation 1
of clusters C_1 and C_2;
4. if $IL_{Max_1} \leq IL_{Max_2}$ then $LeastMaxCluster = C_1$ else $LeastMaxCluster = C_2$;
5. Repeat steps 3 and 4 by replacing Max_1 and Max_2 with Min_1 and Min_2 to create
$LeastMinCluster$;
6. Set $C = C \cup LeastMaxCluster \cup LeastMinCluster$ and
$T' = T' - LeastMaxCluster - LeastMinCluster$;
7. Repeat steps 2-6 until $|T'| < 3k$;
8. if $2k \leq |T'| \leq (3k - 1)$;
(i) Go to step 2;
(ii) Form the $LeastMaxCluster$ cluster with k records in T';
(iii) Form the $LeastMinCluster$ cluster with the remaining $(> k)$ records in T';
9. else;
10. if $T' < 2k$;
(i) Form a new cluster with all the remaining records in T';

5.2   Least Min-Max Distance Microaggregation Algorithm

Based on the information loss measure in Eq. (1), the notion of minimum and maximum distance in Sect. 5.1 and the definition of the microaggregation problem, the Least Min-Max (LMMD) microaggregation algorithm is as follows:.

According to this method, first find the two most distant (Max_1 and Max_2) records and the two closest (Min_1 and Min_2) records in the dataset T using a distance metric. In this paper, the well-known Euclidean distance metric was used, but other distance metric including Manhattan or City-block distances could also be used. The algorithm (see Table 1) first builds two clusters using the Max_1 and Max_2 records as seeds. The first cluster C_{max_1} is built using Max_1 and choosing the nearest $(k-1)$ records from the dataset for which the information loss of the cluster C_{max_1} is the lowest. Similarly, the second cluster C_{max_2} is built using Max_2 and choosing the nearest $(k-1)$ records from the dataset. Now, the information loss is calculated for both C_{max_1} and C_{max_2}. The cluster with the lower information loss is retained and the other one is discarded. Next, two clusters C_{min_1} and C_{min_2} are created in a similar way but this time using Min_1 and Min_2 instead of using Max_1 and Max_2 records. Like before, the cluster with the lower information loss resulting from the two nearest points is kept while the other one is discarded. Therefore, at the end of the first iteration the algorithm will create two clusters (one from Max and the other from Min distant records). This process is repeated until fewer than $3k$ records remain (see steps 2–7 of Table 1). The nearest records in a cluster are chosen in such a way that the inclusion of these records causes less SSE than the other records in the dataset. If between $2k$ and $(3k-1)$ records remain, then first cluster will be formed as before with k records and the second cluster with the remaining records having $k+1$ records to satisfy k-anonymity (see step 8 of Table 1). Finally, if fewer than $2k$ records remain, then just one new cluster is formed with all the remaining records (see step 10 of Table 1).

The proposed algorithms stated above endeavours to repeatedly build two clusters simultaneously using the Min- Max distance based approach which results in significantly reduced information loss than existing techniques (see Sect. 6).

Definition 2 (Least Error Clustering-based Microaggregation Decision Problem). In a given dataset T of n records, there is a clustering scheme $C = \{C_1, C_2, ..., C_c\}$ such that

1. $\mid C_i \mid \geq k, 1 < k \leq n$: the size of each cluster is greater than or equal to a positive integer k, and
2. $\sum_{i=1}^{g} IL(C_i) \leq \epsilon, \epsilon > 0$: the total information loss of the clustering scheme is less than a positive integer ϵ.

where each cluster $C_i(i = 1, 2, ..., p)$ contains the records that are more similar to each other such that the cluster means are close to the values of the clusters and thus cause the least information loss.

6   Experimental Results

This section presents the experimental results and compares the results with several existing techniques. The objective of this experiment is to investigate the effectiveness of the proposed algorithm in terms of measured information loss of represented cluster data. The following three datasets [9], which have been used as benchmarks in previous studies to evaluate various microaggregation methods, were adopted in the experiments.

1. The "Tarragona" dataset contains 834 records with 13 numerical attributes.
2. The "Census" dataset contains 1,080 records with 13 numerical attributes.
3. The "EIA" dataset contains 4,092 records with 11 numeric attributes (plus two additional categorical attributes not used here).

To accurately evaluate our approach, the performance of the proposed algorithm is compared in this section with various microaggregation methods. Tables 2, 3 and 4 show the information losses of these microaggregation methods. The lowest information loss for each dataset and each k value is shown

Table 2. Information loss comparison using Tarragona dataset

Method	$k = 3$	$k = 4$	$k = 5$	$k = 10$
MDAV-MHM	16.9326		22.4617	33.1923
MD-MHM	16.9829		22.5269	33.1834
CBFS-MHM	16.9714		22.8227	33.2188
NPN-MHM	17.3949		27.0213	40.1831
M-d	16.6300	19.66	24.5000	38.5800
μ-Approx	17.10	20.51	26.04	38.80
TFRP-1	17.228	19.396	22.110	33.186
TFRP-2	16.881	19.181	21.847	33.088
MDAV-1	16.93258762	19.54578612	22.46128236	33.19235838
MDAV-2	16.38261429	19.01314997	22.07965363	33.17932950
DBA-1	20.69948803	23.82761456	26.00129826	35.39295837
DBA-2	16.15265063	22.67107728	25.45039236	34.80675148
LeastMinMaxDisPts	**2.16**	**5.12**	**7.01**	**9.19**

Table 3. Information loss comparison using Census dataset

Method	$k = 3$	$k = 4$	$k = 5$	$k = 10$
MDAV-MHM	5.6523		9.0870	14.2239
MD-MHM	5.69724		8.98594	14.3965
CBFS-MHM	5.6734		8.8942	13.8925
NPN-MHM	6.3498		11.3443	18.7335
M-d	6.1100	8.24	10.3000	17.1700
μ-Approx	6.25	8.47	10.78	17.01
TFRP-1	5.931	7.880	9.357	14.442
TFRP-2	5.803	7.638	8.980	13.959
MDAV-1	5.692186279	7.494699833	9.088435498	14.15593043
MDAV-2	5.656049371	7.409645342	9.012389597	13.94411775
DBA-1	6.144855154	9.127883805	10.84218735	15.78549732
DBA-2	5.581605762	7.591307664	9.046162117	13.52140518
LeastMinMaxDisPts	**1.3**	**2.21**	**2.27**	**2.66**

in bold face. The information losses of methods DBA-1, DBA-2, MDAV-1 and MDAV-2 are quoted from [28]; the information losses of methods MDAV-MHM, MD-MHM, CBFS-MHM, NPN-MHM and M-d (for $k = 3, 5, 10$) are quoted from [9]; the information losses of methods μ-Approx and M-d (for $k = 4$) are quoted from [10], and the information losses of methods TFRP-1 and TFRP-2 are quoted from [27]. TFRP is a two-stage method and its two stages are denoted

Table 4. Information loss comparison using EIA dataset

Method	$k = 3$	$k = 4$	$k = 5$	$k = 10$
MDAV-MHM	0.4081		1.2563	3.7725
MD-MHM	0.4422		1.2627	3.6374
NPN-MHM	0.5525		0.9602	2.3188
μ-Approx	0.43	0.59	0.83	2.26
TFRP-1	0.530	0.661	1.651	3.242
TFRP-2	0.428	0.599	0.910	2.590
MDAV-1	0.482938725	0.671345141	1.666657361	3.83966422
MDAV-2	0.411101515	0.587381756	0.946263963	3.16085577
DBA-1	1.000194828	0.84346907	1.895536919	4.265801303
DBA-2	0.421048322	0.559755523	0.81849828	2.080980825
LeastMinMaxDisPts	**2.21**	**0.64**	**5.52**	**4.2**

as TRFP-1 and TRFP-2 respectively. The TFRP-2 is similar to the DBA-2 but disallows merging a record to a group of size over $(4k - 1)$.

Tables 2, 3 and 4 show the information loss for several values of k and the Tarragona, Census and for the EIA datasets respectively. The information loss is compared with the proposed algorithm among the latest microaggregation methods listed above. Information loss is measured as $\frac{SSE}{SST} \times 100$, where SST is the total sum of the squares of the dataset. Note that the within-groups sum of squares SSE is never greater than SST so that the reported information loss measure takes values in the range $[0, 100]$. Tables 2, 3 and 4 illustrate that in all of the test situations, the proposed algorithm causes significantly less information loss than any of the microaggregation methods listed in the table. This shows the utility and the effectiveness of the proposed algorithm.

Analysis: Figure 2 shows how the information loss values changes with k for each dataset. Results indicate that information loss increases with k. This is obvious since the higher number of records in each cluster results in higher sum-of-squared-error (SSE) values due to the fact that each cluster now has more observations and possibly larger variance. Interestingly, there is little correlation between overall information loss of a dataset and its size as evident from the fact that the information loss for CIA dataset (containing 4092 instances) is much lower than the information loss for Tarragona dataset (containing 1082 instances). This may be due to the lower variance in EIA dataset resulting in clusters with lower SSE, hence lower information loss.

Figure 3 shows the how the execution time varies with k and different file sizes. Again, results show that the execution time depends on the value of k. It shows that the execution time increases slightly due to the increased number of permutations that need to be calculated for each cluster for the higher k. Furthermore, as expected the execution is also related to the file size. As shown in

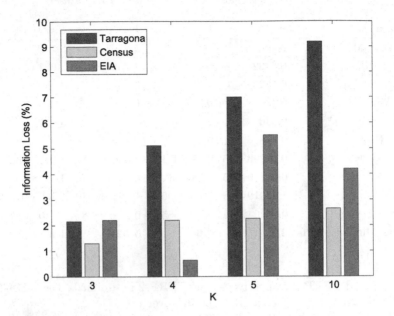

Fig. 2. Information Loss vs k for Tarragona, Census, and EIA datasets

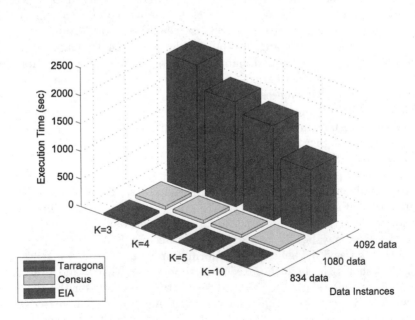

Fig. 3. Execution time vs k

Fig. 3 it takes the longest time to find k-anonymous clusters for the EIA dataset (4092 instances) and quickest time for the census dataset (834 instances).

7   Conclusion

Microaggregation is an effective method in SDC for protecting privacy in micro-data and has been extensively used world-wide. The level of privacy required is controlled by a parameter k, often called the anonymity parameter. For k-anonymization, k is basically the minimum number of records in a cluster. Once the value of k has been chosen, the data protector and the data users are interested in minimizing the information loss. This work has presented a new multi-dimensional sorting technique for numerical attributes. The new method consists of two stages. In the first stage it finds two pairs of Minimum and Maximum distant points. From this, the algorithm creates two k element clusters with the least information loss. In the second stage, it repeatedly creates these clusters until there are $p(k < p \leq 2k)$ records left. In which case, a single cluster is formed with the p points to preserve k-anonymity. A comparison has been made of the proposed algorithm with the most widely used microaggregation methods using the popular benchmark datasets. The experimental results show that the proposed algorithm **out-performs** all the tested microaggregation methods with respect to information loss. Thus the proposed method is very effective in preserving the privacy microdata sets and can be used as an effective privacy preserving k-anonymization method for Statistical Disclosure Control.

References

1. Bezdek, J.C.: Pattern Recognition with Fuzzy Objective Function Algorithms. Academic Publishers, Norwell (1981)
2. Domingo-Ferrer, J., Torra, V.: Privacy in data mining. Data Min. Knowl. Disc. **11**(2), 117–119 (2005)
3. Domingo-Ferrer, J., Mateo-Sanz, J.: Practical data-oriented microaggregation for statistical disclosure control. IEEE Trans. Knowl. Data Eng. **14**(1), 189–201 (2002)
4. Domingo-Ferrer, J., Torra, V.: Extending microaggregation procedures using defuzzification methods for categorical variables. In: 1st international IEEE symposium on intelligent systems, pp. 44–49, Verna (2002)
5. May, P., Ehrlich, H.C., Steinke, T.: ZIB structure prediction pipeline: composing a complex biological workflow through web services. In: Nagel, W.E., Walter, W.V., Lehner, W. (eds.) Euro-Par 2006. LNCS, vol. 4128, pp. 1148–1158. Springer, Heidelberg (2006)
6. Domingo-Ferrer, J., Torra, V.: Towards fuzzy c-means based microaggregation. In: Grzegorzewski, P., Hryniewicz, O., Gil, A. (eds.) Soft Methods in Probability, Statistics and Data Analysis. Advances in soft computing, vol. 16, pp. 289–294. Physica-Verlag, Heidelberg (2002)
7. Domingo-Ferrer, J., Torra, V.: Fuzzy microaggregation for microdata protection. J. Adv. Comput. Intell. Intell. Informatics **7**(2), 153–159 (2003)
8. Domingo-Ferrer, J., Torra, V.: Ordinal, continuous and heterogeneous kanonymity through microaggregation. Data Min. Knowl. Disc. **11**(2), 195–212 (2005)

9. Domingo-Ferrer, J., Martinez-Balleste, A., Mateo-Sanz, J.M., Sebe, F.: Efficient multivariate data-oriented microaggregation. VLDB J. **15**(4), 355–369 (2006)
10. Domingo-Ferrer, J., Sebe, F., Solanas, A.: A polynomial-time approximation to optimal multivariate microaggregation. Comput. Math. Appl. **55**(4), 714–732 (2008)
11. Han, J.-M., Cen, T.-T., Yu, H.-Q., Yu, J.: A multivariate immune clonal selection microaggregation algorithm. In: IEEE international conference on granular computing, pp. 252–256, Hangzhou (2008)
12. Hansen, S., Mukherjee, S.: A polynomial algorithm for optimal univariate microaggregation. IEEE Trans. Knowl. Data Eng. **15**(4), 1043–1044 (2003)
13. Laszlo, M., Mukherjee, S.: Minimum spanning tree partitioning algorithm for microaggregation. IEEE Trans. Knowl. Data Eng. **17**(7), 902–911 (2005)
14. Oganian, A., Domingo-Ferrer, J.: On the complexity of optimal microaggregation for statistical disclosure control. Stat. J. U. Nations Econ. Comm. Eur. **18**, 345–354 (2001)
15. Solanas, A.: Privacy protection with genetic algorithms. In: Yang, A., Shan, Y., Bui, L.T. (eds.) Success in Evolutionary Computation. Studies in Computational Intelligence, vol. 92, pp. 215–237. Springer, Heidelberg (2008)
16. Solanas, A., Martinez-Balleste, A., Domingo-Ferrer, J.: $V-MDAV$: a multivariate microaggregation with variable group size. In: 17th COMPSTAT Symposium of the IASC, Rome (2006)
17. Samarati, P.: Protecting respondent's privacy in microdata release. IEEE Trans. Knowl. Data Eng. **13**(6), 1010–1027 (2001)
18. Sweeney, L.: k-Anonymity: a model for protecting privacy. Int. J. Uncertainty Fuzziness Knowl. Based Syst. **10**(5), 557–570 (2002)
19. Torra, V.: Microaggregation for categorical variables: a median based approach. In: Domingo-Ferrer, J., Torra, V. (eds.) PSD 2004. LNCS, vol. 3050, pp. 162–174. Springer, Heidelberg (2004)
20. Kabir, M.E., Wang, H.: Systematic clustering-based microaggregation for statistical disclosure control. In: IEEE International Conference on Network and System Security, pp. 435–441, Melbourne (2010)
21. Kabir, M.E., Wang, H., Bertino, E., Chi, Y.: Systematic clustering method for l-diversity model. In: Australasian Database Conference, pp. 93–102, Brisbane (2010)
22. Kabir, M.E., Wang, H.: Microdata protection method through microaggragation: a median based approach. Inf. Secur. J. Global Perspect. **20**(1), 1–8 (2011)
23. Ward, J.H.J.: Hierarchical grouping to optimize an objective function. J. Am. Stat. Assoc. **58**(301), 236–244 (1963)
24. Wang, H., Zhang, Y., Cao, J.: Effective collaboration with information sharing in virtual universities. IEEE Trans. Knowl. Data Eng. **21**(6), 840–853 (2009)
25. Willenborg, L., Waal, T.D.: Elements of Statistical Disclosure Control. Lecture notes in statistics. Springer, New York (2001)
26. Zahn, C.T.: Graph-theoretical methods for detecting and describing gestalt clusters. IEEE Trans. Comput. **C−20**(1), 68–86 (1971)
27. Chang, C.-C., Li, Y.-C., Huang, W.-H.: TFRP: an efficient microaggregation algorithm for statistical disclosure control. J. Syst. Softw. **80**(11), 1866–1878 (2007)
28. Lin, J.-L., Wen, T.-H., Hsieh, J.-C., Chang, P.-C.: Density-based microaggregation for statistical disclosure control. Expert Syst. Appl. **37**(4), 3256–3263 (2010)

Securing Sensor Networks by Moderating Frequencies

Pinaki Sarkar[1]([✉]), Priyatosh Mahish[2], Morshed Uddin Chowdhury[3], and Kouichi Sakurai[4]

[1] Department of Mathematics, Techno India University, Kolkata, West Bengal, India
pinakisark@gmail.com
[2] Department of Electrical Engineering, NIST, Berhampur, Odisha, India
priyatosh.priyo@gmail.com
[3] School of Information Technology, Deakin University, Melbourne, VIC, Australia
morshed.chowdhury@deakin.edu.au
[4] Department of Informatics, Kyushu University-Ito Campus, Fukuoka, Japan
sakurai@csce.kyushu-u.ac.jp

Abstract. Security of Wireless Sensor Network (WSN) is a key issue in information security. Most existing security protocols exploit various Mathematical tools to strengthen their security. Some protocols use the details of the geographical location of the nodes. However, to the best authors' knowledge, none of the existing works exploit the constraints faced by the adversary, specifically, tracing a particular frequency from a large range of unknown frequency channels. The current work uses positional details of the individual nodes. Then the aim is to exploit this weakness of tracing frequencies by assigning a wide range of frequency channels to each node. Experiments using Magneto Optic Sensors reveal that any change of the parametric Faraday's rotational angle affects the frequency of the Optical waves. This idea can perhaps be generalized for practically deployable sensors (having respective parameters) along with a suitable key management scheme.

Keywords: Security of wireless sensor networks · Key management schemes · Radio frequency channels · Magneto-optic sensors · Faraday's rotational angle

1 Introduction

The modern generation demands secure transmission of information at a low cost. Thus, security of low cost networks like Wireless Sensor Networks (WSN) have become an important area of study. Such distributed networks consist of numerous identical low cost devices called nodes or sensors along with one or a few powerful Base Stations (BS), connecting the network to the user. The standard method of incorporating hierarchy in such networks is by introducing relatively powerful special nodes called Cluster Heads (CH). For instance, the

© Institute for Computer Sciences, Social Informatics and Telecommunications Engineering 2015
J. Tian et al. (Eds.): SecureComm 2014, Part II, LNICST 153, pp. 173–185, 2015.
DOI: 10.1007/978-3-319-23802-9_15

works [6,16] implements a hierarchy to the classic Transversal Design $(TD(k,p))$ based Key Predistribution Scheme (KPS) [8].

Most existing key management schemes in the literature of WSN concentrate on strengthening their design by the use of Mathematical tools. There are some protocols like [16] which consider the location of the nodes. However, not many, according to the authors' knowledge, have exploited the difficulties faced by the adversary. The main philosophy behind the current work is to exploit the practical hazards faced by the adversary while trying to retrieve the encrypted message. For retrieving any message *encrypted* by the application of a suitable key management protocol and being transmitted in open wireless (Magneto Optical) medium, the attacker primarily does the following:

1. Identify the frequency channels on which the message is being transmitted.
2. Decrypt the encrypted message passing through those frequency channels.

Till date, nodes of a given sensor network are normally configured with specific *frequency channels* or *frequency bands*. The authors suggest preallocating different sensors with varied sets of frequency channels. Of course, for direct communication between any two such sensors preloaded with two distinct sets of (multiple) frequency bands, there should be at least one common band between them. Such a suggestion is certainly practical and cost effective. For instance, mobile phone handsets with multi-Sim card are available at a reasonable price. These handsets generally use different set of frequency channels for different geographical locations (usually for different countries). This justifies the (practical) proposal of manufacturing (numerous) low cost sensor nodes preallocated with different sets of frequency bands.

Once sensors having different frequency channels are available, each node can be preloaded with certain small number (**n**) of channels out of a large number (**N**) of channels meant for the entire network. The adversary may easily trace the entire range of channels for a network. However tracing the exact frequency channels for individual nodes may still be difficult. The concept will be detailed in Sect. 2.

Considering this practical hazard faced by an adversary, the focus shift towards investigating whether the transmission frequencies can be regulated within the nodes; perhaps based on certain parameter(s). For this, experiments have been conducted with Magneto Optic sensors depending on Faraday's Magneto optic effect. The results are plotted in Fig. 2 of Sect. 5. Though such sensor may not suit specific security purpose, the success of the experiments suggest the same can be expected of other application specific sensors with respect to the variations of their respective parameters.

1.1   Related Works

Constraint in resources among the nodes of any WSN generally restricts the use of computationally expensive public key during encryption of messages. Instead, the use of relative inexpensive symmetric key cryptography is preferred. Symmetric key cryptography demands the communicating parties to share the same (or easily derivable) keys prior to message exchange. This emphasizes the importance of adequate key management schemes for such networks. Key Predistribution Schemes (KPS) consisting of preloading the keys before deployment and establishing these symmetric keys immediately afterwards are considered to be one of the best possible management techniques for such networks. Most of the first generation KPS are random in nature which has been well briefed in an excellent technical report [5] authored by Çamtepe and Yener. The same authors initiated the trend of deterministic KPS through their pioneering work [4]. Wei and Wu [17] and Lee and Stinson [7] independently came up with deterministic proposals at almost the same time. The work [17] deduces the general conditions for any scheme to be optimal in terms of connectivity, resilience and memory usage while analyzing existing KPS, and in the process proposes two schemes that can achieve their deduced optimality criteria. The works [7,8,11] establishes that deterministic schemes are better suited than their random counterparts for key establishment post deployment. This motivates the proposal of various deterministic KPS. An updated survey of such schemes can be traced in [11] and the references therein.

Ren et al. [12] proposes a location-aware end-to-end security framework in which each node only stores a few secret keys. These secret keys are determined by the node's geographic location. The property of the location-aware keys successfully limits the impact of compromised nodes to their vicinity. Multifunctional key management framework ensures both node-to-sink and node-to-node authentication along with report forwarding routes. Their one-to-many data delivery approach guarantees efficient en-route bogus data filtering and is robust against many known DoS attacks. However since these keys are bound within a restricted area, the intermediate nodes certainly get access to clear message text, which is not desired.

Simonova et al. (SLW) [16] suggested a localized deployment, where the entire network can be thought to be collection of subnetworks of nodes, each modeled with the design of [8]. Thus this scheme can be visualized as scaling a network built on the classic $TD(k, p)$ KPS [8]. However their amalgamation process enlarges the keyrings of the nodes of the final network. Alternatively, schemes such as [6] scale existing KPS like [8] without overburdening the keyrings of nodes of the ultimate network. Since all such schemes involve solution of higher order polynomial equations for growing networks, the scaling becomes restricted. Another problem faced by many existing KPS is the lack of full connectivity for the entire network. Such issues have been well addressed in the cluster based localized scheme [1]. A certain drawback of this scheme is the use of the special nodes (CH) with extra capabilities. These relatively expensive nodes increases the cost of the entire network, which may not be appropriate for certain applications.

Sarkar et al. [15] proposed the novel idea of distinguishing connectivity and communication of a sensor network while addressing the 'Selective Node Attack' and scalability issues, pertinent to most existing KPS such as [1,6–8,11,12,14–17]. Combination of the generic connectivity model of [15] with any KPS leads to highly secure networks. The UFD based KPS [14] provides a good example.

This KPS is fully connected and capable of supporting a large number of nodes even for small keyrings. One major drawback of this UFD based KPS [14] is its weak resiliency. This issue get appreciably addressed by the connectivity model of [15]. Since these schemes [14,15] uses relatively expensive special nodes with extra capabilities much like the KPS [1], networks designed on such schemes may not be appropriate for a specific application.

Extensive literature survey reveals all existing KPS, such as the ones analyzed in this work [1,6–8,11,12,14–17] and the references therein, try to strengthen the security of their protocol rather than exploiting the practical hazards faced by the adversary. The central idea of this work is to exploit the practical hazards faced by the adversary. One such hazard is the practical difficulties of tracing the frequency bands being used for inter–nodal communication, specially in adverse conditions. The focus then shift towards designing another level of security by assigning various frequency bands for distinct pairs of sensors in the same network. To the best of author's knowledge, this is perhaps the first proposal in WSN literature to propose a security model that exploits this practical weakness of tracing frequencies, encountered by the adversary.

The remaining part of this section is dedicated in reviewing some of the existing works related to Magneto optic sensors and their applications. Bera and Chakraborty [2] propose an experimental application that uses Magneto optic element as a displacement sensor. In this paper Terbium Doped Glass (TDG) has been taken for experimental purpose. A highly sensitive (with in 0.54%) linear micro–displacement sensor with improved performance over an appreciable range of 10 mm and a resolution of 5 μm is achieved. The experimental data is in good agreement with the theoretical study.

Chakraborty and Bera [3] propose an experimental application of magneto optic element as an over-current detector. Over-current detectors (OCDs) are important components in system control but suffer from electromagnetic interference, noise, low response etc. But the potential advantages of using Magneto optic elements of immunity to ElectroMagnetic Interference (EMI), electrical isolation, large bandwidth, ease of integration into digital control system, potentially low cost.

Mahish and Chakraborty [9] proposed an experimental study of the characteristics of Magneto optic sensor using TDG as the magneto optic element. Experiments confirm that the general behavior of this sensor is non–linear. However under certain condition the sensor shows linear nature over a certain range about the operating points, which has been claimed theoretically. The authors suggests using this linear behavior for various applications. This linear behavior of the magneto optic TDG element has been exploited by the present authors while conducting the experiments.

2 Practical Hazard for Adversary: System Design and Analysis

The nodes are to be assigned with different frequency channels, unknown to the adversary. Assignment of different channels that are not known publicly ensures their tracing by the use of 'Selective Filter(s)' becomes inconvenient and hence, expensive for the adversary. The entire network is to be assigned with a large number (N) of frequency channels. The nodes are to be preloaded with a smaller number (n) of frequency channels among the these N channels allocated for the entire network. This assignment is to be executed prior to the deployment of the network. For the sake of simplicity, n may be taken to be uniform (not mandatory) for all the nodes of the network.

Since the n frequency channels allocated to a node are not disclosed publicly, the adversary has to trace at least one of these n channels to get access to the transmitted information. Tracing all the n channels for any given node will naturally reveal all the information transmitted/received by it. Though the upper and the lower bound of the frequency range meant for the entire network may well be easily traceable by the use of an appropriate 'Selective Filter', tracking even one undisclosed band from a large (N) set of frequency bands may be tough in adverse regions. This justifies the usefulness of the proposal of manufacturing nodes with several frequencies channels and allocating distinct pair of band(s) for distinct pair of nodes in the present case.

Further, since nodes can be deployed with different sets of n channels, the adversary has to use the 'Selective Filter' for individual nodes. Thus to nullify the additional security injected by the proposed method, the adversary has to figure out all the n channels of all the nodes. As the standard network size is in the order of thousands, this may be a rather expensive task for the adversary; if at all feasible.

Alternatively, assume a simpler case when the N bands meant for the entire network are somehow known to the adversary. However, the exact number of channels (n) for each individual node is assumed to be still undisclosed. Further assume that no other information concerning the frequency bands is available to the adversary. This may compel the adversary to try and guess the allocated set of n bands for each node by reverting to the exhaustive search technique.

Tracking a single band for certain node may still be difficult task even after possessing the knowledge of all the N bands for the network. This is specially because there are thousands of nodes in the network lying in wide geographic area with varied degree of harshness. Tracing any band will involve tuning the 'Selective Filter(s)' to the exact band out of the N bands. This may be tough in adverse conditions. Clearly, the adversary's task of tracing all the n channels for a given node is not easy even on possessing the knowledge of all N bands of the entire network. This is because finding out all the n preallocated (unknown) bands for any given node among the N (known) bands for the network involve $\binom{N}{n} \approx (N - n)^n$ comparisons. Complexity of computation of any kind involving large numbers ($\approx 2^{80}$ bits) is high and is considered beyond the scope of modern day machine. The possibility of obtaining large value of N is assured by the wide range of Radio frequency (RF). A practical scenario is being described below.

Radio frequency (RF) range varies from around $3\,kHz$ to $300\,GHz$. Each frequency channels of sensor networks may be allocated with a bandwidth of roughly 1 MHz (refer to [10]) to avoid interference (noise). So a practical choice of N may be $3 * 10^5$. For cost effectiveness, one may consider n to be 5. Thus a proposal of nodes having 5 bands amidst a total of $3 * 10^5$ bands for the entire network is being made. Thus even in an unlikely case of knowing all $3 * 10^5$ bands of the network, the adversary's task of tracing the exact 5 channels for each node is certainly difficult. This tracing of all the 5 preallocated (unknown) bands for any given node among the $3 * 10^5$ (known) bands for the network involve $\binom{3*10^5}{5}$ comparisons, which is $\geq (2^{16})^5 = 2^{80}$ comparisons. Such large comparisons is beyond the scope of all existing up-to-date computing devices.

3   Allocation of Frequency Bands: Frequency Graph v/s KPS Graph

Assuming the availability of low cost sensors with different sets of frequency bands, an application of this novel technology is being presented. The *target* is to make the sensors *transmit information automatically* through *various allocated channels* based on the *varying external vibrations* received by them. The parametric variations for an individual sensor may perhaps occur due to some external effect such as a sudden variation of the external impulse received by the node. The 'n' channels of each individual nodes can be paired with a maximum of n different sensors. This gives the flexibility of transmission of information to various nodes depending on *priority*.

For instance, during an emergency which may be indicated by a high external impulse, the sensors in harsh geographical conditions may choose to connect to nodes deployed at relatively safer positions. The phrase 'safer positions/locations' mean locations which are comparatively difficult for the adversary to access. Since the coverage area of any WSN is a large geographical area with varying degrees of harshness, such an argument is practical. This motivates the words 'safer nodes' which consequentially mean sensors falling within such 'safe positions/locations' and hence are less prone to physical capture. Since these 'safer nodes' are expected to be at a relatively distant position from the nodes placed at 'harsh locations', such communications may involve exchange of information through channels with high frequencies. Whereas for normal low external impulse, they may connect to nearby sensors via relatively low frequencies channels for analysis of the data before transmitting to distant 'safer nodes' for further processing. In case, any of the above communications are beyond the radio frequency range of the individual nodes, the encrypted information can be routed to the target entities via intermediate nodes. These 'safer' distant nodes can further analyze the aggregated data before ultimately routing the synchronized information to the BS.

The frequency bands can be *preallocated* in the nodes by the *system designer* to form a separate network graph, distinct from the existing graph of any KPS (key–graph). This separate graph shall be referred to as *frequency graph* of the network. This *frequency graph* imparts a natural *grouping* into the system. The scenario is similar to any *hierarchical* network barring the following key differences:

- Standard cluster based hierarchical network like [1,6,15,16] possessing specially designed nodes (CH) with extra capabilities result in an substantially increased cost of the overall network. These sort of designs generally have different network graphs for different levels of hierarchy.
- There exists odd designs like [16] amalgamates the keyrings of some existing KPS [8], thus burdening the memory of individual nodes of the existing network. This KPS has a inner cluster and a inter cluster graph.
- On the contrary, the current strategy provides a natural subdivision without any extra burden on the existing system. The proposed concept of use of different bands for pairing various node can be combined with an appropriate KPS. This combined resultant network possesses two separate graphs; (i) one owing to the existing KPS; and (ii) the other (*frequency graph*) emerging from the introducing of this novel concept of using separate frequency channels. The practicality of manufacturing sensors with desired small number (**n**) of distinct bandwidths have been justified above.

Thus one may achieve a secure KPS with a natural hierarchy without deploying special nodes with extra capabilities. This, according to the authors, is perhaps the first proposal of a truly distributed scheme achieving a natural hierarchy. This grouping can perhaps be exploited to design KPS with optimal security, i.e. security independent of the protocol design. This motivates the following analysis of the network deployment in order to allocate the various frequency channels for the individual sensors.

Random deployment of any wireless network implies that the nodes fall at varied distance from one another. This distance can be traced by the standard use of a Global Positioning System (GPS). The preallocated (by system designer) frequency channels for each nodes are to be paired with other nodes lying in their communication radius which may vary for individual bands. Since there are **n** channels per node, each of which forms a complete graph comprising of **n** vertex, i.e. nodes here. Thus the network is subdivided into segments of **n** complete graph for each of the **n** channels.

Having proposed partitioning of the network in terms of these varied undisclosed frequency channels, the focus now shifts to visualize a practical demonstration of the idea. Consider a practical example of network proposed for surveillance of enemy movement or another to monitor forest fire. Suppose, in the first case, a particular sensor senses heavy vibrations due to rapid infiltration. Such a case has to be reported immediately to the BS. Instead of analyzing with neighboring sensors, it may be worth to send the information directly to BS by routing via relatively 'safer' distant node(s). Similarly, in case of forest fire, suppose that drastic raise in temperature is noted by some sensor(s). Such an information must be passed onto the BS instantaneously. These real life instances demonstrates the applicability proposed concept.

Due the unavailability of sensors with different sets of multiple frequency bands meant for specific applications in WSN, real life experiments could not be performed. Instead, Magneto Optic sensors depend on Faraday's Magneto optic effect have been utilized to demonstrate the effect of a parametric change on the transmitted frequency.

4   Interplay Between Electromagnetic and Optical Medium

Performance of the Magneto Optic sensors depend on Faraday's Magneto optic effect, which was discovered in the year 1845. This effect says that when plane polarized light is sent through a Magneto Optic element in a direction parallel to the magnetic field, the plane of polarization gets rotated. Polarization of light is the vibration of the light wave in a particular plane. Natural unpolarized light wave vibrates randomly in any plane. So, at a particular time the vibrating plane of a particular wave cannot be determined. If this unpolarized light beam passes through a polarizer, then this permits vibration only in a particular plane. Then that particular wave is said to be a polarized beam for that particular plane. Thus, clearly the performance of these Magneto Optic sensors mainly depend upon the characteristics and properties of light, implying that their speed is as fast as light.

The association between Faraday's rotational angle (θ) related to *Electromagnetic waves* and the frequency of light (ϑ) corresponding to any *Magneto Optic* media is being highlighted in this section. When a linearly polarized light passes through a magneto-optic medium (e.g. a TDG), kept parallel to the magnetic field, the Faraday's rotation is given by the relation mentioned in Eq. 1.

$$\theta = V_{Verdet} B l \tag{1}$$

where V_{Verdet} is the Verdet constant and B is the *magnetic flux density* of the medium. l is the *length* of the *Magneto Optic element (TDG)*. The Verdet constant which is dependent on the wavelength of light can be expressed as:

$$V_{Verdet}(\lambda) = -\frac{e\lambda}{2mc}\left(\frac{dn}{d\lambda}\right) \tag{2}$$

Here, e denotes the *charge of an electron*, m is the *mass of an electron* while c is the *speed of light in vacuum*, which are always constants.

$$n(\lambda) = a + \frac{b}{\lambda^2} \text{ where, } a \text{ and } b \text{ are constants.} \tag{3}$$

n is the refractive index (RI) of the Magneto Optic medium, which depends on the wavelength (λ) of light as well as the Magneto Optic element. So,

$$\frac{\delta n}{\delta \lambda} = -\frac{2b}{\lambda^3} \tag{4}$$

For a particular Magneto Optic element (TDG, here), the refractive index is only function of λ. Thus Eq. 4 can be rewritten as:

$$\frac{dn}{d\lambda} = -\frac{2b}{\lambda^3} \tag{5}$$

Comparing $\frac{dn}{d\lambda}$ values from Eqs. 2 and 5, one concludes:

$$V_{Verdet}(\lambda) = -\frac{e\lambda}{2mc}\frac{2b}{\lambda^3} = -\frac{eb}{mc}\cdot\frac{1}{\lambda^2} = \frac{K_1}{\lambda^2} \text{ where } K_1 = -\frac{eb}{mc}. \tag{6}$$

Again, it is well known that the relation between *wavelength* and *frequency* of any energy source is given by Eq. 7 below:

$$\lambda\vartheta = D(=c), c: \text{ meant for Optical medium}, \tag{7}$$

where D is the velocity of the energy source, which is constant for the given energy source. Since the work deals with Magneto Optics, hence conventionally, D is replaced by the symbol c. Thus in this paper, $D = c$. Combining Eqs. 6 and 7 yield the following Eq. 8.

$$V_{Verdet}(\vartheta) = \frac{K_1}{(c/\vartheta)^2} = \vartheta^2\frac{K_1}{c^2} = K_2\vartheta^2 \text{ where } K_2 = \frac{K_1}{c^2}. \tag{8}$$

So,

$$\theta(\vartheta) = K_2\vartheta^2 Bl \tag{9}$$

When the Faraday's rotation θ is 0° then the polarized optical beam vibrates at particular plane. This plane is called reference plane. Now with the change of θ, the plane of vibration also changes. So at particular rotation if the relative angle between the polarizer and analyzer remains constant then a component of the resultant optical beam will lie on the reference plane. This phenomenon can be expressed by the following equation, popularly known as Malus' law:

$$I = I_0cos^2(\theta - \alpha) \tag{10}$$

where I_0 is the intensity of the optical beam when it vibrates at the reference plane. I is the component of I_0 which lies on a plane different of the reference plane. α is the relative angle between polarizer and analyzer. θ is the angle between the plane of vibration and the reference plane or in other way Faraday's rotational angle. Further, $I \propto V$, where V is the Photodiode voltage output, which can be approximated as a linear function of I. So, Eq. 10 yields:

$$V = V_0cos^2(\theta - \alpha) \tag{11}$$

Combining Eqs. 9 and 11 yields:

$$V(\vartheta) = V_0cos^2(K_2\vartheta^2 Bl - \alpha) \tag{12}$$

V is the voltage output when the optical beam vibrates at the reference plane. V_0 is the voltage output when the optical beam vibrates at the plane different from the reference plane.

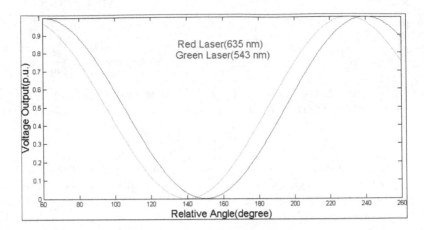

Fig. 1. Theoretical curve of voltage output with changing angle between polarizer-analyzer (Color figure online).

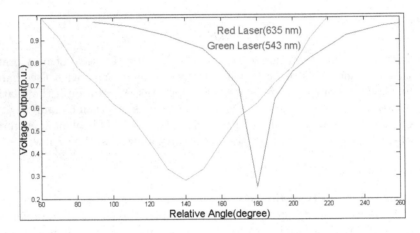

Fig. 2. Experimental curve of voltage output with changing angle between polarizer-analyzer (Color figure online).

5   Experiments and Results

Theoretical results based on Malus' equation have been sketched in Fig. 1. The theoretical figure shows the 10° constant relative difference between these two curves at a particular direction. This causes a 92 nm relative difference between red and green laser. However, the focus should be on the reduction of errors.

Due to limited facility, experiments could be conducted with only two different laser sources, red (635 nm) and green(543 nm). The results of the experiments have been presented in Fig. 2. The graphs in Fig. 2 expresses the change of Faraday's rotational angle with change in the wavelength of the optical wave. According to the change of relative angle between the polarizer and the analyzer, the component of the light intensity at reference plane will vary. This variation helps in tracing the individual curves. From the figure, it is clear that the position of the curve followed by red laser is shifted forward by approximately $40°$ than the curve followed by green laser at relative angle $60° - 180°$. This is caused by the relative difference of wavelengths between two different laser, i.e., $635 - 543 = 92$ nm. Thus it can be concluded that the experimental data resembles the theoretical data. Comparing these two distinct curves in Fig. 2, one may conclude that any change in wavelength of the laser causes variation in the Faraday's rotational angle at a particular direction. This may be generalized for other application specific sensors with corresponding parameters.

6   Conclusion

Unlike most existing works in the literature of WSN security which aims to strengthen their own protocol, this paper focuses on an weakness faced by the adversary; particularly in an adverse deployment zone. A practical hazard may be to trace the frequency channel used for communication between two sensors from a wide range of bands in a harsh geographical locations. Since the RF range is widely varied, use of 'Selective Filter(s)' to trace an unknown frequency may be an expensive affair; if at all feasible. This motivates the authors to think of allocating a large range (N) of frequency bands for the entire network. The low cost nodes are allocated with lesser no. (n) of frequency bands to ensure enhanced security. This concept of allocating various band to the nodes naturally partitions the entire network into groups. This is an added benefit since most existing schemes possessing an hierarchy utilized relatively expensive special nodes like cluster heads for such a subdivision. Unavailability of practically deployable application specific sensors meant that experiments were conducted with Magneto Optic sensors to prove the practicality of the claim that an external impulse may lead to parametric variations, and hence varied transmission of frequency for individual sensors.

7   Future Work

One promising future research direction steaming out of this work is the suggestion of manufacturing sensors with different sets of frequency channels. According to the authors' knowledge, such nodes are still not available commercially. In this connection, one is referred to a standard sensor configuration in [10] which is used universally for WSN applications. The practicality of the suggestion of manufacturing (numerous) nodes with different sets of multiple frequency channels has been set out in Sect. 1 while pointing out the availability of multi-Sim mobile phone handsets at a low cost.

A more challenging task may to construct low cost nodes capable of generating varied range of frequencies within individual sensors. Rohde and Schwarz [13] presents a vector signal generator which may pave a direction towards achieving this goal practically. This generator can act as an all in one test platform for wireless devices. The generator supports cellular, non-cellular as well as broadcast technologies.

Once sensors capable of operating in multiple bands are availability, they may be used for practical implementation of the idea proposed in this paper. Based on an external impulse, transmission can made through desired band of the respective nodes. The varying transmission can be combined with some chosen existing and/or newly proposed KPS to ensure additional security for the encrypted message.

Acknowledgement. This work is partially done during Morshed Chowdhury's visit at Kouichi Sakurai's laboratory in Kyushu University-Ito Campus, Fukuoka, Japan, in June 2014.

References

1. Bag, S., Dhar, A., Sarkar, P.: 100% connectivity for location aware code based KPD in clustered WSN: merging blocks. In: Gollmann, D., Freiling, F.C. (eds.) ISC 2012. LNCS, vol. 7483, pp. 136–150. Springer, Heidelberg (2012)
2. Bera, S.C., Chakrabarty, S.: Study of magneto-optic element as a displacement sensor. Measurement **44**(9), 1747–1752 (2011)
3. Chakrabarty, S., Bera, S.C.: Magneto-optic over-current detection with null optical tuning. Sens. Transducers **87**(1), 52–62 (2008)
4. Çamtepe, S.A., Yener, B.: Combinatorial design of key distribution mechanisms for wireless sensor networks. In: Samarati, P., Ryan, P.Y.A., Gollmann, D., Molva, R. (eds.) ESORICS 2004. LNCS, vol. 3193, pp. 293–308. Springer, Heidelberg (2004)
5. Çamtepe, S.A., Yener, B.: Key distribution mechanisms for wireless sensor networks: a survey. Technical report, Rensselaer Polytechnic Institute, Rensselaer Polytechnic Institute, Lally 310110, 8th Street, Troy, NY 12180–3590 (2005). http://www.cs.rpi.edu/research/pdf/05-07.pdf. Last Accessed: July 14, 2014
6. Chakrabarti, D., Seberry, J.: Combinatorial structures for design of wireless sensor networks. In: Zhou, J., Yung, M., Bao, F. (eds.) ACNS 2006. LNCS, vol. 3989, pp. 365–374. Springer, Heidelberg (2006)
7. Lee, J.-Y., Stinson, D.R.: Deterministic key predistribution schemes for distributed sensor networks. In: Handschuh, H., Hasan, M.A. (eds.) SAC 2004. LNCS, vol. 3357, pp. 294–307. Springer, Heidelberg (2004)
8. Lee, J., Stinson, D.R.: A combinatorial approach to key predistribution for distributed sensor networks. In: WCNC, pp. 1200–1205 (2005)
9. Mahish, P., Chakrabarty, S.: Study of magneto optic sensor using TDG element. Int. J. Innovative Res. Electr. Electron. Instrum. Control Eng. (IJIREEICE) **1**(6), 254–258 (2013)
10. Moteiv Corporation. Tmote sky: Datasheet (2006). http://www.eecs.harvard.edu/konrad/projects/shimmer/references/tmote-sky-datasheet.pdf, Last Accessed: July 14, 2014
11. Paterson, M.B., Stinson, D.R.: A unified approach to combinatorial key predistribution schemes for sensor networks. Des. Codes Cryptography **71**(3), 433–457 (2014)
12. Ren, K., Lou, W., Zhang, Y.: LEDS: Providing Location-Aware End-to-End Data Security in Wireless Sensor Networks. IEEE Trans. Mob. Comput. **7**(5), 585–598 (2008)

13. Rohde and Schwarz. R&S® CMW500 Wideband Radio Communication Tester (2009). http://d3fdwrtpsinh7j.cloudfront.net/Docs/datasheet/rs_cmw500_overview.pdf, Last Accessed: July 14, 2014
14. Sarkar, P., Chowdhury, M.U.: Key predistribution scheme using finite fields and reed muller codes. In: Lee, R. (ed.) Software Engineering, Artificial Intelligence, Networking and Parallel/Distributed Computing 2011. SCI, vol. 368, pp. 67–79. Springer, Heidelberg (2011)
15. Sarkar, P., Saha, A., Chowdhury, M.U.: Secure connectivity model in wireless sensor networks (WSN) using first order Reed-Muller codes. In: MASS, pp. 507–512 (2010)
16. Simonova, K., Ling, A.C.H., Wang, X.S.: Location-aware key predistribution scheme for wide area wireless sensor networks. In: SASN, pp. 157–168 (2006)
17. Wei, R., Wu, J.: Product construction of key distribution schemes for sensor networks. In: Handschuh, H., Hasan, M.A. (eds.) SAC 2004. LNCS, vol. 3357, pp. 280–293. Springer, Heidelberg (2004)

Intelligent Financial Fraud Detection Practices: An Investigation

Jarrod West, Maumita Bhattacharya[✉], and Rafiqul Islam

School of Computing and Mathematics, Charles Sturt University,
Bathurst, Australia
jnwest@netspace.net.au,
{mbhattacharya,mislam}@csu.edu.au

Abstract. Financial fraud is an issue with far reaching consequences in the finance industry, government, corporate sectors, and for ordinary consumers. Increasing dependence on new technologies such as cloud and mobile computing in recent years has compounded the problem. Traditional methods of detection involve extensive use of auditing, where a trained individual manually observes reports or transactions in an attempt to discover fraudulent behaviour. This method is not only time consuming, expensive and inaccurate, but in the age of big data it is also impractical. Not surprisingly, financial institutions have turned to automated processes using statistical and computational methods. This paper presents a comprehensive investigation on financial fraud detection practices using such data mining methods, with a particular focus on computational intelligence-based techniques. Classification of the practices based on key aspects such as detection algorithm used, fraud type investigated, and success rate have been covered. Issues and challenges associated with the current practices and potential future direction of research have also been identified.

Keywords: Financial fraud · Computational intelligence · Fraud detection techniques · Data mining

1 Introduction and Background

Financial fraud is an issue that has wide reaching consequences in both the finance industry and daily life. Fraud can reduce confidence in industry, destabilise economies, and affect people's cost of living. Traditional approaches of fraud detection relied on manual techniques such as auditing, which are inefficient and unreliable due to the complexities associated with the problem. Computational intelligence (CI)-based as well as conventional data mining approaches have been proven to be useful because of their ability to detect small anomalies in large data sets [14].

Financial fraud is a broad term with various potential meanings, but for our purposes it can be defined as the intentional use of illegal methods or practices for the purpose of obtaining financial gain [30]. There are many different types of financial fraud, as well as a variety of data mining methods, and research is continually being undertaken to find the best approach for each case. The common financial fraud

© Institute for Computer Sciences, Social Informatics and Telecommunications Engineering 2015
J. Tian et al. (Eds.): SecureComm 2014, Part II, LNICST 153, pp. 186–203, 2015.
DOI: 10.1007/978-3-319-23802-9_16

categories and the popular data mining as well as computational intelligence-based techniques used for financial fraud detection are depicted in Figs. 1 and 2 respectively.

Advancements in modern technologies such as the internet and mobile computing have led to an increase in financial fraud in recent years [27]. Social factors such as the increased distribution of credit cards have increased spending, but also resulted in an increase to fraud [20]. Fraudsters are continually refining their methods, and as such there is a requirement for detection methods to be able to evolve accordingly. CI and data mining have already been shown to be useful in similar domains such as credit card approval, bankruptcy prediction, and analysis of share markets [16]. Fraud detection is primarily considered to be a classification problem, but with a vast imbalance in fraudulent to legitimate transactions misclassification is common and can be significantly costly [6]. Many data mining approaches are efficient classifiers and are applicable to fraud detection for their efficiency at processing large datasets and their ability to work without extensive problem specific knowledge [19].

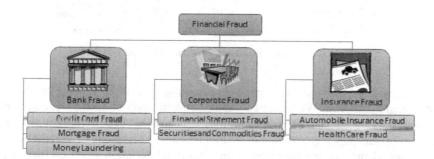

Fig. 1. Common financial fraud categories.

A useful framework for applying CI or data mining to fraud detection is to use them as methods for classifying suspicious transactions or samples for further consideration. Studies show that reviewing 2 % of credit card transactions could reduce fraud losses to 1 % of the total cost of all purchases, with more assessments resulting in smaller loss but with an increase in auditing costs [18]. A multi-layer pipeline approach can be used with each step applying a more rigorous method to detect fraud. Data mining can be utilised to efficiently filter out more obvious fraud cases in the initial levels and leave the more subtle ones to be reviewed manually [18].

Early fraud detection studies focused on statistical models such as logistic regression, as well as neural networks (see [9, 18, 21] and [28] for details). In 1995 Sohl et al. first predicted financial statement fraud using a back-propagation neural network [28]. More recently, in addition to examining financial scenarios such as stock market and bankruptcy prediction, Zhang and Zhou applied various data mining techniques to financial fraud detection in 2004 [29]. In 2005 Vatsa et al. investigated a novel approach using game theory which modelled fraudsters and detection methods as opposing players in a game, each striving to obtain the greatest financial advantage [22]. A process mining approach was used by Yang and Hwang in 2006 to detect health care fraud [26]. In 2007 Yue et al. observed that, to date, classification-based methods are both the most commonly researched techniques as well as the only successful ones [28]. The chronological progression of some of the recent financial fraud detection research has been depicted in Fig. 3.

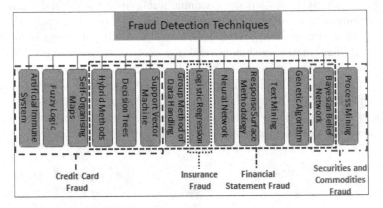

Fig. 2. Detection algorithms used for various fraud categories.

In this paper we provide a comprehensive investigation of the existing practices in financial fraud detection. We present a detailed classification of such practices; aimed at informing development of enhanced financial fraud detection frameworks. The remainder of the paper is structured as follows: Sect. 2 presents a comprehensive classification of the existing practices in financial fraud detection based on fraud type, detection algorithm, success rate and so on. Section 3 offers an insight into issues and challenges associated with financial fraud detection and potential direction for future research. Finally, Sect. 4 presents some concluding remarks.

2 Classification of Financial Fraud Detection Practices

In the following sub-sections we will classify existing financial fraud detection practices based on success rate, detection technique used, and fraud type. This categorisation will enable us to identify trends in current practices, including which have been successful, probable factors influencing the outcomes, and also any gaps in the research.

2.1 Classification Based on Performance

A variety of standards have been used to determine performance, but the three most commonly used are *accuracy, sensitivity,* and *specificity.* Accuracy measures the ratio of all successfully classified samples to unsuccessful ones. Sensitivity compares the amount of items correctly identified as fraud to the amount incorrectly listed as fraud, also known as the ratio of true positives to false positives. Specificity refers to the same concept with legitimate transactions, or the comparison of true negatives to false negatives [3, 19].

Tables 1, 2, and 3 classify financial fraud detection research based on these performance measures. Additionally, Fig. 4 depicts the broad comparative performance of various fraud detection methods.

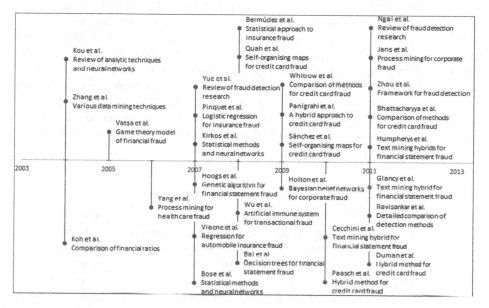

Fig. 3. Chronological progression of recent financial fraud detection research.

In addition to the three performance measures discussed here, several other performance measures have been used in the literature. For example, Duman and Ozcelik chose to show their results for sensitivity in graph form instead of deterministic values, grouped by each set of input parameters [6]. In addition to other forms of graphing [18], some research used software-determined success levels or case-based procedures to determine the success of their fraud detection techniques [11, 20].

From the results we can see that CI methods typically had better success rate than statistical methods. Sensitivity was slightly better for random forests and support vector machines than logistic regression, with comparable specificity and accuracy [3]. Genetic programming, support vector machines, probabilistic neural networks, and group method of data handling outperformed regression in all three areas [19]. Additionally, a neural network with exhaustive pruning was found to be more specific and accurate than CDA [4]. One statistical method seems to contradict this theory however: Bayesian belief networks were reported to be more accurate than neural networks and decision trees [12].

Most of the research showed a large difference between each method's sensitivity and specificity results. For example, Bhattacharyya et al. showed that logistic regression, support vector machines and random forests all performed significantly better at detecting legitimate transactions correctly than fraudulent ones [3]. Support vector machines, genetic programming, neural networks, group method of data handling, and particularly logistic regression were also slightly less sensitive [19]. Also a neural network with exhaustive pruning showed more specificity than sensitivity [4].

As explained previously, fraud detection is a problem with a large difference in misclassification costs: it is typically far more expensive to misdiagnose a fraudulent transaction as legitimate than the reverse. With that in mind it would be beneficial for detection techniques to show a much higher sensitivity than specificity, meaning that these results are less than ideal. Contrary to this belief, Hoogs et al. hypothesised that financial statement fraud may carry higher costs for false positives, and their results reflect this with a much higher specificity [9]. Panigrahi et al. also acknowledged the costs associated with following up credit card transactions marked as fraudulent, focussing their results on sensitivity only [16]. The CDA and CART methods, as well as neural networks, Bayesian belief networks and decision trees performed better in this regard, with all showing a somewhat higher ability to classify fraudulent transactions than legitimate ones [4, 12].

Table 1. Accuracy results for fraud detection practices

Research	Fraud investigated	Method investigated	Accuracy
[3]	Credit card transaction fraud from a real world example	Logistic model (regression)	96.6–99.4 %
		Support vector machines	95.5–99.6 %
		Random forests	97.8–99.6 %
[12]	Financial statement fraud from a selection of Greek manufacturing firms	Decision trees	73.6 %
		Neural networks	80 %
		Bayesian belief networks	90.3 %
[19]	Financial statement fraud with financial items from a selection of public Chinese companies	Support vector machine	70.41–73.41 %
		Genetic programming	89.27–94.14 %
		Neural network (feed forward)	75.32–78.77 %
		Group method of data handling	88.14–93.00 %
		Logistic model (regression)	66.86–70.86 %
		Neural network (probabilistic)	95.64–98.09 %
[7]	Financial statement fraud with managerial statements for US companies	Text mining with singular validation decomposition vector	95.65 %
[5]	Financial statement fraud with managerial statements for US companies	Text mining	45.08–75.41 %
		Text mining and support vector machine hybrid	50.00–81.97 %

(Continued)

Table 1. (*Continued*)

Research	Fraud investigated	Method investigated	Accuracy
[10]	Financial statement fraud with managerial statements for US companies	Text mining and decision tree hybrid	67.3 %
		Text mining and Bayesian belief network hybrid	67.3 %
		Text mining and support vector machine hybrid	65.8 %
[4]	Financial statement fraud with financial items from a selection of public Chinese companies	CDA	71.37 %
		CART	72.38 %
		Neural network (exhaustive pruning)	77.14 %

Remarks: Considering the three performance measures, namely accuracy, sensitivity and specificity, our investigation shows that the computational intelligence-based approaches have generally performed better than the statistical approaches in most cases.

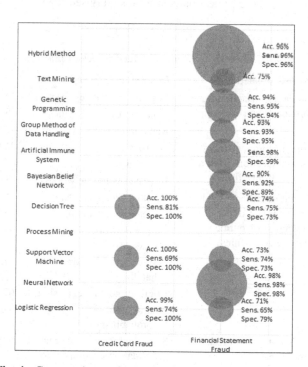

Fig. 4. Comparative performance of various detection methods.

2.2 Classification Based on Detection Algorithm

Classifying fraud detection practices by the detection algorithm used is a useful way to identify the suitable techniques for this problem domain. It can also help us to determine why particular methods were chosen or successful. Additionally, we can identify any gaps in research by looking at algorithms which have not been explored sufficiently. Table 4 shows classification of financial fraud detection practices based on detection algorithm (conventional data mining and CI-based approaches) used.

Previously it was mentioned that early fraud detection research focussed on statistical models and neural networks; however, it may be noted that these methods still continue to be popular. Many used at least one form of neural network [4, 12, 19], some investigated logistic regression [3, 17, 19, 23], while others applied Bayesian belief networks [2, 8, 12]. Application of CDA has been relatively uncommon [4]. Neural networks and logistic regression are often chosen for their well-established popularity, giving them the ability to be used as a control method by which other techniques are tested. Comparatively, more advanced methods such as support vector machines and genetic programming have received substantially less attention. Yue et al. also reported that all the methods mentioned in their research were a form of classification, with no studies performed on clustering or time-series approaches, and that most of the research focussed on supervised learning as opposed to unsupervised [28].

Table 2. Sensitivity results for fraud detection practices

Research	Fraud investigated	Method investigated	Sensitivity
[3]	Credit card transaction fraud from a real world example	Logistic model (regression)	24.6–74.0 %
		Support vector machines	43.0–68.7 %
		Random forests	42.3–81.2 %
[12]	Financial statement fraud from a selection of Greek manufacturing firms	Decision trees	75.0 %
		Neural networks	82.5 %
		Bayesian belief networks	91.7 %
[19]	Financial statement fraud with financial items from a selection of public Chinese companies	Support vector machine	55.43–73.60 %
		Genetic programming	85.64–95.09 %
		Neural network (feed forward)	67.24–80.21 %
		Group method of data handling	87.44–93.46 %
		Logistic model (regression)	62.91–65.23 %
		Neural network (probabilistic)	87.53–98.09 %
[7]	Financial statement fraud with managerial statements	Text mining with singular validation decomposition vector	95.65 %

(*Continued*)

Table 2. (*Continued*)

Research	Fraud investigated	Method investigated	Sensitivity
[4]	Financial statement fraud with financial items from a selection of public Chinese companies	CDA	61.96 %
		CART	72.40 %
		Neural network (exhaustive pruning)	80.83 %
[16]	Credit card fraud using legitimate customer transaction history as well as generic fraud transactions	Bayesian learning with Dempster-Shafer combination	71–83 %
[9]	Financial statement fraud from Accounting and Auditing Enforcement Releases by the Securities and Exchange Commission	Genetic algorithm	13–27 %
[25]	Transactional fraud in automated bank machines and point of sale from a financial institution	Coevolution artificial immune system	97.688–98.266 %
		Standard evolution artificial immune system	92.486–95.376 %

Several of the research focussed on a single form of fraud detection which they advocated above others, such as studying text mining with the singular validation decomposition vector [7], self-organising maps [18], logistic regression [17, 23], and fuzzy logic [20]. Additionally, some researchers focussed solely on classification and regression trees [1], Bayesian belief networks [8], individual statistical techniques [16], or their own hybrid methods [6]. This unilateral approach is useful for demonstrating the ability of the specific method in isolation, but without comparing it to other methods it is difficult to understand the relative performance of the technique. Additional factors such as the fraud type researched and the specific dataset used can influence the results of the experiment. Future research could focus on reviewing these methods against other more established techniques.

A rising trend in fraud detection is the use of hybrid methods which utilise the strengths of multiple algorithms to classify samples. Duman and Ozcelik used a combination of scatter search and genetic algorithm, based on the latter but targeting attributes of scatter search such as the smaller populations and recombination as the reproduction method [6]. A different approach was taken by Panigrahi et al. who used two methods sequentially, beginning with the Depster-Schaefer method to combine rules and then using a Bayesian learner to detect the existence of fraud [16]. Some researchers applied fuzzy logic to introduce variation to their samples, attempting to transform it to resemble real world data before deploying a different technique to actually detect the presence of fraud [11]. The investigators recognised that applying

Table 3. Specificity results for fraud detection practices

Research	Fraud investigated	Method investigated	Specificity
[3]	Credit card transaction fraud from a real world example	Logistic model (regression)	96.7–99.8 %
		Support vector machines	95.7–99.8 %
		Random forests	97.9–99.8 %
[12]	Financial statement fraud from a selection of Greek manufacturing firms	Decision trees	72.5 %
		Neural networks	77.5 %
		Bayesian belief networks	88.9 %
[19]	Financial statement fraud with financial items from a selection of public Chinese companies	Support vector machine	70.41–73.41 %
		Genetic programming	89.27–94.14 %
		Neural network (feed forward)	75.32–78.77 %
		Group method of data handling	88.34–95.18 %
		Logistic model (regression)	70.66–78.88 %
		Neural network (probabilistic)	94.07–98.09 %
[7]	Financial statement fraud with managerial statements	Text mining with singular validation decomposition vector	95.65 %
[4]	Financial statement fraud with financial items from a selection of public Chinese companies	CDA	80.77 %
		CART	72.36 %
		Neural network (exhaustive pruning)	73.45 %
[9]	Financial statement fraud from Accounting and Auditing Enforcement Releases by the Securities and Exchange Commission	Genetic algorithm	98 %–100 %
[25]	Transactional fraud in automated bank machines and point of sale from a financial institution	Coevolution artificial immune system	95.862–97.122 %
		Standard evolution artificial immune system	99.311 %

'fuzziness' to their problem increased the performance of their solution [25]. Similarly, several researchers combined traditional computational intelligence methods with text mining to analyse financial statements for the presence of fraud [5, 10].

Remarks: Based on our investigation, it is apparent that neural networks and statistical algorithms have continued to remain popular through recent years, while hybrid methods are a rising trend in financial fraud detection, combining the strengths of multiple techniques.

2.3   Classification Based on Fraud Type

Given the varying nature of each type of fraud, the problem domain can differ significantly depending on the form that is being detected. By classifying the existing practices on the type of fraud investigated we can identify the techniques more suitable and more commonly used for a specific type of fraud. Additionally we can infer the varieties which are considered the most important for investigation depending on the scope and scale of their impact. Table 5 depicts the classification based on fraud types considered, along with the detection methods used.

With each chosen algorithm, feature selection will differ depending on the problem domain. Specific financial statement fraud exists within individual companies, and as such attribute ratios are used instead of absolute values. Koh and Low provide a good example of the relevant ratios such as net income to total assets, interest payments to earnings before interest and tax, and market value of equity to total assets [13]. In comparison, research into credit card fraud has typically selected independent variables or aggregate values which may be quantitative or qualitative. For example, Bhattacharyya et al. made use of transaction amount, categorical values such as account number, transaction date, and currency, and aggregated properties like total transaction amount per day, and average amount spent at a single merchant [3].

We can see that the existing research has been greatly unbalanced in fraud type studied. The vast majority of research has focussed on two forms of financial fraud: *credit card fraud* and *financial statement fraud*. Only a handful of studies have looked at securities and commodities fraud; also many studies focus on external forms of corporate fraud while neglecting the internal ones [11]. Ngai et al. found that insurance fraud had received the highest coverage during their research [14]: the fact that we identified only a few examples of published literature on this type of fraud since 2007 indicates that research into insurance fraud is declining. Additionally, no studies have been performed directly on mortgage fraud or money laundering. The reason for this disparity may be the differing relevance to stakeholders of each fraud type.

Remarks: Through our investigation we observe a significant imbalance in fraud type studied, with the majority focussing on either financial statement fraud or credit card fraud. Other forms of corporate fraud have received little attention, and hardly any studies have been done into mortgage fraud or money laundering.

Table 4. Classification based on detection algorithm used

Method investigated	Relevant method properties	Fraud Investigated	Research
Neural network	Capable of adapting to new trends, able to handle problems with no algorithmic solution. Typically used for classification and prediction	Financial statement fraud	[4, 12, 19]
Logistic model	Suitable for categorical classification problems	Credit card fraud Insurance fraud	[3] [2, 17, 23]

(Continued)

Table 4. (*Continued*)

Method investigated	Relevant method properties	Fraud Investigated	Research
	like fraud detection. Typically used for regression	Financial statement fraud	[19]
Support vector machine	Able to handle unbalanced data and complicated relationships between variables. Typically used for classification and prediction	Credit card fraud Financial statement fraud	[3, 24] [19]
Decision trees, forests and CART	Easy to use and has a well-documented ability with similar problems. Typically used for classification and prediction	Credit card fraud Financial statement fraud	[3, 24] [1, 4, 12]
Genetic algorithm/programming	Suitable for binary classification as the fitness function can be the accuracy of the population. Typically used for classification	Financial statement fraud	[9, 19]
Text mining	Capable of studying plain text, which offers a new dimension to the problem. Typically used for clustering and anomaly detection	Financial statement fraud	[5, 7]
Group method of data handling	Provides many of the same benefits as neural networks. Typically used for prediction	Financial statement fraud	[19]
Response-surface methodology	Useful for determining which method is best applied to the problem domain	Financial statement fraud	[29]
Self-organizing map	Provide both clustering and classification abilities, similarly to neural networks. Typically used for classification and clustering	Credit card fraud	[18, 20]
Bayesian belief network	Structured and formulaic, used extensively in	Insurance fraud Corporate fraud	[2] [8]

(*Continued*)

Table 4. (*Continued*)

Method investigated	Relevant method properties	Fraud Investigated	Research
	other problems with good results. Typically used for prediction and anomaly detection	Financial statement fraud	[12]
Process mining	Objective and able to work well with large samples of existing data. Typically used for anomaly detection	Securities and commodities fraud	[11]
Artificial immune system	Utilises binary matching rules, shown to be very powerful when paired with fuzzy logic. Typically used for anomaly detection	Credit card fraud	[25]
Hybrid methods	Combines the strengths of multiple standard algorithms into a new, superior method. Can be used for any combination of classification, clustering, prediction, regression, and anomaly detection	Credit card fraud Financial statement fraud	[6, 15, 16] [5, 10]
All/generic	Allows the comparison of multiple methods on a specific problem to discover the benefits and negatives of each. Can be used for any combination of classification, clustering, prediction, regression, and anomaly detection	All/generic	[14, 28]

3   Financial Fraud Detection: Challenges and Future Directions

Financial fraud detection is an evolving field in which it is desirable to stay ahead of the perpetrators. Additionally, it is evident that there are still facets of intelligent fraud detection that have not been investigated. In this section we present some of the key issues associated with financial fraud detection and suggest areas for future research. Some of the identified issues and challenges are as follows:

- *Typical classification problems:* CI and data mining-based financial fraud detection is subject to the same issues as other classification problems, such as feature selection, parameter tuning, and analysis of the problem domain.
- *Fraud types and detection methods:* Financial fraud is a diverse field and there has been a large imbalance in both fraud types and detection methods studied: some have been studied extensively while others, such as hybrid methods, have only been looked at superficially.
- *Privacy considerations:* Financial fraud is a sensitive topic and stakeholders are reluctant to share information on the subject. This has led to experimental issues such as undersampling.
- *Computational performance:* As a high-cost problem it is desirable for financial fraud to be detected immediately. Very little research has been conducted on the computational performance of fraud detection methods for use in real-time situations.
- *Evolving problem:* Fraudsters are continually modifying their techniques to remain undetected. As such detection methods are required to be able to constantly adapt to new fraud techniques.
- *Disproportionate misclassification costs:* Fraud detection is primarily a classification problem with a vast difference in misclassification costs. Research on the performance of detection methods with respect to this factor is an area which needs further attention.
- *Generic framework:* Given that there are many varieties of fraud, a generic framework which can be applied to multiple fraud categories would be valuable.

As a classification problem, financial fraud detection suffers from the same issues as other similar problems. Feature selection has a high impact on the success of any classification method. While some researchers have mentioned feature selection for one type of fraud [3, 13], no comparisons have been made between features for differing

Table 5. Classification based on fraud type investigated

Fraud type	Method applied	Research on the type of fraud
Credit card	Support vector machines; Decision tree; Self-organising maps; Fuzzy logic; Artificial immune system; Hybrid methods	[3] investigated credit card fraud from an international operation; [18] investigated a banking database from the Singapore branch of a well-known international bank; [20] investigated fraud in multinational department stores; [6] investigated typical consumer spending to determine fraud in a major

(Continued)

Table 5. (*Continued*)

Fraud type	Method applied	Research on the type of fraud
		bank in Turkey; [16] investigated variation in legitimate customer transaction behaviour with synthesised credit card data; [25] investigated automated bank machines and point of sale from an anonymous financial institution; [24] investigated credit card transactions
Securities and commodities and other Corporate	Bayesian belief network; process mining	[11] investigated internal transactional fraud from a successful, anonymous European financial institution; [8] Investigated emails and discussion group messages to detect corporate fraud
Insurance Fraud	Logistic model	[2, 17] and [23] all investigated motor insurance claims from Spanish insurance companies
Financial statement	Response-surface methodology; Neural networks; Decision trees; Bayesian belief networks; Support vector machine; Genetic algorithms; Group method of data handling; Logistic model (regression); Text mining; Hybrid methods	[29] investigated financial statement fraud in general; [12] investigated a selection of Greek manufacturing firms; [1, 4], and [19] investigated a series of public Chinese companies; [7] and [10] investigated managerial statements from official company documents; [5] and [9] investigated Accounting and Auditing Enforcement Releases authored by a selection of US companies

problem domains. Also, one of the major benefits of the computational intelligence and data mining methods is their ability to be adjusted to fit the problem domain. Existing research has rarely used any form of customisation or tuning for specific problems; however, tuning is an important factor in the context of an algorithm's performance. For example, the number of nodes and internal layers within a neural network has a large impact on both accuracy and computational performance. Similarly the kernel function chosen will considerably alter the success of a support vector machine and parameters such as the fitness function, crossover method, and probability for mutation will impact the results of a genetic programming algorithm. Research on customisation or tuning of the computational methods is required to truly comprehend the ability of each method. Further, in other data mining cases the solution algorithm is selected based on its performance within the problem domain, which for financial fraud detection is the type of fraud investigated. Studies on the suitability of various methods for each fraud category are necessary to understand which attributes of each algorithm make them appropriate for detecting financial fraud.

From the existing literature it is apparent that there are some forms of fraud that have not been investigated as extensively as others. Financial statement fraud has been considerably investigated, which is understandable given its high profile nature, but there are other forms of fraud that have a significant impact on consumers. Credit card fraud often has a direct impact on the public and the recent increase in online transactions has led to a majority of the U.S. public being concerned with identity theft [3]. A benefit of this close relation to the user is that credit card fraud is typically detected quickly, which gives researchers access to large datasets of unambiguous transactions. Other forms of fraud which have not been covered in depth include money laundering, mortgage, and securities and commodities fraud. A lack of sufficient sample size may be the reason for the lack of research in these areas [14]. Future studies that focussed on these types of fraud detection would be beneficial.

The private nature of financial data has led to institutions being reluctant to share fraudulent information. This has had an affect both on the fraud types that have been investigated as well as the datasets used for the purpose. In the published literature many of the financial fraud simulations consisted of less than a few hundred samples, typically with comparable amounts of fraudulent and legitimate specimens. This is contrary to the realities of the problem domain, where fraud cases are far outweighed by legitimate transactions [3]. Undersampling the problem domain like this can cause biases in the data that do not accurately represent real-world scenarios [9]. There is a definite need for further studies with realistic samples to accurately depict the performance of each method [7].

Some forms of financial fraud occur very rapidly, such as credit card fraud. If a fraudster obtains an individual's credit card information it's very likely that they will use it immediately until the card limit is reached. The ability to detect fraud in real-time would be highly beneficial as it may be able to prevent the fraudster from making subsequent transactions. Computational performance is therefore a key factor to consider in fraud detection. Though some researchers have noted the performance of their particular methods [3, 18], most studies were simulations performed on test datasets. Further research focussing on the computational as well as classification performance is required.

Unlike many classification problems, fraud detection solutions must be capable of handling active attempts to circumvent them. As detection methods become more intelligent, fraudsters are also constantly upgrading their techniques. For example, in the last few decades credit card fraud has moved from individuals stealing or forging single cards to large-scale phone and online fraud perpetrated by organised groups [3]. It is therefore necessary for fraud detection methods to be capable of evolving to stay ahead of fraudsters. Some researchers have considered models for adaptive classification, however further research is required to fully develop these for use in practical fraud detection problems [30].

As explained previously fraud has a large cost to businesses. Additionally, fraud detection has associated costs: systems require maintenance and computational power, and auditors must be employed to monitor them and investigate when a potential fraud case is identified [12]. The expense of a false positive, in misclassifying a legitimate transaction as fraud, is typically far less than that of a false negative [14]. Insufficient study has been performed on the disproportionate nature of these costs, with attention typically focussing on the traditional classification performance methods outlined in Sect. 2.1. Considering the accuracy of each fraud detection method, focus should be on achieving an optimum balance for each technique such that the expense is smallest. Research specifically focused on finding this balance would add significant real-world value to financial fraud detection.

Given the diversity of common categories of fraud it would be useful to have some form of generic framework that could apply to more than one fraud category. Such a framework could be used to study the differences between various types of fraud, or even specific details such as differentiating between stolen and counterfeit credit cards [3]. A ubiquitous model could also be used to determine which specific fraud detection method is applicable given the problem domain. This approach has been investigated slightly with response surface methodology [30], but more detailed research is desirable.

4 Conclusion

Fraud detection is an important part of the modern finance industry. In this research, we have investigated the current practices in financial fraud detection using intelligent approaches, both statistical and computational. Though their performance differed, each technique was shown to be reasonably capable at detecting various forms of financial fraud. In particular, the ability of CI methods such as neural networks and support vector machines to learn and adapt to new situations is highly effective at defeating the evolving tactics of fraudsters.

There are still many aspects of intelligent fraud detection that have not yet been the subject of research. Some types of fraud, as well as some data mining methods, have been superficially explored but require future study to be completely understood. There is also the opportunity to examine the performance of existing methods by using customisation or tuning, as well as the potential to study cost benefit analysis of computational fraud detection. Finally, further research into the differences between each type of financial fraud could lead to a generic framework which would greatly enhance the scope of intelligent detection methods for this problem domain.

References

1. Bai, B., Yen, J., Yang, X.: False financial statements: characteristics of China's listed companies and CART detecting approach. Int. J. Inf. Technol. Decis. Making 7, 339–359 (2008)
2. Bermúdez, L., Pérez, J., Ayuso, M., Gómez, E., Vázquez, F.: A Bayesian dichotomous model with asymmetric link for fraud in insurance. Insur. Math. Econ. 42, 779–786 (2008)

3. Bhattacharyya, S., Jha, S., Tharakunnel, K., Westland, J.C.: Data mining for credit card fraud: a comparative study. Decis. Support Syst. **50**, 602–613 (2011)
4. Bose, I., Wang, J.: Data mining for detection of financial statement fraud in Chinese companies. In: Paper presented at the International Conference on Electronic Commerce, Administration, Society and Education, Hong Kong (15–17 August 2007)
5. Cecchini, M., Aytug, H., Koehler, G.J., Pathak, P.: Making words work: using financial text as a predictor of financial events. Decis. Support Syst. **50**, 164–175 (2010)
6. Duman, E., Ozcelik, M.H.: Detecting credit card fraud by genetic algorithm and scatter search. Expert Syst. Appl. **38**, 13057–13063 (2011)
7. Glancy, F.H., Yadav, S.B.: A computational model for financial reporting fraud detection. Decis. Support Syst. **50**, 595–601 (2011)
8. Holton, C.: Identifying disgruntled employee systems fraud risk through text mining: a simple solution for a multi-billion dollar problem. Decis. Support Syst. **46**, 853–864 (2009)
9. Hoogs, B., Kiehl, T., Lacomb, C., Senturk, D.: A genetic algorithm approach to detecting temporal patterns indicative of financial statement fraud. Intell. Syst. Account. Finan. Manag. **15**, 41–56 (2007)
10. Humpherys, S.L., Moffitt, K.C., Burns, M.B., Burgoon, J.K., Felix, W.F.: Identification of fraudulent financial statements using linguistic credibility analysis. Decis. Support Syst. **50**, 585–594 (2011)
11. Jans, M., van der Werf, J.M., Lybaert, N., Vanhoof, K.: A business process mining application for internal transaction fraud mitigation. Expert Syst. Appl. **38**, 13351–13359 (2011)
12. Kirkos, E., Spathis, C., Manolopoulos, Y.: Data mining techniques for the detection of fraudulent financial statements. Expert Syst. Appl. **32**, 995–1003 (2007)
13. Koh, H.C., Low, C.K.: Going concern prediction using data mining techniques. Manag. Auditing J. **19**, 462–476 (2004)
14. Ngai, E., Hu, Y., Wong, Y., Chen, Y., Sun, X.: The application of data mining techniques in financial fraud detection: a classification framework and an academic review of literature. Decis. Support Syst. **50**, 559–569 (2011)
15. Paasch, C.A.: Credit Card Fraud Detection Using Artificial Neural Networks Tuned by Genetic Algorithms. Hong Kong University of Science and Technology, Hong Kong (2010)
16. Panigrahi, S., Kundu, A., Sural, S., Majumdar, A.K.: Credit card fraud detection: a fusion approach using Dempster-Shafer theory and Bayesian learning. Inf. Fusion **10**, 354–363 (2009)
17. Pinquet, J., Ayuso, M., Guillen, M.: Selection bias and auditing policies for insurance claims. J. Risk Insur. **74**, 425–440 (2007)
18. Quah, J.T., Sriganesh, M.: Real-time credit card fraud detection using computational intelligence. Expert Syst. Appl. **35**, 1721–1732 (2008)
19. Ravisankar, P., Ravi, V., Raghava Rao, G., Bose, I.: Detection of financial statement fraud and feature selection using data mining techniques. Decis. Support Syst. **50**, 491–500 (2011)
20. Sánchez, D., Vila, M., Cerda, L., Serrano, J.-M.: Association rules applied to credit card fraud detection. Expert Syst. Appl. **36**, 3630–3640 (2009)
21. Sohl, J.E., Venkatachalam, A.: A neural network approach to forecasting model selection. Inf. Manag. **29**, 297–303 (1995)
22. Vatsa, V., Sural, S., Majumdar, A.: A game-theoretic approach to credit card fraud detection. In: Jajodia, S., Mazumdar, C. (eds.) ICISS 2005. LNCS, vol. 3803, pp. 263–276. Springer, Heidelberg (2005)
23. Viaene, S., Ayuso, M., Guillen, M., Van Gheel, D., Dedene, G.: Strategies for detecting fraudulent claims in the automobile insurance industry. Eur. J. Oper. Res. **176**, 565–583 (2007)

24. Whitrow, C., Hand, D.J., Juszczak, P., Weston, D., Adams, N.M.: Transaction aggregation as a strategy for credit card fraud detection. Data Min. Knowl. Disc. **18**, 30–55 (2009)
25. Wu, S.X., Banzhaf, W.: Combatting financial fraud: a coevolutionary anomaly detection approach. In: Proceedings of the 10th Annual Conference on Genetic and Evolutionary Computation, pp. 1673–80. ACM (2008)
26. Yang, W.-S., Hwang, S.-Y.: A process-mining framework for the detection of healthcare fraud and abuse. Expert Syst. Appl. **31**, 56–68 (2006)
27. Yeh, I., C-h, L.: The comparisons of data mining techniques for the predictive accuracy of probability of default of credit card clients. Expert Syst. Appl. **36**, 2473–2480 (2009)
28. Yue, D., Wu, X., Wang, Y., Li, Y., Chu, C.-H.: A review of data mining-based financial fraud detection research. In: International Conference on Wireless Communications, Networking and Mobile Computing, WiCom 2007, pp. 5519–22. IEEE Press (2007)
29. Zhang, D., Zhou, L.: Discovering golden nuggets: data mining in financial application. IEEE Trans. Syst. Man Cybern. Part C Appl. Rev. **34**, 513–522 (2004)
30. Zhou, W., Kapoor, G.: Detecting evolutionary financial statement fraud. Decis. Support Syst. **50**, 570–575 (2011)

Network Traffic Pattern Analysis Using Improved Information Theoretic Co-clustering Based Collective Anomaly Detection

Mohiuddin Ahmed[✉] and Abdun Naser Mahmood

School of Engineering and Information Technology, UNSW Canberra,
Canberra, ACT 2600, Australia
Mohiuddin.Ahmed@student.adfa.edu.au, Abdun.Mahmood@unsw.edu.au

Abstract. Collective anomaly is a pattern in the data when a group of similar data instances behave anomalously with respect to the entire dataset. Clustering is a useful unsupervised technique to identify the underlying pattern in the data as well as anomaly detection. However, existing clustering based techniques have high false alarm rates and consider individual data instance behaviour for anomaly detection. In this paper, we formulate the problem of detecting DoS (Denial of Service) attacks as collective anomaly detection and propose a mathematically logical criteria for selecting the important traffic attributes for detecting collective anomaly. Information theoretic co-clustering algorithm is advantageous over regular clustering for creating more fine-grained representation of the data, however lacks the ability to handle mixed attribute data. We extend the co-clustering algorithm by incorporating the ability to handle categorical attributes which augments the detection accuracy of DoS attacks in benchmark KDD cup 1999 network traffic dataset than the existing techniques.

Keywords: Network traffic analysis · Information theory · Co-clustering · Collective anomaly detection · Pattern mining

1 Introduction

Internet is a modern day communication platform which provides a diverse range of services. Applications like e-mail, real time video and voice communication, file transfers and storage, web based contents are the most common applications on Internet. Consequently, there is a growing demand for efficient algorithms to detect important trends and anomalies in network traffic data. For example, network managers need to understand user behavior in order to plan network capacity.

One important concern in today's networking environment is Internet security. The network administrators have to handle a large variety of intrusion attempts by individuals with malicious intent [1]. Although research in security domain is growing significantly, the threats are yet to be mitigated. According

J. Tian et al. (Eds.): SecureComm 2014, Part II, LNICST 153, pp. 204–219, 2015.
DOI: 10.1007/978-3-319-23802-9_17

to Symantec Internet Security Threat Report, 2013 is considered as a year of mega breach and the size of DoS attacks underwent a rapid increase [2]. Stuxnet stands out of all because of the destructive and malicious behavior, discovered in June 2010 [3]. The technology giant Google was also attacked along with numerous other companies in 2010 [5]. With the increasing number of cyber security experts, the number of individual with detrimental motif is also raising. According to Verizon's Data Breach Investigation Report 2014, 63437 security incidents were carried out by hackers [4]. In addition to that, the expertise required to commit such crimes have decreased due to easily available tools. So, the detection of network attacks has become the highest priority in today's Internet. In this paper, we present a co-clustering scheme for identifying significant traffic flow patterns such as DoS(denial of service) attacks. The contributions in this paper can be summarized as follows-

- We propose a novel framework for the detection of the DoS(denial of service) attacks.
- The characteristics of DoS attacks are analysed and considered as collective anomaly (a group of similar data instances behaving abnormal) unlike the traditional anomaly detection techniques [6–8] where an individual data instance is considered as anomalous.
- We propose a method for selecting the important traffic attributes for detecting collective anomaly.
- Additionally, we extend the co-clustering algorithm [9,10] by incorporating the ability to handle categorical attributes which augments the detection accuracy of DoS attacks in benchmark KDD cup 1999 network traffic dataset [11] than the existing techniques.

The roadmap of this paper is as follows. In Sect. 2, we describe the anomaly detection and different aspects of it. Section 3 contains the formulation of anomaly detection problem for network traffic analysis and a framework for important network traffic attribute selection. In Sect. 4, we discuss the information theoretic co-clustering and our proposed extension incorporating the ability to handle categorical data. Section 5 contains the analysis of the experimental results on benchmark KDD cup 1999 intrusion detection dataset [11] and followed by related works in Sect. 6. We conclude our paper stating the future works in Sect. 7.

2 Anomaly Detection and Network Traffic Analysis

In this Section we provide a brief discussion on traditional anomaly detection and categories of anomaly. Next, we describe various assumptions of anomaly detection for network traffic analysis.

2.1 Different Types of Anomaly

Anomaly detection is an important aspect of data mining, where the main objective is to identify anomalous or unusual data from a given dataset. Anomaly detection is interesting because it involves automatically discovering interesting and rare patterns from datasets. Anomaly detection has been widely studied in statistics and machine learning, also known as outlier detection, deviation detection, novelty detection, and exception mining [12]. Anomalies are considered to be important because they indicate significant but rare events, and they can prompt critical actions to be taken in a wide range of application domains. For example, an anomaly in an MRI image may indicate the presence of a malignant tumour. Similarly, abnormal behaviour in a credit card transaction could indicate fraudulent activities, an unusual traffic pattern in a network could mean that a computer is hacked or under attack, e.g., using worms and Denial of Service attacks. An important aspect of anomaly detection is the nature of anomaly. Anomalies can be categorized in the following ways.

1. **Point Anomaly:** When a particular data instance deviates from the normal pattern of the dataset, it can be considered as a point anomaly. For a realistic example, we can consider expenditure on car fuel. If the usual car fuel usage of a person is five litres/day but if it becomes fifty litres in any random day then it is a point anomaly.
2. **Contextual Anomaly:** When a data instance is behaving anomalous in a particular context, but not in other context, then it is termed as a contextual anomaly, or conditional anomalies. For example, the expenditure on credit card during a festive period, e.g., Christmas or New Year, is usually higher than the rest of the year. Although, the expenditure during a festive month can be high, it may not be anomalous due to the high expenses being contextually normal in nature. On the other hand, an equally high expense during a non-festive month could be deemed as a contextual anomaly.
3. **Collective Anomaly:** When a collection of similar data instances are behaving anomalously with respect to the entire data set, then this collection is termed as collective anomaly. It might happen that the individual data instance is not an anomaly by itself, but due to its presence in a collection it is identified as an anomaly [13].

2.2   Anomaly in Network Traffic and Assumptions

Reliance on computer network and the increasing connectivity of these networks also raised the probability of damage caused by various types of network attacks. Network attacks, also named as intrusions are difficult to detect and prevent networks, with security policies due to the rapid change of system and applications. Simply, a threat/attack refers to anything which has the detrimental characteristics to compromise a host or network. Poor design of network, carelessness of users, misconfiguration of software or hardware cause the vulnerabilities. According to Kendall et al. [14], the attacks can be classified into four major categories discussed below.

– **Denial of Service (DoS):** It is a type of misuse of the rights to the resources of a network or a host. These are targeted to disrupt the normal computing environment and make the service unavailable. A simple example of DoS attack is denial of access to a web service to legitimate users, when the server is flooded with numerous connection requests. Performing DoS attack need no prior access to the target and thus considered to be a dreaded attack (Fig. 1 illustrates the DoS attack execution)

- **Probe:** These attacks are used to gather information about a target network or host. More formally, these attacks are used for reconnaissance purpose. The reconnaissance attacks are quite common for gathering information about types and number of machines connected to a network, a host can be attacked to find out the types of softwares installed or application used. The probe attacks are considered as first step of an actual attack to compromise the host or network. There is no specific damage caused by these attacks but considered as serious threat to any corporation because it might give useful information to launch another dreadful attack.

- **User to Root:** When the attacker aims to gain illegal access to administrative account to manipulate or abuse important resources, user to root attacks are launched. To launch such attacks, using social engineering approaches or sniffing password, the attacker access a normal user account. Then exploits some vulnerability to gain the super user privilege.

- **Remote to Local:** When an attacker wants to gain local access as an user of a targeted machine, the R2L attacks are launched. The attacker have the privilege to send packets over network to the target machine. Most commonly the attacker tries hit and trial password guessing by automated scripts, brute force method etc. There are also some sophisticated attacks where attacker installs a sniffing tool to capture password before penetrating the system

Fig. 1. DoS attack execution. The attacker is labelled red and a huge amount of special requests are sent to the server to make the service unavailable to other legitimate users (labelled green), adapted from Internet [15] (Color figure online)

It is a research challenge to efficiently identify such attacks/intrusions in network traffic to prevent the network from probable damages. Anomaly detection is one such technique to identify abnormal behaviour and analyse further. The basic assumptions for anomaly detection from network traffic are as follows-

- **Assumption 1:** *'The majority of the network connections are normal traffic, only a small percentage of traffic are malicious'*[16].
- **Assumption 2:** *'The attack traffic is statistically different from normal traffic'* [17].

In recent years, the traditional philosophy of using a knowledge base or external supervision is superseded by unsupervised anomaly detection. Unsupervised anomaly detection techniques are based on purely fundamental topics of data mining such as clustering. Without relying on expert supervision, unsupervised anomaly detection uses clustering techniques to divulge the underlying structure of unlabelled data as well as unknown behaviour. The clustering based anomaly detection follows similar assumptions as below-

- **Premise 1:** We can create clusters of normal data only, subsequently, any new data that do not fit well with existing clusters of normal data are considered as anomalies. For example, density based clustering algorithms do not include noise inside the clusters. Here noise is considered as anomalous.
- **Premise 2:** When a cluster contains both normal and anomaly data, it has been found that normal data lie close to the nearest cluster centroid but anomalies are far away from the centroids [6]. Under this assumption, anomalous events are detected using a distance score. For example, Mohiuddin et al. [6] considered an outlier according to a points distance from its centroid. If the distance is a multiple of mean distances of all other data points from the centroid then it is considered as an outlier. Formally, *'an object o in set of n objects is an outlier if the distance between o and the centroid is greater than to p times the mean of the distances between centroid and other objects'*. They also showed that removing outliers from clusters can significantly improve clustering objective function.
- **Premise 3:** In a clustering where there are clusters of various sizes, smaller and sparser can be considered as anomalous and dense clusters can be considered normal. The instances belonging to clusters whose size and/or density is below a threshold are considered as anomalous. Amer et al. [7] introduced Local Density Cluster-Based Outlier Factor (LDCOF) which can be considered as a variant of CBLOF [8]. The LDCOF score Eq. (4) is calculated as the distance to the nearest large cluster divided by the average distance to the cluster center of the elements in that large cluster. LDCOF score will be **A** when $p \in C_i \in SC$ where $C_j \in LC$ and **B** when $p \in C_i \in LC$.

$$distance_{avg}(C) = \frac{\sum_{i \in C} d(i, C)}{|C|} \tag{1}$$

$$A = \frac{min(d(p, C_j))}{distance_{avg}(C_j)} \tag{2}$$

$$B = \frac{d(p, C_i)}{distance_{avg}(C_i)} \tag{3}$$

$$LDCOF(p) = A \mid B; \tag{4}$$

3 DoS Attack as Collective Anomaly and Relevant Attribute Selection

In this Section, we discuss more about the how DoS attack can be considered as collective anomaly and propose a criteria for finding the relevant attributes for their detection. At first, we look at the data distribution of the benchmark KDD cup 1999 network intrusion dataset to understand the impact of these aforementioned attacks. The rationale behind using this dataset is quite logical in a sense that, the taxonomy used to classify attack types for intrusion detection evaluation is relevant today regardless of the advent of newer attacks. Additionally the scarcity of labelled network traffic datasets for intrusion detection evaluation is a major issue. Although being outdated, this dataset has been used widely for benchmarking purposes [18].

3.1 DoS Attack as Collective Anomaly

From Table 1, it is evident that, the Probe, R2L and U2R attack types are quite insignificant in size and traditional machine learning approaches shown poor performance on these rare classes of attack [19,20]. However, in this paper we are addressing the issue of detecting the DoS attacks as collective anomaly. Following the data distribution of KDD cup 1999 dataset and the anomaly detection assumptions discussed previously (Sect. 2.2), we observe a complete mismatch. For network traffic analysis, DoS attacks do not follow these assumptions. Considering the characteristics of DoS attack and the size we can come to a conclusion that, DoS attack can be considered as a group of network traffic instances affecting the network as well as collective anomaly (Sect. 2.1). DoS attack has few variants and can be classified into two major groups based on their distribution. There are six variants of DoS attack as follows-

- **Back:** It is an attack against the Apache web server.
- **Land:** It is an effective attack where the attacker sends a packet with same source and destination address.
- **Neptune:** This attack makes the TCP/IP implementations vulnerable.
- **POD:** In *ping of death* attack, the size of ICMP packets are longer than 64000 bytes.
- **Smurf:** When there is a large number of 'echo replies' sent to a machine without any 'echo request' can be considered as Smurf attack.
- **Teardrop:** This attack has the ability to exploit the flaws in the implementations of IP fragmentation re-assembly code.

Table 1. Class distribution of KDD Cup 1999 dataset [11]

Class Label	Full training dataset (%age)	10 % of Training dataset (%age)	Test dataset (%age)
DoS	79.28	79.24	73.9
Probe	0.84	0.83	1.34
U2	0.001	0.01	0.02
R2L	0.023	0.23	5.26
Normal	19.86	19.69	19.48

The Table 2 displays the distribution of different types of DoS attack in KDD cup dataset. Considering the volume of DoS attack and their characteristics, we can come to an understanding that, DoS attack cannot be treated as point anomaly and in this regard treating the same as collective anomaly is a better idea for more accurate results.

Table 2. DoS attack distribution of KDD Cup 1999 dataset [11]

Attack	No. of instance
Smurf	280790
Neptune	10720
Back	2203
Teardrop	979
POD	264
Land	21

From the Table 2, it is evident that there exists predominant two classes of DoS attack based on the size. We can also summarize in the way that, clustering these different attacks will result in two classes. Next, we discuss the technique to select the attributes responsible for differentiating DoS from normal traffic.

3.2 Traffic Attribute Selection

In this Section, we investigate the behaviour of DoS and normal traffic attributes. Since, there is a huge amount of network traffic corresponding to DoS attack, we can consider the similarity in instances and the difference in standard deviation between the normal and DoS instances as important factor for attribute selection. It is mathematically logical that, if there are more similar instance in a group then the difference of standard deviation will be less with the other group with smaller number of similar instances. Lets give an example to show that our hypothesis. Consider the dataset D has two attributes and contains only DoS and normal instances. Now, as we know, DoS attack is a collective anomaly and outnumber the normal instances, we need to identify the attributes which play important role for differentiating DoS and normal instances. Additionally, these huge number of traffic instances are linearly scaled between [0,1] for avoiding the impact of distance function of clustering algorithms. Let A and B be two attributes where A = (1,....,100000) and B = (1,....,100). The range is defined as range(i) = max(i)- min(i), consequently the range(A) = 100000 and range(B) = 100. When Euclidean distance Eq. (5) will be used for clustering the dataset, the attribute A will have a greater impact than the attribute B. Table 3 displays the sample dataset where instances corresponding to DoS and normal are labelled.

$$D(C_1, C_2)) = \sqrt{\sum_{i=1}^{d} D_i(C_1, C_2)^2} \qquad (5)$$

Table 3. Sample dataset

Label	A1	A2
DoS	0.11	0.88
DoS	0.33	0.11
DoS	0.44	0.33
DoS	0.55	0.44
DoS	0.88	0.11
Normal	0.11	0.94
Normal	0.94	0.33
Normal	0.22	0.11

In the Table 3, the similarity of instances between DoS and normal for attribute A1 is 1 and for A2 is 2. The standard deviation difference between DoS and normal for attribute A1 is 0.1661 and for A2 is 0.1453. In Eq. (6) *Sim* indicates the number of similar instances in DoS and normal. In Eq. (7) *Stdev* indicates the standard deviation Eq. (8) and *d* is the difference.

$$Sim_{A1}(DoS, Normal) < Sim_{A2}(DoS, Normal) \qquad (6)$$

$$d(Stdev_{A1}(DoS, Normal)) > d(Stdev_{A2}(DoS, Normal)) \qquad (7)$$

$$\sigma = \sqrt{\frac{1}{N} \sum_{i=1}^{N} (x_i - \mu)^2} \qquad (8)$$

Once we have the similarity and difference in standard deviation for the original dataset, clustering algorithm is applied to find out the underlying pattern from the data with $D(Sim_i, d_i)$, where $i=1$ to n, the number of attributes in the dataset. Here we propose to apply *x-means* clustering algorithm which is a variant of basic *k-means* and use bayesian information criterion Eq. (9) to identify the number of clusters in the data [13]. Where l_j (D) is the log-likelihood of the data according to the j_{th} model and taken at the maximum likelihood point, p_j is the number of parameters in M_j, which refers to a family of alternative models. R refers to the size of dataset D.

$$BIC(M_j) = l_j(D) - \frac{p_j}{2} \times \log R \qquad (9)$$

Now, the cluster with lowest similarity and highest difference in standard deviation contains the expected attribute set of the data which can be used for differentiating DoS attack as well as collective anomaly from the normal instances with better accuracy than using the attributes which can exacerbate the detection accuracy. (Sect. 5.1 includes more details on the experimental analysis)

4   Improved Information Theoretic Co-clustering

In this Section, we briefly discuss about the co-clustering technique at first, then we describe the information theoretic co-clustering framework. Finally, we highlight the issue of mixed attribute dissimilarity measure for co-clustering and integrate such measure for information theoretic co-clustering to improve it's ability to handle network traffic.

4.1   Co-clustering

Co-clustering can be simply considered as a simultaneous clustering of both rows and columns. Co-clustering can produce a set of **c** column clusters of the original columns **C** and a set of **r** row clusters of original row instances **R**. Unlike other clustering algorithms, co-clustering also defines a clustering criterion and then optimizes it. In a nutshell, co-clustering finds out the subsets of rows and columns simultaneously of a data matrix using a specified criterion. Co-clustering has been widely applied in various application domain such as text clustering, gene-microarray analysis, natural language processing and many more [10]. The benefits of co-clustering over the regular clustering are the following-

1. Simultaneous grouping of both rows and columns can provide a more compressed representation and preserve information contained in the original data.
2. Co-clustering can be considered as a dimensionality reduction technique and suitable for creating new features.
3. Significant reduction in computational complexity. For example, traditional *k-means* algorithm has the $\mathcal{O}(mnk)$ as computational complexity where $m=$ number of rows, $n =$ number of columns and k is the number of clusters. But in co-clustering the computational complexity is $\mathcal{O}(mkl + nkl)$, here l is the number of column clusters. Obviously $\mathcal{O}(mnk) \gg \mathcal{O}(mkl + nkl)$.

4.2 Information Theoretic Co-clustering

Information theoretic co-clustering is first proposed by Dhillon [9] where it is modeled as the joint probability distribution. According to their approach an optimal co-clustering confirms the loss minimization of 'Mutual Information' as follows in Eq. (10).

$$min(I(X;Y) - I(\hat{X};\hat{Y})) \tag{10}$$

Banerjee et al. [10] pointed out that the information theoretic co-clustering uses the joint probability distribution which may not be known and calculated from contingency table or co-occurrence matrix. Additionally the data matrix may contain negative entries and distortion measure other than KL-divergence may be more appropriate. Banerjee et al. [10] extended the information theoretic co-clustering [9] in three directions as follows-

- Nearness is measured by Bregman divergence.
- Allows multiple co-clustering schemes.
- Generalization of maximum entropy approach.

Bregman co-clustering tries to minimize the information loss in the approximation of a data matrix X, in terms of a predefined bregman divergence function. For a given co-clustering (R, C) and a matrix approximation scheme M, a class of random variables which store the characteristics of data matrix X is defined. The objective function tries to minimize the information loss on the approximation of X for a co-clustering R, C. The Bregman information of X can be defined as follows

$$I_\phi(X) = E\left[log\left(\frac{X}{E[X]}\right)\right] \tag{11}$$

Here, the matrix approximation scheme is defined by the expected value and the bregman divergence d_ϕ for a optimal co-clustering as follows

$$(R^*, C^*) = arg\ min\ E[d_\phi(X, X)] \tag{12}$$

Here, d_ϕ, can be considered in two ways as follows.

$$\mathbf{I - Divergence} : d_\phi(x_1, x_2) = x_1 log(\frac{x_1}{x_2}) - (x_1 - x_2) \tag{13}$$

$$\mathbf{EuclideanDistance} : d_\phi(x_1, x_2) = (x_1 - x_2)^2 \tag{14}$$

4.3 Co-clustering Mixed Attribute Data

Since, we are inspired to use the co-clustering for network traffic analysis, we find that, these co-clustering techniques are not using any nearness measures for mixed attribute data instances such as the data matrix with both categorical and numerical data. However, network traffic instances contain both categorical and numerical data. For example, the protocols of traffic instances are categorical and port numbers are numerical in nature. In this scenario, we incorporate the mixed attribute distance measure for co-clustering network traffic as well as collective anomaly detection. There are various measures for similarity calculation of categorical data [21] but for simplicity we just consider that, the dissimilarity between two data instances is 1 when they mismatch and zero otherwise Eq. (15). The following Table 4 displays the concept for the network traffic protocols which are categorical data. As a whole, for numerical data, we simply use the Euclidean distance and for categorical data we consider the similar data instance has distance zero and dissimilar data has distance one Eq. (16).

Table 4. Nearness calculation for categorical data [21]

Label	TCP	UDP	ICMP
TCP	0	1	1
UDP	1	0	1
ICMP	1	1	0

$$D(X_k, Y_k) = \begin{cases} 0 \; if \; X_k = Y_k \\ 1 \; otherwise \end{cases} \quad [For \; Categorical \; data] \qquad (15)$$

$$[Mixed \; Attribute \; Distance \; Measure] \quad D(X,Y) = \sqrt{\sum_{k=1}^{d} D_k(X_k, Y_k)^2} \quad (16)$$

Consequently the distance between two traffic instances $d_1 = (TCP, 0.11, 0.78), d_2 = (ICMP, 0.33, 0.74)$ will be calculated as Eq. (16) $\sqrt{(TCP - ICMP)^2 + (0.11 - 0.33)^2 + (0.78 - 0.74)^2} = \sqrt{1 + 0.0484 + 0.0016} = 1.02$. As a result, bregman co-clustering is extended for handling dataset with both categorical and numerical data and is suitable for applying on network traffic datasets.

5   Experimental Analysis

As discussed earlier, we use the KDD cup 1999 dataset for the experimental evaluation. The first part of our experiment contains the attribute selection for collective anomaly detection and then we show the effectiveness of improved information theoretic co-clustering for network traffic analysis.

Table 5. Attribute selection results

Attributes	$Sim(DoS,Normal)$	$d_{stdev}(DoS, Normal)$
1-20,23,24,25,26,28,29,35,37	257	255.50
21,22,30,31	1056	111.05
27,32,33,34,36,38,39	536	115.10

5.1 Attribute Selection from KDD Cup 1999 for Collective Anomaly Detection

The KDD cup 1999 dataset has 41 attributes which can be classified into four main groups as the basic, time, host, content features. Since, we are using the normalized data which is linearly scaled between 0 and 1, it is important to use the attributes which has the ability to distinguish DoS attack from normal instances. We calculate the standard deviation of the DoS and normal data instances from labelled data and measure the difference as $d_{stdev}(DoS, Normal)$. Also, the number of similar number of data instances in both category of the data as $Sim(DoS,Normal)$. Then we apply x-$means$ algorithm on the dataset as x-$means(d_{stdev}(DoS, Normal), Sim(DoS,Normal))$. The following Table 5 depicts the results after the clustering and it is clear that, the cluster which has less similar data instances and higher standard deviation will be suitable group of attributes for collective anomaly detection. For the space scarcity, we represent the attributes with the numbers serially.

5.2 Collective Anomaly Detection Using Improved Co-clustering

Once we have the desired attribute set, next we apply the improved information theoretic co-clustering which can handle both the numeric and categorical data. Since, we are focusing on detecting DoS attacks and in Sect. 3.1 it was discussed that in KDD cup has predominant 2 groups of attack according to size. So, the input row as three for the co-clustering will be appropriate and based on the attributes the number of column clusters will be four. We consider the smaller cluster will be the cluster containing normal instances and the larger clusters as attack clusters or collective anomaly. We measure the accuracy of our approach using the standard confusion metrics. The metrics are listed as True Positive (TP = Attack correctly identified as attack.), False Positive (FP = Normal traffic incorrectly identified as attack.), True Negative (TN = Normal traffic correctly identified as normal), False Negative (FN = Attack incorrectly identified as normal.). Table 6 displays the possible test outcomes and the confusion metrics.

The accuracy is computed using Eq. (17).

$$Accuracy = \frac{TP + TN}{TP + TN + FP + FN} \tag{17}$$

We also consider the *Precision, Recall* and *F-measure* for evaluation. In pattern mining, precision is referred as the fraction of retrieved instances that are

Table 6. Standard confusion metrics

Actual traffic label	Normal	Attack
Normal	TN	FP
Attack	FN	TP

Table 7. Evaluation results

Accuracy	Precision	Recall	F-measure	Attack cluster purity	Normal cluster purity
92.82%	0.9236	0.9923	0.96	92.36%	95.6%

relevant, while recall is the fraction of relevant instances that are retrieved. F-measure combines precision and recall as the harmonic mean of precision and recall Eq. (18). We also consider cluster purity as another evaluation criterion Eq. (19).

$$F - measure = 2 * \frac{Precision * Recall}{Precision + Recall} \tag{18}$$

$$Cluster\ Purity = \frac{Number\ of\ Attack/Normal\ Instances}{Size\ of\ the\ cluster} \tag{19}$$

Table 7 contains the evaluation results of all the metrics discussed above. The experimental results are quite satisfactory, however, it is not worthy to compare our results with other clustering based techniques because the concept of collective anomaly detection is proposed by ourselves for the first time and not considered by others. The closest approach [1] which used co-clustering for network anomaly detection considered only cluster purity for evaluation and only seven numerical attributes for co-clustering. However, our proposed technique outperforms their approach with the cluster purity as well considering both normal and attack cluster purity (Table 8).

Table 8. Cluster purity comparison

Purity	Our proposed technique	Network anomaly detection using co-clustering [1]
Normal	95.6%	75.84%
Attack	92.36%	92.44%

6   Related Works

In this Section, we provide a brief description on the existing techniques for network anomaly detection. There are various approaches to deal with the network

Table 9. Network anomaly detection accuracy using clustering algorithm [23]

Algorithm	Accuracy	False positive
k-means	57.81 %	22.95 %
Improves k-means	65.40 %	21.52 %
k-medoids	76.71 %	21.83 %
EM clustering	78.06 %	20.74 %
Distance based outlier detection	80.15 %	21.14 %

anomaly detection, however we focus on the clustering based network anomaly detection since our approach is of this category.

To the best of our knowledge, we are the first to propose collective anomaly detection using co-clustering. Although in [1], co-clustering is used for anomaly detection however considered the numerical attributes for co-clustering. So, the comparison is not logical due to different set of attributes. Also, the cluster purity, accuracy of our approach is significantly better than their approach. Portnoy et al. [16] proposed clustering based on width to classify data instances. The width is a constant and remains same for all the clusters. Once the clustering is done, based on the assumption that normal instances constitute overwhelmingly large portion of the entire dataset, N percent of clusters are normal and other are anomalous. Using the assumption of Portnoy et al. [16], Kingsly et al. [22] proposed a density-based and grid-based clustering algorithm which is suitable for unsupervised anomaly detection. Iwan et al. [23] described the advantages of using the anomaly detection approach over the misuse detection technique in detecting unknown network intrusions or attacks. It also investigates the performance of various clustering algorithms when applied to anomaly detection (Shown in Table 9). Four different clustering algorithms: k-means, improved k-means, k-medoids, Expectation Maximization(EM) clustering and distance-based outlier detection algorithms are used. The anomaly detection module produced high false positive rate (more than 20 %) for all four clustering algorithms. None of these techniques considered collective anomaly detection and avoids the volume issue of DoS attacks, consequently performing poor than our proposed approach.

7 Conclusion

In this paper, we have proposed to solve the network intrusion detection problem using a set of emerging data mining and machine learning techniques. Our contribution includes detection of the DoS attacks due to its volume and detrimental impact on the network. The characteristics of these type of attacks are analysed and considered as collective anomaly unlike the traditional anomaly detection techniques. We propose a method for selecting the traffic attributes responsible for detecting collective anomaly. We also explore the effectiveness of information theoretic co-clustering algorithm which is advantageous over regular clustering for creating more fine-grained representation. Additionally, we extend the co-clustering algorithm by incorporating the ability to handle categorical attributes. Experimental results show that our proposed approach have better results on various evaluation metrics using benchmark KDD cup 1999 network traffic dataset than the existing techniques. In future, we will focus on creating concise and informative network traffic summaries using co-clustering techniques.

References

1. Papalexakis, E.E., Beutel, A., Steenkiste, P.: Network anomaly detection using co-clustering. In: Proceedings of the 2012 International Conference on Advances in Social Networks Analysis and Mining (ASONAM 2012), pp. 403–410. IEEE Computer Society, Washington, DC (2012)
2. Symantec Internet Security Threat Report. http://www.symantec.com/content/en/us/enterprise/
3. Stuxnet. http://www.stuxnet.net/
4. Verizon's Data Breach Investigation Report 2014. http://www.verizonenterprise.com/DBIR/2014/
5. Google hack attack was ultra sophisticated, new details show. http://www.wired.com/2010/01/operation-aurora/
6. Ahmed, M., Naser, A.: A novel approach for outlier detection and clustering improvement. In: 2013 8th IEEE Conference on Industrial Electronics and Applications (ICIEA), pp. 577–582 (2013)
7. Goldstein, M., Mennatallah A.: Nearest-neighbor and clustering based anomaly detection algorithms for rapidminer. In: Proceedings of the 3rd RapidMiner Community Meeting and Conference (RCOMM 2012), pp. 1–12. Shaker Verlag GmbH, Aachen, August 2012
8. He, Z., Xu, X., Deng, S.: Discovering cluster based local outliers. Pattern Recogn. Lett. **2003**, 9–10 (2003)
9. Dhillon, I.S., Mallela, S., Modha, D.S.: Information-theoretic co-clustering. In: Proceedings of the Ninth ACM SIGKDD International Conference on Knowledge Discovery and Data Mining, KDD 2003, pp. 89–98. ACM, New York (2003)
10. Banerjee, A., Dhillon, I., Ghosh, J., Merugu, S., Modha, D.S.: A generalized maximum entropy approach to Bregman co-clustering and matrix approximation. J. Mach. Learn. Res. **8**, 1919–1986 (2007)
11. 1999 kdd cup dataset. www.kdd.ics.uci.edu
12. Ahmed, M., Mahmood, A., Hu, J.: Outlier detection. In: The State of the Art in Intrusion Prevention and Detection, pp. 3–23. CRC Press, USA
13. Ahmed, M., Mahmood, A.: Network traffic analysis based on collective anomaly detection. In: 2014 IEEE 9th Conference on Industrial Electronics and Applications (ICIEA), pp. 1141–1146, June 2014
14. Kendall, K.: A database of computer attacks for the evaluation of intrusion detection systems. In: DARPA Off-line Intrusion Detection Evaluation, Proceedings of DARPA Information Survivality Conference and Eexposition (DISCEX), pp. 12–26 (1999)
15. How to survive botnet attacks - Understanding Botnets and DDOS attacks. https://www.youtube.com

16. Portnoy, L., Eskin, E., Stolfo, S.: Intrusion detection with unlabeled data using clustering. In: Proceedings of ACM CSS Workshop on Data Mining Applied to Security (DMSA-2001), pp. 5–8 (2001)
17. Valdes, A., Javitz, H.S.: The nides statistical component: description and justification. Technical report (1993)
18. Ahmed, M., Mahmood, A.N., Islam, M.R.: A survey of anomaly detection techniques in financial domain. Future Generation Computer Systems (2015)
19. Levin, I.: KDD-99 classifier learning contest LLSoft's results overview. SIGKDD Explor. Newsl. **1**(2), 67–75 (2000)
20. Agarwal, R., Joshi, M.V.: Pnrule: A new framework for learning classifier models in data mining (a case-study in network intrusion detection). Technical report, IBM Research Report, Computer Science/Mathematics (2000)
21. Boriah, S., Chandola, V., Kumar, V.: Similarity measures for categorical data: a comparative evaluation. In: Proceedings of the Eighth SIAM International Conference on Data Mining, pp. 243–254
22. Leung, K., Leckie, C.: Unsupervised anomaly detection in network intrusion detection using clusters. In: Proceedings of the Twenty-Eighth Australasian Conference on Computer Science, ACSC 2005, vol. 38, pp. 333–342. Australian Computer Society Inc, Darlinghurst (2005)
23. Syarif, I., Prugel-Bennett, A., Wills, G.: Unsupervised clustering approach for network anomaly detection. In: Benlamri, R. (ed.) NDT 2012, Part I. CCIS, vol. 293, pp. 135–145. Springer, Heidelberg (2012)

A Survey on Mining Program-Graph Features for Malware Analysis

Md. Saiful Islam[1]($\boxtimes$), Md. Rafiqul Islam[2], A.S.M. Kayes[1], Chengfei Liu[1], and Irfan Altas[3]

[1] Swinburne University of Technology, Melbourne, Australia
{mdsaifulislam,akayes,cliu}@swin.edu.au
[2] Charles Sturt University, Alburry, Australia
mislam@csu.edu.au
[3] Charles Sturt University, Wagga Wagga, Australia
ialtas@csu.edu.au

Abstract. Malware, which is a malevolent software, mostly programmed by attackers for either disrupting the normal computer operation or gaining access to private computer systems. A malware detector determines the malicious intent of a program and thereafter, stops executing the program if the program is malicious. While a substantial number of various malware detection techniques based on static and dynamic analysis has been studied for decades, malware detection based on mining program graph features has attracted recent attention. It is commonly believed that graph based representation of a program is a natural way to understand its semantics and thereby, unveil its execution intent. This paper presents a state of the art survey on mining program-graph features for malware detection. We have also outlined the challenges of malware detection based on mining program graph features for its successful deployment, and opportunities that can be explored in the future.

Keywords: Program graph · Graph features · Malware detection

1 Introduction

Malwares are one of the most severe problems witnessed by the modern computer society everyday. Malware is a malevolent software that either tries to disrupt the normal computer operation or gather sensitive information from private computer systems by spying on users' behavior and compromising their privacy. The malware writers also apply various code obfuscation techniques on previous malwares, changing their internal structures while keeping their original functionalities unchanged known as *polymorphic malwares*, to evade detection. The obfuscation techniques also facilitate widespread proliferation of various instances of the same malware without getting detected. David Perry from Trend Micro reported that some antivirus (AV) vendors are seeing 5,000 distinct malware samples per day [32]. A malware detector determines the malicious intent

© Institute for Computer Sciences, Social Informatics and Telecommunications Engineering 2015
J. Tian et al. (Eds.): SecureComm 2014, Part II, LNICST 153, pp. 220–236, 2015.
DOI: 10.1007/978-3-319-23802-9_18

of a program and thereafter, stops its execution if it is malicious. In malware detection based on mining graph features, a program graph is constructed by considering System and/or API calls, sub-programs and targets of jump instructions as nodes and their calling relationships as connections or links. A program graph may come in various formats and names, e.g., call graphs, control-flow graphs, code graphs etc. Once constructed, a program graph can be mined to extract important graph-based-features which can be intelligently learned into a classifier to detect malicious intent of the unknown program.

While a substantial number of malware detection techniques based on static and dynamic analysis has been studied for decades ([13,22] for survey), malware detection based on mining program graph features is not established yet. However, it is commonly believed that graphs can be used to represent complex program behavior efficiently [36], which may not be possible in traditional static and dynamic behavior analysis [12,18]. For example, code obfuscations are easily detectable through mining program graph features. Therefore, graph based representation of program behavior and thereby mining important graph features for malware detection has attracted recent attention [1,7,8,10–12,15,18,23,26, 28,34,41]. Though, a number of research efforts has been made for malware detection based on mining program graph features, this is still in its premature stage. In this survey paper, we report only representative and important state of the art research works that develop malware detection techniques based on mining program graph features. We also provide necessary background on malware detection based on program graph analysis and outline important research directions that can be explored in the future.

The main contributions of this survey paper are given as follows:

- We provide the background on the program graph, its construction and mining program graph features for malware detection.
- We present a survey on representative works that develop malware detection techniques based on mining program graph features.
- We provide a comparative study of the existing works under the variants of program graph and a summary of them.
- We outline the future challenges that need to be addressed for successful deployment of malware detectors based on mining program graph features.

The rest of the paper is organized as follows: Sect. 2 presents related surveys; Sect. 3 provides preliminaries on program graphs and mining program graph features; Sect. 4 describes the modules of a generalized malware detection system based on mining program graph features; Sect. 5 presents the surveyed works; Sect. 6 presents the limitation of the existing works and the future challenges of malware detection based on mining program graphs; and finally, Sect. 7 concludes the paper.

2   Related Surveys

Survey on Malware Analysis Techniques: In [37], Siddiqui et al. present a survey on malware detection based on data mining techniques. The surveyed works learn the detection model by mining the file features extracted from the binary programs. The authors categorize the surveyed works based upon the analysis type (static and dynamic) and detection type (misuse and anomaly). In [35], Shabtai et al. present a taxonomy of malware detection methods that rely on machine learning classifiers (which utilize static features extracted from executables) to detect malwares. The authors also address various aspects of the detection challenge such as file representation and feature selection methods, classification algorithms, weighting ensembles, the imbalance problem, active learning and chronological evaluation. In [17] Felt et al. survey the current state of mobile malware in the wild. The authors collect malware samples from iOS, Android, and Symbian mobile platforms to analyze the incentives and possible defenses of them. They classify collected malwares by analyzing their behavior and describe the incentives that actually promote each type of malicious behavior. They also present defenses that disincentivize some of the behaviors of these malwares. In [13], Egele et al. provide an overview of techniques based on dynamic analysis that are used to analyze potentially malicious samples.

Survey on Code Obfuscation Techniques: In [3], Balakrishnan and Schulze analyze the different code obfuscation techniques in connection with the protection of intellectual property and the hiding of malicious code. In [30], Majumder et al. provide an overview of obfuscation and highlight that the dispatcher model and opaque predicates transforms have provable security properties. In [46], You and Yim present a survey on malware obfuscation techniques by reviewing the encrypted, oligomorphic, polymorphic and metamorphic malwares.

Survey on Botnet Detection Techniques: A botnet is a collection of compromised computers, which are remotely controlled by hackers to perform various network attacks, such as denial-of-services and information phishing. In [16], Feily et al. present a literature survey on botnet and four classes of botnet detection techniques: (a) signature-based (b) anomaly-based (c) DNS-based and (d) mining-based. In [2], Bailey et al. provide a brief survey on existing botnet research, the development and trends of botnets as well as different types of networks that approach the botnet problem with differing goals and visibility. In [48], Zhang et al. survey the latest botnet attacks and defenses by introducing the principles of fast fluxing and domain fluxing, and explain how these techniques were employed by the botnet owners. In [38], Silva et al. presents a comprehensive survey on the botnet problem by briefly summarizing the previous works from the literature. Then, the authors supplement these works by covering an extensive range of discussion of recent works and providing solution proposals.

Survey on Intrusion Detection Techniques: In [19], Garcia-Teodoro et al. present a survey of the most well-known anomaly-based intrusion detection techniques. The authors also present the available platforms, systems under development and research projects in the area. Finally, the authors outline the main challenges that need to be addressed for the wide scale deployment of anomaly-based intrusion detectors. In [40], Tavallaee et al. review the experimental practice in the area of anomaly-based intrusion detection by surveying

276 studies published during the period of 2000–2008. Finally, the authors summarize their observations, e.g., why anomaly-based intrusion-detection methods are not adopted by the industry and identify the common pitfalls among the surveyed works.

To the best of our knowledge, there exists no other paper that provides a complete survey on program graphs and malware analysis based on mining graph features. The purpose of this paper is to provide a tutorial on program graphs and mining graph features, as well as survey the existing works that extract program graph features for malware analysis. We also summarize the limitation of existing works and give challenges to explore further in this direction.

3   Preliminaries

In this section, we present the generalized definition of program graph, properties and common features mined on such graphs.

Definition 1 *(Program Graph). A program graph, denoted by g, is represented as $g = (V, E, l_v, l_e)$, where V is the set of nodes and E is the set of links. A directed link (u, v) will be in E if there is a directed relationship from u to v, where both u and v is in V. The l_v denotes a labeling function that returns the label of the nodes in V, i.e., $l_v : V \to \Sigma_v$. The l_e denotes another labeling function that returns the label of the links in E, i.e., $l_e : E \to \Sigma_e$. A path p is a sequence of nodes $v_1, v_2, ..., v_k$ such that there is a link between the successive pair of nodes in this sequence. If the start and end nodes are the same, we call it a cycle c.*

The nodes in V may consist of system or API calls, targets of jump instructions, procedure calls and jump targets of a program, even a code fragment of a program including program instructions itself [7,15,24,28]. The links in E may represent the calling relationships (i.e., who calls whom) and/or information flows between nodes. The nodes and links are summarized in Table 1.

Table 1. Nodes and links of program graphs

Type	Value(s)
Nodes	System&API Calls, Procedure Calls, Jump Instructions, Targets of Jump, Code Fragments, Program Instructions
Links	Calling Relationships, Information Flows

The generalized definition of program graph given in Definition 1 can be made specific for call graphs, control-flow graphs (CFGs), code graphs etc. as shown in Fig. 1. The nodes and links in differ-

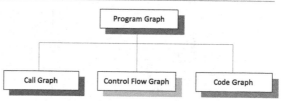

Fig. 1. Variants of program graph

ent variant of program graphs are shown in Table 2. An example of a program call graph (who-calls-whom), which is directed, is shown in Fig. 2.

Table 2. Nodes and links in different program graphs

Program graph	Nodes	Links	Σ_v	Σ_e
Call graph	Sub-functions, API/System Calls	$u \rightarrow v$ (u calls v), where u, v are nodes	Sub-function and API or System Call names	$l_v(u) \rightarrow l_v(v)$, where (u, v) is a link
Control-flow graph	Sub-functions, API/System Calls, Targets of jump-instructions	$u \rightarrow v$ (u calls v or u jumps to v), where u, v are nodes	Sub-function and API or System Call names, Jumps	$l_v(u) \rightarrow l_v(v)$, where (u, v) is a link
Code graph	Opcodes or Instructions	$u \rightarrow v$ (v follows u), where u, v are nodes	Opcode or Instruction names	$l_v(u) \rightarrow l_v(v)$, where (u, v) is a link

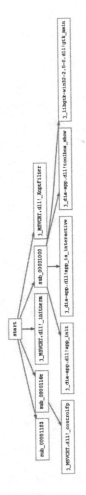

Fig. 2. A sample call (who-calls-whom) graph

The root node "start" in the call graph is the node from where execution begins and is the same for every program call graph. The success of a malware detector based on mining program graph features depends on the accurate construction of the corresponding program graph and the information encoded in it [24,27]. In [27], Kruegel et al. propose an approach for identifying the program control-flow-graph and program's instruction information based on its initial control flow graph and statistical methods. Generally, the construction of program graph is accomplished as a preprocessing step by the detectors [24].

Definition 2 (Graph Isomorphism). *Given two program graphs $g_1 = (V_1, E_1, l_v, l_e)$ and $g_2 = (V_2, E_2, l_v, l_e)$, g_1 is said to be subgraph isomorphic to g_2, if there is an injective function $\mu : V_1 \rightarrow V_2$ such that (1) $\forall u, v \in V_1$ and $u \neq v$, we have $\mu(u) \neq \mu(v)$. (2) $\forall v \in V_1$, we have $\mu(v) \in V_2$ and $l_v(v) = l_v(\mu(v))$. (3) $\forall (u, v) \in E_1$, $(\mu(u), \mu(v)) \in E_2$ and $l_e((u, v)) = l_e((\mu(u), \mu(v)))$. We say that g_1 is a subgraph of g_2 and g_2 is a supergraph of g_1. Given two program graphs g_1 and g_2, graph g_{12} is said to be a common subgraph of g_1 and g_2, if g_{12} is subgraph isomorphic to both g_1 and g_2, respectively.*

Proving subgraph isomorphism is NP-complete [20], which urges for approximate matching between program graphs in large datasets. To facilitate this approximate matching for nodes and links between pair of program graphs, the node label function l_v and link label function l_e can be enhanced to return additional information about nodes and links beyond their labels. Approximate/inexact graph matching also urges an efficient indexing mechanism in the databases for storing program graphs. The advanced graph indexing techniques proposed elsewhere [43,50] can be borrowed to serve this purpose.

Definition 3 (Graph Database). *The database D is a collection of program graphs, $\{g_1, g_2, ..., g_n\}$, where each g_i can have either labels "malware" (m) or "benign" (b), i.e., $l_g : D \rightarrow \Sigma_g$, where $\Sigma_g = \{m, b\}$ and l_g is a labeling function.*

Definition 4 (Graph Pattern). *A graph feature, f_i, is a pattern mined from program graphs in D that is highly discriminative for characterizing samples in either class. A pattern space, F, is a collection of highly discriminative patterns.*

In general, graph features are extracted by applying special techniques on nodes, links, paths and cycles of the program graph, and thereby, to generate signatures that can represent the corresponding program efficiently. The performance of the detector system largely depends on the intelligent selection of features and/or construction of signatures [15,18].

Definition 5 (Malware Detection Based on Mining Program Graph Features). *Given the database of program graphs (D) and the pattern space (F), a malware detector learns a classifier or model, C, that can correctly return the label of an unknown program graph.*

By learning a classifier or model in the above definition we mean gathering enough information (i.e., graph features) from existing graphs in D so that C can classify an unknown program as either *malware* or *benign*. This can be modeled as both *lazy* and *eager* learning approach or a combination of both for developing a multi-step/multi-evidence based malware detectors [47]. For example, we can adopt *lazy* learning approach for k-nearest neighbor (kNN) classification where an unknown program is labeled based on the labels of its k nearest neighbors [49]. Though, we can apply eager learning approach for learning the appropriate value of k from D. In classifiers like SVM, we need to adopt *eager* learning approach to learn an appropriate weight function W from D for classifying an unknown program graph [45]. The adoption of a specific learning approach depends on the learned classifier used by the detector system.

4   A Generalized Malware Detection System Based on Program Graph Analysis

We depict a generalized conceptual framework of a malware detection system based on mining program graph features in Fig. 3. The framework shows important modules and the information flow between them by dividing the whole system into two main parts: (a) detector system and (b) user interface. The detector system classify or label an unknown program based on the learned classifier/model in general. The purpose of user interface is to include user feedback in the detection system to make it more usable and transparent to end user [39].

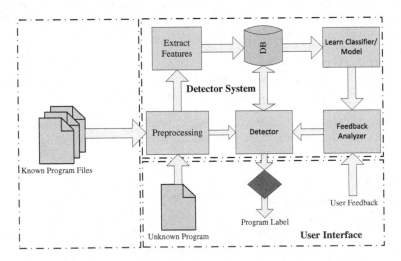

Fig. 3. Conceptual block diagram of a generalized malware detection system based on mining program graph features

The functions of individual modules are described below in detail:

- **Preprocessing:** This module preprocess and construct program graphs from program files. To do so, this module first dissemble the input binary (e.g., program executables) and then, gather information to construct the corresponding program graph (e.g., call graph, control-flow graph, code graph etc.).
- **Extract Features:** This module extract features by mining program graphs and store them into the database (DB). The database may be equipped with specialized data indexing techniques to facilitate efficient access.
- **Learn Classifier/Model:** This module learn classifier/model from features stored in DB. This module may rerun if there is a need to tune performance of the detector system.
- **Feedback Analyzer:** This module analyze user feedback to facilitate feedback driven detection and performance tuning of the system.
- **Detector:** This module classify and label an unknown program based on learned classifier/model and analyzed user feedback.

In this paper, we present a brief survey of the state-of-the-art important works under the variants of program graph and the generalized program graph-based malware detection system shown in Fig. 3.

5   Surveyed Works

This section presents the surveyed works under the variants of program graph and the generalized graph-based malware detection system shown in Fig. 3.

5.1   Control-Flow Graph Based Systems

- In [42] Wagner and Dean propose a technique in which a control flow graph for a program is constructed from its system call trace. Then at run time, this graph is compared with the known system call sequences to check for any violation. The authors apply both static analysis and dynamic monitoring to combat malwares and claim that this combination yields better results.
- In [5], Bruschi et al. propose a strategy that can detect the metamorphic malicious code inside a program P. To do so, they compare the control flow graphs of P against the set of known malwares' control flow graphs. Firstly, they unveil the flow connections between the benign and the malicious code within P after disassembling and performing a set of normalization operations on P. Then, they build the corresponding *labeled inter-procedural control flow graph* for P. This control flow graph of P is then compared against the control flow graphs of known malwares to see whether P contains a subgraph isomorphic to the control flow graphs of the known malwares. The authors also provide an encouraging experimental results to support their approach.
- In [26], Kruegel et al. propose an approach for detecting structural similarities between variations of a polymorphic worm based on control flow information. A fingerprinting technique is developed based on a coloring scheme of the

control flow graph, which characterizes the high-level structure of a worm executable. The authors claim that their proposed system is more robust to polymorphic modifications of a malicious executable and is capable of detecting some previously unknown, polymorphic worms.

- Cesare and Xiang [7] propose a system for detecting polymorphic malwares using control-flow graphs. They apply an existing approximated flow graph matching algorithm [6] to estimate graph isomorphisms at the *procedure level*. The similarity between programs is then quantified by identifying the underlying isomorphic flow graphs. Firstly, the approach applies depth-first ordering technique to order the nodes in the control flow graph. Then, a signature is constructed as a list of graph links for the ordered nodes, where the node ordering is used as node labels. This signature is represented as a string. To classify an unknown program, Dice coefficient is computed as the similarity score between the set of the flow graph strings of the unknown program and each set of flow graphs associated with malware stored in the database.
- In [8] Cesare and Xiang propose a similarity search technique for malwares using novel distance metrics. A malware signature is described by a set of control flow graphs contained in the malware. Then, a feature vector is constructed by decomposing these control flow graphs into either fixed size k-subgraphs, or q-gram strings of the decompiled high-level source. A distance metric between two sets of control-flow graphs is then computed based on the minimum matching distance between the corresponding feature vectors of the sets. The minimum matching distance utilizes the string edit distance and the minimum sum weight matching between two sets of graphs. The authors claim that the above technique runs in real time and detects more malware variants in comparison with other existing malware variant detection techniques.
- In [14,15], Eskandari and Hashemi propose a control-flow graph based malware detection method by converting the sparse matrix of the control-flow graph into a vector where they save only the situations of nonzero items. Then, a feature vector for each program graph is constructed by taking the API number as data-item and edge number as feature. Among different classifiers, the authors observe that random forest attains best result.
- In [10] Cesare et al. propose "Malwise" for malware classification. A fast application-level emulator is used to reverse engineering the code packing transformation. To classify a malware, two flow-graph based matching techniques are proposed. The exact flow-graph matching algorithm adopts string-based signatures. Firstly, they use depth first ordering technique to order the nodes in the control flow graph. A signature subsequently consists of a list of graph links for the ordered nodes, where the node ordering is used as node labels. Then, the similarity between two flow graphs with signatures x and y is calculated as 1 iff $x = y$, otherwise 0. The approximate flow graph matching algorithm uses string edit distance to quantify the similarity between two flow graphs. To generate string-based signatures, they apply the decompilation technique of structuring. The intuition is that malware variants share similar high-level structured control flow. The authors claim that the probability of detecting the new malware as the variant of existing malware is 88 %.

5.2   Code Graph Based Systems

- In [24], Jeong and Lee proposed a code graph based malware detection system by analyzing the instructions related to the system-call sequence in binary executables and then demonstrating their outcomes in the form of a topological graph. These topological graphs are used to preview the effects of programs on a system. Application programs are then tested with the code graph system to extract their distinctive characteristics. These distinctive characteristics are then used to separate malwares (worms and botnets) from normal programs. The authors claim to detect 67 % of unknown malwares from normal programs.

- In [1], Anderson et al. present a code graph-based malware detection technique by dynamically collecting instruction traces of the executables. The instructions represent nodes in the graph. To transform the graphs into Markov chains, the links are labeled with transition probabilities, where the transition probabilities are estimated from the data contained in the trace. A similarity matrix between the graphs is constructed by using a combination of graph kernels. To perform the classification, the similarity matrix is then sent to a support vector machine. The above technique significantly outperforms the signature-based and many other machine learning based detection methods.

- Runwal et al. [34] present a method for computing the similarity of executable files, based on opcode graphs. This opcode graph based technique is similar but simpler than the one based on instruction trace graphs proposed in [1]. Instead of using graph kernels to generate scores and SVMs for classifications, the authors directly compare the opcode graphs and compute the similarity scores. The authors then propose to apply these similarity scores to detect metamorphic malwares and claim that their approach can outperform a previously developed technique in [44] based on hidden Markov models.

5.3   Call Graph Based Systems

- In [4], Bergeron et al. propose a malware analysis technique based on program graph, which consists of three major steps. Firstly, the binary code of the program is transformed into an internal intermediate form. Secondly, the intermediate form is converted to various relevant graphs, e.g., control-flow graph, data-flow graph, call graph and critical-API graph via flow-based analysis. Finally, these graphs are checked and verified against the security policy.

- Lee et al. [28] propose to reduce the call graphs of malwares into code graphs for extracting semantic signatures. To do so, they consider only API calls in the call graphs. They produce 128 groups (32 objects 4 behaviors) to reduce the sizes of the call graphs. During this reduction step, links represented call relationships are maintained. Finally, a code graph is represented by a 128×128 adjacent matrix and saved. To estimate the similarity between two code graphs, they divide the number of links of the union graph with the number of links of the intersection graph. A suspicious program is identified by computing its code graph similarity score with the code graphs of the known malwares. The authors claim that their proposed mechanism achieves 91 % detection ratio of real-world malwares and detects 300 metamorphic malwares that can evade anti-virus (AV) scanners.

- In [21] Han et al. propose a metamorphic malware classification method using the sequential characteristics of API calls used. The authors also present experimental results using the proposed method with some malware samples.

5.4   Other Graph Based Systems

- Fredrikson et al. [18] present an automatic technique for extracting optimally discriminative specifications, which can be used by a behavior-based malware detector based on graph mining and concept analysis. To do so, they first divide the positive (benign) set of programs into disjoint subsets of behaviorally similar programs. Then, a dependence-graph is constructed for each malware and benign application to represent its behavior. Then, significant behaviors specific to each positive subset are mined. A significant behavior is a sequence of operations that distinguishes the programs in a positive subset from all of the programs in the negative (malware) subset. The author use *structural leap mining* to identify multiple distinct graphs that are present in the dependence graphs of the positive subset and absent from the dependence graphs of the negative set. The significant behaviors mined from each positive subset are combined via *concept analysis* to obtain a discriminative specification for the whole positive set. A specification is said to be discriminative if it matches malicious programs but does not match benign programs and therefore, can be used in the detection of unknown malware. The authors claim to achieve an 86 % detection rate on new, unknown malware, with 0 false positives.

- The authors in [23] present a system called JACKSTRAWS, which automatically extracts and generalizes graph templates to capture the core of different kinds of command and control (C&C) activities. Then, these C&C templates are matched against the behavioral graphs produced by other bots. Firstly, the authors record the activities (e.g., system calls) on the host system that are related to data that is sent over and received via each network connection. These activities are then used to construct the behavioral graphs. One graph is constructed for each connection. Then, all behavioral graphs that are constructed during the execution of a malware sample are checked against the templates of different types of C&C communication. When a sufficiently close match is found, the corresponding connection is reported as C&C channel. The authors claim that JACKSTRAWS can accurately detect C&C connections, even for bot families that were not previously used to generate the templates.

- The authors in [11] present Polonium, which is a novel semantic technology for detecting malicious programs via large-scale graph inference. Polonium applies scalable belief propagation algorithm to compute the reputation of program files and program files with low reputations are identified as malwares. They generate an undirected and unweighted bipartite machine-file graph from the raw data. A link exists between a file and a machine that has the file. The links are unweighted and there exists at most one link between a file and a machine. The algorithm predicts the label of a node from some prior knowledge about the node and from its neighbor nodes. The idea is that good files are supposed to appear on many machines and bad files appear only on few machines.

6   Future Challenges

This section presents the future challenges of mining program graphs under the generalized malware detection framework depicted in Fig. 3.

6.1   Efficient Construction of (Lossless) Program Graph

A malware can damage the host as soon as it starts its execution. Therefore, the most effective means of protecting the host system is to detect and block the malware before it starts executing. Graph based representation of program is a natural way to understand its semantics [18] and also facilitate unveiling its execution intent [42]. In connection with this, a program graph must satisfy the following properties: (a) it should characterize the program accurately and include all important information needed by the feature extraction module of the detectors to reduce the false positives/negatives; (b) it should be easily comprehensible by a human being to facilitate user feedback in the system; (c) it should be easy to identify the similarity/dissimilarity of multiple program graphs to increase the accuracy and also for detecting polymorphic malwares; and (d) it should be easy to distinguish the program graphs of different groups to separate malwares from benign programs. Most of the existing works propose detection techniques that apply various noise reduction/node summarization techniques (e.g., [28]) and are therefore, lossy. It should be noted that properties (c) and (d) are quite hard to ensure in the program graph (*one diminishes the other*) and therefore, a very challenging problem. The study made by Cesare and Xiang in [9] may help towards addressing the above problem.

6.2   Exact Matching vs. Approximate Matching

In exact graph matching, we test whether a program graph is a subgraph or supergraph of another program graph and is important for detecting polymorphic malwares [7]. However, testing subgraph or supergraph isomorphism is an NP-hard problem [20]. This problem becomes more hard as polymorphic malwares add noise (e.g., obfuscated codes) into the original version of the malware program, which urges an efficient noise reduction techniques before feeding the program graph to the matching algorithm and also, approximate matching techniques between program graphs in large datasets. To facilitate approximate matching for nodes and links between pair of program graphs, the node labeling function l_v and link labeling function l_e in the program graph g can be enhanced to return additional information about nodes and links beyond their labels. For example, the sub-function nodes in the program graph can itself represent another sub-program graph which can be used to match sub-function node of another program graph that has a different node label. Approximate graph matching also urges an efficient indexing mechanism in the databases for storing program graphs. The approximate matching techniques proposed in the existing works are either insufficient or inapplicable in large scale datasets. The advanced graph indexing techniques proposed elsewhere [43,50] can be borrowed to serve this. We can also transform the pair-wise similarity problem into a similarity search problem over the database.

6.3 Behavioral Patterns and Malware Signatures

The success of malware detection based on mining program graphs depends on discovering discriminative and important behavioral program graph patterns/features that can separate malwares from benign programs [18]. The system-call calling sequences encoded in the program graph paths and information encoded in it can be exploited to serve this. Frequent paths can be treated as behavioral patterns. However, polymorphic codes may transform the frequent path to be infrequent. To solve this, a path can be represented by a string and thereafter, approximate string matching [31] along with noise reduction [28] techniques can be applied to find frequent paths from the program graphs. Also, frequent-subgraph idea can be implemented to discover frequent patterns and thereby, to identify metamorphic code in the program. The authors in [25] propose to relax the rigid structure constraint of frequent subgraphs by introducing connectivity to frequent itemsets, which can eases the detection of metamorphic code in the malware program. The malware detectors must also conform properties such as soundness and completeness [33] of them. The challenge is to incorporate these techniques in an integrated manner. None of the existing techniques works in this direction.

6.4 Non-executable Code

There are worms that do not rely on executable codes, rather these worms are written in non-compiled scripting languages. These kind of worms urge specialized techniques to detect their behavioral patterns through program graph. We believe that the generalized program graph construction techniques [18,36] and features of binary programs [9] can be customized to serve this purpose. An obvious challenge is to analyze malware program in heterogeneous environments e.g., matching a polymorphic malware in a platform that is different from the known malware's platform (i.e., inter-platform comparability).

6.5 Other Graphs

There are works based on graphs, other than the control-flow or code-graphs, utilizes information not only encoded in the program itself, but also its host [11] and its command and control activities [23]. A hybrid approach can be implemented to have the positive aspects of both of these techniques.

6.6   User Feedback

To the best of our knowledge, user feedback is not studied in graph based malware detection techniques. Li et al. [29] develop a malware (virus) detection technique with *real-valued negative selection* (RVNS) algorithm. The authors propose to utilize the arguments of process calls to train the detector and integrate user feedback for tuning the threshold between normal files and viruses. User feedback can be used not only for improving the system performance as described above but can also be tied to improve the usability and transparency of the system. Stumpf et al. [39] demonstrate that it is possible to improve the accuracy of the machine learning system as well as gain the trust of the users by gathering various forms of user feedback, e.g., collecting user feedback on *why* the prediction was wrong after explaining *how* the reasoning made by the system. We propose to utilize such forms of user feedback from graph construction (e.g., nodes/links selection) to feature and system's parameters selection. The challenge is to develop a model that requires minimal user involvement and is also capable of integrating it to tune the model parameters successfully.

7   Conclusion

This paper presents a brief survey on malware detection techniques based on mining program graph features. We have outlined the variants of program graph, their properties and presented the surveyed works under them. We have also presented the challenges that have not been addressed yet as future research direction. To the best of our knowledge there are no other surveys on malware detection based on program graph analysis. We believe that the tutorial and future research challenges presented in this paper may serve as the collective knowledge base among the malware research community.

Acknowledgement. M.S. Islam and C. Liu are supported by the Australian Research Council (ARC) discovery project no. DP140103499.

References

1. Anderson, B., Quist, D., Neil, J., Storlie, C., Lane, T.: Graph-based malware detection using dynamic analysis. J. Comput. Virol. **7**(4), 247–258 (2011)
2. Bailey, M., Cooke, E., Jahanian, F., Xu, Y., Karir, M.: A survey of botnet technology and defenses. In: Cybersecurity Applications & Technology Conference for Homeland Security, pp. 299–304. IEEE Computer Society, Washington, DC (2009)
3. Balakrishnan, A., Schulze, C.: Code obfuscation literature survey (2005). http://pages.cs.wisc.edu/~arinib/writeup.pdf
4. Bergeron, J., Debbabi, M., Desharnais, J., Erhioui, M.M., Lavoie, Y., Tawbi, N.: Static detection of malicious code in executable programs. Int J. of Req. Eng. **2001**, 184–189 (2001)
5. Bruschi, D., Martignoni, L., Monga, M.: Detecting self-mutating malware using control-flow graph matching. In: Büschkes, R., Laskov, P. (eds.) DIMVA 2006. LNCS, vol. 4064, pp. 129–143. Springer, Heidelberg (2006)

6. Carrera, E., Erdélyi, G.: Digital genome mapping-advanced binary malware analysis. In: Virus Bulletin Conference (2004)
7. Cesare, S., Xiang, Y.: A fast flowgraph based classification system for packed and polymorphic malware on the endhost. In: AINA, pp. 721–728 (2010)
8. Cesare, S., Xiang, Y.: Malware variant detection using similarity search over sets of control flow graphs. In: TrustCom, pp. 181–189 (2011)
9. Cesare, S., Xiang, Y.: Static analysis of binaries. In: Software Similarity and Classification. SpringerBriefs in Computer Science, pp. 41–49. Springer, London (2012)
10. Cesare, S., Xiang, Y., Zhou, W.: Malwise - an effective and efficient classification system for packed and polymorphic malware. IEEE Trans. Comput. **62**(6), 1193–1206 (2013)
11. Chau, D.H., Nachenberg, C., Wilhelm, J., Wright, A., Faloutsos, C.: Large scale graph mining and inference for malware detection. In: SDM, pp. 131–142 (2011)
12. Chen, C., Lin, C.X., Fredrikson, M., Christodorescu, M., Yan, X., Han, J.: Mining graph patterns efficiently via randomized summaries. PVLDB **2**(1), 742–753 (2009)
13. Egele, M., Scholte, T., Kirda, E., Kruegel, C.: A survey on automated dynamic malware-analysis techniques and tools. ACM Comput. Surv. **44**(2), 6:1–6:42 (2008)
14. Eskandari, M., Hashemi, S.: Metamorphic malware detection using control flow graph mining. Int. J. Comput. Sci. Netw. Secur. **11**(12), 1–6 (2011)
15. Eskandari, M., Hashemi, S.: A graph mining approach for detecting unknown malwares. J. Vis. Lang. Comput. **23**(3), 154–162 (2012)
16. Feily, M., Shahrestani, A., Ramadass, S.: A survey of botnet and botnet detection. In: Third International Conference on Emerging Security Information, Systems and Technologies, pp. 268–273 (2009)
17. Felt, A.P., Finifter, M., Chin, E., Hanna, S., Wagner, D.: A survey of mobile malware in the wild. In: Proceedings of the 1st ACM Workshop on Security and Privacy in Smartphones and Mobile Devices, pp. 3–14 (2011)
18. Fredrikson, M., Jha, S., Christodorescu, M., Sailer, R., Yan, X.: Synthesizing near-optimal malware specifications from suspicious behaviors. In: IEEE Symposium on Security and Privacy, pp. 45–60 (2010)
19. Garcia-Teodoro, P., Díaz-Verdejo, J.E., Maciá-Fernández, G., Vázquez, E.: Anomaly-based network intrusion detection: techniques, systems and challenges. Comput. Secur. **28**(1–2), 18–28 (2009)
20. Garey, M.R., Johnson, D.S.: Computers and Intractability: A Guide to the Theory of NP-Completeness. W. H. Freeman, New York (1979)
21. Han, K.S., Kim, I.K., Im, E.: Malware classification methods using api sequence characteristics. In: Kim, K.J., Ahn, S.J. (eds.) Proceedings of the International Conference on IT Convergence and Security 2011. Lecture Notes in Electrical Engineering, vol. 120, pp. 613–626. Springer, Netherlands (2012)
22. Islam, R., Tian, R., Batten, L.M., Versteeg, S.: Classification of malware based on integrated static and dynamic features. J. Netw. Comput. Appl. **36**(2), 646–656 (2013)
23. Jacob, G., Hund, R., Kruegel, C., Holz, T.: Jackstraws: picking command and control connections from bot traffic. In: USENIX Security Symposium (2011)
24. Jeong, K., Lee, H.: Code graph for malware detection. In: ICOIN, pp. 1–5 (2008)
25. Khan, A., Yan, X., Wu, K.L.: Towards proximity pattern mining in large graphs. In: SIGMOD Conference, pp. 867–878 (2010)
26. Kruegel, C., Kirda, E., Mutz, D., Robertson, W., Vigna, G.: Polymorphic worm detection using structural information of executables. In: Valdes, A., Zamboni, D. (eds.) RAID 2005. LNCS, vol. 3858, pp. 207–226. Springer, Heidelberg (2006)

27. Kruegel, C., Robertson, W., Valeur, F., Vigna, G.: Static disassembly of obfuscated binaries. In: USENIX Security Symposium, p. 18 (2004)
28. Lee, J., Jeong, K., Lee, H.: Detecting metamorphic malwares using code graphs. In: SAC, pp. 1970–1977 (2010)
29. Li, Z., Liang, Y., Wu, Z., Tan, C.: Immunity based virus detection with process call arguments and user feedback. In: Bio-Inspired Models of Network, Information and Computing Systems, pp. 57–64 (2007)
30. Majumdar, A., Thomborson, C., Drape, S.: A survey of control-flow obfuscations. In: Bagchi, A., Atluri, V. (eds.) ICISS 2006. LNCS, vol. 4332, pp. 353–356. Springer, Heidelberg (2006)
31. Navarro, G.: A guided tour to approximate string matching. ACM Comput. Surv. **33**(1), 31–88 (2001)
32. Perry, D.: Here Comes the Flood or end of the Pattern file. Virus Bulletin, Ottawa (2008)
33. Preda, M.D., Christodorescu, M., Jha, S., Debray, S.: A semantics-based approach to malware detection. SIGPLAN Not. **42**(1), 377–388 (2007)
34. Runwal, N., Low, R.M., Stamp, M.: Opcode graph similarity and metamorphic detection. J. Comput. Virol. **8**(1–2), 37–52 (2012)
35. Shabtai, A., Moskovitch, R., Elovici, Y., Glezer, C.: Detection of malicious code by applying machine learning classifiers on static features: a state-of-the-art survey. Inf. Secur. Tech. Rep. **14**(1), 16–29 (2009)
36. Sherwood, T., Perelman, E., Hamerly, G., Calder, B.: Automatically characterizing large scale program behavior. SIGARCH Comput. Archit. News **30**(5), 45–57 (2002)
37. Siddiqui, M., Wang, M.C., Lee, J.: A survey of data mining techniques for malware detection using file features. In: ACM Southeast Regional Conference, pp. 509–510 (2008)
38. Silva, S.S.C., Silva, R.M.P., Pinto, R.C.G., Salles, R.M.: Botnets: a survey. Comput. Netw. **57**(2), 378–403 (2013)
39. Stumpf, S., Rajaram, V., Li, L., Wong, W.K., Burnett, M.M., Dietterich, T.G., Sullivan, E., Herlocker, J.L.: Interacting meaningfully with machine learning systems: three experiments. Int. J. Hum.-Comput. Stud. **67**(8), 639–662 (2009)
40. Tavallaee, M., Stakhanova, N., Ghorbani, A.A.: Toward credible evaluation of anomaly-based intrusion-detection methods. Trans. Sys. Man Cyber. Part C **40**(5), 516–524 (2010)
41. Wagener, G., State, R., Dulaunoy, A.: Malware behaviour analysis. J. Comput. Virol. **4**(4), 279–287 (2008)
42. Wagner, D., Dean, D.: Intrusion detection via static analysis. In: Proceedings of the 2001 IEEE Symposium on Security and Privacy, pp. 156–169 (2001)
43. Wang, X., Ding, X., Tung, A.K.H., Ying, S., Jin, H.: An efficient graph indexing method. In: ICDE, pp. 210–221 (2012)
44. Wong, W., Stamp, M.: Hunting for metamorphic engines. J. Comput. Virol. **2**(3), 211–229 (2006)
45. Ye, Y., Wang, D., Li, T., Ye, D.: Imds: intelligent malware detection system. In: ACM SIGKDD, pp. 1043–1047 (2007)
46. You, I., Yim, K.: Malware obfuscation techniques: a brief survey. In: BWCCA, pp. 297–300. IEEE (2010)
47. Yu, Z., Tsai, J.J.: Intrusion Detection: A Machine Learning Approach, vol. 3. Imperial College Pr., London (2010)

48. Zhang, L., Yu, S., Wu, D., Watters, P.: A survey on latest botnet attack and defense. In: TrustCom, pp. 53–60 (2011)
49. Zhang, M.L., Zhou, Z.H.: Ml-knn: a lazy learning approach to multi-label learning. Pattern Recogn. **40**(7), 2038–2048 (2007)
50. Zhu, Y., Qin, L., Yu, J.X., Cheng, H.: Finding top-k similar graphs in graph databases. In: EDBT, pp. 456–467 (2012)

Defence Against Code Injection Attacks

Hussein Alnabulsi[1], Quazi Mamun[1], Rafiqul Islam[1], and Morshed U. Chowdhury[2(✉)]

[1] School of Computing and Mathematics, Charles Sturt University, Albury, Australia
{halnabulsi,qmamun,mislam}@csu.edu.au
[2] School of Information Technology, Deakin University, Melbourne, Australia
muc@deakin.edu.au

Abstract. Code injection attacks are considered serious threats to the Internet users. In this type of attack the attacker injects malicious codes in the user programs to change or divert the execution flows. In this paper we explore the contemporary defence strategies against code injection attacks (CIAs) and underline their limitations. To overcome these limitations, we suggest a number of countermeasure mechanisms for protecting from CIAs. Our key idea relies on the multiplexing technique to preserve the exact return code to ensure the integrity of program execution trace of shell code. This technique also maintains a FIFO (first in first out) queue to defeat the conflict state when multiple caller method makes a call simultaneously. Finally, our technique can provide better performance, in terms of protection and speed, in some point compared to the CFI (control flow integrity) as well as CPM (code pointer masking) techniques.

Keywords: Security · Code injection attacks · Malicious

1 Introduction

Code injection attack is a malicious activity where a malware code placed by hacker in the memory of a system either to cause damage on the system, spy on the user, or to steal user's information. An attacker tries to take the control of the program flow using code injection attacks by changing the return address of shell code. An example of code injection attacks is the stack-based buffer overflow, which overwrites the return address. In addition, more advanced techniques are exist such as indirect pointer overwrites, and heap-based buffer overflows, where a code pointer can be overwritten to divert the execution control to the attacker's shell code. According to National Institute of Standards and Technology (NIST 2013) [1], code injection attack represents a high priority of all types of vulnerabilities and that must be mitigated. According to (NIST) (9.86 % of attacks is buffer over flow) came after SQL injection attacks and XSS attacks (16.54 % of attack, 14.37 % of attack) respectively [1].

There are many countermeasures techniques are available against code injection attacks but each has limitations. Below, we describe them briefly:

1. StackGuard: In this technique a canary secret value is placed between the buffer and the return address. Thus when an intruder tries to change the return address in the

J. Tian et al. (Eds.): SecureComm 2014, Part II, LNICST 153, pp. 237–251, 2015.
DOI: 10.1007/978-3-319-23802-9_19

victim program StackGuard detects these changes. As the canary value is random 32-bit wide then it is very hard for an attacker to guess the value of the canary. The canary value is usually chosen at the time when program starts. There are four types of canaries that have been used: Random Canary, Random XOR Canary, Null Canary, Terminator Canary [9, 11, 14].

The limitation of StackGuard is that this technique does not work well when indirect pointer overwrite attacks occurred. In this type of attack the attacker overwrites an unprotected pointer and then inserts a value in the stack. Whenever, the application changes the pointer and overwrites the value with the integer, the attacker writes a random value in any location in the memory by manipulating the pointer and the integer. Thus, the attacker can write any value over the return address of the stack. Moreover, StackGuard technique is incompatible with Linux kernel [4, 8, 11].

2. Address Space Layout Randomization (ASLR): This technique is used to protect the system from buffer over flow attacks. It works by randomizing the base address of structures such as the heap, stack, and libraries, making it hard for an attacker to find injected shell code in memory of the system. Also if an attacker succeeds in over-writing a code pointer, the attacker does not know where to point it [10]. Windows Vista provides Address Space Layout Randomization as a basis on a per image, so any executable image which have a PE header, such as (.dll or .exe) can be used in Address Space Layout Randomization (ASLR) [13].

    Limitation of the Address Space Layout Randomization countermeasure is that an attacker may use a new technique called heap-spraying, in this technique an attacker fills the heaps with many copies of the malicious shell code, and then jumps any location in the memory, this operation gives a good probability to an attacker that he will access to his shell code in memory [4]. However Address Space Layout Randomization is not effective against exploit code for single flaw, and for brute force attack [12].

3. Memory Management Unit Access Control Lists (MMU ACLs): it allows applica-tions to mark memory pages as non-executable memory, and supported by Control Processing Units (CPUs). In this technique, memory semantic consists of three components: the first component separates readable and writable pages, the second component makes stack, heap, anonymous mapping, and mark memory pages as non-executable memory, the third one is enforcing ACL (Access Control List, which is a set of data that informs the operating system (OS) about permissions, access rights, and privileges (read, write, and execute) for users in the computer system object [15]), which control the operation of converting the non-executable memory to executable memory and vice versa or denying the conversion [1, 14].

    However, the MMU ACLs are not supported by some processors, as the technique breaks applications which expect the heap or stack to be executable. It is possible that an attacker injects a crafted fake stack, then an application will unwind the fake stack instead of the original calling stack, the attacker then directs the processor to arbitrary function in program code or library, and it is also possible that the attacker marks the memory where he injected his shell code as executable and jumping to it [1].

4. StackShield: it is developed from StackGuard to protect against stack smashing attacks, and exploitation of stack based buffer overflows. This technique applies a random

secret canary value. This technique is comparatively better, however it cannot protect against indirect pointer overwriting attacks [8, 17].

5. Control Flow Integrity (CFI): This technique provides a good guarantee against code injection attacks, it determines control flow graph for every program, and to each control flow destination of a control flow transfer it gives a unique ID. The CFI will know if there are code injection attacks by comparing the destination ID with expected ID before transferring the control flow to destination, if they are not equal, the application will kill. Otherwise the program will proceed as normal.
    In comparison with other countermeasures CFI is considered very slow [2, 4].

6. CPM (masking code pointers) is a countermeasure against code injection attacks, CPM does not detect memory corruption or prevent overwriting code pointer, but it is hard for an attacker to make a successful code injection attack. It provides a mask to every return addresses and function pointer of the program and masks the global offset table, the masking operation relies on logic operation such as OR, AND operations to prevent code injection in the memory of the system [1]. The limitation of CPM (masking code pointers) is that it does not give a good guarantee of protection against code injection attacks.

Our key idea relies on the multiplexing technique to preserve the exact return code to ensure the integrity of program execution trace of shell code. This technique also maintains a FIFO (first in first out) queue to defeat the conflict state when multiple caller method makes a call simultaneously.

To alleviate the aforementioned problems with the existing countermeasures, we propose a technique which relies on the multiplexer idea. To preserve the exact return code to ensure the integrity of program execution trace of shell code. As each method has a particular ID, using the multiplexer method an attacker will not be able to divert the return address to the attacker's shell code. This technique also maintains a FIFO (first in first out) queue to defeat the conflict state when multiple caller method makes a call simultaneously. The proposed technique has some similarity with the CFI; however it improves the main problem of the CFI, which is being slow.

The rest of paper is organized as follows: The next section provides related work. Section 3 illustrates the idea of our approach. Section 4 provides complexity analysis between CFI methodology and multiplexer methodology, and between CPM methodology and Counter methodology. Finally, the paper is concluded in Sect. 5.

2 Related Work

According to [3] the authors presented a design of MoCFI (Mobile CFI) and implemented a framework of Smartphone platforms, the standard platform that they focused is ARM architecture. The ARM architecture is standard platform of smartphones. It prevents control flow attacks by using control flow integrity (CFI) method. In the paper authors showed the enforcement of CFI that applied on the ARM platform, and implemented CFI framework for Apple iOS. The result showed that the application mitigates Control Flow Attacks. The limitation of MoCFI is that it can only applicable in mobile phone applications.

In [4] authors presented a CPM countermeasure against code injection attacks which does not depend on secret value (stack canaries), but relies on masking the return address functions, masking function pointer, and masking global offset table. However it gave a good protection against code injection attacks but there are some scope for an attacker to success his attack, therefore it does not give a full protection against code injection attacks.

Lee *et al.* [5] presented secure return address stack (SRAS) which is hardware-based to prevent code injection attacks by verifying modification of return address. To apply this methodology needs low cost modification of the processor and operating system (OS), the hardware protection can be applied to executable code and new program. The impact of performance of the applications using this hardware-based is negligible, it does not impact on performance of return instructions and procedure call. However SRAS requires a hardware modification that some time hard to apply because of compatibility with the processor and operating system (OS) of the system.

Zhang *et al.* [6] presented a new protection method called Compact Control Flow Integrity and Randomization (CCFIR), to solve the limitation of CFI by collecting all targets of indirect control transfers instructions in a section called "Springboard" in a random order. By using "Springboard" section CCFIR will ensure indirect transfers easier than CFI. Result showed that CCFIR eliminate control flow attacks such as return-into-libc and ROP, but this technique still use the same approach of CFI.

In [7] Xia *et al.* presented a system called CFIMon, which is the first system can detect a control flow attacks without any changes to applications (binary code or source) and it does not require any special hardware. It works by collecting legal control flow transfers and uses branch tracing store mechanism to analyse runtime traces, and detects the code injection attacks. The CFIMon uses two phases: offline phase which builds a set of target addresses for every branch instruction, and online phase that applied a number of rules to diagnoses possible attacks. The limitation of CFIMon is that it gives a false alarm (false positive or false negative) when detecting code injection attacks.

The motivation of our work is to improve CFI speed by applying a multiplexer to divert every return addresses to its address memory locations, and overcome problem with CPM which did not give a complete guarantee to protect against code injection attacks by using a counter of one's in return addresses. Our approaches addresses these issues and have a significant countermeasures to protect against code injection attacks.

3   Our Proposed Approaches

In this section, we propose two different approaches to protect the code injection attacks. The first approach is a *multiplexer application approach*, which can protect the return address of each legitimate method, residing in a non-writable memory location. In our second approach we apply a matrix to keep the number of 1s of the return addresses of each legitimate method, and later we compare it with the calling method for similarity testing. The following subsections describe our approaches in details.

Multiplexer approach:

In this approach we apply a software module called *MUX_App* and every method in the system must call the *MUX_App* to get its return address. Each legitimate method is provided with a unique ID and will have its own return address. Our assumption is to keep *MUX_App* in a memory location which is non-writable. As a result the *MUX_App* remains protected from the attackers to divert the program execution (Fig. 1).

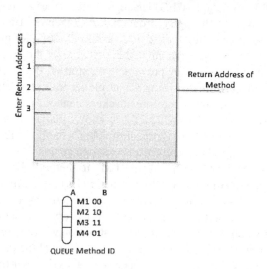

Fig. 1. Multiplexer with the return address of the method

We provided a queue (first-in first-out) to the multiplexer application to manage calling operations to prevent multiple calls for the multiplexer application in the same time. Therefore it will give a protection from code injection attacks and will improve speed significantly compare to CFI technique.

Figure 2 shows the assembly code for the CFI method. Note that, the code contains a comparison operation (cmp [ecx], 12345678h), which make the CFI method slower compared to the proposed multiplexer approach.

Source			destination		
Bytes (opcodes)	x86 assembly code	Comment	Bytes (opcodes)	x86 assembly code	Comment
FF E1	jmp ecx	; a computed jump instruction	8B 44 24 04	mov eax, [esp+4]	; first instruction of destination code
81 39 78 56 34 12	cmp [ecx], 12345678h	; compare data at destination	78 56 34 12	DD 12345678h	; label ID, as data
75 13	jne error_label	; if not ID value, then fail	8B 44 24 04	mov eax, [esp+4]	; destination instruction
8D 49 04 FF E1	lea ecx, [ecx+4] jmp ecx	; skip ID data at destination ; jump to destination code			

Fig. 2. CFI low-level language code [2]

The policy of our methodology is that the software execution must follow a path of Control Flow Graph (CFG) which determined ahead of time as shown in Fig. 3. The definition of Control Flow Graph (CFG) is a representation using graph notation, of all paths that might be traversed through a program during its execution. The CFG can be defined by analysing source code, or execution profile [2, 16]. Our methodology based on CFG; its enforcement can be implemented in software as shown in Fig. 3. It is very close to CFI in execution, it works by preventing an attacker divert code execution, by diverting to a static return addresses using a multiplexer for every return addresses and every static application program. Therefore attackers cannot divert the code execution to their shell code as shown in Fig. 4. The figure shows that an attacker tried to divert the execution method M1 by calling it from an attacker's method M2, but when method M1 calling the multiplexer to get its return address then an attacker will fail because the multiplexer will give the right return address of M1 to method M1.

The difference between our methodology with CFI, is that our methodology is faster because it diverts the return address methods immediately by using a multiplexer's application that contains a static return addresses for every application's methods, but the CFI is working by comparing the ID of the destination with expected ID, and if they are not equal, the program will be killed, but if they are equal the program proceeds as normal as shown in Fig. 2. The comparing operation takes a longer time than our methodology [1].

Figure 5 illustrates how the attacker can successfully inject shell code in process.

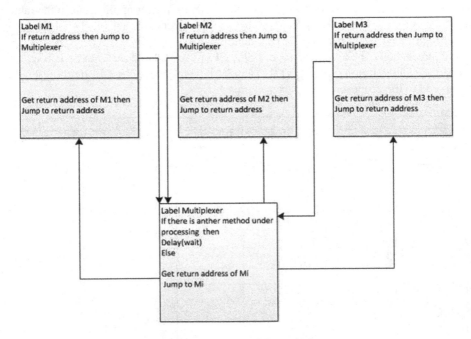

Fig. 3. CFG control flow graph

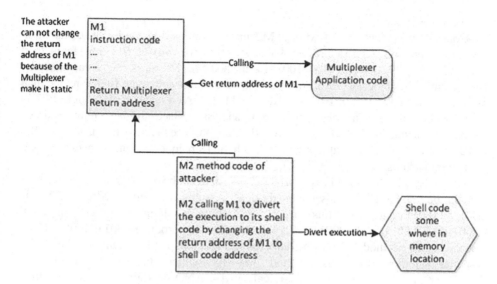

Fig. 4. An attacker tries to divert the execution to his shell code

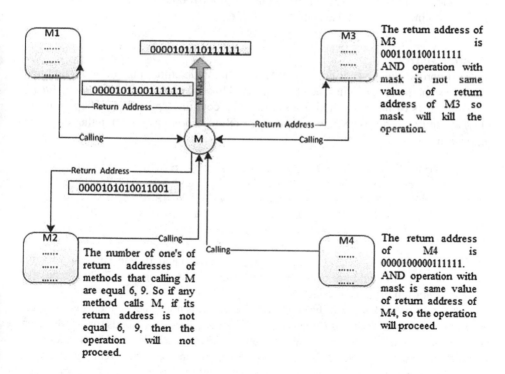

Fig. 5. Explaining for example 1

Example 1:

Consider two caller methods M1 and M2 and a call method M. During the compilation the system knows the return addresses of M say $0 \times 0B3F$ (0000101100111111) for method M1, and $0 \times 0A99$ (0000101010011001) for method M2. The mask can be calculated by performing bitwise logical OR operations of the two return addresses. Therefore, the final mask is calculated as $0 \times 0BBF$ (0000101110111111). As a result, bitwise logical AND operation between the final mask and a return address produces the same return address. On the other hand, an invalid return address does not produce the same return address after AND operation with the final mask. This is a basic technique to identify incorrect/malicious return address, as proposed in [1].

However, this technique fails to protect the system all the time. For instance, assume a malicious method M3 calls the method M. Assume the return address of M3 is 0001101100111111. In this case, the bitwise logical AND operation 0000101110111111 && 0001101100111111 does not produce 0001101100111111. Therefore, the method M3 will be detected as malicious method. On the other hand, consider another malicious method M4 for which the return address is 0000100000111111. Performing a logical bitwise AND operation between the final mask and the return address does produce the correct return address 0000100000111111 && 0000101110111111 = 0000100000111111. Therefore, the method M4 increases the false negative instance.

Counter Matrix:

To improve the possibility to identify a malicious method, our proposed solution uses the same masking technique [1] after an additional phase, called *Counter Matrix*, of counting 1s of the return addresses. In this bit counting "process numbers of one's (1's) are counted and compare with that of the return address as shown in the following algorithm.

```
if (bit_count())==0  // compare the number of ones
       return False; // Malicious method identified
else run CPM(); // the system will consider the     //
             method as vulnerable and will
             // call CPM process.
```

For example, the return addresses of M1, M2 have 6 and 10 one-bits respectively. Therefore M4, M5 could not call M3 because the number of one's is 7, 3 respectively and the operation process will kill.

After counting operation if the code injection attack is not detected, then a mask operation will be done by using OR operation with return addresses methods that is M3, then AND operation will conduct with every return address methods of M3, therefore our method will improve the time. Because it - kills the operation if the counting operation detect differences in count of one's for each method, and it will ensure security. The security is enhanced because the masking operation (CPM) is conducted after counting operation. However if still there is a small space for the attacker to pass his attack then it will fail because we use two techniques together (Counter of One's technique and CPM technique). Therefore, it is not needed more time in execution if the first technique (Counter of One's technique) detects an attack operation it will kill the operation of method without executing second technique (CPM technique). Here we preview example 2 with its Fig. 6.

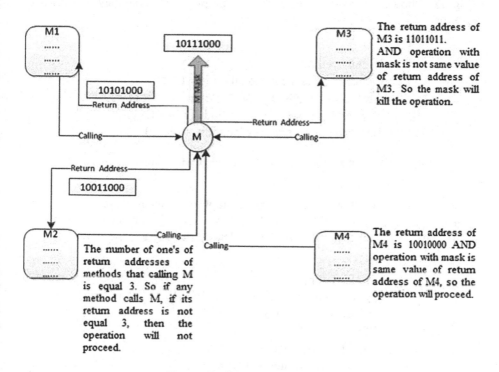

Fig. 6. Explaining for example 2

Consider a method M which is being called by two other methods M1 and M2. The mask of M is calculated by performing logical bitwise OR operation of the return addresses of M1 and M2.

Thus, Masking M = 10101000 OR 10011000 = 10111000.

We consider a method M3, which contains malicious code and this method wants to call the M.

Therefore when AND operation conducted with the return address of M3 (11011011) with the making code 10111000, we will not get the same return address value of M3 (11011011), thus the attacker cannot continue his attacks, and he cannot divert the return address of method M into his shell code in memory and cannot execute it because the application will kill. In the same Fig. 6 illustrate a preview example of masking failure, Consider M4 as a malicious code that want to call the method M.

The AND operation of the return address of M4 with the mask of M, the result will be the same value of the return address of M4, so the application will continue.

Therefore if we apply our technique in this problem it will count the numbers of 1's for every return addresses that has called method M. In this example its 3 (1's), and the return address of M4 is 4, and for M3 is 6.

By applying this technique the application will kill, because the number of (1's) of M3 and M4 are not equal with 3 (1's).

Figure 7 shows our propose algorithm of multiplexer methodology with its time execution.

> **If call method => O(1)**
> **Going to Multiplexer location => O(1)**
> **Give ID of method to Multiplexer => O(1)**
> **Get return address for method ID => O(1)**
> **Jump to return address location => O(1)**

Fig. 7. Algorithm of multiplexer methodology with its time execution

The total execution time for multiplexer methodology is equal $O(1) + O(1) + O(1) + O(1) + O(1) => O(1)$ as shown in Fig. 7. Our algorithm of counter methodology with its time execution is illustrated in Fig. 8.

> **If call method => O(1)**
> **Going to counter location => O(1)**
> **Compare count of one's => O(n)**
>   **If true = > O(1)**
>   **Go to mask location => O(1)**
>   **AND Operation => O(n)**
>   **If true => O(1)**
>   **Go to return address location => O(1)**
>   **else**
>   **error kills operation => O(1)**
>   **else**
>   **error kills operation => O(1)**

Fig. 8. Algorithm of counter methodology with its time execution

The execution time for counter methodology according to Fig. 8 is $O(N) + O(N) + O(1) + O(1) + \ldots + O(1) = O(2\,N)$. Figure 9 shows an assembly code for counter methodology.

```
for (int i=0; i<a.length; i++)
051E6B40: 04        iconst_0              //get 0                       : A
051E6B41: 3E        istore_3              //  store it in i
051E6B42: A70011    goto       0x051E6B53 //go to test i<a.length near bottom

          if (a[i] = n)
051E6B43: 2B        aload_1               //get a's base address : B
051E6B44: 1D        iload_3               //  get i
051E6B45: 2E        iaload                //  get a[i]
051E6B46: 1C        nload_2               //get n
051E6B47: A70011    goto       0x051E6B52 //go to increment C
051E6B49: A40007    if_icmple  0x051E6B50 //go to test near bottom if <=

051E6B50: 840301    iinc                  //increment i                 : C

      Count=Count+1
051E6B51: 1E        Cload_4               //get count                   : D
051E6B52: 840303    Cinc                  //increment C                 : E
051E6B53: 1D        iload_3               //get i                       : F
051E6B54: 2B        aload_1               //get a's
051E6B55: BE        arraylength           //  length
051E6B56: A1FFED    if_icmplt  0x051E6B43 //go to if above if <
Compare Count with count of one's in method
051E6B57: 2E        Cload_5               //get count from method       : G
          if (b[s] = C)
051E6B58: 2B        bload_1               //get b base address : H
051E6B59: 1D        sload_1               //  get s
051E6B60: 2E        sbload                //  get b[s]
051E6B61: 1C        cload_3               //get c
Then same operations of mask methodology
```

Fig. 9. An assembly code for counter methodology [19]

Figure 9 also shows the implementation of the countermeasure technique, which requires 21 assembly instructions. Although the implementation of the proposed technique requires few extra instructions, the proposed technique detects more anomalies than the CPM technique. This is because the proposed technique uses parity checking in addition to the masking technique.

Figure 10 shows use of C code for quicksort algorithm to illustrate our multiplexer methodology; we preview the following C function, this function code return the median value of an array of integers [18].

```
int median (int* data, int len, void* cmp )
{ int tmp [MAX_LEN];
Memcpy ( tmp, data, len*sizeof(int) );
Qsort ( tmp, len, sizeof (int), cmp );
Return tmp [len/2];
}
```

Fig. 10. Quicksort algorithm [18]

The time complexity of quicksort algorithm is O (N*log N) [20]. In Figs. 11, 12 and 13 show assembly codes of quicksort algorithm, quicksort with CFI, and quicksort with our multiplexer technique respectively.

```
Regular_qsort:
...
push  ebx
mov  eax, esi
call  shortsort
add  esp, 0ch
...
push  edi   ; an attack is
push  edx   ; possible by
call  [esp+comp_fp]  ;   Going to X
add  esp,  8
test  eax,  eax
jle  lable_lessthan


Regular_library_function:
mov  edi, edi
push  ebx
mov  ebx, esp
push  ecx
...
pop  ebp
X:  mov  esp, ebx
pop  ebx
ret
```

Fig. 11. Quicksort assembly code [18]

The Qsort algorithm code is vulnerable as shown in Fig. 11. Figure 12 shows the assembly code of Qsort with CFI. If an attacker overwrites the comparison function cmp before it is passed to Qsort, an attacker can exploits this point to divert the execution to his shell code when the Qsort method calls the corrupted comparison function cmp. This has been labelled as X in Figs. 11, 12, and 13.

The Qsort with CFI assembly code in Fig. 12 includes ID checks before call instructions, therefore CFI methodology will prevent the exploiting Qsort code from an attacker, because of the ID checks will happen before call instructions and this prevents any exploitation in calling instructions in the code.

In Fig. 13 shows Qsort with multiplexer methodology that will protect from an attacker exploiting because when call function has happened, an attacker has changed the return address of method. Therefore, next instruction is to get the return address from a multiplexer (prefetchnta [AABCCDEEh]: line 5 in Fig. 13) which means to go to this location in memory to get the return address of the method. As a result incorporating multiplexer technique is able to protect from attacking such as CFI methodology, but also improves execution time [18].

Qsort_with_CFI

...

```
push ebx
mov eax, esi
call shortsort
prefetchanta [AABCDDEEh]   ; tacking data from this location
add esp, 0Ch
...
push edi
push ebx
mov eax, [esp+comp_fp]
cmp [eax+4], 12345678h      ; CFI check
jne error lable             ; Prevents
call eax                    ; going to X
prefetchanta [AABCDDEEh]    ; tacking data from this location
add esp, 8
test eax, eax
jle label_lessthan
...
```

Fig. 12. Quicksort assembly code with CFI [18]

Qsort_with_Our_ methodology

...

```
push ebx
mov eax, esi
call shortsort
prefetchanta [AABCCDEEh]   ; tacking data from this location
add esp, 0Ch
...
push edi
push ebx
mov eax, [esp+comp_fp]
call eax                    ; going to X
prefetchanta [AABCCDEEh]    ; tacking data from this location
add esp, 8
...
```

Fig. 13. Quicksort assembly code with multiplexer methodology [18]

4 Complexity Analysis Between CFI, Multiplexer Methodologies and CPM, Countermeasure Methodologies

It also shows in Figs. 12 and 13 that our multiplexer methodology requires only 11 lines of code instead of 12 lines of code used in CFI for implementation, which is an evidence of improving execution time. Table 1 shows a complexity analysis between our method, CFI and CPM. Our method gives better results compare to other methods.

Table 1. Complexity analysis between CFI, Multiplexer methodologies and CPM, Counter-measure methodologies

	Execution time	Security	Lines of code
CFI	$O(n)$	No vulnerability	15 lines of code* (N time)
Multiplexer	$O(1)$	No vulnerability	11 lines of code* (N time)
CPM	NA	Good protection	NA
Counter	$O(2n)$, or $O(2n) + $ CPM execution time	It uses 2 approaches together (Counter-measure + CPM)	21 + CPM's line of code

5 Conclusion

In this paper we propose two approaches to defence against code injection attacks. One of the approaches augments '1' bit counting technique to modify the Masking Code Pointer (CPM) [1]. The augmentation technique improves the probability of identifying malicious code compared to CPM. The proposed technique provides more protection without introducing time complexity.

The second methodology relies on the multiplexer technique, which is based on the Control Flow Integrity (CFI) however performs faster than the CFI technique. The time complexity of the proposed multiplexer technique is $O(n)$ compared to the time complexity of the CFI which is $O(2n)$.

In our future work, we will apply our counter technique and multiplexer technique using a Linux environment and SPEC CPU2006 Integer benchmarks.

References

1. Philippaerts, P., Younan, Y., Muylle, S., Piessens, F., Lachmund, S., Walter, T.: CPM: masking code pointers to prevent code injection attacks. ACM Trans. Inf. Syst. Secur. (TISSEC) **16**(1), Article No. 1 (2013)
2. Abadi, M., Budiu, M., Erlingsson, U., Ligatti, J.: Control flow integrity principles, implementations, and applications. ACM J. **13**, 4 (2006)
3. Davi, L., Dmitrienko, A., Egele, M., Fischer, T., Holz, T., Hund, R., Nurnberger, S., Sadeghi, A.: MoCFI : a framework to mitigate control-flow attacks on smartphones. IETF J. **4**, 32–44 (2012)

4. Philippaerts, P., Younan, Y., Muylle, S., Piessens, F., Lachmund, S., Walter, T.: Code pointer masking: hardening applications against code injection attacks. In: Holz, T., Bos, H. (eds.) DIMVA 2011. LNCS, vol. 6739, pp. 194–213. Springer, Heidelberg (2011)

5. Lee, R.B., Karig, D.K., McGregor, J.P., Shi, Z.: Enlisting hardware architecture to thwart malicious code injection. In: International Conference on Security in Pervasive Computing (SPC 2003), pp. 237–252, Boppard, Germany (March 2003)

6. Zhang, C., Wei1, T., Chen, Z., Duan, L., Szekeres, L., McCamant, S., Song, D., Zou, W.: Practical control flow integrity and randomization for binary executables. In: 34th IEEE Symposium on Security and Privacy (Oakland), San Francisco (May 2013)

7. Xia, Y., Liu, Y., Chen, H., Zang, B.: CFIMon: detecting violation of control flow integrity using performance counters. In: 42nd Annual IEEE/IFIP International Conference, pp. 1–12 (2012)

8. Richarte, G.: Four different tricks to bypass StackShield and StackGuard protection. J. Comput. Virol. 7(3), 173–188 (2002)

9. Etoh, H., Yoda, K.: Protecting from stack-smashing attacks. IBM Research Division, Tokyo Research Laboratory (June 2000)

10. Bhatkar, S., DuVarney, D.C., Sekar, R.: Address obfuscation: an efficient approach to combat a broad range of memory error exploits. In: 12th USENIX Security Symposium, USENIX Association (2003)

11. Cowan, C., Beattie, S., Day, R.F., Pu, C., Wagle, P., Walthinsen, E.: Protecting systems from stack smashing attacks with StackGuard (May 2005)

12. Shacham, H., Page, M., Pfaff, B., Goh, E., Modadugu, N., Boneh, D.: On the effective of address-space randomization. In: CCS 2004 Proceedings of the 11th ACM Conference on Computer and Communications Security, pp. 298–307 (October 2004)

13. Whitehoue, O.: An analysis of address space layout randomization on Windows Vista. Symantec Adv. Threat Res. (February 2007)

14. Silberman, P., Johnson, R.: A Comparison of Buffer Overflow Prevention Implementations and Weaknesses. iDEFENSE Inc., Dallas (2004)

15. ACL (2014). http://www.webopedia.com/TERM/A/ACL.html

16. Control flow graph (April 2014). http://en.wikipedia.org/wiki/Control_flow_graph

17. Youna, Y., Pozza, D., Piessens, F., Joosen, W.: Extended Protection Against Stack Smashing Attacks Without Performance Loss, pp. 194–213. Springer, Berlin (2006)

18. Abadi, M., Budiu, M., Erlingsson, U., Ligatti, J.: Control flow integrity principles, implementations, and applications. ACM J. 13(1), Article 4 (2009)

19. Pattis, R.E.: https://www.cs.cmu.edu/afs/cs/Web/People/pattis/15-1XX/15-200/lectures/aa/index.html. Accessed June 2014

20. How to find time complexity of an algorithm. http://stackoverflow.com/questions/11032015/how-to-find-time-complexity-of-an-algorithm

False Data Injection Attack Targeting the LTC Transformers to Disrupt Smart Grid Operation

Adnan Anwar$^{(\boxtimes)}$, Abdun Naser Mahmood, and Mohiuddin Ahmed

School of Engineering and Information Technology, UNSW Canberra,
Canberra, ACT 2600, Australia
adnan.anwar@adfa.edu.au, Abdun.Mahmood@unsw.edu.au,
mohiuddin.ahmed@student.adfa.edu.au

Abstract. Load Tap Changing (LTC) Transformers are widely used in a Power Distribution System to regulate the voltage level within standard operational limit. In a SCADA connected network, the performance of LTC transformers can be improved by utilizing a closed loop monitoring and control mechanism. The widely used SCADA communication protocols, including Modbus and DNP3, have been proven vulnerable under cyber attack. In this paper, we conduct a vulnerability analysis of LTC transformers under malicious modification of measurement data. Here, we define two different attack strategies, (i)attack targeting energy system efficiency, and (ii) attack targeting energy system stability. With theoretical background and simulation results, we demonstrate that the attack strategies can significantly affect the power distribution system operations in terms of energy efficiency and stability. The experiments are performed considering IEEE benchmark 123 node test distribution system.

Keywords: False Data Injection · Smart grid FDI attacks · Cyber security · OpenDSS · LTC transformer

1 Introduction

Voltage stability has been identified as one of the major concerns of power distribution system planning and operation [1]. Traditionally, the power distribution system is designed such a way that the voltage continues to drop with the increase of the feeder length. At peak load or the heavily loaded conditions, the voltage drop phenomena may affect the distribution system stability significantly which can further lead to a voltage collapse situation [2]. Due to voltage stability or collapse problems, a large blackout may occur in a distribution system which can again lead to a cascading failure in the transmission system resulting huge customer sufferings and significant financial losses. In order to improve of voltage stability of a distribution system, Load Tap Changing (LTC) transformers are widely used which regulates the voltage profiles by changing the tap locations [3]. In a traditional setup, LTC transformers rely on the current and voltage measurement data which are obtained using the local information of that node

© Institute for Computer Sciences, Social Informatics and Telecommunications Engineering 2015
J. Tian et al. (Eds.): SecureComm 2014, Part II, LNICST 153, pp. 252–266, 2015.
DOI: 10.1007/978-3-319-23802-9_20

where LTC transformer is connected. Although this local measurement based LTC operation can control the voltage profile at a upstream node where LTC transformers are connected, still downstream nodes of a traditional radial distribution feeder may suffer from poor voltage magnitudes due to lack of observability of the total system. Hence, in a smart grid environment, the operation of the LTC transformers are improved by utilizing an End-of-Line (EoL) voltage feedback with the aid of remote monitoring devices (voltage sensors) and communication networks [4]. This closed loop adaptive voltage control method improves the overall voltage profiles and ensures Conservation Voltage Reduction (CVR) of a smart distribution grid but may introduce new security vulnerabilities as control signals are passed through a communication network. In an Advanced Metering Infrastructures (AMI) based Smart Grid environment, end-user measurement data from smart sensors may also be used to take the voltage control decisions which is again proven vulnerable to spoofing attacks or man-in-the-middle attacks, typically known as False Data Injection (FDI) attacks in the Smart Grid community. These *Data Integrity* attacks targeting the LTC transformers to disrupt the stable voltage operation will have two major consequences- (i) *failure or decrement of the lifetime of LTC transformers*, and (ii) *Service interruptions and system failures resulting poor customer reliability and huge financial loss*. In the following paragraphs, we discuss recent cyber related anomalies in different components and operational modules of a Smart Grid and then draw the connections of these new yet alarming FDI attacks on the LTC transformers which can be launched to disrupt the stable voltage operations.

1.1   Cyber Attacks on the Smart Grid

We classify the Smart Grid vulnerabilities into four broad classes, discussed below:

(i) Cyber Attacks on the Communication Channels: Smart Grid is a cyber-physical infrastructure where both communication networks and physical power grid are highly coupled. Under a Supervisory Control And Data Acquisition (SCADA) controlled Smart Grid environment, traditional communication protocols (e.g., Modbus, DNP3, etc.) are proven vulnerable to cyber attacks [5–7]. For example, vulnerability of Modbus protocols are discussed in [5], where authors also propose a bloom filter based Intrusion Detection System (IDS) to protect the field devices of a SCADA system. Queiroz et al. propose a Smart Grid simulator where they discuss a scenario considering Modbus attacks to disrupt the operations of a SCADA connected wind farm [6]. Vulnerabilities of DNP3 protocols are discussed in [7] where authors design firewalls based on the monitoring and analysis of the system states. A detailed surveys of the cyber security issues of the Smart Grid is discussed in [8].

(ii) Cyber Attacks on the Smart Grid Operational Modules: A good number of research works have been conducted on the security issues of the Smart

Grid operational modules. State estimator, which is an important tool for determining system states, may produce misleading operational decision under a FDI attack. Authors in [9] have developed some heuristic approaches that have been proven to be successful in attacking the DC state estimation in such a way so that the malicious changes in the data cannot be detected by the state estimation module, hence the attach remains undetected. Further enhancement of the work can be found in [10]. While the research work [9,10] focuses on how to develop these types of unidentifiable attack, other research work are related to the development of a defense model [11,12]. Databases of the Smart Grid operation centre are also vulnerable to cyber attacks. This database manipulation attack may be undetected if proper security actions are not taken, as discussed in [13,14].

(iii) Cyber Attacks on the Sensor Devices: By gaining the access of the sensors (e.g., Smart meters) and Intelligent Electronic Devices (IEDs), an intruder can inject or manipulate wrong information. Various threats of AMI devices are discussed in [16,17]. Authors in [16] propose an adaptive tree based method to identify the malicious meters in a Smart Grid. A hybrid IDS for theft detection of AMI smart meters is proposed by Lo et al. in [17].

(iv) Cyber Attacks on the Actuators of a Control Device: The Automatic Generation Control (AGC) utilizes the power flow and frequency measurement data obtained from the remote sensors to regulate the system frequency within a specified bound. Esfahani et al. discuss the cyber attack scenarios of the AGC devices from the attacker's point of view [18]. To defend against these types of attacks targeting AGC, a model-based attack detection and mitigation strategy is proposed by Sridhar et al. in [19]. A detailed discussion and review of different Smart Grid cyber attacks can be obtained from [20,21]

1.2   Contribution

Although significant research works have been conducted considering the above top three types of security issues, there is still enough opportunity to further investigate the impact of cyber attacks on different actuators in a physical Smart Grid. Hence, we consider the remote node monitoring capability based adaptive voltage control of a LTC transformer to analyse the impacts of the FDI attacks. Specifically, the contributions of this paper are as follows:

(1) First, we discuss the voltage drop phenomena of a typical power distribution system and then show how the LTC operations can improve the voltage profile of the system. Then, we investigate the impact of the remote monitoring facilities under a Smart Grid consideration and explore how it can further improve the voltage profile of the whole radial system by ensuring the observability of the most distant node from the LTC transformer.

(2) Finally, the operation of the LTC transformer is analysed under FDI attacks. With extensive experiments, we show that the FDI attacks on the measurement data of the LTC controller will decrease the system efficiency and

stability. To the best of our knowledge, this paper, for the first time considers the FDI attacks on the operation of a LTC transformer. Here, we define two different attack strategies where measurement data are maliciously manipulated such a way it decreases the system efficiency or stability. For example, if the downstream node voltages are very close to the minimum operational threshold and they need LTC operations to boost up the voltages, the measurement data are modified such a way that the LTC controller takes the decision to decrease the actuator taps further instead of boosting up. As a results, voltage profiles in the physical downstream nodes will go beyond the minimum threshold of voltage stability limit.

1.3   Organization

The organization of this paper is as follows- In Sect. 2, the voltage drop phenomena of a distribution system and the corresponding LTC operations for voltage regulations are discussed. Adaptive LTC control operation with remote node monitoring mechanism is discussed in Sect. 3. Our proposed attack definitions and their impacts on the LTC operations towards disrupting energy system operation is discussed in Sect. 4. The paper concludes with some brief remarks in Sect. 5.

2   Preliminaries

In this section, we explain the voltage drop phenomena of a typical radial power distribution system. Then the construction and operational procedures of a LTC transformer based on local measurement data is discussed.

2.1   Voltage Drop of a Power Distribution System

Voltage stability has been a subject of great interest in recent years in attempts to ensure secure power system operations [22]. It refers to the ability of a power system to maintain steady voltages at all its nodes when there is a progressive or uncontrollable drop in its voltage magnitude after a disturbance, increase in load demand or change in operating conditions [23]. Voltage instability can lead to a voltage collapse which can be defined as a point in time at which the voltage becomes uncontrollable after a voltage instability [2]. Two major symptoms of voltage collapse are a low voltage profile and inadequate reactive power support. Generally, a distribution system is a low-voltage network which is very prone to the voltage collapse phenomena when it experiences increases in its load demand. Traditionally, distribution networks have been modelled for power delivery and consumption as a passive network considering the voltage drop phenomena. Actually, the R/X ratio of a transmission system is very low but, as the resistance of the conductors in a distribution system is very high, this leads to voltage drops along the distribution lines from the substation to load centre. To exemplify the effect of voltage drop, we consider IEEE benchmark 123 node test distribution system [24]. Under peak load condition, the voltage profiles of *phase-A* of the 123 node test system is plotted in the Fig. 1 using the sign 'o'. In the current setup we show the voltage drop phenomena without considering any LTC control. As seen from the figure, a good number of downstream nodes are below the minimum voltage stability threshold.

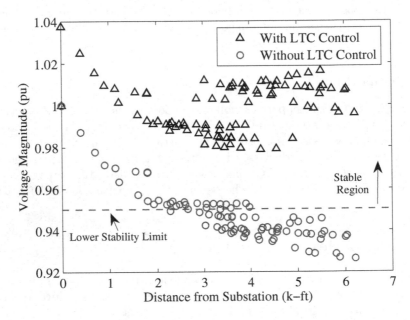

Fig. 1. Voltage profile of 123 node test system with and without LTC control

2.2   LTC Operation

In order to improve the voltage profile of downstream nodes, voltage regulation mechanism can be used. Traditionally, voltage regulation is performed based on an autotransformer with LTC mechanism. The desired voltage level is obtained by changing the taps of the series windings of the autotransformer [25]. The decision of the position of the desired tap is determined using a control circuit equipped with Line Drop Compensator (LDC). Generally, there are 32 taps in an LTC transformer and each tap changes the voltages by 0.00625 pu on a 120 V base   [25]. Throughout the operation of the LTC transformers, ANSI/IEEE C57.15 standard is maintained to limit the voltage within the voltage stability ratings. The operations blocks of the LTC transformer is shown in Fig. 2.

We simulate the impact of LTC operation on the voltage profile of IEEE 123 node test system. The parameter settings of the LTC transformer and their

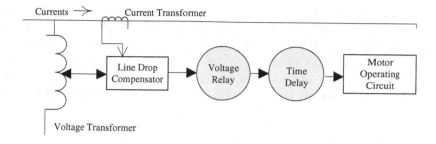

Fig. 2. LTC transformer block used for voltage regulation [25]

definitions are given in the Appendix. Using four LTC transformers, we obtain the voltage profile that maintain ANSI/IEEE C57.15 standard and remain within the stability margin. The *phase-A* voltage magnitudes are plotted in the Fig. 1 using the sign '$\triangle$'

3   Adaptive LTC Controller with Remote Monitoring Capabilities

In a traditional setup, the control decision of a LTC transformer is processed based on the local measurements of currents and voltages. As a result, the optimal control decision is not possible as the *Voltage Control Processor (VCP)* lacks full observability of the distribution system. Typically, the distribution systems are radial in nature where the voltage drops gradually and the *EoL* node faces the maximum voltage deviations. Therefore, monitoring the *EoL* node, the performance of the LTC operations can be further improved. In a Smart Grid, the

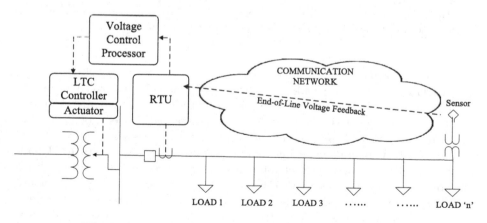

Fig. 3. Operational diagram of an adaptive LTC controller

sensor connected with the *EoL* node sends the measurement data or control input through a communication channel to the Intelligent Electronic Devices (IEDs) connected with the LTC transformers. The VCP within the IED takes intelligent decisions based on the input data. This is a *closed loop* process which takes adaptive control decisions based on the change of the input measurements. An operational diagram of this adaptive LTC control technique is given in Fig. 3.

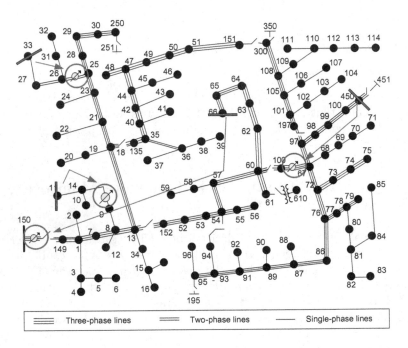

Fig. 4. LTC transformer locations and their corresponding remote monitoring node. Here, the *red circle* represents the LTC transformers and the *red* marked nodes are the remote nodes being monitored and controlled (Color figure online).

To simulate the impact of the adaptive LTC controller on the voltage profile, we consider a typical load profile of 24-hr period obtained from [26]. We run the power flow using Electric Power Research Institutes's (EPRI) OpenDSS [26] for the 24-hr period considering local measurement based LTC operations following the parameter settings described in the Appendix. For the same load profile, we use adaptive LTC operations using remote monitoring of node voltages. There-fore, the monitoring buses are set following the Fig. 4, where the target voltage of remote controlled node is set to 116 V with a 2 V bandwidth. Here, the remote nodes are being monitored by the LTC controller in the IED and control deci-sions are taken accordingly to run the system in a lower voltage level, which is welly known as CVR. Due to this adaptive LTC operations with measurement data feedback, the system efficiency is increased upto 1.8 % and an average of 1.4 % as shown in Fig. 5.

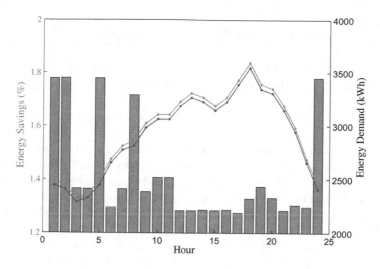

Fig. 5. Energy savings in a typical day using adaptive LTC transformers

4 FDI Attacks: Constructions and Impact

Although this remote monitoring based adaptive LTC control increases the efficiency, they introduce new vulnerabilities. In a SCADA connected network, sensors and actuator communicate with each other using Modbus, DNP3 or IEC 61850 standard protocols. The Modbus, DNP3 has already proven vulnerable under different types of cyber attacks, e.g., spoofing attacks [5–7]. Besides, with the advancement of Smart Grid, LTC operations can be further improved using closed loop measurement feedback from AMI smart meters. Widespread use of smart meters need the use of TCP/IP protocols, which is again vulnerable to cyber attacks [27,28]. In Fig. 6, the closed loop operation of adaptive LTC control under the attack uncertainty is shown.

In our analysis, we demonstrate two different types of attack strategies, discussed below:

(i) *Attacking Energy Efficiency:* Attacker maliciously modify the voltage measurement data such a way that the system operates at a higher voltage level which will need more power supply from the substation. As a result, it will increase cost and decrease the system efficiency as more energy is needed under an attack scenario compared with the base case. One simple example is demonstrated to illustrate the scenario. Suppose, the base voltage of the LTC is set to 120 V with a bandwidth of 2 V ($120 \pm 1V$). As the LTC has 32 taps, around 0.75 V change occurs due to per tap change [25]. Now we consider a situation where monitored node voltage is below the minimum voltage regulation limit of the LTC ($120V - 1V$). Therefore, the desired number of *tap operation* the LTC needs to control, can be calculated as follows:

$$Number\ of\ tap\ change,\ \ k_t^a = \frac{V_{reg}^{low} - V_{meas}}{\Delta V_{tap}} \qquad (1)$$

here, $V_{reg}^{low} = 119\ V$ and $\Delta V_{tap} = 0.75$. For any measurement voltage, $V_{meas} = 114.6\ V$, the LTC needs the following tap operations:

$$k_t^a = \frac{119 - 114.6}{0.75} = +5.47 \approx +6\ taps \qquad (2)$$

here, '+' sign indicates that the actuator will increase the tap and approximation to 6 is made as tap number must be an integer value. Now, if the measurement voltage information V_{meas} is manipulated such a way that the original measurement values are decreased (e.g., $V_{FDI} < V_{meas}$), the required number of tap operations will be increased following the Eq. (1). For example, if the LTC controller receive the measurement value $V_{FDI} = 112V$ instead of the true measurement value $V_{meas} = 114.6V$, the required number of tap operations will be calculated as $k_t = 14$. As the manipulated measurement information V_{FDI} does not represent the actual quantity of voltage (note, the true value is V_{meas}), the overall system will be operated at a higher voltage level due to the increase of tap operations. As the aim of the CVR is to lower the voltage level (by maintaining the standard stability limit) to increase the efficiency, operation at a higher voltage level will violate the CVR principles, hence the system efficiency will be degraded.

Based on the above discussions, we define the attack model towards energy inefficiency as follows:

$$V_{FDI}(t) = \begin{cases} V_{reg} - \Delta V_{tap} * k_t^a(t), & if\ no\ attack \\ V_{reg} - \Delta V_{tap} * k_t^m(t), & if\ attack\ exists \end{cases} \qquad (3)$$

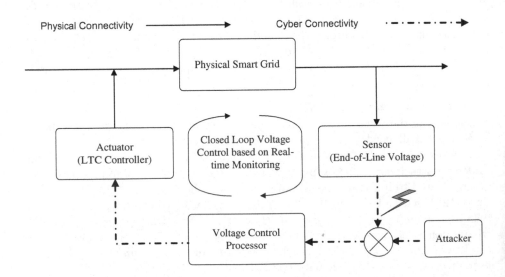

Fig. 6. Closed loop voltage control based on real-time monitoring

s.t.,

$$k_t^{max} > k_t^m(t) > k_t^a(t)$$

here, $k_t^m(t)$ is the intended number of tap operations chosen by the attacker and k_t^{max} is the maximum number of tap operations possible by the LTC transformer (generally, $k_t^{max}=16$ in one direction). Other symbols have their usual meaning defined above. Any value of $k_t^m(t)$ that is greater than k_t^a will represent a malicious modification of the measurement data which will initiative an attack scenario. The maximum value of $k_t^m(t)$ must not exceed the maximum possible tap operation value. Any value of $k_t^m(t)$ that is equal to k_t^a will produce the same corrupted measurement equal to the original measurement (hence, it does not represent an attack scenario). Note, all the values of k_t^{max}, $k_t^m(t)$, and k_t^a are integer as number of taps can't be a fraction. A larger value of k_t^a represents a greater attack magnitudes in terms of energy inefficiency.

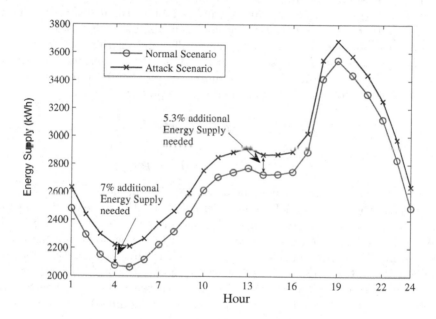

Fig. 7. Attack targeting energy system efficiency

Based on the load data, first we simulate the LTC operations with remote node voltage monitoring facilities using OpenDSS. Then, the corrupted measurements are generated following the Eq. (3), considering $k_t^m(t) = +8$. The total power supplied by the substation under normal situation and attacked scenario is plotted in Fig. 7. After the attack, we see that the total amount of energy supply is increased significantly, which is around 5.5 % in an average and maximum 7 % increase of the normal case. As the operational cost is a quadratic function of supply energy, the overall operational cost of the system will increase due to the need of the additional energy resulting from the attack vectors. Hence, the system efficiency will decrease significantly.

(i) *Attacking Energy Stability:* Now we recall the examples and the procedures of calculating desired tap value from the measurement data discussed in the previous section. If the measurement voltage is 114.6 V, the LTC controller takes the decision to increase the tap positions by 6 steps as calculated in Eqs. (1) and (2). Now, we observe that the measurement value V_{meas} is already at the lower half of the stability region, hence, the corresponding node voltage needs to be boost up by the LTC operations. However, if the LTC tap positions are further decreased rather than boosting up, the downstream node voltages of the LTC will decrease further which may go beyond the minimum voltage stability limit recommended by ANSI/IEEE. As a result, voltage collapse and system instability may occur resulting poor reliability of the system. So, the attacker may wish to target the system stability and reliability by maliciously manipulating the voltage measurement information such a way that it further decrease the LTC taps. Therefore, the attacker may utilize the relation of voltage measurements and tap numbers described in Eq. (4) to take intelligent decisions to disrupt the voltage stability of the system. Based on the above discussions, we define the attack model to unstable the system as follows:

$$V_{FDI}(t) = V_{reg} + \Delta V_{tap} * \lambda(t) \tag{4}$$

where,

$$\lambda(t) \in [+1, +16] \quad and \quad \lambda(t) > k_t^a(t) \tag{5}$$

here, $\lambda(t)$ is an attack factor defined using Eq. (5). For the value of $\lambda = 0$, $V_{FDI} = V_{meas} = V_{reg}$, therefore, the LTC controller calculates the value of $k_t^a = 0$ using Eq. (1). For the above example, where the measurement voltage is 114.6 V, the value of k_t^a is +6 obtained from the Eqs. (1) and (2). Now, following the attack definition in Eq. (4), we consider $\lambda = +8$ which is obviously greater than the calculated $k_t^a = +6$. Therefore, the attacker can modify the original measurement voltage with the new V_{FDI} which is 127 V. Once the LTC controller receives the measurement data (which is actually maliciously modified), it calculates the expected number of tap operations following below:

$$k_t^a(t) = \frac{V_{reg}^{up} - V_{meas}}{\Delta V_{tap}} = \frac{121 - 127}{0.75} = -8 \tag{6}$$

After the tap number is calculated, the actuator decreases 8 taps (downwards) to decrease the voltage level. As the original voltage was only 114.6 V, further decrement will force the node voltage to remain below the stability limit as shown in Fig. 8.

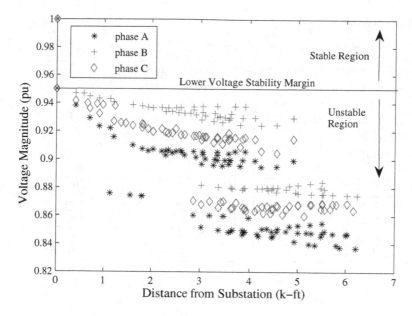

Fig. 8. Attack targeting energy system stability

5   Conclusion

In this paper, we have discussed the voltage drop phenomena of a traditional distribution system and the effect of LTC transformers to regulate the voltage level within stability margin. The advantages of closed loop adaptive LTC control based on the remote node monitoring is also explained. As the operation the this closed loop LTC control is highly dependent on the measurement data from a remote node, we show how the malicious modification (*FDI attacks*) of the measurement data can lead to distribution system operational disruptions. Here, we define two different types of attacks, one aiming to decrease the energy efficiency by demanding additional power from the substation and the another one is targeting the system stability by forcefully placing all node voltages under the lower stability margin. For the first type of attack, we see that a typical attack scenario can increase the need of power supply by 7 %. For the second attack type, every node of the distribution system goes below the stability threshold under a typical attack situation.

The scope of this paper is to define and study these new attack templates that target the LTC transformers to disrupt distribution system operations from an attacker's perspective. An Intrusion Detection System (IDS) to defend against these types of attacks is under preparation.

6   Appendix

Regulator ID:	1
Line Segment:	150 - 149
Location:	150
Phases:	A-B-C
Connection:	3-Ph, Wye
Monitoring Phase:	A
Bandwidth:	2.0 volts
PT Ratio:	20
Primary CT Rating:	700
Compensator:	Ph-A
R - Setting:	3
X - Setting:	7.5
Voltage Level:	120

Regulator ID:	2
Line Segment:	9 - 14
Location:	9
Phases:	A
Connection:	1-Ph, L-G
Monitoring Phase:	A
Bandwidth:	2.0 volts
PT Ratio:	20
Primary CT Rating:	50
Compensator:	Ph-A
R - Setting:	0.4
X - Setting:	0.4
Voltage Level:	120

Regulator ID:	3	
Line Segment:	25 - 26	
Location:	25	
Phases:	A-C	
Connection:	2-Ph, L-G	
Monitoring Phase:	A-C	
Bandwidth:	1 volts	
PT Ratio:	20	
Primary CT Rating:	50	
Compensator:	Ph-A	Ph-C
R - Setting:	0.4	0.4
X - Setting:	0.4	0.4
Voltage Level:	120	120

Regulator ID:	4		
Line Segment:	160 - 67		
Location:	160		
Phases:	A-B-C		
Connection:	3-Ph, L-G		
Monitoring Phase:	A-B-C		
Bandwidth:	2 volts		
PT Ratio:	20		
Primary CT Rating:	300		
Compensator:	Ph-A	Ph-B	Ph-C
R - Setting:	0.6	1.4	0.2
X - Setting:	1.3	2.6	1.4
Voltage Level:	124	124	124

References

1. Roy, N.K., Pota, H.R., Anwar, A.: A new approach for wind and solar type DG placement in power distribution networks to enhance systems stability. In: 2012 IEEE International Power Engineering and Optimization Conference (PEOCO), Melaka, Malaysia, 6–7 June 2012, pp. 296–301 (2012)
2. Johansson, S., Sjogren, F.: Voltage collapse in power systems, Ph.D. thesis, Chalmers University of Technology (1995)
3. Dzafic, I., Jabr, R.A., Halilovic, E., Pal, B.C.: A sensitivity approach to model local voltage controllers in distribution networks. IEEE Trans. Power Syst. **29**(3), 1419–1428 (2014)
4. Uluski, R.W.: VVC in the smart grid era. IEEE Power Energy Soc. Gen. Meet. **2010**, 25–29 (2010)
5. Parthasarathy, S.; Kundur, D.: Bloom filter based intrusion detection for smart grid SCADA. In: 25th IEEE Canadian Conference on Electrical & Computer Engineering (CCECE), pp. 1–6 (2012)
6. Queiroz, C., Mahmood, A., Tari, Z.: SCADASim - a framework for building SCADA simulations. IEEE Trans. Smart Grid **2**(4), 589–597 (2011)

7. Fovino, I.N., Coletta, A., Carcano, A., Masera, M.: Critical state-based filtering system for securing SCADA network protocols. IEEE Trans. Ind. Electron. **59**(10), 3943–3950 (2012)

8. Wang, Wenye, Zhuo, Lu: Cyber security in the smart grid: survey and challenges. Comput. Netw. **57**, 1344–1371 (2013)

9. Liu, Y., Ning, P., Reiter, M.K.: False data injection attacks against state estimation in electric power grids. In: Proceedings of the 16th ACM Conference on Computer and Communications Security, pp. 21–32. ACM (2009)

10. Ozay, M., Esnaola, I., Vural, F., Kulkarni, S., Poor, H.: Sparse attack construction and state estimation in the smart grid: centralized and distributed models. IEEE J. Sel. Areas Commun. **31**, 1306–1318 (2013)

11. Hug, G., Giampapa, J.: Vulnerability assessment of AC state estimation with respect to false data injection cyber-attacks. IEEE Trans. Smart Grid **3**, 1362–1370 (2012)

12. Qin, Z., Li, Q., Chuah, M.-C.: Defending against unidentifiable attacks in electric power grids. IEEE Trans. Parallel Distrib. Syst. **24**, 1961–1971 (2013)

13. Valenzuela, J., Wang, J., Bissinger, N.: Real-time intrusion detection in power system operations. IEEE Trans. Power Syst. **28**, 1052–1062 (2013)

14. Mousavian, S., Valenzuela, J., Wang, J.: Real-time data reassurance in electrical power systems based on artificial neural networks. Electr. Power Syst. Res. **96**, 285–295 (2013)

15. Grochocki, D.; Huh, J.H.; Berthier, R.; Bobba, R.; Sanders, W.H.; Cardenas, A.A.; Jetcheva, J.G.: AMI threats, intrusion detection requirements and deployment recommendations. In: IEEE Third International Conference on Smart Grid Communications (SmartGridComm), 5–8 November 2012, pp. 395–400 (2012)

16. Xiao, Z., Xiao, Y., Du, D.H.: Exploring malicious meter inspection in neighborhood area smart grids. IEEE Trans. Smart Grid **4**(1), 214–226 (2013)

17. Lo, C.-H., Ansari, N.: CONSUMER: a novel hybrid intrusion detection system for distribution networks in smart grid. IEEE Trans. Emerg. Top. Comput. **1**(1), 33–44 (2013)

18. Esfahani, P.M., Vrakopoulou, M., Margellos, K., Lygeros, J., Andersson, G.: A robust policy for automatic generation control cyber attack in two area power network. In: 49th IEEE Conference on Decision and Control (CDC) (2010)

19. Sridhar, S., Govindarasu, M.: Model-based attack detection and mitigation for automatic generation control. IEEE Trans. Smart Grid **5**(2), 580–591 (2014)

20. Anwar, A.; Mahmood, A.: Cyber security of smart grid infrastructure. In: The State of the Art in Intrusion Prevention and Detection, CRC Press, USA, 2014, CRC Press, Taylor & Francis Group, pp. 139–154

21. Anwar, A., Mahmood, A.: Vulnerabilities of smart grid state estimation against false data injection attack. In: Hossain, J., Mahmud, A. (eds.) Renewable Energy Integration. Green Energy and Technology, pp. 411–428. Springer, Singapore (2014)

22. Yorino, N., Sasaki, H., Masuda, Y., Tamura, Y., Kitagawa, M., Oshimo, A.: An investigation of voltage instability problems. IEEE Trans. Power Syst. **7**, 600–611 (1992)

23. Kundur, P., Paserba, J., Ajjarapu, V., Andersson, G., Bose, A., Canizares, C., Hatziargyriou, N., Hill, D., Stankovic, A., Taylor, C., Van Cutsem, T., Vittal, V.: Definition and classification of power system stability - IEEE/CIGRE joint task force on stability terms and definitions. IEEE Trans. Power Syst. **19**, 1387–1401 (2004)

24. Distribution System Analysis Subcommittee Radial Test Feeders. http://ewh.ieee.org/soc/pes/dsacom/testfeeders/index.html
25. Kersting, W.: Distribution System Modeling and Analysis. CRC Press, Boca Raton (2002)
26. Smart Grid Resource Center, Simulation Tool OpenDSS. http://www.smartgrid.epri.com/SimulationTool.aspx
27. Liu, C.-C., Stefanov, A., Hong, J., Panciatici, P.: Intruders in the grid. IEEE Power Energy Mag. 10(1), 58–66 (2012)
28. Xie, Y., Yu, S.-Z.: A large-scale hidden semi-markov model for anomaly detection on user browsing behaviors. IEEE/ACM Trans. Netw. 17(1), 54–65 (2009)

A Domain-Based Multi-cluster SIP Solution for Mobile Ad Hoc Network

Ala' Aburumman[✉] and Kim-Kwang Raymond Choo

Information Assurance Research Group, School of Information Technology and Mathematical Sciences, University of South Australia, South Australia, Australia
ala_fahed.aburumman@mymail.unisa.edu.au,
raymond.choo@unisa.edu.au

Abstract. Mobile Ad Hoc Networks (MANETs) are an active and challenging area in computer network research. One emerging research trend is the attempts in implementing or adapting existing voice protocols over MANETs. Successful implementation of voice over MANETs would allow an autonomous way to communicate. Session Initiation Protocol (SIP) is one of the most widely-used signaling protocols used in VoIP services. In order to implement a voice protocol over MANETs, SIP is generally required to be adapted for use over the decentralized environment instead of the overlay infrastructure-based networks. This paper proposes a Domain-Based Multi-cluster SIP solution for MANET. Our proposed solution eliminates the shortcomings of centralized approaches such as single point of failure and provides a scalable and reliable implementation. In addition, it reduces the overhead in existing fully distributed approaches. We then simulate and evaluate the proposed solution under different conditions and using metrics such as Trust Level, Proxy Server (PS) Load, Network Delay, Success Rate, and Network Management Packet.

Keywords: Mobile ad hoc networks (MANETs) · Session initiation protocol · Wireless ad hoc networks · Voice over IP (VoIP) · Voip over manets · Domain-Based Multi-cluster SIP

1 Introduction

In the past decade, there have been significant advances in the wireless arena and, consequently, we have witnessed an increase in consumer adoption of wireless technologies. An example of a widely used consumer product is Voice over IP (VoIP) that delivers multimedia over Internet Protocol (IP) networks (rather than using the Public Switched Telephone Network - PSTN). The two most popular signalling protocols for an IP-based network are the H.323- defined by the ITU, and the Session Initiation Protocol (SIP) - defined by the IETF. Increasingly, SIP is becoming more popular than H.323, mainly due to SIP's flexibility and relative simplicity [1]. Due to the popularity of 802.11/Wi-Fi enabled devices with more powerful built-in capabilities such as smart mobile devices (e.g. iOS and Android devices), Ad hoc networks can be used to support VoIP and other applications. For example, students physically present on the same

© Institute for Computer Sciences, Social Informatics and Telecommunications Engineering 2015
J. Tian et al. (Eds.): SecureComm 2014, Part II, LNICST 153, pp. 267–281, 2015.
DOI: 10.1007/978-3-319-23802-9_21

campus can communicate with each other using MANET-based VoIP [2]. However, implementing VoIP services over MANETs remains a challenge due to the inherent characteristics of MANETs (e.g. self-configuration of IP addresses).

One possible solution is to modify VoIP signalling services in order to support decentralized infrastructure-less networks. However, we would need to modify existing SIP services for deployment in a peer-to-peer (P2P) communication environment without compromising on availability, flexibility and efficiency (e.g. accepted call ratio) [1, 3].

In this paper, we propose a secure domain-based multi-cluster SIP solution for mobile Ad hoc network (MANET) that achieves scalability, reliability and availability.

In our proposed solution, we build a cluster-based logical overlay network on top of the network's nodes using a mechanism to minimize the overhead on the cluster heads by splitting and merging the cluster into smaller clusters in the same domain (see Sect. 3). This is designed to allow SIP users to communicate with each other either directly or to request for contact information from the logical SIP servers distributed among the network; allowing us to solve the bottleneck issue due to a standalone SIP server serving numerous client requests. In addition, our proposed solution employs security mechanism on different levels (i.e. servers and clients). To the best of our knowledge, this is one of very few publications to date that supports the secure use of SIP over MANETs. This is, probably, due to the fact that SIP has its own architecture that is based on several servers, which is more suitable for networks with a predefined infrastructure.

This paper is organized as follows: Sect. 2 reviews the background and related work. Section 3 describes our proposed domain-based cluster-based SIP solution for MANET. Our experiment setup and findings are presented in Sect. 4. Finally, Sect. 5 concludes this paper.

2   Background and Related Work

2.1   Background

The term VoIP refers to the use of IP to transfer voice. SIP, an application layer open standard developed by the IETF, is defined in RFC3261 [4]. It is a transport-independent, text-based, request-response paradigm and flexible signalling protocol, initially designed to accommodate multimedia sessions. Fundamentally, SIP is used for initiating, managing and terminating the multimedia sessions for voice and video across packet switched networks. SIP sessions generally involve one or more participants with SIP-enabled devices [4, 5].

SIP builds an overlay network on top of regular infrastructure IP-network by using the set of (following) entities communicated via SIP messages.

- User Agent (UA) is a SIP endpoint that interacts with the user.
- Servers (Proxy, Registrar and Redirect) communicate with each other or with the UA providing service.
- Gateway translates SIP into other protocols. Usually, gateways are used to connect SIP networks to the PSTN [4, 5].

An overview of a typical SIP overlay network architecture is illustrated in Fig. 1.

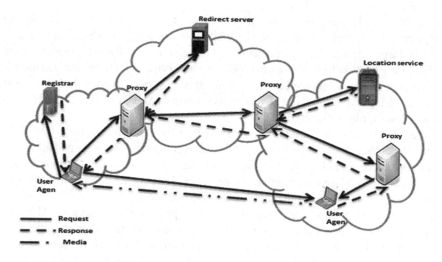

Fig. 1. SIP overly network architecture.

An Address of Record (AoR) is a SIP User Resource Identifier (URI), which is the SIP's addressing schema to call SIP users. AoR points to a domain with a location service that maps the URI to another where the user might be available [4].

It is important to differentiate between securing SIP-enabled sessions and SIP security. The former is ensuring the security of media data exchanged between parties. The latter is concerned with the exchanged SIP signaling. Like other protocols on the IP stack, SIP may suffer from various vulnerabilities. Despite the diverse security mechanisms that have been proposed for SIP-based applications [4, 6], securing SIP-based applications remain an active research challenge.

Wireless ad hoc networks are collections of autonomous nodes forming a temporary network without any centralized administration. They differ from traditional wired networks in several characteristics. For example, wireless nodes must track changes in the network in the absence of an administrator point in the network [2, 3]. Thus, establishing a secure VOIP session in such a distributed environment is a challenging task. Since SIP is the dominating signaling protocol for VoIP service, it is more practical to deploy secure SIP (rather than another signaling protocol) in a real-world implementation.

2.2 Related Work

Rebahi et al. [7] proposed the integration of a fully distributed certification authority (FDCA) as the underlying protocol for the public key infrastructure mechanism. FDCA makes use of a threshold scheme to maintain a secure SIP for Ad hoc networks' entities. It assumes the existence of a Certification Authority (CA), which issues certificates and maintains the certificate database. However, Rehabi et al.'s proposed security mechanism adds a significant overhead and the scalability factor was not considered in the implementation.

Leggio et al. [8] proposed a solution that inserts a set of the basic functionalities of a SIP proxy and registrar server in every mobile node forming a MANET. In this mechanism, the Registrar functions as an access port to manage the SIP location service entity, whereas Proxy Servers logically access the location service. User terminals can use their SIP clients in MANETs as well as in infrastructure networks. Although this proposed solution has a logical distribution of voice service over MANET, scalability and security were not thoroughly considered.

Bai et al. [9] presented a test-bed infrastructure for distributed wireless VoIP SIP servers. The architecture consists of centralized servers, and a SIP server and an Authentication, Authorization, and Accounting (AAA) server. However, the proposal used a centralized approach based on distributed servers, which may not be suitable for deployment in a decentralized environment (e.g. Ad hoc networks).

Bah [10] proposed a business model for service provision in standalone MANETs, which defines the business roles and the relationship, and interfaces between them. Bah also proposed (1) a service invocation and execution architecture to implement the business model based on the overlay network, and (2) a distribution scheme of the SIP servlets engine. The overlay network enables self-organization and self-recovery to take into account MANET's characteristics. The proposed solution is designed for a business model in a closed environment setting, which is much easier to deal with as long as the distribution of the voice service and security mechanisms is pre-agreed. It may not, however, be a viable option for everyday use in an open environment.

Kagoshima et al. [11] proposed an emulator architecture and local multipath routing suitable for SIP services. Their MANET emulator implementation demonstrated the feasibility of operating a SIP service from the time a request for session establishment is received to the establishment of voice packets and to the end of the session. The implementation also suggested that the local multipath routing provides a high probability of retaining the required path using an enhanced adaptive AODV routing protocol adaptive considering SIP service. However, this is only a simple test bed with limited nodes to implement voice and video services in Ad hoc networks. In addition, their work did not consider various important factors such as performance analysis, scalability and security.

Alshingiti [12] proposed an enhanced security mechanism for SIP over Ad hoc networks, by introducing an extension to the SIP header. This is done by combining Cryptographically Generated Addresses with the social network paradigm to provide authentication and message integrity. The proposed mechanism includes a reasonably secure mechanism to distribute an adaptive voice service for MANETs, but it adds a significant overhead and, again, the scalability factor was not considered.

Leggio et al. [13] proposed an architecture for MANET emulator in SIP service deployment (SIP_MANET emulator), which uses AODV protocol as the underlying routing protocol. A simulation of a test implementation to deliver voice and video services in Ad hoc networks was conducted using a small number of nodes. However, the study did not consider factors such as performance analysis, scalability and security.

In our previous work [14], we presented a secure nomination–based solution to implement SIP functionality in Ad hoc networks by combining Distributed SIP Location Service with two security techniques, namely; the Digest Authentication Access (DAA) and Simple/Multipurpose Internet Mail Extensions(S/MIME). Both DAA and S/MIME are used to provide secure log in service for users and data exchanged between proxies respectively. In the proposed solution, a node is elected to be a proxy server (PS) that handles SIP functionality and another node, Change D'affair (CD), is elected to be a backup for the server. The proxy is set to be the first node in the network, and then it will broadcast an election message to select a CD to be the next proxy after the PS delivers the task to the elected CD.

Abdullah et al. [15] proposed a secure cluster-based SIP service over Ad hoc network to protect the adapted SIP service from several types of attacks. This research eliminates the shortcomings of centralized approaches such as single point of failure, as well as reducing the overhead presented in fully distributed approaches.

It is clear from the literature that improving the scalability and security of SIP services on MANETs is an ongoing research challenge. This is not surprising as SIP relies on the resources of server functions, and unfortunately in a MANET environment, servers have limited resources. As the size of the network increases, the load on the servers increases, and consequently, this decreases their reliability and availability. In addition, the dynamic, unpredictable and self-configuring nature of MANETs complicates efforts to maximize the scalability and security of SIP services over MANETs.

The aim and novelty of this paper is the proposed solution to overcome the scalability shortcoming of MANETs in a secure manner. This is done by implementing a mechanism on the organizational level of the application layer using a domain-based dynamic clustering with a built-in reputation function to maintain the best selection of the servers based on a feedback from the network core and key ranking equation to implement an adaptive SIP solution over MANETs.

3   Our Proposed Solution

This section describes our proposed Domain-Based Multi-cluster SIP solution for MANET, which allows calls to be established between peer-nodes ubiquitously using infrastructure-less environment. It is assumed that the SIP application can perform at least one hop message broadcasting (Fig. 2).

In the proposed solution, SIP entities comprise SIP User Agent (UA) and SIP Proxy (a combination of SIP Registrar and SIP Discovery Server - SIP DS), and are implemented on the protocol stack. Nodes can also function as Registrar or as DS to register other SIP UAs or provide address-of-record (AoR) resolution respectively.

We note that a number of researchers have demonstrated that cluster-based solutions can address various limitations associated with Ad hoc networks such as in routing, traffic coordination and fault-tolerance [5]. Therefore, our proposed solution builds logical clusters over the SIP network at the application level. The formation of SIP network's clusters is based on nodes' positions within the network and the neighborhood degree. This approach eliminates the need for additional message types as it reuses the well-known SIP messages by adding special headers. The latter is used to indicate the nature of the exchanged message. The clusters consist of Cluster Head (CH) nodes which act as SIP DS. The terms CH and SIP DS (or SIP server) are used interchangeably in this paper.

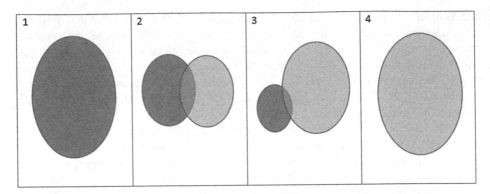

Fig. 2. Logical diagram – cluster splitting and merging. (1) Cluster reaches saturation limit. (2) Cluster splits into two separate clusters. (3) A cluster reaches minimal count. (4) Merges with an appropriate cluster.

Naturally, we assume that the network is vulnerable to attacks. For example, external attackers can launch various attacks targeting the availability of the SIP network (e.g. poisoning information to SIP users so that the SIP network is unable to establish calls). We also assume that SIP users will pre-share or establish their security associations with each other (e.g. they have exchanged their security keys offline or via other secure means). All SIP users are capable of using basic security algorithms such as Message Authentication Code algorithm.

The aim of our solution is to support both standard and ad-hoc SIP operations with the following design goals:

- Enabling Ad hoc node peers to establish calls over the decentralized environment of Ad hoc network based on SIP;
- Overcoming existing limitations of relying on static, fixed, and centralized entities;
- Preventing unnecessary expensive overheads (e.g. eliminating the need to distribute all SIP functionalities over the entire network) without affecting scalability or resulting in higher energy and bandwidth consumption; and
- Compatibility with the standard SIP.

Next, we will outline the modifications required to the standard components in MANETs to implement our proposed solution.

3.1   MANET Clustering

For MANET networks to utilize SIP for VoIP, we need SIP servers for the initialization and teardown of the P2P sessions as well as AoR resolution. Since MANET is a flexible network without any supporting infrastructure, the selected server needs to be one of the nodes within the MANET. These nodes typically have relatively little CPU power and battery life, and consequently, limiting the number of users in this service before latency issue occurs. To address this limitation, we use a clustering mechanism to dynamically elect or retire servers to load balance based on demand (see Sect. 3.4), which ensures a uniform service level.

3.2   Proposed Server Functionality

Primary Server (PS) is a node elected to act as a SIP Proxy and Registrar server to transmit and receive P2P connection requests for the nodes in the cluster that it manages.

This server maintains three different tables containing node data (Local Node, Global Node and Server). The PS has other duties, namely: servicing special invite requests of new nodes and merging and splitting the cluster based on the node count.

The Backup Server (BS) is a backup node that will take over or be promoted to act as the PS if the PS goes offline as well as supporting the PS with load balancing functionality. The BS keeps an identical set of the tables containing node data.

3.3   Reputation-Based Election

Using a reputation-based technique to select a PS or BS ensures that the chosen server is a trusted entity [12]. However, in such an approach, the preference of a server needs to be updated each time they are elected, affecting the stable operation of the network. To avoid this limitation, we propose a priority algorithm (see Eq. (1)) that takes into account the amount of time that a server has been operational when increasing its priority. This is to ensure that reliable servers are selected in preference to others.

Our proposed priority algorithm is as follows:

$$Priority = RPC + ((SU2)/10) \tag{1}$$

In the algorithm, RPC denotes the Reputation Point Count and SU denotes the Server Uptime. The initialization value of RPC for both the Backup server and the primary server needs to be different. For example, in our experiment, RPC is initialized to 1 when computing the priority value of the Backup server and RPC is initialized to 3 for the primary server, and an SU of 10 units will result in a priority value of 11 for the Backup server or 13 for the primary server.

The priority algorithm computes the reputation of selected functioning servers, which is used to determine their eligibility to serve as the PS or BS. To achieve a higher priority score, potential servers will have to either serve longer in the network (SU) or maintain higher roles (PS, BS). Our priority algorithm gives preference to a longer serving server than one who has served for a shorter period in different roles.

3.4   Proposed New Clustering Mechanism

The proposed clustering mechanism assigns one server to a specified set of nodes referred to as a cluster head. Each cluster has a maximum and a minimum saturation limit of nodes, which is used to trigger the respective cluster split and merge sequences. In a cluster split sequence, the BS node becomes the PS in the new cluster taking half of the nodes and then performing an election to select a BS. Once a cluster falls below the minimum saturation limit, the PS of that cluster will send merge requests to other clusters to amalgamate into an efficient cluster size.

3.5 Server's AoR Entities

The Local Node Table holds records of the local in-cluster nodes installed on every server and contains the Name, Status, Priority and Offline duration for all nodes in the cluster. This table is stored on both on PS and BS to keep track of all nodes in the cluster. The Global Node Table contains a list of all registered nodes in the domain, and each node can only be updated by their respective PS or BS. The table is distributed and installed on all in-domain active servers (participating clusters).

The Server Table contains information about the cluster servers such as Type, Public keys, Cluster ID, Server name and Priority. The priority field of the server cannot, however, be updated by itself – this field can only be updated by the in-domain active servers (cluster heads).

4 Experiment Setup and Findings

4.1 How Does the Proposed Solution Work?

Startup: The first node to initiate the service with a domain-name is the PS acting as a CH. In addition to the role of PS, the CH functions as the Registrar to maintain the AoR (generally a device-independent long-term identity of a user, such as an email address). The process is outlined in Fig. 3.

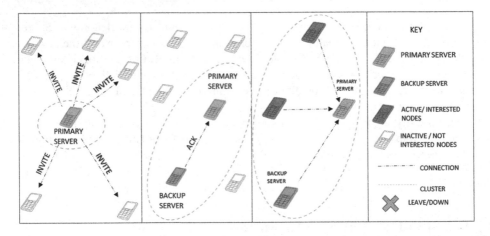

Fig. 3. Startup

On startup, the node initiating the service will advertise to all other nodes that are in range of the service. The first interested and eligible node to act as the BS will respond with an ACK command, which will be authenticated (e.g. using S/MIME security mechanism [12]). Once this node has been accepted as the BS, all subsequent nodes that send ACK's will be added as regular nodes to the service.

Primary Server Leave/Down Procedure: Should the PS exit the service (e.g. due to insufficient battery power), the BS will be promoted to be the new PS by the departing PS. The new PS sends an Election message to all registered and currently logged in nodes in the cluster to select a new BS and this must be done before any new node can be registered with this cluster.

The new BS is selected based on its priority. If no trusted node can be found to be elected to act as a BS, then a node will be selected by the new PS to act as the BS.

The handover process should not affect any client node cluster affiliation or the progress of already initialized SIP P2P communications, although there might be minor delays for nodes in the process of sending messages to the server. If the server goes offline unexpectedly or the BS does not hear from the PS for a pre-determined duration, then the BS is automatically promoted to be the PS temporarily until a server election is performed to select new servers (see Fig. 4).

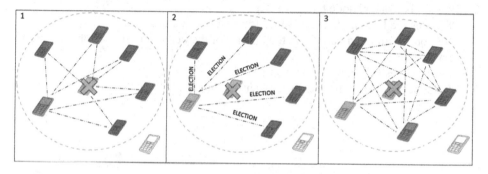

Fig. 4. Primary server leave/down procedure

Backup Server Leave/Down Procedure: If the BS exits the service:

- The BS will send a LEAVE message to the PS, and
- The PS will send an Election message to all registered and currently logged in nodes in the cluster to select a new BS and this must be done before any new node can be registered with this cluster

The new BS is selected using the procedure described in the previous Section. If no trusted node can be found to be elected to act as a BS, then a handshake is performed with an adjacent node to the PS and this node is now the BS.

The handover process should not affect any client node cluster affiliation or the progress of already initialized SIP P2P communications, although nodes sending messages to the server may experience minor delays. If the server goes offline unexpectedly and the PS does not hear from the BS for a pre-determined duration, then the PS triggers another server election to select a new BS.

Clustering Function: If the cluster reaches its saturation limit of nodes, the PS splits the table giving half the nodes to the BS, and the BS adds these nodes to a new Local Node table. BS will then create a new cluster and notify all his/her nodes with a new Cluster ID and Server ID. Both servers will also notify the other servers in the domain of the updates to their global node and server tables. An election is done in both clusters to ensure the best selection of servers.

Merging Function: When the Cluster reaches a minimum count threshold, the PS will find another cluster to join. Note that PS1 and PS2 denote the Local Primary Server and the Remote Primary Server respectively.

1. PS1 sends a GETCOUNT message to all other PS in the domain, which will respond with their node count;
2. PS1 selects the cluster with the smallest count of nodes;
3. PS1 sends a MERGE command to the selected cluster's PS (PS2);
4. If an ACK message is received from PS2, PS1 will notify his/her nodes providing PS2's Cluster ID and Server ID. Otherwise, PS1 will send a merge request to the next smallest cluster This process will repeat until PS1 successfully join a cluster;
5. PS1 sends its local node table to PS2;
6. PS2 adds the local node table values to its table and cluster;
7. PS2 notifies all other servers in the domain of the updates to their global node and server tables;
8. PS1 dissolves to a regular node; and
9. PS2 calls election in the merged cluster (see Fig. 5).

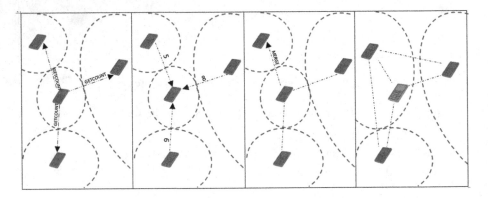

Fig. 5. Cluster heads merge/join procedure

When a node goes offline, the PS will remove their entry from the local node table prior to notifying other servers in the domain. The entry will only exist in the global node table for the period of 24 h (or a pre-determined duration). The node will then need to apply again as a new node when rejoining the network. For security reasons, only the PS and BS are able to update the state of a node and this is cross-checked against the Server table.

Server authentication is an important consideration to ensure the security and integrity of the services. For example, a strong server authentication will prevent low priority nodes masquerading as high priority ones to rig their own election. The use of a CHAP handshake when a server is being elected could be an effective authentication method, as the selected server would come into direct contact with the server that is electing it. This would prevent man in the middle attacks. Real-time blocking of accounts which was found to be in violation of policies (e.g. multiple logins from different locations and on different devices) is another effective way to mitigate risks associated with compromised accounts in a timely manner.

4.2 Findings

Our simulation of the proposed solution is described in this section, and we evaluate using the following evaluation metrics and parameters:

- PS Load: The number of messages received by the PS.
- Success Rate: The number of invitations successfully delivered to the intended recipient over time.
- Scalability: The behavior of the proposed mechanism when the number of nodes is increased.
- Stability: Shows the consistency with increasing number of nodes and its effect on the service request time.
- Time: The amount of time in seconds for the running of the network. For each second of run-time, the power of the nodes is decreased by one unit to take into consideration that the simulation time is not equivalent to one second in real-time network.
- Power: The measurement of power consumed in each node.
- Mobility: The movement of the node and its effect on the node.

We conducted 100 simulations under different conditions, and computed the average of the findings (also taking into consideration that all the nodes are changing position (mobility) with time).

Figure 6 presents the findings of the effect of PS load over the lifetime of the network. When the cluster was first established, the number of nodes within the cluster will increase (due to new registration) and eventually reach a point of stability. Once the threshold values are reached, the clustering process (i.e. merge or split) will commence. For example, as shown between the values of 115–134 on the X-axis of Fig. 6, the Merge process is triggered, and between the values of 248–267 on the X-axis, the Split process is triggered resulting into the forming of another cluster.

As shown in Fig. 7, the success rate is consistent and does not degrade over time. This is due to the network load being divided by the dynamic multi-clustering mechanism, resulting in a fair distribution of the load carried by each cluster. It is recommended that the threshold values (that trigger the Merge and Split process) be determined only after an in-depth analysis of the network behaviour to provide an optimal performance.

As shown in Fig. 8, our multi-clustering approach has significantly increased the number of participating nodes; addressing one of the challenging issues of MANETs (i.e. the overall management of the voice service was divided into clusters to evenly share the network load on dynamic clusters in the same domain). It is also worth pointing out that the cluster may fail to register nodes in the merge process occasionally, which may cause a visible drop in the number of nodes such as the example between the values

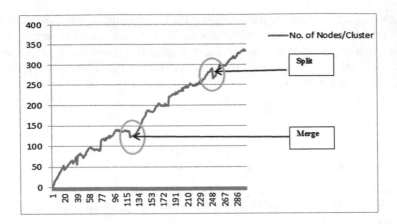

Fig. 6. Number of nodes per cluster over time

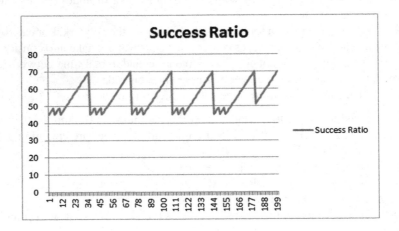

Fig. 7. Stability (success rate)

of 37–49 on the X-axis of Fig. 8. Those nodes can, however, re-register directly under any other cluster in the same domain and will be connected and added to the global table record. The noticeable sudden increase in the number of nodes between the values of 133–145 on the X-axis is due to the increase in the number of nodes interested in joining the network (e.g. peak/rush hour), which results in multiple splits of the clusters to register more nodes.

Figure 9 shows the reputation (server uptime) which ensures nonlinear growth of priority over time for this disparity between time, and points rewarded ensures the most stable servers are preferred (i.e. based on number of times the cluster heads and backup server were selected).

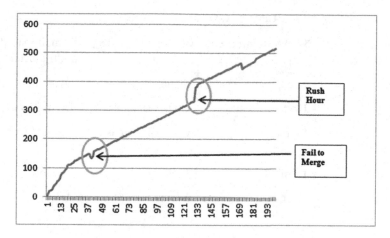

Fig. 8. Scalability (number of nodes against the simulation time)

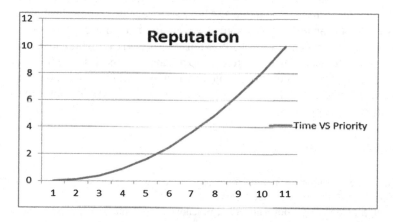

Fig. 9. Reputation (server uptime)

Our proposed mechanism has addressed issues previously identified in [14, 15]. As shown in Table 1, the domain-based dynamic clustering solution significantly enhanced the scalability factor of MANETs by adapting a SIP solution on the application layer to virtually organize and administrate the network in a dynamic way based on pre-determined thresholds to trigger the point of optimal performance. The security of the solution is also enhanced by the integration of our proposed priority algorithm as a way of quantifying the trust level. While the number of nodes in our previous mechanisms [14] was limited to a maximum of 50 nodes, this proposed solution can accommodate up to 350 nodes. In addition, our proposed solution has reduced the average number of management packets and provides a more flexible way to divide the overhead over the network, which stabilized the network and maintained an optimal performance.

Table 1. Comparative summary

	Nomination-based [17]	Cluster-based [18]	Domain-based multi-cluster
Priority	Static	Static	Dynamic
Scalability	Up to 50 nodes	Up to 80 nodes	Up to 350 nodes
Av. No. management packets	Stable	Gradual increase	Gradual increase
Stability	Limited	Limited	Flexible
Overhead	High	Varies	Average

5   Conclusion and Future Work

In this paper, we proposed a Domain-Based Multi-cluster SIP Solution for MANET that results in a stable, secure and scalable MANET service. Our proposed solution includes an advanced clustering technique designed to overcome the shortcomings of the adapted nomination-based mechanism in our previous work [14]. We simulated our solution under different settings and using different metrics and parameters. The findings demonstrated the utility of our proposed solution. Future work includes conducting user studies where we implement and evaluate our solution with student and staff mobile participants on the University campus.

References

1. Garber, M.: Securing session initiation protocol over ad hoc network. Master thesis, Institute for Pervasive Computing, Zurich (2005)
2. Basagni, S., Conti, M., Giordano, S., Stojmenovic, I.: Mobile Ad Hoc Networking. Wiley, New York (2004)
3. Stuedi, P., Bihr, M., Remund, A., Alonso, G.: SIPHoc: efficient SIP middleware for ad hoc networks. In: Cerqueira, R., Campbell, R.H. (eds.) Middleware 2007. LNCS, vol. 4834, pp. 60–79. Springer, Heidelberg (2007)
4. Rosenberg, J., et al.: SIP: session initiation protocol. RFC 3261, IETF (2002)
5. Sparks, R.: SIP basics and beyond, estacado systems. ACM Queue 5(2), 22–33 (2007)
6. Arkko, J., Torvinen, V., Camarillo, G., Niemi, A., Haukka, T.: Security mechanism agreement for the session initiation protocol (SIP), RFC 3329. In: IETF (2003)
7. Rebahi, Y., et al.: SIP-based multimedia services provision in ad hoc networks. In: MAGNET Workshop on My Personal Adaptive Global Net: Visions and Beyond, Shanghai, China (2004)
8. Leggio, S., et al.: Session initiation protocol deployment in ad-hoc networks: a decentralized approach. In: 2nd International Workshop on Wireless Ad-hoc Networks (IWWAN 2005) (2005)

9. Bai, Y., Aminullah, S., Han, Q., Wang, D., Zhang, T., Qian, D.: A novel distributed wireless VoIP server based on SIP. In: IEEE International Conference on Multimedia and Ubiquitous Engineering (MUE 2007), pp. 958–962 (2007)
10. Bah, S.: SIP servlets-based service provisioning in MANETs. Concordia University (2010)
11. Kagoshima, T., Kasamatsu, D., Takami, K.: Architecture and emulator in ad hoc network for providing P2P type SIP_VoIP services. In: 2011 IEEE Region 10 Conference (TENCON 2011), pp. 164–168 (2011)
12. Alshingiti, M.: Security Enhancement for SIP in Ad Hoc Networks. Carleton University, Ottawa (2012)
13. Leggio, S., Miranda, H., Raatikainen, K., Rodrigues, L.: SIPCache: a distributed SIP location service for mobile ad-hoc networks. In: Third Annual International Conference on Mobile and Ubiquitous Systems: Networking and Services, pp. 1–8 (2006)
14. Aburumman, A, Choo, K.-K.R., Lee, I.: Nomination-based session initiation protocol service for mobile ad hoc networks. In: Gaertner, P., Bowden, F., Piantadosi, J., Mobbs, K. (eds) 22nd National Conference of the Australian Society for Operations Research (ASOR 2013), pp. 149–155. The Australian Society for Operations Research, Adelaide, 1–6 December 2013
15. Abdullah, L., Almomani, I., Aburumman, A.: Secure cluster-based SIP service over ad hoc networks. In: 2013 IEEE Jordan Conference on Applied Electrical Engineering and Computing Technologies (AEECT 2013), pp. 1–7 (2013)

DAPRO 2014 and SSS 2014
International Workshop on Data Protection in Mobile and Pervasive Computing (DAPRO) International Workshop on Secure Smart Systems (SSS)

virtio-ct: A Secure Cryptographic Token Service in Hypervisors

Le Guan[1,2,3]([✉]), Fengjun Li[4], Jiwu Jing[1,2], Jing Wang[1,2], and Ziqiang Ma[1,2]

[1] State Key Laboratory of Information Security,
Institute of Information Engineering, Chinese Academy of Sciences, Beijing, China
{lguan,jing,jwang,zqma13}@is.ac.cn
[2] Data Assurance and Communication Security Research Center,
Chinese Academy of Sciences, Beijing, China
[3] University of Chinese Academy of Sciences, Beijing, China
[4] Department of Electrical Engineering and Computer Science,
The University of Kansas, Lawrence, USA
fli@ku.edu

Abstract. Software based cryptographic services are subject to various memory attacks that expose sensitive keys. This poses serious threats to data confidentiality of the stakeholder. Recent research has made progress in safekeeping these keys by employing isolation at all levels. However, all of them depend on the security of the operating system (OS), which is extremely hard to guarantee in practice. To solve this problem, this work designs a virtual hardware cryptographic token with the help of virtualization technology. By pushing cryptographic primitives to ring -1, sensitive key materials are never exposed to the guest OS, thus confidentiality is retained even if the entire guest OS is compromised. The prototype implements the RSA algorithm on KVM and we have developed the corresponding driver for the Linux OS. Experimental results validate that our implementation leaks no copy of any sensitive material in the "guest-physical" address space of the guest OS. Meanwhile, nearly 1,000 2048-bit RSA private requests can be served per second.

Keywords: Virtual cryptographic token · KVM · Virtio

1 Introduction

In computer and communications systems, data confidentiality is often provided by encryption. The strength of encryption mechanisms depend on both the security of the encryption algorithm and the secrecy of cryptographic keys. Over the years, there has been several encryption algorithms that withstand continuous cryptographic analyses. However, in a practical deployment, various reasons may cause the exposure of keys. For instance, key manager's dereliction of duty, improper software implementations, permeate attacks, etc. all put the keys at risk.

© Institute for Computer Sciences, Social Informatics and Telecommunications Engineering 2015
J. Tian et al. (Eds.): SecureComm 2014, Part II, LNICST 153, pp. 285–300, 2015.
DOI: 10.1007/978-3-319-23802-9_22

In particular, software vulnerabilities that leak memory regions to unauthorized subjects are main threats against the confidentiality of the keys. They extend to every level of the software stack and are often difficult to detect, due to the complication of computer systems. The sensitive data spread across the whole memory space (both kernel and user spaces) for longer than traditionally thought, even if the used memory is freed [1–3]. Applications designed with security in mind that zeros memory space containing the keys may also be fooled by the compiler, as such "superfluous" operations may be removed as a result of optimization [1]. Mobile-devices hoard a mass of sensitive information in plain-text in both RAM and stable storage. These data are very likely to be leaked once the device is lost [4]. The recently discovered OpenSSL vulnerability, namely Heartbleed [5], allows remote attackers without any privileged credentials to steal private keys. The bug is attributed to the loose inspection on the request packet that triggers a buffer over-read. Moreover, there are numerous subversions at the OS level that leak arbitrary kernel space memory to user space [6–8].

To migrate these attacks, threshold cryptosystems [9] and intrusion-resilient cryptosystems [10] are designed to withstand disclosure of some portion of the keys. In [11], keys are scrambled and dispersed in memory, but re-assembled in x86 SSE XMM registers when cryptographic computation is needed. Nikos et al. proposed implementing a cryptographic framework inside Linux kernel and providing cryptographic service to user space through a proven secure interface [12]. Unfortunately, all the above solutions only mitigate the problem to some extent. If the entire memory image is obtained by the attacker somehow, all "hidden" information is disclosed.

One of the most efficient and effective ways to safekeep keys is to employ hardware security modules (HSM). For example, Luna G5 is an usb-attached device that uses a dedicated chip to store user keys and perform cryptographic computation [13]. The keys are well protected both logically (keys cannot be legally accessed through the software interface) and physically (illegal physical invasion cannot obtain the keys). Optionally, whenever a cryptographic key is used, a LED flickers to alert the user that the key is being accessed. Since such approaches are secure and efficient, especially in insecure environments, they are often adopted in the industry, e.g., for authentication in online banking. However, hardware-based solutions all require additional costs, and are vendor dependent.

Motivation. We observe that hardware virtualization technology (VT-x for Intel and SVM for AMD) has been widely supported in commodity computers. By running a virtual machine, another layer of software isolation is added. The compromise of the guest OS does not harm the security the virtual machine monitor (VMM) or hypervisor. Based on this property, it is feasible to emulate a "HSM" in VMM for the guest OS such that arbitrary malicious code running in guest OS (including ring 0 malware) does not harm the key security.

In this paper, we present `virtio-ct`, a software virtual cryptographic token that aims to inherit some key advantages of a HSM. In particular, on top of virtualization technology, a `virtio-ct` virtual device:

- provides guest OS with RSA cryptographic service using emulated PCI interface.
- decouples cryptographic keys from the guest OS.
- is OS agnostic.
- audits all the accesses to the keys and emits physical signals in a mandatory way.

Like a real HSM, by designing an interface only for requests and responses, the cryptographic keys are never exposed to the guest OS. So even kernel compromise cannot retrieve the keys. At the same time, as `virtio-ct` is a software solution, users benefit from its flexibility, low costs and easy use.

The prototype is implemented on top of Kernel-based Virtual Machine (KVM) [14] and uses QEMU [15] as its user space device emulator. The communication channel is based on `virtio` [16], the de-facto standard for paravirtualization I/O. Experimental results show that `virtio-ct` achieves nearly 1,000 2048-bit RSA private key encryptions per second on an Intel core i7-4770S CPU.

Limitations. `virtio-ct` resembles a real HSM in many aspects, except that it is not resilient to physical attacks. A HSM defeats invasive physical attack by enclosing the key information in a tamper-sensing device. However, when a machine running `virtio-ct` services falls into an attacker's hand, this attacker could launch physical attacks to the RAM chip, for example, cold-boot attack [17].

`virtio-ct` only provides cryptographic key storage and computation services. A full Trusted Platform Module (TPM) also offers many other capacities like remote attestation [18]. Virtual TPM (vTPM) is a superset of `virtio-ct`. However, our work makes sense because of the following reasons: (1) vTPM needs a physical TPM to establish trust while `virtio-ct` does not rely on it. (2) A full vTPM is relatively error prone and may encounter many challenges because of its complexity. (3) System programmer needs expertise to work with TPM. In contrast, the application programming interface (API) of `virtio-ct` is much simpler: we provide services through the OpenSSL API by encapsulating several `ioctl` system calls.

Outline. The remainder of our paper is structured as follows: First, Sect. 2 introduces related works in this field. Then we describe the system model and applications of `virtio-ct` and clarify the attack model of it in Sect. 3. Next we give background information about VMM and `virtio` in Sect. 4. We introduce the design and implementation of `virtio-ct` in Sect. 5. Evaluations in terms of performance and security are presented in Sect. 6. Finally, Sect. 7 draws the conclusion.

2   Related Work

Protecting cryptographic keys from unauthorized access is a prerequisite for the security of the entire cryptographic system. Toward this, there are two generic ways. The first one keeps keys in the same memory space of the OS, while depends on software mechanisms to ensure strong isolation. Chow et al. proposed a secure deallocation mechanism to minimize the exposure of the keys [1]. Nikos et al. proposed a cryptographic framework inside Linux kernel to provide cryptographic service to user space through a proven secure interface [12]. Intel Software Guard Extension (SGX) solves the problem in hardware [19]. Specifically, it supplies new instructions to seal legitimate software inside an enclave and protected environment, irrespective of the privilege level of the malware.

virtio-ct falls into the second category, which escrows the key to a trusted third party. The keys are accessed either through network, PCI-E or usb interface in HSM solution. CleanOS [4] on the other hand, evicts the key that was used to encrypt sensitive data locally to the cloud when the data is not in active use. vTMP [18] emulates a TMP device in the cloud environment. It extended the current TPM V1.2 command set with virtual TPM management commands that allow users to create and delete instances of TPMs. Each created instance of a TPM holds an association with a VM throughout its lifetime on the platform. Compared with vTMP, virtio-ct provides a small yet important subset in the perspective of cryptographic computing. virtio-ct is more flexible (no dependance on real TPM) and efficient.

3   System Model and Threat Model

System Model. virtio-ct is designed to isolate cryptographic computation from the OS in commodity platform. For a secure conscious user, he or she would expect to run untrusted applications in an isolated environment to avoid possible infection to the host, while access sensitive data through a secure interface. To this end, the user may create a VM to execute that application while employ virtio-ct to request cryptographic service. Whenever the guest OS accesses the cryptographic keys, virtio-ct emits physical signals to notify the user, just like a real HSM.

Threat Model. We consider an attacker who can execute arbitrary code in the legacy OS – both in user space and kernel space. The attacker can achieve this by injecting customized code via buffer overflow attacks or implanting system level rootkits and Trojans. This implies that the attacker is able to manipulate page tables to access all desired memory regions.

We assume the attacker has no physical access to the computer. Otherwise, hardware-based attacks such as cold-boot attacks [17] or even bus-probing could be used to harm the security of the RAM chips.

We also assume that the underlying VMM is mostly safe. The compromise of the guest OS cannot escape from the VMM. That is to say, the adversary cannot interfere with Virtual Machine Control Structures (VMCSs), Extended Page Tables (EPTs) and other sensitive structures that require higher privilege. Note that a trend in designing VMMs is that the code size is reducing. For example, the Xen hypervisor [20] has approximately 100 kilo lines of code (KLOC) while BitVisor [21] has only 20 KLOC. The result is that it is easier to verify the security of VMM itself.

4   Background

This section first gives an overview of several popular virtualization solutions, with detailed description of Kernel-based Virtual Machine (KVM). Then virtio, a de-facto standard for para-virtualization I/O devices is explained. `virtio-ct` is implemented on top of both solutions.

4.1   VMMs and KVM

VMM is a software layer that abstracts isolated virtual hardware platforms on which several independent guest OSes run in parallel. These virtual machines (VMs) share the same set of physical resources with VMM acting as resource manager and device emulator. VMM guarantees that VMs cannot access each other's resources, including memory regions.

With the prevalence of hardware virtualization extensions, most instructions of the guest OS can be executed directly in the CPU. Unlike those in the host OS, they are executed in a separated non-root mode. In this mode, certain predefined events that are considered risky can be intercepted by the VMM, for example, privileged instructions, interrupts and I/O instructions. In this way, VMM runs in a more privileged level because it can decide whether or not these guest-issued sensitive operations can be executed. In both modes, the executable can run in either of the four privilege levels defined in the x86 platform. So traditional OSes that employ separated privilege levels do not have to modify its code to accommodate the virtualized environment.

There are two types of VMM architectures. Type I VMMs run natively on the bare-metal hardware and implement all the VMM functions itself. This include Xen, VMware ESX/ESXi, Hyper-V, etc. On the contrary, Type II VMMs run in the context of the host OS. This simplifies the design of the VMM because many of the host OS's functionalities can be used readily. Most notable implantations among these are VMware Workstation, Oracle VirtualBox and KVM.

KVM. KVM is implemented as a loadable kernel module originally for Linux on the x86 platform, but later ported to PowerPC, System z (i.e., S/390) and ARM platforms. The KVM module is the core of the KVM solution. It initializes the CPU hardware and provides a serial of VMM management interfaces through the `ioctl` system call, for instance, creating a VM, mapping the physical address of the VM, and assigning virtual CPUs (vCPUs). A dedicated user space program, namely QEMU, provides for PC platform emulation and calls the KVM interface to execute guest OS code.

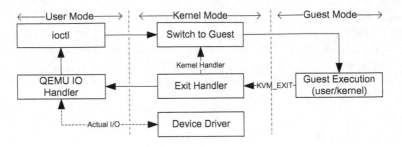

Fig. 1. Three vCPU modes in which the guest OS runs

In KVM, a guest OS is presented as a normal QEMU process and each vCPU is a thread. A QEMU process has three execution modes, namely, guest mode, kernel mode and user mode, as shown in Fig. 1. In guest mode, guest OS executes most of its instructions, either in user space or kernel space. Certain event causes a VM-EXIT and is intercepted by the KVM module. Then the QEMU process is in kernel mode. Based on the event that causes the trap, the exit handler deals with it inside the kernel or transfers it to user space. The former is called a lightweight exit while the latter is called a heavyweight exit, because the transfer leads to inter-ring switches. In user mode, QEMU accomplishes the exit handler and then calls the ioctl system call to resume the guest.

4.2 Virtio

In a full virtualization environment, the guest OS is unaware of being virtualized and requires no change of code. However, when encountering I/O operations, emulating hardware at the lowest level is inefficient. Conversely, in a paravirtualization environment, the guest and the VMM can work cooperatively to boost the I/O performance. Correspondingly, device drivers of guest OS should be modified (Fig. 2).

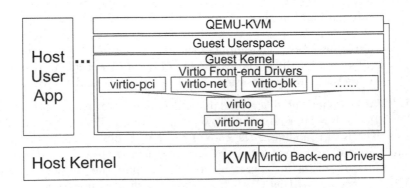

Fig. 2. Virtio architecture

Many virtualization solutions have their own para-virtualization I/O drivers with varying features and optimizations. `virtio`, developed by Rusty, aims to provide a standardized virtual I/O mechanism that works on multiple VMMs. To this end, virtio abstracts a common set of emulated devices and the VMM exports them through a common application binary interface (ABI). In this way, a particular device driver in guest OS can work with multiple VMMs as long as these VMMs implement the required behaviors in their back-ends.

Current virtio implements a virtio-over-PCI model to discovery virtio devices. Each virtio device is driven by two-layered guest-to-VMM communication.

Device Discovery. Because of the universal use of PCI devices, most VMMs support some forms of PCI emulation and most OSes have easy-to-use PCI driver model. A virtio-over-PCI model simplifies the coding of both sides in the virtualization environment.

Any PCI device with vendor ID of 0x1AF4 and Device ID 0x1000 through 0x10FF is recognized as a virtio device. The `probe` function of the PCI driver first allocates necessary resource (port I/O, MMIO regions and interrupt number) for the PCI device, and then calls `register_virtio_device()`, which puts the device on a virtual bus, namely `virtio-bus`. Virtio drivers pick up the devices on `virtio-bus` and recognize the particular `virtio` device based on the subsystem vendor and device ids of its underlying PCI device.

Virtio. The `struct virtio_device` passed in to the virtio driver contains a `virtio_config_ops` struct, which is an array of function pointers. These functions can be used to configure/reset the device by reading/writing a configuration space in the first I/O region of the PCI device. In addition, a dedicated function `find_vq()` can be used to instantiate several `virtqueues` which conceptually attach front-end drivers to back-end drivers.

Transport Abstraction and Virtio_ring. Virtqueue is the second abstraction layer for transport. There are functions on it to (1) write new buffers (2) get used buffers (3) notify VMM that new buffers have been added, etc. In addition, when VMM consumes the data and feeds back results to the guest, a callback function is called as an interrupt handler. This callback function is assigned by function `find_vq()` when the `virtqueue` is instantiated.

Theoretically, this layer can be implemented in any way, provided that the guest and the VMM abide by the same rule. Current virtio implements `virtio_ring`, a simple ring-based scheme. The buffers are represented as scatter-gather list, which are chained by the `vring_desc` data structure. Newly added buffers and used buffers are indicated by `available_ring` and `used_ring` respectively. The addresses of the buffers are allocated dynamically inside the guest. To inform the VMM of these addresses, guest writes "guest-physical" addresses to the configure space. The actual "host-virtual" addresses can be calculated by simply adding an offset.

5   Design and Implementation

As shown above, `virtio` exhibits an extreme slim architecture and a flexible interface that greatly reduce the effort to port it to other platforms. Although its original purpose is to standardize virtual I/O devices, we find that it has the building block to implement a virtual cryptographic device. Indeed, `virtqueue` is an ideal place to exchange requests and responses.

In this section, we first explain the design goals of `virtio-ct`. Then we show the way we export keys to the VM. Next, we describe the implementation of actual cryptography service. Finally, the user API and usage are demonstrated.

5.1   Design Goals

The most primary design goal of virtio-ct is that cryptographic keys and sensitive intermediate state during computation should never be accessible by the VM. To this end, the shared buffers that are accessible by both sides should be restricted to those only contain the input/output of the computation. The actual RSA keys and its context should never be exposed to the memory space of the VM.

Meanwhile, every access to the key should be strictly audited and notified. Otherwise, malicious processes could stealthily sign any data it wants to sign once the OS kernel is compromised.

5.2   Key Initialization

`virtio-ct` instantiates two pairs of `virtqueues` during initialization. A pair of `virtqueues` is a channel between VMM and VM: one for transmission and one for receiving. One pair of them serves for the cryptographic computation. The left one is reserved for the purpose of key management, which communicates between VMM and VM about the key information as shown in Fig. 3.

Management Channel. By default, a `virtio-ct` device only contains a management channel and a pair of `virtqueues`. The actual RSA token is specified as a separate device, namely `virtio-ct-token`. A `virtio-ct-token` device is

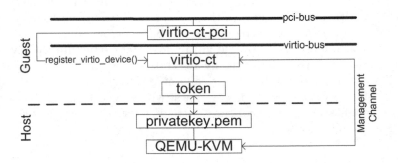

Fig. 3. `virtio-ct` architecture

back-ended by a RSA private key file in PEM format, which is decrypted by a pass phrase when the VM is launched. During initialization of `virtio-ct`, it sends management messages through the reserved management channel to add the token to `virtio-ct` dynamically. In particular, we define the following commands:

- VIRTIO_CT_READY: VM notifies VMM that `virtio-ct` is ready for use.
- VIRTIO_CT_TOKEN_ADD: VMM sends information about `virtio-ct-token` to the VM.
- VIRTIO_CT_TOKEN_READY: VM acknowledges VMM of the added token.
- VIRTIO_CT_TOKEN_NAME: VMM sends VM a user friendly string that describes a given token.
- VIRTIO_CT_TOKEN_PUBKEY: VMM sends VM the plain-text public key of a given token.

The management message has the following structure (`len` is variable, so this code will not compile):

```
struct virtio_ct_management {
    __u16 cmd;  /* command */
    __u8 buffer[len];  /* command data */
};
```

We do not support hot-plugging and changing RSA keys when VM is running. These features may be useful for VM migration but is not of particular importance in our scenario.

5.3   Cryptographic Service

VM and VMM exchange cryptographic requests/responses though a `virtqueue` pair. VMM calls the OpenSSL cryptographic library to do the actual computation. The request message is sent in the following layout (`in_len` is variable, so this code will not compile):

```
struct virtio_ct_request {
    __u16 cmd;
    __u16 padding;
    __u16 in_len;
    __u8 buffer[in_len];
};
```

`cmd` decides which of the 4 following operations should be performed: (1) encryption with public key (2) decryption with public key (3) encryption with private key (4) decryption with private key. `padding` denotes the padding modes. They are PKCS1, OAEP, SSLV23 or NO-PADDING. All of them are supported by OpenSSL. We note that public key calculations are completely unnecessary to be pushed in VMM, because public keys are safe to be store in VM. User should consider perform public calculation directly in VM instead of in VMM for efficiency. We

enable CRT, sliding windows and Montgomery multiplication to boost performance, and also RSA-blinding to defeat against timing side channel attack on
RSA keys [22].

The response message is much simpler:

```
struct virtio_ct_response {
    __u16 out_len;
    __u8 buffer[out_len];
};
```

If an error occurs (different padding methods have different restrictions on input
length), out_len is 0 and buffer is omitted.

Audit. Although the primary goal of virtio-ct is not on access control of
the cryptographic service, we do not want unauthorized RSA operations to be
performed stealthily without the RSA key owner knowing about it. We write a
log whenever VM requests for cryptographic service. Meanwhile, just like a real
HSM, virtio-ct makes a sound by driving the *pc-speaker* that is a standard
component of the PC platform to notify the user. Note that audit is accomplished
in the VMM, so the VM cannot suppress this when it issues cryptographic
request.

5.4 Use Case

This section first demonstrates the user interface to launch a VM with virtio-ct
support. Then we show the application programming interface (API) for Linux
developers. The implementation of windows driver is in progress.

User Interface. virtio-ct consists of a virtual PCI device (virtio-ct) and
a cryptographic token (virtio-ct-token) that is logically attached to it. To
add cryptographic token support to a VM, users append a virtio-ct-pci
and a virtio-ct-token option to the QEMU command line. virtio-ct-pci
is interpreted into a virtio-ct virtual device as shown in Fig. 3 while
virtio-ct-token is the actual token, which requires a PEM formatted private key file as back-end. In Fig. 4, the VM is assigned a cryptographic token
that is associated with a distinct printable identifier "key0" thought the **name**
argument and an encrypted private key file "/data/prikey0.pem" through the
privatekeypath argument.

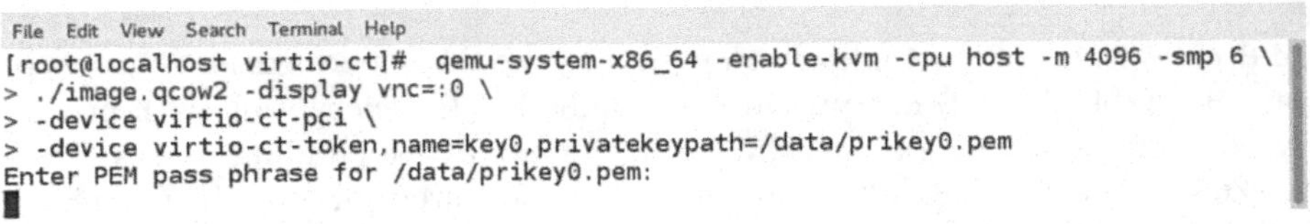

Fig. 4. virtio-ct command line options

API Structure. `virtio-ct` supports two categories of APIs. The `sysfs` attributes are used to export token's name and public key. These are useful for device identification. For example, `udev` rules can be configured to create symlink to the token device by its name (Fig. 5).

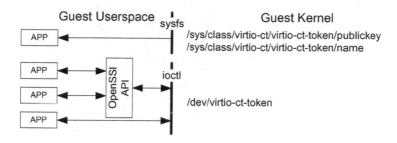

Fig. 5. `virtio-ct` API

The other category of API is used for the actual cryptographic services described in Sect. 5.3. Accordingly, there are 4 kinds of `ioctl` commands to perform a public/private encryption/decryption. The used padding mode is included in the `ioctl` messages. Furthermore, we encapsulate this device specific API to a universal applicable module – an OpenSSL engine. When the RSA key is loaded through the function `ENGINE_load_private_key()`, the corresponding virtual token can be used to do cryptographic computation by calling widely used OpenSSL routines. This would be useful for the easy integration of `virtio-ct` into other cryptographic programs.

6   Evaluation

6.1   Performance

We show the throughput of the `virtio-ct` prototype, and compare it with the native OpenSSL implementation inside the VM. In addition, we measured the system load of both the VMM and VM when calling `virtio-ct` service. All the experiments were conducted using 2048-bit RSA keys to do a private key encryption, and the padding mode is `PKCS1`. The target machine is a Lenovo PC with an Intel core i7-4770S CPU and 8 GB memory. The used CPU has 4 physical cores with hyper-threading support.

Throughput was measured in multi-core mode. Specifically, we enabled hyper-threading on the host and assigned 6 vCPUs and 4 GB memory to the VM. Each thread requests for private key encryption in an infinite loop. In Fig. 6, we can see that the throughput of `virtio-ct` does not grow as the concurrency level increases, instead, it decreases slightly. This is because only one I/O thread can execute in the VMM and the increased threads only adds the burden of

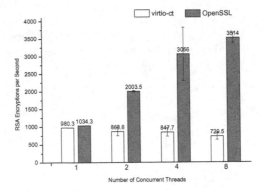

Fig. 6. Throughput

task scheduling. We will expand this in the next section. One interesting observation is that the standard deviations of both solution are extraordinarily high when there are more threads. We attribute it to hyper-threading. In fact, when 2 threads are running in the same physical core, the speed is degraded as these two logical threads share the same set of execution unit.

We next measured the latency for each cryptographic request. To minimize the effect of hyper-threading and task scheduling, we assigned a single thread to the VM and disabled hyper-threading on host. The average latencies are 1041.3 ms and 964.9 ms for `virtio-ct` and OpensSSL respectively. These values are very close to the average processing time drawn in Fig. 6. This is somehow expected: `virtio-ct` works in blocking mode and the RSA computation time is much more than the time spent on context switching.

We then used the `top` utility to record the CPU load of both the host and guest machine when there is one `virtio-ct` thread. Obviously, one thread achieves the maximum throughput. System loads were recorded per second for 1000 s, and the statistics on average were calculated as shown in Table 1. Apart from idle state, VM spent most of time in kernel mode and on handling hardware interrupts. Note that VMM notifies VM of the returned data by virtual-interrupt injection. In contrast, VMM spent most of time in user space. Indeed, RSA computation runs inside the QEMU process which is in user mode.

Table 1. CPU state percentages for VM and VMM. The host machine has 4 physical cores with hyper-threading enabled. VM is attributed 6 vCPUs and launches a single thread to call `virtio-ct` service in an infinite loop.

	User*	Kernel	Idle	Wait for I/O	Hardware interrupts	Software interrupts
VM	0.043	13.830	74.334	2.372	8.819	0.602
VMM	24.987	1.142	73.735	0.098	0.032	0.006

*User state presents time running both niced and un-niced user processes.

Efficiency Issues. As shown above, the maximum throughput of `virtio-ct` is close to that of native OpenSSL library with one vCPU, regardless of the attributed number of vCPUs. This indicts that the current QEMU implementation can only execute one I/O thread simultaneously. Figures 7 and 8 list some code snaps that handle I/O events. I/O could be served either in a dedicated QEMU I/O thread or in vCPUs threads. However, there is a global mutex that synchronizes core QEMU code across them. That is, only one thread can execute code that handles I/O that may operate on global structures of QEMU. Note that when there is not much I/O events, vCPU is in the guest mode for most of the time, so several vCPUs can runs in parallel for computation-intensive programs.

The current QEMU thread structure is sufficient for real I/O tasks when most of CPU time are waste waiting for I/O completion. For virtual I/O that does not involve real peripheral, like `virtio-ct`, the constraint that all the I/O must be serialized is a big hit for performance. One of our future work is to allocate more threads that are isolated from the QEMU context, so that cryptographic service can be executed in parallel in these extra threads. In fact, VNC [23] and SPICE [24] display protocols which involve intensive computation (video codecs, display encryption, etc.) have adopted similar solutions.

6.2   Security

We performed extensive tests that observe the memory space of the VM to ensure that there is no occurrence of private RSA keys. Inside the QEMU console, we used the `dump-guest-memory` command to dump the memory image of the VM and the `info registers` command to obtain register contents, and then used various ways to find RSA keys. We first invoked an automatic tool called RSAKeyFinder [25]. It searches for the patterns of DER-encoded RSA keys to find suspicious memory contents. We successfully find out some occurrences of RSA keys, but none of them is that used in `virtio-ct`. On the contrary, when we ran the tool on the memory dump of the QEMU process, all the used keys were recovered.

```
int main_loop_wait(...)
{
    ......
    qemu_mutex_unlock_iothread();
    g_poll_ret = qemu_poll_ns(
        poll_fds, ...);
    qemu_mutex_lock_iothread();
    if(g_poll_ret > 0)
    /* process I/O */
}
```

```
int kvm_cpu_exec(CPUState *cpu)
{
    ......
    qemu_mutex_unlock_iothread();
    run_ret = kvm_vcpu_ioctl(cpu,
        KVM_RUN, 0);
    qemu_mutex_lock_iothread();
    kvm_arch_post_run(cpu, run);
    /* process I/O */
}
```

Fig. 7. Dedicated I/O thread

Fig. 8. vCPU thread

The second method is using a simple binary matching program `bgrep`. As we know the plain-text of the keys, we used `bgrep` to match the key string (including p, q, d and other CRT elements). It turned out that we never found a binary sequence that overlaps for more than 3 bytes with any key. These experiments proves that there will be no occurrence of escrowed RSA key copies when employing `virtio-ct`. The compromise of guest OS will not effect the secure storage of keys, provided that the VMM is implemented correctly.

7   Conclusions and Future Work

We present `virtio-ct`, a virtual cryptographic token in the KVM virtualization environment. `virtio-ct` assembles a real HSM in that it never exposes the real keys to the guest OS, so that the compromise of the guest OS will not threaten the secrecy of the keys. Moreover, audit is enforced in a mandatory way when the `virtio-ct` service is called. Because `virtio-ct` is a software solution and most personal computers have support for hardware virtualization, it is more flexible and economical to achieve cryptographic key isolation, compared with HSM solutions. Our prototype achieves nearly 1,000 times RSA private operations per second on a mainstream Intel desktop processor.

Future Work. We intend to extend the prototype with the following features.

1. Dedicated cryptographic threads to boost performance.
2. Physical memory attack resistance: We are resorting to solutions such as PRIME [26] and Copker [27] to add cold-boot resistent in the VMM. As a result, `virtio-ct` achieves comparable security strength with HSM in all aspects.
3. Conformation to the PKCS#11 standard [28]. We plan to support more cryptographic algorithms through this widely used standard API.

Acknowledgments. The authors would like to thank the anonymous reviewers for their helpful suggestions and valuable comments. Le Guan, Jiwu Jing, Jing Wang and Ziqiang Ma were partially supported by National 973 Program of China under award No. 2014CB340603. Fengjun Li was partially supported by NSF under Award No. EPS0903806 and matching support from the State of Kansas through the Kansas Board of Regents, and the University of Kansas Research Investment Council Strategic Initiative Grant (INS0073037).

References

1. Chow, J., Pfaff, B., Garfinkel, T., Rosenblum, M.: Shredding your garbage: reducing data lifetime through secure deallocation. In: 14th USENIX Security Symposium (2005)
2. The MITRE Corporation, CWE-226: Sensitive information uncleared before release (2013). https://cwe.mitre.org/data/definitions/226.html
3. The MITRE Corporation, CWE-212: Improper cross-boundary removal of sensitive data (2013). https://cwe.mitre.org/data/definitions/212.html

4. Tang, Y., Ames, P., Bhamidipati, S., Bijlani, A., Geambasu, R., Sarda, N.: Cleanos: Limiting mobile data exposure with idle eviction. In: 10th USENIX Symposium on Operating Systems Design and Implementation (OSDI 12), Hollywood, CA, pp. 77–91 (2012)
5. National Vulnerability Database, CVE-2014-0160. http://web.nvd.nist.gov/view/vuln/detail?vulnId=CVE-2014-0160
6. Engler, D., Chen, D., Hallem, S., Chou, A., Chelf, B.: Bugs as deviant behavior: a general approach to inferring errors in systems code. In: 18th ACM Symposium on Operating Systems Principles, pp. 57–72 (2001)
7. Lafon, M., Francoise, R.: CAN-2005-0400: Information leak in the Linux kernel ext2 implementation (2005). http://www.securiteam.com
8. Guninski, G.: Linux kernel 2.6 fun, Windoze is a joke (2005). http://www.guninski.com
9. Desmedt, Y.G., Frankel, Y.: Threshold cryptosystems. In: Brassard, G. (ed.) CRYPTO 1989. LNCS, vol. 435, pp. 307–315. Springer, Heidelberg (1990)
10. Itkis, G., Reyzin, L.: SiBIR: signer-base intrusion-resilient signatures. In: Yung, M. (ed.) CRYPTO 2002. LNCS, vol. 2442, pp. 499–514. Springer, Heidelberg (2002)
11. Parker, T.P., Xu, S.: A method for safekeeping cryptographic keys from memory disclosure attacks. In: Chen, L., Yung, M. (eds.) INTRUST 2009. LNCS, vol. 6163, pp. 39–59. Springer, Heidelberg (2010)
12. Mavrogiannopoulos, N., Trmač, M., Preneel, B.: A linux kernel cryptographic framework: decoupling cryptographic keys from applications. In: Proceedings of the 27th Annual ACM Symposium on Applied Computing, ser. SAC 2012, pp. 1435–1442 (2012)
13. Safe Net, Luna g5 usb-attached hsm. http://www.safenet-inc.com/data-encryption/hardware-security-modules-hsms/luna-hsms-key-management/luna-G5-usb-attached-hsm/. Accessed July 2014
14. Kernel Based Virtual Machine. http://www.linux-kvm.org/page/Main_Page
15. QEMU open source processor emulator. http://wiki.qemu.org/Main_Page
16. Russell, R.: Virtio: towards a De-facto standard for virtual I/O devices. SIGOPS Oper. Syst. Rev. 42(5), 95–103 (2008)
17. Halderman, J., Schoen, S., Heninger, N., Clarkson, W., Paul, W., Calandrino, J., Feldman, A., Appelbaum, J., Felten, E.: Lest we remember: cold boot attacks on encryption keys. In: 17th USENIX Security Symposium, pp. 45–60 (2008)
18. Berger, S., Cáceres, R., Goldman, K.A., Perez, R., Sailer, R., van Doorn, L.: vTPM: virtualizing the trusted platform module. In: 15th USENIX Security Symposium, vol. 15 (2006)
19. Intel Corporation, Intel software guard extensions. https://software.intel.com/en-us/intel-isa-extensions#pid-19539-1495. Accessed July 2014
20. Barham, P., Dragovic, B., Fraser, K., Hand, S., Harris, T., Ho, A., Neugebauer, R., Pratt, I., Warfield, A.: Xen and the art of virtualization. SIGOPS Oper. Syst. Rev. 37(5), 164–177 (2003)
21. Shinagawa, T., Eiraku, H., Tanimoto, K., Omote, K., Hasegawa, S., Horie, T., Hirano, M., Kourai, K., Oyama, Y., Kawai, E., Kono, K., Chiba, S., Shinjo, Y., Kato, K.: Bitvisor: a thin hypervisor for enforcing i/o device security. In: Proceedings of the 2009 ACM SIGPLAN/SIGOPS International Conference on Virtual Execution Environments, pp. 121–130 (2009)
22. Brumley, D., Boneh, D.: Remote timing attacks are practical. Comput. Netw. 48(5), 701–716 (2005)
23. Virtual Network Computing. http://www.realvnc.com/

24. SPICE: Simple Protocol for Indenpendent Enviroment. http://www.spice-space.org/
25. Heninger, N., Feldman, A.: RSAKeyFinder. https://citp.princeton.edu/research/memory/code/
26. Garmany, B., Müller, T.: PRIME: private RSA infrastructure for memory-less encryption. In: 29th Annual Computer Security Applications Conference (2013)
27. Guan, L., Lin, J., Luo, B., Jing, J.: Copker: Computing with private keys without RAM. In: 21st ISOC Network and Distributed System Security Symposium (2014)
28. RSA Laboratories, PKCS#11: Cryptographic Token Interface Standard. http://www.emc.com/emc-plus/rsa-labs/standards-initiatives/pkcs-11-cryptographic-token-interface-standard.htm

Blind Format String Attacks

Fatih Kilic$^{(\boxtimes)}$, Thomas Kittel, and Claudia Eckert

Technische Universität München, München, Germany
{kilic,kittel,eckert}@sec.in.tum.de

Abstract. Although Format String Attacks (FSAs) are known for many years there is still a number of applications that have been found to be vulnerable to such attacks in the recent years. According to the CVE database, the number of FSA vulnerabilities is stable over the last 5 years, even as FSA vulnerabilities are assumingly easy to detect. Thus we can assume, that this type of bugs will still be present in future. Current compiler-based or system-based protection mechanisms are helping to restrict the exploitation this kind of vulnerabilities, but are insufficient to circumvent an attack in all cases.

Currently FSAs are mainly used to leak information such as pointer addresses to circumvent protection mechanisms like Address Space Layout Randomization (ASLR). So current attacks are also interested in the output of the format string. In this paper we present a novel method for attacking format string vulnerabilities in a blind manner. Our method does not require any memory leakage or output to the attacker. In addition, we show a way to exploit format string vulnerabilities on the heap, where we can not benefit from direct destination control, i.e. we can not place arbitrary addresses onto the stack, as is possible in stack-based format string.

Keywords: Security · Format string attacks

1 Introduction

Format string vulnerabilities are known for many years and are assumed to be easy to detect. But unfortunately there still exist applications, that are vulnerable to this kind of attack. According to the CVE database [17], the number of vulnerabilities that can be classified as format string vulnerability has decreased in the last 10 years. Over the course of the last 5 years, however, it appears to stay on a constant level.

These was, for example, a severe format string flaw in sudo versions 1.8.0 through 1.8.3p1 which was found in the sudo_debug() function (CVE-2012-0809). In Linux kernel through 3.9.4 existed a bug which allowed an attacker to gain privilege rights, which could be exploited by using format strings in device names (CVE-2013-2851). There also existed an exploitable format string bug in the Linux kernel before 3.8.4 in the function ext3_msg() which could be used to get higher privileges or crash the system (CVE-2013-1848). Therefore, we can

© Institute for Computer Sciences, Social Informatics and Telecommunications Engineering 2015
J. Tian et al. (Eds.): SecureComm 2014, Part II, LNICST 153, pp. 301–314, 2015.
DOI: 10.1007/978-3-319-23802-9_23

Table 1. Number of format string attacks in the last five years

Year	2009	2010	2011	2012	2013
Number	26	14	9	18	14

assume, that format string bugs will still be present in the future. Table 1 lists the number of registered format strings vulnerabilities over the last 5 years.

Since the first methods for a FSA were released, system wide protection mechanisms like Non Executable Bit (NX) and ASLR are implemented in many operating systems. Also compiler-based protections like stack-cookies and FOR-TIFY_SOURCE should protect from binary exploitation. All these protection mechanisms make exploitation more difficult nowadays. Nevertheless, Planet [13] has shown that FORTIFY_SOURCE can be circumvented and Payer et al. [12] have shown, that NX can also be bypassed.

All generic exploiting techniques shown in the past are relying on two mature constraints. First, the input buffer that is used by the attacker has to be placed on the stack, and secondly, the attacker requires knowledge about the output of the format string. In this paper, we instead assume, that the attacker is blind regarding to the output of the application. He will not receive any memory leakage by the exploited application. In addition, we also show that with our technique, the attackers payload may also be located on heap, instead of the stack.

In this paper we make the following contributions:

- We introduce a novel mechanism that enables an attacker to write to arbitrary memory locations using an FSA without the requirement to place the format string onto the stack.
- We describe a technique to redirect the control flow of an FSA vulnerable function in a blind fashion.
- We describe a Proof Of Concept (POC) implementation of our attack conducted with enabled protection mechanisms.

The rest of this work is structured as follows: First we introduce related work and various protection mechanisms in Sect. 2 and thereby motivate that format strings are still an issue in modern systems. Secondly, we describe the classical version of format string attacks in Sect. 3. We continue by showing our novel method to exploit format string attacks even without receiving any output in Sect. 4. In Sect. 5 we then present a POC that is able to use our method to execute arbitrary code on the victims machine. Finally we conclude our work in Sect. 6.

2   Related Work

The topic of FSAs is already known in the academic world for over a decade. The basic concept was first introduced by Newsham back in the year 2000 [11].

The concept was then extended and described in more detail in 2001 by Teso [14]. The attack has been enhanced by Haas [9] and Planet [13] in 2010. Haas is showing, that the memory leak of a format string can be used to calculate all relevant memory address to build the exploit string without any bruteforce, whereas Planet is showing a way to bypass the FORTIFY_SOURCE protection using format string attacks. We will describe the basic concepts of these attacks in the next section. In the recent years, however, this topic gained less interest. Payer et al. [12], recently describes a method for applying both Return Oriented Programming (ROP) [15] and Jump Oriented Programming (JOP) [5] to format string attacks described by Haas and Planet and also discusses different protection mechanisms.

We now describe protection mechanisms that have been established to mitigate memory write attacks. We hereby differ between two classes of protections mechanisms: Compiler-based and system-based protections. A commonly used compiler-based defense mechanism against control flow violations are stack cookies. The basic idea behind stack cookies is, that, in order to overwrite the return address of a function, a user has to overflow a buffer on the stack and thus overwrite everything between this buffer and the return address. If the compiler places a stack cookie between the buffer and the return address, the attacker also has to overwrite this cookie. As an attacker is unable to know the content of this cookie in advance, it is possible to detect the modification of the return address, if the cookie was overwritten by an attacker. This cookie can be circumvented by FSAs easily, because the place to be written can be directly controlled by the attacker. Another compiler-based protection mechanism is the compiler flag RELocation Read-Only (RELRO). This mechanism is resolving all addresses at the beginning and mapping the Global Offset Table (GOT) read-only, so an attacker cannot overwrite the function pointer and redirect the control flow.

A further mechanism that specifically protects against a FSA is using the FORTIFY_SOURCE option at compile time. The idea behind FORTIFY_SOURCE is to check the source code for the usage of certain insecure functions. These are common functions (e.g. strcpy) that use a given buffer and expect it to be delimited by a null terminator, which is not always the case. If the compiler detects the usage of such an insecure function (like strcpy), it tries to identify the size of the destination buffer and replaces the vulnerable function with a more secure function. A call to the printf function is replaced with a more secure function, so that the compiled program can handle a possible attack at runtime. If an attacker, for example, tries to use the %n parameter in a format string, the program will crash. Although this is a good idea, Planet has shown that this protection can be circumvented by overwriting the IO_FLAGS2_FORTIFY bit in the file stream by controlling the nargs value in the format string [13]. Another compiler-based protection is pointer encryption. This technique is used to encrypt instruction pointers with a simple encryption function which is not known by the attacker and thus prevents a pointer manipulation by the attacker [7]. This approach is thereby somehow similar to the stack-cookie approach. Although even if the algorithm uses XOR the attacker can easily find the key if he knows a pair of plain and encrypted text. Furthermore, instruction set randomization uses the same idea in which the attacker does not know the instruction set [8].

After we now described some compiler-based approaches, we now look at common system-based mitigation approaches. One approach is ALSR. ALSR randomizes the memory addresses of both the executed code as well as the stack. Unfortunately, it only randomizes the prefix of entire pages, thus in case of $4K$ pages (which is common on the intel architecture), the last 12 bits of an address are not randomized. On modern systems we also see more randomization added to some mappings. They extend it to 20 bits and therefore only the last 4 bits are not randomized. This does not ensure security in 32 bit systems because the address can still be bruteforced. The reason for this is the limited number of randomized bits [1,3,4,10,16]. Another system-based protection mechanism is NX or Data Execution Prevention (DEP). Its goal is to hinder the execution of code that is located on a page that is supposed to contain data. Thus it hinders an attacker to prepare, for example his shellcode on the stack or heap.

Libsafe is a library which which can be used to protect against overwriting the stack at run-time. Equal to FORTIFY_SOURCE it replaces vulnerable functions like *printf() with secure versions. If there is an possible attack the library will kill the process and log the event. The disadvantage of this approach is that it works only for limited amount of functions [2].

FormatGuard is a patch for glibc which counts the arguments which are given to the printf function at run-time and compares it to the number of format specifiers (%). If the format string uses for more arguments then the actual number of printf arguments then a attack is assumed and the program will be terminated. To use this protection the programmer has to re-compile the program with FormatGuard. A problem with this approach is that it can only detect if the number of specifiers is changing but not if the variables are reordered. This kind of attack can not be recognized by FormatGuard [6].

3   Classical Attack

To give the reader a background in the topic of this work, we now describe the classical FSA attack that has evolved throughout the recent years. The classical FSA exploits the behavior of *printf functions, which are a class of functions that use formatting information to specify the format of the output. Since the printf function family are variadic c-functions, the number of format specifiers within the format strings is controlling the number of parameter which are used by the function and are thus popped from the stack[1]. The most important format specifiers for exploiting format string vulnerabilities are listed below:

%x - pop address from stack
%s - pop address and dereference
%n - write printed char count to address on stack

---

[1] e.g. *printf("id: %d, size:%d, name: %s",id,size,name)* consumes three arguments.

%hn - write to lower 16 bits (short)
%hhn - write to lower 8 bits (byte)

A basic format string vulnerability just passes a single argument to the *printf* function. This is illustrated in Line 5 of Fig. 1 were a user controlled buffer is given to the `printf` function as a single argument. In the classical exploit the buffer is defined as a character array on the stack. If the buffer contains user controlled input, an attacker can fill this buffer with arbitrary format specifiers, as listed above, and the function will access the next immediate value on the stack for each format identifier within the buffer. Depending on the used specifier, different actions will be executed on the stack. The attacker can, for example, shift the stack by using a *%x* operator or can dereference a memory address to access the content that is referenced by that address by using the *%s* operator. But the most important format specifier for having a generic way for exploiting this vulnerability is the *%n* operator. This specifier takes an address from the top of the stack, dereferences it and writes the total number of printed characters into the specified location. This allows an attacker to write arbitrary values to an arbitrary memory location, assuming that the vulnerable input buffer is located on the stack[2]. The chosen address could be the address of the saved return value, the address to an address in the GOT or an entry in the list of the destructors (*.dtors*). Thereby the attacker is able to change the control flow of the application, if she redirects such a pointer to some shellcode that she also prepared in advance.

4 New Attack Methods

After we discussed the classical FSA in the last section, we now describe a novel technique to apply an FSA even in an environment where the exploit string is placed on the heap and in addition, the user has no direct control over the stack content. Afterwards we will also describe, how it is possible to exploit this blindly, even without any feedback by the vulnerable program.

As this paper is about describing a blind FSA, we now want to define the term "Blind Attack": A blind attack is a network-based attack that is executed remotely without any local access to the attacked system. In addition, the attack does not require the attacking entity to receive any data from the attacked system. In the case of FSA this especially means that the output of the attacked *printf* function is not available to the attacker. Nevertheless, we assume, that the attacker is in possession of the executed binary beforehand. This is a legit restriction because most software is custom of the shelf software, that is not self developed and is available for the public.

---

[2] An input to a buffer like "$\backslash x78\backslash x4f\backslash x9e\backslash xbf$", "*%5u*", "*%10\$hhn*" will, for example, write the value $0x9$ to the least significant byte at the address $0xbf9e4f78$, because in this example the tenth value on the stack is containing our user input.

```
1   void logfunc(char *buf) {
2       char * pch;
3       pch = strtok (buf,"|");
4       while (pch != NULL) {
5           printf(pch);
6           pch = strtok (NULL, "|");
7       }
8   }
9   int parse(char *buf, int log) {
10      if (log == ENABLELOGGING)
11          logfunc(buf);
12      /* Do something using local stack variables */
13  }
14  int handle(clientsocket) {
15      char *buf = (char*)malloc(SIZE);
16      // ...
17      recv(clientsocket, buf, SIZE-1, 0);
18      parse(buf,1);
19      free(buf);
20      // ...
21  }
22  int func(serversocket) {
23      // ...
24      while(1) {
25          pid = fork();
26          if(pid == 0) { /* ... */ handle(clientsock); /* ... */
27          }
28          // ...
29      }
30      // ...
31  }
```

Fig. 1. Format string vulnerability on the heap

4.1 Exploitstring on Heap

To exploit a FSA vulnerability, an attacker traditionally needs to store her attack
payload in a buffer inside the vulnerable program. In Sect. 3 we have shown how
a FSA is applied if the user input is saved on the stack. Within related work
it is assumed, that it is required, that this buffer is located on the stack of the
attacked system. This is an optimistic assumption, as is not always the case in
practice. The problem with a heap based FSA is, that the attacker can only
write to addresses which are already saved on the stack using the %n specifier.
In this case the attacker can not place the destination address of the write on
the stack to dereference it directly.

Stack-based FSAs, however, rely on user controlled input on the stack. The
attacker places the exploit string, which contains the address of the write destination, directly inside the user input buffer. This address can then be directly
accessed by the $ operator or using the %x operator many times to pop all values

from top of stack until the attacker controlled data is at the top of stack. In our case we do not require attacker controlled input on the stack. This means only application controlled data is referenced on the stack. We therefore assume that there is no other input channel to place data on the stack, which would make the exploitation easier.

4.2   Arbitrary Write

Above, we described how to write to application controlled locations by deref-erencing the memory addresses on the stack and writing to it using the %n specifier. Now we focus on a generic exploitation concept to achieve arbitrary writes into application memory. The basic idea of our novel approach is to use the saved frame pointer, which is stored on the stack once a new function is called. If the application is not compiled with specific flags like *-fomit-frame-pointer* every function will save/push the last frame pointer on the stack in the prologue and restore it in the epilogue. We benefit from this fact because this address is always pointing to another location in the stack, which is also writeable. There-fore, no protection mechanisms like NX, stack cookies or ASLR will protect the system from an attacker writing to that location. Whenever an application is using the saved frame pointer feature, one frame pointer is pointing to the next frame pointer like a linked list. The next frame is therefore also located on the stack on higher addresses which can also be written to.

The goal of our mechanism is to use this list of saved frame pointers to achieve an arbitrary write to an arbitrary location within the system. With current FSA mechanisms we are only able to write to locations, which are already referenced on the stack of the current application. But by leveraging the linked list property of the saved frame pointers, we are able to modify the saved frame pointers on the stack according to our needs and thus achieve a situation in which we are able to write to an arbitrary location in memory. First we are using the saved base pointer (BP) on a lower address to overwrite the value of the next saved BP to point it to an arbitrary address like the GOT. In the second step we this location can be written to with an arbitrary value.

4.3   Changing the Control Flow

As we now are able to write to arbitrary memory locations, we describe how it is possible to hijack the applications control flow using an FSA. This still requires exact knowledge about the addresses, that have to be modified in order to control the execution flow. In the case of a blind attack, with no feedback from the attacked application and with ASLR activated at the same time, it is impossible to guess the exact address of our destination in advance. Entries like GOT are mainly at constant addresses but as mentioned in Sect. 2 the compiler flag RELRO will protect this locations from write access. In our approach we will only write to the stack, which is always writeable, to change the execution flow of the application. A generic way of controlling the execution flow is to overwrite the saved instruction pointer on the stack, so that an address is getting executed on a *ret* command that was chosen by an attacker. As we already described above, the stack frames are connected with a linked list with directed pointers. Our goal is control the pointers in a way, that we can write to arbitrary locations on the stack.

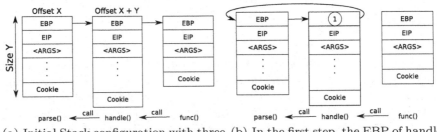

(a) Initial Stack configuration with three functions.

(b) In the first step, the EBP of handle() is redirected to the EBP of parse().

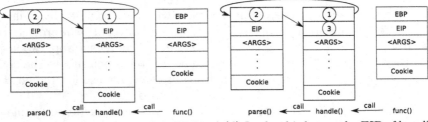

(c) In the second step, the EBP of parse() is redirected to the EIP of handle().

(d) In the third step, the EIP of handle() is redirected to the attackers code.

Fig. 2. Sequence of overwrites to modify the return address

We will now describe our mechanism in more detail. To illustrate our mechanism first imagine a chain of three function calls like shown in Fig. 1. In this example a function `handle` calls a vulnerable function `parse` which in turn forwards the attackers buffer to an internal log function wrapper `logfunc`. This is a common scenario in both the Linux kernel and userspace applications. The initial stack layout of this scenario is depicted in Fig. 2(a). If we consider a format string like %6$*hhn*, we will write to the destination of the 6th value on the stack. The number six would be the *offset* in our explanation. The size is given as multiples of the architecture size, in our case 32 bit. *EBP* is the saved extended base pointer of the calling function. We do not have to care about the stack cookie protection, but if there is a cookie it will be at the bottom of the box, which we assume in our case as part of the frame content like the used stack variables. As the stack is growing to lower addresses, it is possible to overwrite the contents of the stack frames of the function `handle` and `parse` from within the log function. The attack consists of three format string overwrites, that use the pointers in *EBP*.

Note that the linked list of saved frame pointers is corrupted by this attack. An attacker may, nevertheless, reconstruct it after he is able to execute his own code, if it is required. This is only the case if the function is using local variables after the overwrite and before the return. Otherwise the application flow is changed and the attacker succeeded.

Table 2. Overview of required overwrites.

	Offset in format string	Dereferenced offset	Value written (address of)
1	X	$X + Y$	X
2	$X + Y$	X	$X + Y + 1$
3	X	$X + Y + 1$	Address of ROP gadget

In the first overwrite, the saved EBP of the function `handle` (1) will be modified to point to the saved EBP of the function `parse`. This is achieved by using the offset X in the format specifier and change the content at offset $X + Y$ with the address of offset X. Now we can directly address the saved EBP of `parse` as shown in Fig. 2(b). The next overwrite then replaces the contents of the saved EBP of `parse`, located at offset X (2) to the EIP of the function `handle`, located at offset $X + Y + 1$ by using the offset $X + Y$, as shown in Fig. 2(b). As a result of these first two steps an attacker generated a pointer on the stack, that points to the return address. In the third step the attacker overwrites this return address using offset X (3) to point to either the shellcode or some ROP chain, that the attacker prepared in advance. This final step is depicted in Fig. 2(c). After the vulnerable function finishes, the control flow will switch to a sequence of instructions that was chosen by an attacker. An overview over the conducted overwrites is given in Table 2.

4.4   Pointer Modification with ASLR Enabled

In our approach we leverage the saved frame pointer feature as it contains pointers that can be used during an FSA. In case the attacked system has stack ASLR enabled, an attacker is unable to guess the address he has to write to the stack. Unfortunately in its simple version, ASLR is not randomizing the whole address. For example all addresses inside a page will be constant, as ASLR only randomizes the beginning of the stack on page granularity. This means that effectively the least significant 12 bits, we assume a page size of $4K$ as described in Sect. 2, of the address will be constant and not randomized. In the case of an FSA an attacker can benefit from this behavior as he only needs to overwrite the least significant bytes of the frame pointer and redirect it to another frame pointer. Thus she modifies the least significant bytes of an address that is already pointing to the right location. Depending on the frame size the attacker has to overwrite one or two bytes. In the case of a good alignment and a distance less than 256 Bytes, an attacker does not need to care about ASLR, because only one byte

write is required. We can only write a multiple of eight bits using the %n operator. This means that in case of a two byte overwrite, four bits of randomization
are overwritten by the FSA. In a practical exploit this is not a problem and an
attacker is able to brute force these four bytes because of two reasons. First, if
we have a network related application, each connection is transfered into its own
process. This feature can be leveraged in a way that the attacker is able to crash
the process without crashing the whole application. In case the exploit is not
successful, the attacker can simply reconnect and try again. The second reason
is, that only four bits of ASLR randomization is not a barrier for an attacker in
this case, because the value only has to be found once. Every other write will also
be at the same randomized four bytes and can thus be calculated beforehand.
Note that as the connection handler is forked for every connection the stack will
also be at the same address until the main application is restarted. In contrast
to the 12 bit ASLR randomization, some systems use 20 bits of randomization
for the stack. In this case an attacker has to bruteforce more bits, but as we
will show this case in our POC, even with 20 bits of randomization the attack
is practicable in a short time.

5   Proof of Concept

After we have introduced a novel technique to change the control flow of an
application in a blind way using an FSA, we now introduce our POC implementation. In the following we assume the attack to be conducted on a 32 bit
Linux system on the x86 architecture. In our tests we used an Ubuntu 14.10
system with the latest security patches applied. Therefore we assume that our
binary is compiled with gcc in version 4.8. As already described, our vulnerable
application consists of a networking daemon that forks a new process once it
receives a new network connection. Each connection is than handled inside the
newly created process. Our test system has the following protections activated:
ASLR for stack, heap and libraries, NX on stack and heap, and RELRO. The
stack addresses, where the BP are stored is randomized with 20 bit. After a
local analysis of the attacked binary we will get the following values for the
stack frame sizes: $X = 48$ Bytes and $Y = 48$ Bytes. This means that we will
only require a one byte write if the least significant byte (LSByte) of the saved
BP of *handle()* is between $0x60(= X + Y)$ and $0xfc(= 0x100 - 4)$. Otherwise it
has to be a two byte write. As it is the more complex case, we will only consider
the case of two byte writes and show, that this technique is feasible even with
bigger frame sizes.

First of all we will start with a simple bruteforce using three phases: In
Phase 1, we will iterate over all possible values for the LSByte and restore the
saved BP of *handle()*. Since the addresses on the stack are 32bit aligned, there
are only 64 possible values for the LSByte. If the value that is currently checked
does not match, we assume that the application crashes and the server socket is
closed. We can recognize this behavior once we do not get any feedback. On the
other hand we also have to take into account that not all successful tries imply a

correct guess of the correct LSByte. value. Thus after this step there can still be a number of false positives that we have to filter in the next step. Therefore, we will collect all checked LSByte. values that do not crash the server immediately in the first phase and verify them in the second phase.

In the second phase we reduce the number of possible values that we received in the first phase by verifying the integrity of those values. In our POC we designed four different verification tests that can be divided into two category. In the first category we try to rewrite pointers on the stack by building a chained list of pointers. For example, as we know the stack layout we can calculate the relative addresses of the saved frame pointers of other frames or any other variables within the frames and to overwrite their contents. In this case we do not expect the application to crash. In the second category we also use those addresses where we assume pointers on the stack and redirect the pointer chain to point to a non mapped memory location at the end, so *printf()* will crash during the memory write. After this verification process we have the exact address of the LSByte.

The third phase is then required to obtain the value of the second byte. Thus this phase is only needed if we have a two byte write. In this phase we are writing to the second byte, which has 256 possible values in total. Since we now modify the saved BP by a multiple of $4K$, the probability of having false positives is small. In our POC we did not get any false positives during our experiments. Our attack thus requires $256 + 64 + \delta^3$ connections in the worst case, which only takes few seconds in total. As the exploit strings used in this phase are small and can thus be executed very fast after *printf()* is called and the connections can also be multi-threaded, this step can be conducted in a short time.

After having the exact LSBytes of our address, we can now calculate all other stack addresses and build our exploit string to achieve an arbitrary write as describe in Sect. 4.3. The stack layout of our POC is illustrated in Fig. 3, where every column represents the stack layout in one of the described three stages of our attack. In Stage 3, we are overwriting the saved instruction pointer of *handle()* to return to a previously chosen destination. This destination could be the first ROP chain. Putting the whole ROP chain into the stack would assume, that we have enough space on the stack for all gadgets. It would also require more space in the input buffer or many calls to *printf()* for many writes using the format string vulnerability. Therefore the ROP chain should be located within the buffer itself and the number of the written gadgets by *printf()* should be small. It should only be used to switch the stack to the heap and to execute another ROP chain. But this technique has a big constraint. Since the *libc* is randomized, the non randomized gadgets are only available in the text section. We cannot guarantee, that we can find enough gadgets in the text section, especially if the binary is small. It has been proven that the libc gadgets are turing complete by Schacham [15], so we set our focus to use the libc gadgets here. As our technique is based on a remote connection, the Procedure Linkage Table (PLT) contains network related functions like *send()* and *recv()*. We are going to

---

[3] δ = false positive count * (# of verification tests).

use this feature for constructing a memory leak and to extract the address of the libc back to the attacker. The addresses of the used library functions like *send()* are stored in the GOT at a constant and readable address. The call to a library function is done inside the text segment, which is not randomized. We can either call it by returning to the text segment or we can call it directly using the PLT entry, which is also on constant addresses. Overwriting the return value with *send@PLT* and leveraging the send function also requires that we now the value of *clientsocket*, to return the information to the right client. This value could be bruteforced, but in many cases it is stored on the stack. In our POC, for example, the clientsocket is a parameter of the *handle()* function. We are using a gadget to lift the stack to the position of clientsocket and return to *send@PLT* with the arguments *(clientsocket, send@GOT, 4, 0)*. This sends the address of *send@libc* to the attacker, who in the next step is able calculate all addresses inside the libc and build an exploit for a successful attack.

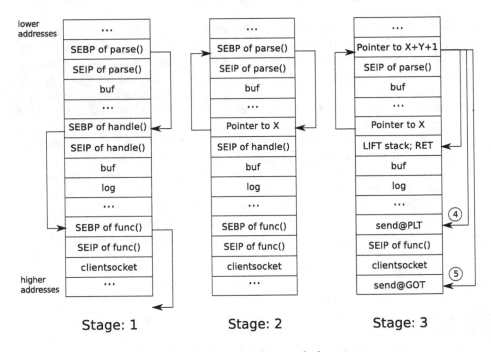

Fig. 3. Stacklayout for the proof of concept

6   Conclusion

In this paper we have shown, that format string attacks are still a security issue in recent history. We proposed a new approach, which does not require a memory leakage to exploit a format string vulnerability. Using our approach, we can exploit an FSA blindly without having any output channel to the attacker or access to the local system. Our concept extends the classical FSAs to write to arbitrary memory locations even in cases where the format string is not stored on the stack but instead resides on the heap. We especially show that is is possible to redirect the control flow of an application using and modifying only pointers that are already present on the stack. We have also considered the most known protection mechanisms like ASLR, NX, RELRO and have shown that blind format string attacks are feasible even with activated protections.

References

1. Homepage of the pax team. http://pax.grsecurity.net/. Accessed 15 November 2013
2. Baratloo, A., Singh, N., Tsai, T.K.: Transparent run-time defense against stack-smashing attacks. In: USENIX Annual Technical Conference, General Track, pp. 251–262 (2000)
3. Bhatkar, S., DuVarney, D.C., Sekar, R.: Address obfuscation: an efficient approach to combat a broad range of memory error exploits. In: Proceedings of the 12th USENIX Security Symposium, vol. 120, Washington, D.C. (2003)
4. Bhatkar, S., Sekar, R., DuVarney, D.C.: Efficient techniques for comprehensive protection from memory error exploits. In: Proceedings of the 14th USENIX Security Symposium, pp. 271–286 (2005)
5. Bletsch, T., Jiang, X., Freeh, V.W., Liang, Z.: Jump-oriented programming: a new class of code-reuse attack. In: Proceedings of the 6th ACM Symposium on Information, Computer and Communications Security, ASIACCS 2011, pp. 30–40. ACM, New York (2011)
6. Cowan, C., Barringer, M., Beattie, S., Kroah-Hartman, G., Frantzen, M., Lokier, J.: Formatguard: automatic protection from printf format string vulnerabilities. In: USENIX Security Symposium, vol. 91, Washington, D.C. (2001)
7. Cowan, C., Beattie, S., Beattie, S., Kroah-Hartman, G., Frantzen, M., Lokier, J.: Pointguardtm: protecting pointers from buffer overflow vulnerabilities. In: USENIX Security Symposium, vol. 91, Washington, D.C. (2001)
8. Gadaleta, F., Younan, Y., Jacobs, B., Joosen, W., De Neve, E., Beosier, N.: Instruction-level countermeasures against stack-based buffer overflow attacks. In: Proceedings of the 1st EuroSys Workshop on Virtualization Technology for Dependable Systems, pp. 7–12. ACM (2009)
9. Haas, P.: Advanced format string attacks. DEFCON 18 (2010)
10. Müller, T.: Aslr smack & laugh reference. In: Seminar on Advanced Exploitation Techniques (2008)
11. Newsham, T.: Format string attacks. Guardent Inc., September 2000
12. Payer, M., Gross, T.: String oriented programming. In: Proceedings of the 2nd ACM SIGPLAN Program Protection and Reverse Engineering Workshop, PPREW 2013. ACM (2013)
13. Planet, C.: A eulogy for format strings. Phrack magazine, 14(67), November 2010
14. Scut. Exploiting format string vulnerability. http://crypto.stanford.edu/cs155/papers/formatstring-1.2.pdf
15. Shacham, H.: The geometry of innocent flesh on the bone: return-into-libc without function calls (on the x86). In: Proceedings of the 14th ACM Conference on Computer and Communications Security, CCS 2007, pp. 552–561. ACM, New York (2007)

16. Shacham, H., Page, M., Pfaff, B., Goh, E.-J., Modadugu, N., Boneh, D.: On the effectiveness of address-space randomization. In: Proceedings of the 11th ACM Conference on Computer and Communications Security, pp. 298–307. ACM (2004)
17. The MITRE Corporation: Common vulnerabilities and exposures. https://cve.mitre.org/data/downloads/allitems.csv

An Empirical Evaluation of Software Obfuscation Techniques Applied to Android APKs

Felix C. Freiling, Mykola Protsenko, and Yan Zhuang[✉]

Department of Computer Science,
Friedrich-Alexander University Erlangen-Nürnberg (FAU), Erlangen, Germany
{felix.freiling,mykola.protsenko,yan.zhuang}@cs.fau.de

Abstract. We investigate the problem of creating complex software obfuscation for mobile applications. We construct complex software obfuscation from sequentially applying simple software obfuscation methods. We define several desirable and undesirable properties of such transformations, including idempotency and monotonicity. We empirically evaluate a set of 7 obfuscation methods on 240 Android Packages (APKs). We show that many obfuscation methods are idempotent or monotonous.

Keywords: Software obfuscation · Mobile security · Android · Software protection · Reverse engineering · Software metrics

1 Introduction

Software obfuscation is a common tool to protect software from reverse engineering, and it is particularly relevant for architectures that execute *bytecode* because bytecode is much easier to decompile (and therefore to reverse engineer) than native machine code. The Android platform is a prominent and practically relevant example of such an environment. In Android, applications (or "apps") are shipped in the Android Package format. An Android Package (APK) contains *dex bytecode* for which it is rather easy to reconstruct the original Java source code using decompilers. There are multiple software obfuscation frameworks for Java in general (such as Sandmark [9]) and Android in particular (such as ProGuard [15]). In this paper, we focus on PANDORA [19], an obfuscation framework that contains a representative selection of obfuscating transformations specifically for Android. PANDORA is based on the Soot framework [20] which is a Java optimization tool working on source code. Therefore, PANDORA has to transform the dex file into a Java archive (jar) file, then applies obfuscation and finally tansforms the resulting program back into a dex file again.

Intuitively, software obfuscation transforms a program in such a way such that

- the original program semantics are preserved (maybe with a negligible delay in performance) and
- the resulting program is harder to understand as the original one.

© Institute for Computer Sciences, Social Informatics and Telecommunications Engineering 2015
J. Tian et al. (Eds.): SecureComm 2014, Part II, LNICST 153, pp. 315–328, 2015.
DOI: 10.1007/978-3-319-23802-9_24

The problem of theoretical and practical definitions is to capture what it means for a program to be "harder to understand". While there exist some obfuscation methods that are provably hard to reverse [3, 21], the general understanding is that strong obfuscation for general programs is impossible (for reasonable definitions of "strong") [1]. Despite theoretical advances of the field [13, 14], we must therefore continue to approximate the strength of practical obfuscation methods *empirically*.

Most practical methods are designed with an "idea" in mind of why the resulting program is harder to understand, but for most techniques there is no empirical evaluation, especially in comparison to other obfuscation methods. Emirically, the hardness to understand a piece of code can only be checked by human experiment [4] or (as an approximation) by using specific software complexity/quality metrics. In this paper, we focus on software obfuscation for the Android platform and empirically evaluate the obfuscation techniques of PANDORA [19].

The research question we investigate in this paper is the following: *Considering the basic obfuscation techniques of* PANDORA, *does obfuscation improve if we apply the same obfuscation technique multiple times?* Since obfuscation methods are usually applied only once to a piece of code this might appear as a strange and unusual question. However, our aim is not primarily to build better obfuscation techniques but rather to *understand* the behavior of existing techniques better. Rephrasing the question, we ask: What are the characteristics of software if obfuscation methods are reused?

To answer our questions empirically, we have built an Android software obfuscation framework that allows us to automate the task of obfuscation and software complexity measurement. In designing this framework, we formalized the problem of building complex obfuscation methods from simpler ones. This allowed us to identify a set of desirable properties which practical program transformations should satisfy and to classify the investigated obfuscation techniques in this respect.

In this paper we make the following contributions:

1. We formally define what it means to apply a sequence of obfuscation methods to a program and identify desirable and undesirable structural properties. For example, we identify *idempotency* and *monotony* as desirable properties of obfuscation functions.
2. We empirically evaluate 7 obfuscation methods with respect to 8 software complexity metrics on a set of 240 Android Packages (APKs). Following our research question, we restrict our investigation to properties inherent to a single obfuscation function, i.e., we only investigate iterative applications of the same obfuscation methods to a given program.
3. We show that most obfuscation methods exhibit "stable" properties when used iteratively, i.e., they are idempotent or monotonous. However, a single obfuscation method usually exhibits different stable properties with respect to different complexity metric, i.e., it might be idempotent regarding one metric and monotonous regarding a second metric.

Related Work. According to Collberg and Nagra [7], to measure the strength of practical obfuscation techniques, a definition is required that allows to compare the *potency* of two transformations. Preda and Giacobazzi [10], for example, give a definition that classifies a transformation as potent when there exists a property that is not preserved by the transformation. Of course, *some* properties of a program must be preserved since the obfuscated program should compute the same functionality. In practice, however, the definition of Preda and Giacobazzi [10] only allows to compare simple transformations in isolated environments. To compare the strength of two obfuscated real-world programs, their framework cannot be applied.

Seminal work of Collberg et al. [8] surveyed different obfuscation techniques and classified them mainly into three categories: data obfuscations, control obfuscations, and layout obfuscations. They also investigated the effect of single obfuscation steps on different software metrics and even proposed a Java obfuscation framework (named Kava [8, Sect. 3]) designed to systematically obfuscate a program such that certain quality criteria are satisfied. We are, however, not aware of any empirical evaluation of the framework.

Outline. This paper is structured as follows: We first give some background in Sect. 2. We then define desirable properties of obfuscation functions in Sect. 3. After giving an overview of our obfuscation framework in Sect. 4 we provide the results and a discussion in Sect. 5. Section 6 concludes the paper.

2   A Brief Tour of the Obfuscation and Metric Zoo

This section provides a brief overview of the obfuscation techniques and the software complexity metrics we used in our evaluation. Where appropriate, we give an akronym as a shorthand in the later discussion.

Obfuscation Methods. In total, we considered 10 obfuscation techniques that were available in the PANDORA obfuscation tool [19] for Android. These techniques represent a broad selection of specialized and general obfuscation methods. They can be classified into 4 transformations at the method level and 6 transformation at the class level.

At the method level, we considered the following techniques:

- *Array index shift* obfuscates the use of the arrays by shifting the indices with a constant shift value.
- *Compose locals* groups the method's local variables of the same type and composes them to a single container variable, such as array or map. For the latter one random keys of the types string, character or integer are used.

At the class level, we considered the following obfuscation methods:

- *Drop modifiers* is one of the most simple transformations: It discards the access-restricting modifiers like `private`, `protected`, or `final` for classes, methods, and fields.

- *Extract methods* "outlines" the bodies of the methods, the signatures of which cannot be changed due to restrictions laid down by the application design, e.g., methods called in response to the system and user events, like the `onCreate` of the Android `Activity` class.
- *Move fields* changes the hosting class of the field and replaces all accesses correspondingly. Note that for non-static fields a reference object to the new host class is required. Such objects are created and initialized in each constructor of the class.
- In analogy to move field, *move methods* moves a method from one class to another. If the method makes use of the implicit `this` parameter, it must be added to the explicit parameter list of the method.
- *Merge methods* replaces two methods of the same class and the same return type with a single method. It interleaves both parameter lists and the bodies of the methods. Furthermore, an additional `key` parameter is added in order to differentiate which of the bodies is to be executed at runtime.

Software Complexity Metrics. The set of software complexity metrics used in our evaluation contains measurements of the control flow complexity and data flow complexity of the methods, as well as the usual object-oriented design (OOD) metrics suite. We now give a very brief description of these metrics.

At the method level, we used two metrics to measure the complexity of the control flow and data flow: McCabe's Cyclomatic Complexity and Dependency Degree, respectively. Cyclomatic Complexity [16] of the method corresponds to the number of the linearly independent circuits in the control flow graph (CFG). It can be computed as $v = e - n + p$, with e, n, and p being the number of edges, nodes, and connected components of the CFG respectively.

The Dependency Degree metric (abbreviated as DepDegree), proposed by Bayer and Fararooy [2], is defined with help of the *dependency graph*, which is constructed for the given CFG as follows. The nodes correspond to the instructions of the method, and the edges reflect the dependencies between them. One instruction is said to depend on the another if it uses some values defined by that instruction. Then, the Dependency Degree of the method is defined as the number of edges in the corresponding dependency graph.

The measurement of OOD complexity is performed with a suite containing 6 metrics by Chidamber and Kemerer [5]. These metrics measure complexity on the class level:

- *Weighted Methods pro Class* (WMC): the number of the methods defined in a class.
- *Depth of Inheritance Tree* (DIT): the number of classes along the path from the given class to the root in the inheritance tree.
- *Number of Children* (NOC): the number of direct subclasses.
- *Coupling Between the Object classes* (CBO): the number of coupled classes. Here, two classes are considered coupled, if one of them uses methods or instance variables of the other one.
- *Response Set for a Class* (RFC): the number of declared methods plus the number of methods the declared ones call.

- *Lack of Cohesion in Methods* (LCOM): Given a class C declaring methods $M_1, M_2, ..., M_n$ and a set of instance variables used by the method M_j denoted as I_j, define $P = \{(I_i, I_j) | I_i \bigcap I_j = \emptyset\}$ and $Q = \{(I_i, I_j) | I_i \bigcap I_j \neq \emptyset\}$. Then $LCOM = max\{|P| - |Q|, 0\}$.

3   Obfuscation as a Function

In this section, we formally define what it means to apply a sequence of obfuscation methods to a program and identify desirable and undesirable structural properties.

(Complex) Obfuscation Methods. We consider a finite set of obfuscation methods $\Omega = \{\omega_1, \omega_2, ...\}$. Each such method is defined as a program transformation for a particular domain. Let $\mathcal{P}$ denote the set of all programs from that domain (e.g., all programs written in C). Then formally, every ω_i is defined as a function

$$\omega_i : \mathcal{P} \mapsto \mathcal{P}$$

such that $\omega_i(p)$ computes the same functionality as p without being exponentially slower or larger than p.

A complex obfuscation method can be defined by applying first a specific simple obfuscation method ω_i and then another simple obfuscation method ω_j. From the perspective of obfuscation as a function this is the *composition* of functions, i.e., $\omega_j(\omega_i(p))$.

We now define what it means to apply a *sequence* of obfuscation methods from Ω to a program. We denote by Ω^+ the set of all finite sequences of elements of Ω (including the empty sequence). An example sequence is $\langle \omega_1, \omega_2, \omega_1 \rangle$. For two sequences $\alpha, \beta \in \Omega^+$ we denote by $\alpha \cdot \beta$ the concatenation of α and β and by $\alpha \sqsubset \beta$ that α is a strict (i.e., shorter) prefix of β.

We now define a general notion of obfuscator composition $\mathcal{O}$ that uses individual methods from Ω to create new (and possibly better) variants of obfuscation methods.

Definition 1. Complex obfuscator composition *is a function* $\mathcal{O} : \mathcal{P} \times \Omega^+ \mapsto \mathcal{P}$ *that satisfies the following conditions for all* $p \in \mathcal{P}$:

1. $\mathcal{O}(p, \langle \rangle) = p$
2. *For all* $\alpha \in \Omega^+$: $\mathcal{O}(p, \alpha \cdot \omega) = \mathcal{O}(\omega(p), \alpha)$

As an example, let $\alpha = \langle \omega_1, \omega_2, \omega_1, \omega_3 \rangle$. Then we have:

$$\mathcal{O}(p, \alpha) = \omega_1(\omega_2(\omega_1(\omega_3(p))))$$

Properties. We now define a set of properties that complex obfuscation methods can satisfy. These properties sometimes refer to software metrics such as those defined in Sect. 2. We formalize them as a finite set of functions $M = \{m_1, m_2, ...\}$. Each metric is a function that takes a program and maps to into a totally ordered metrical space like the natural numbers. A simple complexity metric is *lines of code* for which the metrical space is the set of natural numbers and the ordering relation is $\leq$.

The first property of idempotency refers to the effect of an individual obfuscation function and intuitively states that applying the function more than once does not improve the obfuscation result regarding a particular metric.

Definition 2. *An obfuscation function ω is* idempotent *with respect to metric $m \in M$ iff for all $p \in \mathcal{P}$ holds that $m(\omega(\omega(p))) = m(\omega(p))$.*

Note that some obfuscation methods such as *drop modifiers* are idempotent for all metrics since they satisfy the stronger property of $\omega(\omega(p)) = \omega(p)$. We call such methods simply *idempotent*. An obviously non-idempotent method is *extract methods*, since it creates a new methods with every invocation.

We now define an additional property of obfuscation functions: monotony. Intuitively, monotonous obfuscation functions continuously increase (or decrease) the value of the considered metrics. Obviously, all idempotent obfuscators are monotonous. For non-monotonous obfuscators, there are metrics which are unstable, i.e., which rise and later decrease or vice versa.

Definition 3. *An obfuscation function ω is* monotonous *with respect to metric $m \in M$ iff the following holds: Let α and β be sequences of ω: If $\alpha \sqsubseteq \beta$ then $m(\mathcal{O}(p,\alpha)) \leq m(\mathcal{O}(p,\beta))$, where $\leq$ is the order on the metrical space of m.*

While idempotency is rather easy to understand, monotony is more complex since the effect of an obfuscation method on a particular metric is not always clear. In general, we believe that "good" obfuscation methods should be either idempotent or at least monotonous for most metrics considered. Idempotency is a good property because it makes an obfuscation method easy to apply and it facilitates control of its effects. Monotony is positive, because it corresponds to the expectation that obfuscation methods make analysis (increasingly) "harder".

We will evaluate the obfuscation methods presented in Sect. 2 and show that most of them satisfy these desirable properties.

4   An Android Obfuscation Framework

We have designed and implemented a framework with which we can automatically apply and evaluate complex obfuscation methods composition to Android APKs. The structure of the framework is depicted in Fig. 1. The framework is based on three modules which we use to apply and evaluate obfuscation methods:[1]

1. PANDORA [19] is an Android obfuscation tool that implements the obfuscation techniques introduced in Sect. 2. It operates on jar files that are the main ingredient of APKs.

---

[1] Although we rely heavily on PANDORA, please note that our framework does not implement any obfuscation methods or metrics itself and can be extended with other obfuscation tools (such as Sandmark) later. It therefore is rather a "meta framework".

2. SSM, a supplementary function to PANDORA [19], is a measurement tool for computing the different software complexity metrics mentioned in Sect. 2. SSM computes these metrics on every class and method in a jar file.
3. Androsim [18] is a tool written in Python for measuring the similarity between APKs. It is part of the Androguard APK analysis toolset [11]. The basis for similarity measurement is the *compression distance* between different APKs. To compute this distance, APKs are compiled into an intermediate representation focusing much on the control flow and abstracting from identifier names. The resulting strings of the two APKs are then compared by computing the *normalized compression distance* (NCD) [6]. We use the resulting value as a reference value for the SSM metrics.

We now explain how APKs are processed in our framework. The starting point is a set of APKs stored in the file system of our analysis machine (top of Fig. 1). The APK is transformed into a jar file that is subsequently processed by PANDORA. The resulting jar file, which is a obfuscated version of the original jar file, goes through the post-processing section (e.g., it is checked whether it contains valid JVM code using the *jasmin* tool [17]). To distinguish both files in the file system, we append the name of the applied obfuscation method to the original filename of the jar file (*_ω.jar, where ω is an identifier of the obfuscation method record in our database). After that, the jar file is turned into a dex file and compressed into an Android package which is again stored in the file system. In the meantime, we use Androsim and SSM to compare and compute different metrics on the original and transformed jar files and APKs (see Fig. 1). All the generated data is inserted into a database.

The above processing refers to one step of the complex obfuscation composition of Definition 1. To apply multiple obfuscation techniques in sequence, the framework will perform the same iteration with another obfuscation techniques to the same APK. The selection of the input files as well as the iteration and

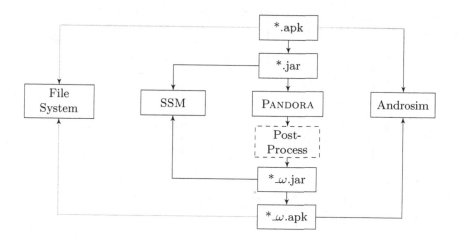

Fig. 1. Structure of the Android Obfuscation Framework.

type of obfuscation techniques applied on the APKs are totally automated using Python.

5   Results

We applied the obfuscation transformations described in Sect. 2 to 240 APKs which we randomly selected from a set of more than 1000 APKs which we downloaded from the open source Android application market *F-Droid* [12]. With more time we would have chosen more APKs for the computation of our results but we consider 240 a large enough set such that our results have some significance.

Idempotent Transformations. As introductory example for a clearly idempotent transformation, we show two metrics (CBO and LCOM) of *drop modifiers* in

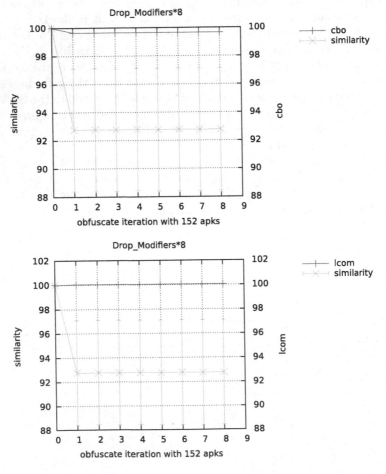

Fig. 2. CBO and LCOM measurements of *drop modifiers* (Color figure online).

Fig. 2. In these (and the following) graphs, the horizontal axis denotes the number of transformation iterations and the vertical axis denotes the percentage of the original APK's complexity or similarity. The red and green lines correspond to the given complexity metric and the similarity measured with Androsim,

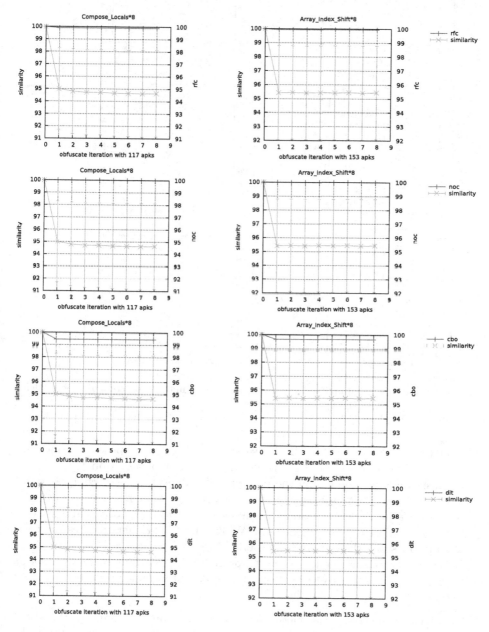

Fig. 3. Selection of OOD metrics for *compose locals* (left) and *array index shift* (right).

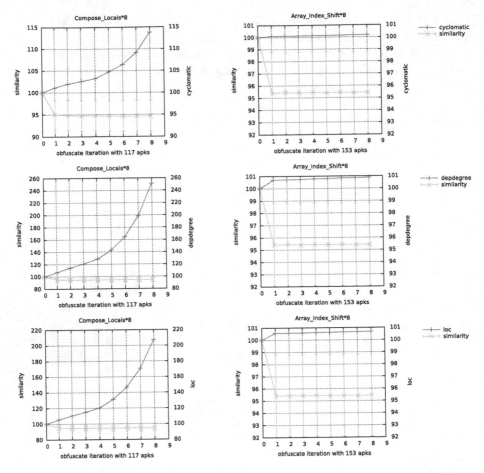

Fig. 4. Cyclomatic complexity, DepDegree and LOC metrics for *compose locals* (left) and *array index shift* (right).

respectively. The values of similarity serve the reference purposes and indicate the overall change of the program structure caused by obfuscation.[2]

Transformations applied on the intraprocedural level, namely *compose locals* and *array index shift*, are as expected idempotent with respect to all OOD metrics. *Move fields* is idempotent for all metrics. *Move methods* exhibits idempotency for cyclomatic complexity and WMC, since it neither changes the code of the methods nor their overall number.

Transformations applied on the intraprocedural level, namely *compose locals* and *array index shift*, are as expected idempotent with respect to all OOD metrics. This can be seen in Fig. 3.

---

[2] In the following figures, we have scaled down the graphs to improve the visual "overview" impression with multiple graphs on one page. The caption repeats the method and metric for readability.

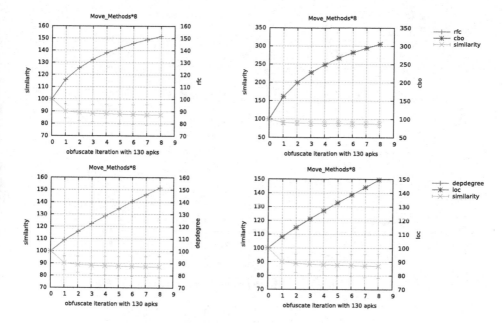

Fig. 5. RFC, CBO, DepDegree and LOC metrics for *move methods*.

Monotonous Transformations. Many of the evaluated obfuscation transformations were found to be monotonous, i.e., their continuous application keeps increasing some of the complexity metrics. In particular, the method-level obfuscations *compose locals* and *array index shift* are monotonous for the method-level metrics Cyclomatic complexity, DepDegree and LOC (shown in Fig. 4). For *compose locals* the complexity growth was superlinear for all three metrics, whereas *array index shift* shows very slow linear increase reaching less than 101 % of the original complexity after 8 transformations.

Move methods is monotonous for the OOD metrics RFC and CBO as well as DepDegree and LOC (in Fig. 5). As mentioned earlier, with respect to the cyclomatic complexity this transformation is idempotent. This is because moving non-static methods requires a reference object to the target class, which is stored in the class field and copied to the local variable before the method invocation. Since this does not add any branches, cyclomatic complexity stays unchanged, however, new instructions and variables are added, which increases the other two method-level metrics.

Merge methods is monotonous with respect to DepDegree and LOC: It adds new instructions and operations on variables. However, allthough it adds an additional branch per merge operation, the cyclomatic complexity (shown in Fig. 6) remains constant, since the number of circuits in the merged code equals the sum of the circuits of the merged methods.

Unstable Transformations. Some of the obfuscation transformations did not fit the definitions of monotonicity or idempotency for certain metrics. These

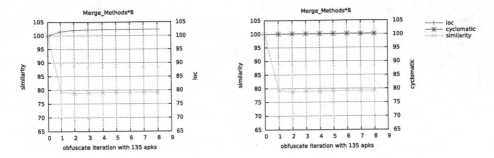

Fig. 6. *Merge methods*: measurements for metrics LOC (left) and Cyclomatic complexity (right).

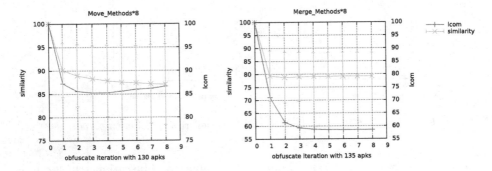

Fig. 7. A comparison of LCOM for *move methods* (left) and *merge methods* (right).

unstable transformations are particularly interesting. One example is *merge methods* which exhibits monotonicity and idempotency for CBO and DepDegree, respectively, but is unstable in WMC, RFC, and LCOM (see Fig. 7, right). *Move methods* showed interesting unstable behavior with respect to the LCOM too: After decreasing within the first 3 obfuscation runs, LCOM increases again (see Fig. 7, left). The key to understanding of this phenomenon lies in the random application of the transfomation and the nature of the metric: Recall that LCOM increases with the number of class methods operating on different sets of instance variables and decreases with the number of those operating on the intersecting sets of instance variables. Since the movement process of *move methods* is randomized, a repeated application of the transfomation can result in both more and less cohesive method layouts, therefore decreasing or increasing the metric.

6   Conclusions and Future Work

In this paper, we experimentally evaluated obfuscation methods when they are applied iteratively and we defined and revealed some structural properties of these methods regarding different software complexity metrics. While the results are interesting and show that most obfuscation methods we have used exhibit rather "stable" properties, the general picture is rather complex since a single obfuscation method usually exhibits different properties (i.e., monotonicity or idempotency) regarding different complexity metrics. Interestingly, a few obfuscation methods have unstable properties regarding some of the metrics.

More experiments are needed to understand this behavior better. A more thorough understanding of the behavior of obfuscation methods is the basis for a more intelligent application of these methods in practice. For example, following an idea of Collberg et al. [8], a detailed understanding of the effects of certain obfuscation methods on complexity metrics would allow to transform programs in such a way that specific "target" complexity requirements are reached with a minimum number of obfuscation steps. Our obfuscation framework is a good basis for such investigations.

Acknowledgments. We wish to thank Tilo Müller for his comments on a prior version of this paper. This work was partly supported by the German Research Foundation (DFG) as part of the Transregional Collaborative Research Centre "Invasive Computing" (SFB/TR 89), the "Bavarian State Ministry of Education, Science and the Arts" as part of the FORSEC research association, and by a scholarship of the Chinese State Scholarship Fund.

References

1. Barak, B., Goldreich, O., Impagliazzo, R., Rudich, S., Sahai, A., Vadhan, S.P., Yang, K.: On the (im)possibility of obfuscating programs. J. ACM **59**(2), 6 (2012)
2. Beyer, D., Fararooy, A.: A simple and effective measure for complex low-level dependencies. In: Proceedings of the 2010 IEEE 18th International Conference on Program Comprehension, ICPC 2010, pp. 80–83. IEEE Computer Society, Washington, DC (2010)
3. Canetti, R., Dakdouk, R.R.: Obfuscating point functions with multibit output. In: Smart, N. (ed.) EUROCRYPT 2008. LNCS, vol. 4965, pp. 489–508. Springer, Heidelberg (2008)
4. Ceccato, M., Penta, M., Falcarin, P., Ricca, F., Torchiano, M., Tonella, P.: A family of experiments to assess the effectiveness and efficiency of source code obfuscation techniques. Empirical Softw. Eng. **19**(4), 1040–1074 (2013)
5. Chidamber, S.R., Kemerer, C.F.: Towards a metrics suite for object oriented design. SIGPLAN Not. **26**(11), 197–211 (1991)
6. Cilibrasi, R., Vitányi, P.M.B.: Clustering by compression. IEEE Trans. Inf. Theory **51**(4), 1523–1545 (2005)
7. Collberg, C., Nagra, J.: Surreptitious Software: Obfuscation, Watermarking and Tamperproofing for Software Protection. Addison-Wesley Longman, Amsterdam (2009)
8. Collberg, C., Thomborson, C., Low, D.: A taxonomy of obfuscating transformations. Technical Report 148, Department of Computer Sciences, The University of Auckland, July 1997
9. Collberg, C.S., Myles, G., Huntwork, A.: Sandmark-a tool for software protection research. IEEE Secur. Priv. **1**(4), 40–49 (2003)

10. Dalla Preda, M., Giacobazzi, R.: Semantics-based code obfuscation by abstract interpretation. J. Comput. Secur. (JCS) **17**(6), 855–908 (2009)
11. Desnos, A., Gueguen, G.: Android: From reversing to decompilation. In: Black Hat, Abu Dhabi (2011)
12. F-Droid Ltd., F-droid. https://f-droid.org/
13. Garg, S., Gentry, C., Halevi, S., Raykova, M., Sahai, A., Waters, B.: Candidate indistinguishability obfuscation and functional encryption for all circuits. In: FOCS, pp. 40–49. IEEE Computer Society (2013)
14. Gentry, C.: Fully homomorphic encryption using ideal lattices. In Proceedings of the Forty-First Annual ACM Symposium on Theory of Computing (STOC), pp. 169–178. ACM, New York (2009)
15. Lafortune, E.: Proguard homepage, June 2014. http://proguard.sourceforge.net/
16. McCabe, T.: A complexity measure. IEEE Trans. Softw. Eng. **SE-2**(4), 308–320 (1976)
17. Meyer, J., Reynaud, D.: Jasmin. http://jasmin.sourceforge.net/
18. Pouik and G0rfi3ld: Similarities for fun and profit, April 2014. http://phrack.org/issues/68/15.html
19. Protsenko, M., Müller, T.: Pandora applies non-deterministic obfuscation randomly to android. In: MALWARE, pp. 59–67. IEEE (2013)
20. Vallée-Rai, R., Gagnon, E., Hendren, L.J., Lam, P., Pominville, P., Sundaresan, V.: Optimizing java bytecode using the soot framework: is it feasible? In: Watt, D.A. (ed.) CC/ETAPS 2000. LNCS, vol. 1781, pp. 18–34. Springer, Heidelberg (2000)
21. Wee, H.: On obfuscating point functions. In: Proceedings of the Thirty-Seventh Annual ACM Symposium on Theory of Computing (STOC), Baltimore, MD, USA, pp. 523–532. ACM, April 2005

Towards Privacy-Preserving Web Metering via User-Centric Hardware

Fahad Alarifi[✉] and Maribel Fernández

Department of Informatics, King's College London, Strand,
London WC2R 2LS, UK
{fahad.alarifi,maribel.fernandez}@kcl.ac.uk

Abstract. Privacy is a major issue today as more and more users are connecting and participating in the Internet. This paper discusses privacy issues associated with web metering schemes and explores the dilemma of convincing interested parties of the merits of web metering results with sufficient detail, and still preserving users' privacy. We propose a web metering scheme utilising user-centric hardware to provide web metering evidence in an enhanced privacy-preserving manner.

Keywords: Web metering · Privacy · Secure embedded hardware

1 Introduction

Consider a service provider, which in the context of this paper will simply be a *webserver*, and a *user*, who is a person using a platform to access the webserver through an open network. The *web metering problem* is the problem of counting the number of visits done by such user to the webserver, additionally capturing data about these visits. A *web metering scheme* produces the number of visits and supporting evidence to interested enquirers, mainly for *Online Advertising* applications. The web metering scheme can be run by an *Audit Agency* or a less trusted third party *Metering Provider*. There are three different classes of web metering schemes, each with its own problems. Web metering schemes are classified as user-centric, webserver-centric or third-party-centric, depending on the entity controlling the scheme or having a major role in setting up the scheme. We consider a hostile environment where the adversary is motivated to fake users' visits or can invade users' privacy. The adversary can be a corrupt webserver or an outside attacker.

Privacy is the right of individuals to control or influence what information related to them may be collected and stored and by whom; and to whom that information may be disclosed [17]. There are trade-offs between designing secure web metering schemes and preserving users' privacy. The schemes become more difficult to design when the main interacting party is not interested to participate and operations need to be carried out transparently. To satisfy such *transparency* property, the scheme needs to execute inside or behind another existing action or property so it does not require a new explicit action from the user.

© Institute for Computer Sciences, Social Informatics and Telecommunications Engineering 2015
J. Tian et al. (Eds.): SecureComm 2014, Part II, LNICST 153, pp. 329–340, 2015.
DOI: 10.1007/978-3-319-23802-9_25

Contributions. We propose a new web metering scheme that uses a hardware device at the user side to provide web metering evidence in a privacy-preserving manner. To the best of our knowledge, the proposed scheme is the first generic hardware-based user-centric web metering scheme. We show that the proposed scheme has the required security properties and enhances the privacy of users. In addition, we show that, aside the presence of the hardware component, the scheme can be implemented in a way that makes web metering transparent to the user. We also use privacy measurements to analyse and compare different categories of web metering schemes, showing the benefits of the proposed scheme.

2   Web Metering via User-Centric Hardware

2.1   High Level Description of Proposed Scheme

Inspired by the webserver-centric hardware-based web metering scheme in [4] and the use of secure user-centric hardware-based broadcasting technique (e.g. pay television) in [10], we propose here a new web metering scheme that relies on a hardware device at the user side.

Definition 1. *A **secure device** is an abstraction for an integrated circuit that can securely store a secret value. To access that secret value, a processor is needed which can be inside that device or inside an attached computing platform. The device has to be equipped with a technique (e.g. zeroization) so that the secret key cannot be extracted. In addition to the secured secret key, we assume that another signature secret key will be stored inside or outside the device.*

Examples of such hardware devices are a smart card or an enhanced version e.g. a Trusted Platform Module (TPM) [16]. The adversary could still *purchase* devices for "fake" users' identities. The cost should typically be higher than the gained benefits, as in [14].

Our generic web metering scheme operates in an environment which consists of a webserver, a user, who owns a device, and an Audit Agency. The three parties follow the protocol specified below. First, we define hardware authentication which will be used as a step in the generic scheme.

Definition 2. *Hardware authentication is a unilateral authentication [12] in which the Audit Agency is assured of the communicating user's identity.*

The following is a generic protocol for the proposed web metering scheme.

1. **User** → **Webserver** :   Access request
2. **Webserver** → **User** :   Certificate request
3. **User** → **Audit Agency** :   Hardware certificate
4. **User** ↔ **Audit Agency** :   Hardware authentication
5. **User** → **Audit Agency** :   New key
6. **Audit Agency** → **User** :   Certificate for new key
7. **User** ↔ **Webserver** :   Certificate & signature
8. **Webserver** ↔ **Audit Agency** :   Verification key & evidence

In step 1, the user sends an access request to the webserver. In step 2, the webserver checks whether the user has submitted a valid (attestation) certificate. If not, the webserver requests a certificate (to be issued from the Audit Agency). In step 3, the user checks if she holds a valid certificate. If so, step 7 is instead executed. Otherwise, the user sends to the Audit Agency, the certificate for the secret key embedded in the device. In step 4, the Audit Agency checks the validity of the received certificate (e.g. not revoked) and whether the user holds the corresponding secret key in relation to the certificate. For this step, the user is asked to encrypt fresh nonces using the embedded secret key. In step 5, the user generates a new signature key pair and sends the public part of it (verification key) to the Audit Agency. This step can be executed for x number of key pairs. In step 6, the Audit Agency signs the received verification key ("blindly" if privacy is required) using its signature key and sends the produced signature (requested certificate) to the user. In step 7, the user forwards the received certificate in step 6 to the visited webserver or convinces the webserver that she has obtained a certificate. The user also sends her verification key to the webserver if it is not included in the submitted certificate. The user also signs a webserver identifier (e.g. URL) and possibly other information (e.g. time) and sends the *evidential signature* to the webserver. In step 8, the webserver checks that the certificate was somehow *signed* using Audit Agency verification key. The webserver also checks (possibly using a privacy-preserving protocol) that the received signature was signed by the user's new signature key. If both checks succeed, the webserver stores the certificate and signature as web metering evidence.

2.2 Security and Privacy Assumptions and Attacks

We assume that number of corrupt users is small as done in [3]. In particular, the webserver cannot convince significant number of users to collude with it, to create fake web metering evidence. The rationale behind this assumption here is that the number of users captured by web metering evidence should typically be large and unlikely for the webserver to be able to cost-effectively motivate a considerable number of users into colluding.

User-centric hardware-based web metering schemes have a potential to overcome user impersonation attacks and can be designed to preserve users' privacy. This can be achieved by involving the Audit Agency in the user setup or increasing the cost of webserver faking visits, as followed in the lightweight security approach in [14]. The use of hardware increases the cost for a corrupt webserver to fake visits by requiring it to own a device for each fake user. At the same time, the scheme has to ensure that it is impossible for a corrupt webserver with one authentic device to be able to generate an unlimited number of evidences e.g. using a periodic hardware authentication with a limit of issued certificates. Therefore, we need a device at the user side containing a secret key. Also, the secret keys certificates and public cryptographic values have to be available to the Audit Agency as they are required in step 3. In steps 3 and 7, the user is assumed to be securely redirected and may not necessarily be aware of this ongoing web metering operation, if a privacy-preserving scheme is being used in a *transparent* mode.

A summary of the assumptions we followed in this paper are as follows.

1. Number of corrupt users is far less than the total number of metered users.
2. User owns a secure device (as in Definition 1).
3. The Audit Agency can obtain a list of valid devices certificates (e.g. from Intel) and recognise revoked or expired ones. Alternatively, users could be incentivised to register their authentic hardware devices for privacy-preserving browsing.
4. The web metering environment is where the user's privacy is a concern.
5. There is limited value of the online content (affecting the cost for webserver owning devices).

In the rest of this section we further describe attacks that can happen during a hostile web metering operation and then highlight the required security goals to counter such attacks. We derive the following security attacks from the adversary capabilities described in Dolev-Yao threat model [13]: replay, impersonation and man in the middle attacks.

Attack 1. *A replay attack occurs when an adversary captures data sent from the user to the Metering Provider, the Audit Agency or the webserver and sends the data again. Similarly, an adversary captures data sent from the webserver to the Metering Provider or the Audit Agency and sends the data again.*

If a replay attack is not detected, the visits number may be increased.

Attack 2. *An adversary in an impersonation attack (which is more powerful than the replay attack scenario where attack effect is limited to captured data), creates fake data and sends it to the Metering Provider or the Audit Agency impersonating a valid webserver or user. Or an adversary creates a fake request to a webserver impersonating a valid user.*

If an impersonation attack is not detected, the visits number may be increased or the evidence data may have invalid properties.

Attack 3. *Man in the middle attack occurs when an adversary receives data from the user or the webserver not intended to him and modifies it before forwarding it to the intended party.*

If such attacks are not detected, the visits number may be increased or the data have invalid properties.

Besides the three communication attacks, there is also a threat that a corrupt webserver may not follow the required **web metering operations**. A corrupt webserver is inherently motivated to change the number of visits. Also, a corrupt webserver can be motivated to change some metering operations without changing number of visits. For example, a corrupt webserver intentionally changes a webpage identifier, which is going to be recorded in web metering evidence, to a different webpage that charges higher fees for advertisements.

To preserve user's privacy, in step 6, the Audit Agency has to blindly sign the new user's key and send the blind signature (i.e. certificate) to the user. Owing to the blind signature production, the Audit Agency does not know the user's key. In step 7, the user submits a form of the received signature or proves to the webserver that she possesses an Audit Agency signature on the new web metering signature key. The webserver would store the signatures as evidence for number of visits that are done by users carrying authentic devices. In Sects. 4 and 5, we provide a more detailed analysis of security and privacy properties of the scheme and show that the attacks are not possible.

2.3   Practical Aspects

The use of hardware devices is common today. Commercial hardware tokens can be used in the proposed scheme as long as they hold a *zeroizable* secret for authentication. A relevant application that uses hardware decoders but not for web metering purposes, is pay television. Here, the user has to have hardware decoders to get multimedia content sent by a broadcasting server. Only authorised users' decoders can decrypt the broadcast content, using the embedded decryption keys. The server encrypts the broadcast content, which will be decrypted using the corresponding decryption key, inside the hardware decoder. The technique can also have other security properties like a tracing capability to detect rogue decoders that share the decryption keys [10].

In case the user is not motivated to explicitly participate in the web metering scheme but still have an applicable hardware device, the scheme can still be run transparently to the user, where a program (or a script) anonymously attests the user. For example, the *BitLocker program* uses the TPM public key for disk encryption, allowing the decryption (by TPM private key) if baseline platform measurements are met again. Another current application requiring TPMs are *digital wallets*. Potential motivations for such a wallet over credit cards could be finding better deals or further authenticating communicating users with customised information set in the wallet. On the other hand, an organisation might want to restrict accesses to their local network once users have certain devices in a fashion similar to Virtual Private Network (VPN) connections. For example, distributed devices can provide the required connectivity and privacy-preserving web metering results. On a larger scale another non-transparent scenario could be to distribute free zeroizable devices to users (e.g. USB storage sticks) which they could use for privacy-preserving web browsing. There is also a trend of developing hardware devices (rather than traditional Personal Computers or mobile phones) for various desirable functions e.g. *Google Glass*. Along the main functions like cameras or games, accessing certain webservers can be an additional function using a privacy-preserving web metering scheme.

3   Techniques to Implement the Proposed Scheme

In this section, we start by describing mechanisms to implement each step in the proposed generic scheme.

Steps 1 and 2 can be implemented using standard mechanisms for issuing requests e.g. HTTP requests. **Steps 3 and 4** address the identification and authentication of the device. As mentioned in Sect. 2.1, a TPM can be used as a web metering hardware device for the required hardware authentication step. A *trusted computing* platform is a device which has an embedded TPM, which has Endorsement Key (EK) and a certificate on the public part of it to prove the platform is genuine. We can follow with such device the lightweight security approach, where it is still possible for an adversary to construct fake web metering evidence but its cost does not offset the earned benefit.

Steps 5, 6 and 7 are included in the proposed scheme to take into account the privacy requirements. In Sects. 3.1 and 3.2, we describe existing protocols and schemes that can be used to implement steps 5, 6 and 7 in the web metering scheme defined in Sect. 2.1. Using them, we obtain a technique to implement the scheme, satisfying both the security and users' privacy requirements. **Step 8** is optional depending on whether the webserver needs to contact the Audit Agency for certificates or evidence redemption.

3.1   Security and Privacy Techniques for Steps 5, 6 and 7

To provide a privacy-preserving web metering scheme, the user has to commit to a new key for step 5 in the generic scheme e.g. using Pedersen commitment scheme [21]. For the next step, an Audit Agency has to blindly sign the committed value (once the user is authenticated) and allow the user to prove its possession, without revealing it. For step 7, the user uses the new signature value, without linking it to the former authenticated credential.

A general view of the privacy-preserving technique required in step 5 can be two interacting entities in which one can prove to the other that it holds a secret without revealing it. New secrets can be generated with the help of a trusted third party while the former secret is "buried away" in another value. For example, using *Schnorr* zero-knowledge protocol [23], a secret s can be embedded in a smart card and used for signing such that $y = g^s mod\ p$ where g is a group generator and p and q are two large prime numbers such that q is a divisor of $p-1$ (y, g, p and q are public values). A commitment scheme can be used in constructing a zero-knowledge protocol. In the web metering context, the user can convince the Audit Agency that the interacted messages are correctly formed using zero-knowledge proof of knowledge of a discrete logarithm. We discuss in Sect. 3.2 a technique to implement step 6 in the generic scheme where the Audit Agency has to document the result as a "redeemable" privacy-preserving certificate. Then, for step 7, the zero-knowledge protocol has to run again between the user and the webserver.

3.2   Direct Anonymous Attestation Protocol for Steps 5, 6 and 7

Direct Anonymous Attestation (DAA) protocol [7] can fortunately provide the needed public commitment, signature scheme and zero-knowledge proofs techniques. DAA protocol uses Camenisch-Lysyanskaya signature scheme [8] to provide a blind signature on the committed value and allow the user to prove its possession, through a zero-knowledge proof of knowledge of the committed value. According to DAA protocol described in [7], communication between user and Audit Agency can be done using *Join Protocol* and communication between user and webserver can be done using *Sign/Verify Protocol*.

The user gets authenticated to Audit Agency using EK (steps 3 and 4 in the generic scheme) and then receives a certificate as follows. In step 5, during Join Protocol, the user generates a secret key f and computes $U = z^f x^{v1} mod\ n$ where $v1$ is used to blind f and (n, x, y, z) is public key of Audit Agency. (z can be set-up as $x^{r2} mod\ n$ where $r2$ is random number so that the Audit Agency chosen random number will be multiplied by the secret f and added to the blind $v1$). Also, the user computes $N = Z^f mod\ p$ where Z is derived from Audit Agency identifier and p is a large prime. Then, the user sends (U, N) to the Audit Agency and convinces the Audit Agency that they are correctly formed using a proof knowledge of a discrete logarithm. We assume that the challenges and messages are securely chosen and constructed as specified in [7]. Then, in step 6 in the generic scheme, the Audit Agency computes $S = (y/(Ux^{v2}))^{1/e} mod\ n$ where $v2$ is random number and e is a random prime. Then, the Audit Agency sends $(S, e, v2)$ to the user to have (S, e, v) as a TPM certificate where $v = v1 + v2$. More than one secret can be generated here to guarantee unlinkability in case the Audit Agency is offline. The join phase is the heavy work phase of the scheme and can be periodically done for different requirements.

In step 7 in the generic scheme, during Sign/Verify Protocol, the user signs messages using the secret key f and Audit Agency certificate (S, e, v) received in Join Protocol. The user also computes $N2 = Z_2^f mod\ p$ where Z_2 is a group generator that can be configured for a required anonymity level. Z_2 can be fixed for a limited period of time in synchronisation with Audit Agency certificate issuance to determine unique number of users. For example, to determine unique users for a period of one hour, the Audit Agency has to keep a record of hardware authentications so the user cannot generate another key f, and Z_2 has to be fixed, for that period of time. Also, Z_2 can be chosen by the webserver, reflecting its true identity. The b bit can be specified in DAA protocol to indicate that the signed message was chosen by the user.

The user can provide a proof that she has a certificate for the secret values (f and v) by providing a zero-knowledge proof of the secret values, such that the following equation holds: $S^e z^f x^v \equiv y\ mod\ n$. Then, the user sends the signature to the webserver and convinces the webserver that she knows f, S, e and v. The webserver checks the signature and if valid, the webserver stores $N2$ along the result of the zero-knowledge proof as web metering evidence, proving interactively the communicated user's TPM was genuine.

4   Security Analysis of Proposed Scheme

We assume that the user owns a secure device and number of corrupt users is small (as in Sect. 2.2). Thus, hardware authentication (as in Definition 2) can only succeed by interactively proving the ownership of the physical device containing the built-in secret key. Valid evidence cannot be created in the absence of the subsequent committed signature key in step 5 (i.e. f). Consequently, the adversary has to own a device in order to create valid web metering evidence. Moreover, we assume that the challenges and messages in steps 5, 6, and 7 are securely chosen and constructed as specified in Sects. 3.1 and 3.2. Therefore, evidential integrity goal is achieved.

Depending on the Audit Agency setup, x certificates can be issued to the user after the successful hardware authentication, and valid for a limited period and cannot be reused. We assume that user's secret keys are used to encrypt nonces or time stamps, as specified in Sects. 3.1 and 3.2, to ensure freshness as a countermeasure against impersonation and replay attacks for an observed user. Any captured messages that are resent again during Join Protocol will be rejected by Audit Agency as they will not fit in the current window of acceptable responses. Similarly, captured and resent messages during Sign/Verify Protocol will not enable webserver to construct new valid evidence N2 as they will not fit in the required window. Therefore, security goal is achieved. Using zero-knowledge proof of a discrete logarithm [23], the adversary will not be able to learn the built-in secret key to pass the required authentication in Join Protocol nor be able to learn the corresponding secret signature key in Sign/Verify Protocol. Therefore, observing messages sent by a user will not enable the adversary to get the secret values to impersonate a valid user or hijack the session. Consequently, the following proposition holds.

Proposition 1. *An adversary capturing all communicated messages, but not owning the device, cannot:*

1. *create fake web metering evidence (i.e., N2, see Sect. 3.2);*
2. *impersonate an existing user.*

5   Privacy Analysis of Proposed Scheme

By Definition 1, after hardware authentication, the Audit Agency is assured that the communicating user can securely access the secret key inside the device and consequently can confirm the user's identity. Then, the zero-knowledge protocol [23] is used to convince the Audit Agency that constructed commitment messages were formed correctly without disclosing the secret value f. We assume that during Sign/Verify phase, the user keeps the Audit Agency certificate (S, e, v) secret and only uses it to convince the webserver of the knowledge of the chosen secret key f. Similarly, there has to be a non-predictable difference in time or no pattern between user committing to a new signature key and using it. This is initially achieved by the two roles of Audit Agency and webserver when their involvement is separated by time. (Any introduced random delay should be minimal as not to affect the user browsing experience). Therefore, the proposed scheme protects any captured identifying information. With our assumptions, the following proposition holds.

Proposition 2. *The proposed DAA-based web metering scheme protects any identifying information captured from the authentic certificate of the user's hardware secret key.*

6   Related Work

User-centric Web Metering Schemes. User-centric schemes can use *digital signatures* and hash chaining to construct non-repudiation evidences of visits as proposed by Harn and Lin [15]. To exempt the user from producing a costly signature for each visit, a hash chain is proposed. That is, the webserver uses the received signature and the hash values as evidence for the number of visits. However, the received signature can be linked to the user's identity, which is a privacy problem.

To avoid the apparent privacy problem with digital signatures, *Secret Sharing schemes* were proposed by Naor and Pinkas [20] and used in many works e.g. by Masucci [5,6] and others [19,25]. As evidence of the visits, the webserver here needs to receive a specific number of shares from users to be able to compute a required result using a Secret Sharing scheme e.g. Shamir Secret Sharing [24]. However, the user has to be authenticated (which is another privacy problem) so that the webserver cannot impersonate him and have the required shares. Also, if the Metering Provider is generating and sending the shares, it has to be trusted not to collude with the webserver to link user identity with visits. Similarly, an adversary can observe and correlate user authentication data with the visits. The users' identities have also to be revealed to the Audit Agency to resolve disputes about collected shares by the webserver which can potentially be linked to the visits.

Webserver-centric Web Metering Schemes. A webserver-centric *voucher* scheme uses e-coupons [18] as an attempt to map traditional advertisements models into the electronic ones. The user has to be authenticated when forwarding the e-coupon to the issuing party to stop the webserver from forwarding the e-coupons itself. Also, a questionable Metering Provider can potentially use received e-coupons and authentication data and collude with the webserver to link the information to visits. Or an adversary can observe and correlate authentication data and e-coupons with the visits. Another webserver-centric *processing-based* scheme was proposed by Chen and Mao [9] which uses computational complexity problems like prime factorisation. These computational problems attempt to force the webserver to use users resources in order to solve them and consequently provide web metering evidence via the produced result. However, besides using users' resources, an adversary can still fake users' visits.

The use of a physical web metering *hardware* box attached to the webserver was proposed in [4]. The webserver connects to an audited hardware box which intercepts users requests and stores a log. Randomly, the box also produces a Message Authentication Code (MAC) on a user request which is then redirected to the Audit Agency as an additional verification step. The Audit Agency verifies the MAC code and the request and if valid, the received request is redirected back to the webserver. User impersonation is still a successful attack here in which the webserver can inflate the number of visits.

Third-party-centric Web Metering Schemes. A third-party-centric scheme was proposed in [2] which tracks the user using an *HTTP proxy*. The intercepting HTTP proxy adds a JavaScript code to returned HTML pages to track users actions e.g. mouse movements. Consequently, all visits have to go through the proxy, which does not preserve users privacy. Another scheme is *Google Analytics (GA)* [1] which can provide more granular information than the number of visits. However, during the user-webserver interaction, GA captures private information about the user e.g. Internet Protocol (IP) address to provide geographic results. During users' visits, referenced web metering code is loaded into the webserver script domain. The code is executed under the webserver control, setting a *webserver-owned* cookie [22] to track returning users to the webserver and not Google-Analytics.com. Despite the privacy improvement of webserver-owned cookie of not figuring out users visiting different webservers incorporating GA script, returning users will still be identified to the webserver and Google-Analytics.com. Also, the referenced code captures private data about the user e.g. user's Internet Protocol (IP) address to provide geographic results.

Privacy Comparison. The World Wide Web Consortium (W3C) Platform for Privacy Preferences Project (P3P) [11] provides a framework regarding privacy issues in accessing webservers by allowing them to express their privacy practices in a standard format. We have analysed representative web metering schemes according to relevant metrics described in P3P. A summary of the P3P analysis is shown in Table 1. From two extremes, a particular private information can be either *required* by the scheme or *protected*. We use the symbol ✗ to denote the

Table 1. Privacy comparison

Scheme	Identifiers	State	Interactive	Location	Computer	Navigation
Digital Signature [15]	✗	†	✔	✔	✔	✔
Secret Sharing [20]	✗	†	✔	✔	✔	✔
Webserver Voucher [18]	✗	†	✔	✔	✔	✔
Processing [9]	✔	✗	✔	✔	†	†
Webserver Hardware [4]	✔	†	✗	✔	✔	✔
HTTP Proxy [2]	†	†	†	†	✔	†
Google Analytics [1]	†	✗	✔	†	†	†
This paper (DAA [7])	✔	†	✔	✔	✔	†

scheme cannot operate without the corresponding required private information in order to provide web metering result or evidence. On the other hand, we use the symbol ✔ to denote that the private information can be protected and not accessed by the adversary under secure user setup. Such setup can be achieved with countermeasures that can prevent the adversary from getting the private information. The countermeasures can be provided by the scheme itself or can be potentially provided by other techniques. We use the symbol ┦ to denote that the private information is not always or necessarily required by the web metering scheme; however, it is *available* and can still be captured by the adversary due to an implementation (or a variation) of the scheme.

7 Conclusion

We proposed a new user-centric web metering scheme using hardware to enhance users' privacy. We built a proof of concept implementation[1] on a traditional computer to evaluate efficiency and transparency of running operations. The tests showed feasible results. It took around 1650 nanoseconds to execute U and around 515 nanoseconds to execute N. Besides operational cost from Audit Agency and webserver sides, main barrier for a wide deployment is that users should accept the device. However, in many contexts, gain in privacy will offset the costs. We discussed how user hardware assumption can be realistic in today's and future computing devices and showed different options.

Future work includes exploring techniques for discovering rogue devices, and implementing the scheme with different settings to provide the evidential signature e.g. hash chaining. Various options for counting the number of unique users can be further explored for different advertising applications. Future work also includes analysing the performance of the proposed scheme using handheld devices. Formal validation of the proposed scheme is left for future work as well.

References

1. Google analytics blog. Official weblog offering news, tips and resources related to google's web traffic analytics service. analytics.blogspot.com
2. Atterer, R., Wnuk, M., Schmidt, A.: Knowing the user's every move: user activity tracking for website usability evaluation and implicit interaction. In: WWW 2006: Proceedings of the 15th International Conference on World Wide Web, pp. 203–212. ACM, New York (2006)
3. Barwick, S.G., Jackson, W.-A., Martin, K.M.: A general approach to robust web metering. Des. Codes Crypt. **36**(1), 5–27 (2005)
4. Bergadano, F., De Mauro, P.: Third party certification of HTTP service access statistics (Position Paper). In: Christianson, B., Crispo, B., Harbison, W.S., Roe, M. (eds.) Security Protocols 1998. LNCS, vol. 1550, pp. 95–99. Springer, Heidelberg (1999)

---

[1] at National Center for Digital Certification (NCDC): Research & Development. www.ncdc.gov.sa.

5. Blundo, C., Bonis, A.D., Masucci, B.: Bounds and constructions for metering schemes. Commun. Inf. Syst. **2**, 1–28 (2002)
6. Blundo, C., Martn, S., Masucci, B., Padr, C.: A linear algebraic approach to metering schemes. Cryptology ePrint Archive, Report 2001/087 (2001)
7. Brickell, E., Camenisch, J., Chen, L.: Direct anonymous attestation. In: Proceedings of the 11th ACM Conference on Computer and Communications Security, CCS 2004, pp. 132–145. ACM, New York (2004)
8. Camenisch, J.L., Lysyanskaya, A.: Dynamic accumulators and application to efficient revocation of anonymous credentials. In: Yung, M. (ed.) CRYPTO 2002. LNCS, vol. 2442, pp. 61–76. Springer, Heidelberg (2002)
9. Chen, L., Mao, W.: An auditable metering scheme for web advertisement applications. In: Davida, G.I., Frankel, Y. (eds.) ISC 2001. LNCS, vol. 2200, pp. 475–485. Springer, Heidelberg (2001)
10. Chor, B., Fiat, A., Naor, M., Pinkas, B.: Tracing traitors. IEEE Trans. Inf. Theory **46**(3), 893–910 (2000)
11. Cranor, L., Dobbs, B., Egelman, S., Hogben, G., Humphrey, J., Langheinrich, M., Marchiori, M., Presler-Marshall, M., Reagle, J., Schunter, M., Stampley, D.A., Wenning, R.: The platform for privacy preferences. W3C Recommendation, November 2006
12. Dent, A.W., Mitchell, C.J.: User's Guide to Cryptography and Standards. Artech House Computer Security. Artech House Inc., Norwood (2004)
13. Dolev, D., Yao, A.C.: On the security of public key protocols. Technical report, Stanford, CA, USA (1981)
14. Franklin, M.K., Malkhi, D.: Auditable metering with lightweight security. J. Comput. Secur. **6**(4), 237–256 (1998)
15. Harn, H., Lin, L.: A non-repudiation metering scheme. IEEE Commun. Lett. **37**(5), 486–487 (2001)
16. International Organization for Standardization: ISO 11889–1:2009. Information technology - Trusted Platform Module - Part 1: Overview, May 2009
17. International Organization for Standardization: ISO 7498–2:1989. Information processing systems - Open Systems Interconnection - Basic Reference Model - Part 2: Security Architecture (1989)
18. Jakobsson, M., MacKenzie, P.D., Stern, J.P.: Secure and lightweight advertising on the web. Comput. Netw. **31**(11–16), 1101–1109 (1999)
19. Laih, C.-S., Fu, C.-J., Kuo, W.-C.: Design a secure and practical metering scheme. In: International Conference on Internet Computing, pp. 443–447 (2006)
20. Naor, M., Pinkas, B.: Secure and efficient metering. In: Nyberg, K. (ed.) EUROCRYPT 1998. LNCS, vol. 1403, pp. 576–590. Springer, Heidelberg (1998)
21. Pedersen, T.P.: Non-interactive and information-theoretic secure verifiable secret sharing. In: Feigenbaum, J. (ed.) CRYPTO 1991. LNCS, vol. 576, pp. 129–140. Springer, Heidelberg (1992)
22. Roesner, F., Kohno, T., Wetherall, D.: Detecting and defending against third-party tracking on the web. In: Proceedings of the 9th USENIX Conference on Networked Systems Design and Implementation, NSDI 2012, p. 12. USENIX Association, Berkeley (2012)
23. Schnorr, C.-P.: Efficient identification and signatures for smart cards. In: Brassard, G. (ed.) CRYPTO 1989. LNCS, vol. 435, pp. 239–252. Springer, Heidelberg (1990)
24. Shamir, A.: How to share a secret. Commun. ACM **22**(11), 612–613 (1979)
25. Wang, R.-C., Juang, W.-S., Lei, C.-L.: A web metering scheme for fair advertisement transactions. Int. J. Secure. Appl. **2**(4), 453–456 (2008)

Towards Efficient Update of Access Control Policy for Cryptographic Cloud Storage

Weiyu Jiang[1,2,3]([✉]), Zhan Wang[1,2], Limin Liu[1,2], and Neng Gao[1,2]

[1] State Key Laboratory of Information Security,
Institute of Information Engineering, Chinese Academy of Sciences, Beijing, China
{wyjiang,zwang,lmliu,gaoneng}@lois.cn
[2] Data Assurance and Communication Security Research Center
of Chinese Academy of Sciences, Beijing, China
[3] University of Chinese Academy of Sciences, Beijing, China

Abstract. To protect sensitive data from unauthorized access, encrypting data at the user end before outsourcing them to the cloud storage, has become a common practice. In this case, the access control policy is enforced through assigning proper cryptographic keys among collaborators. However, when the access control policy needs to be updated (e.g. new collaborators join or some collaborators leave), it is very costly for the data owner or other parties to re-encrypt the data with a new key in order to satisfy the new policy. To address this problem, we propose a dual-header structure and batch revocation, which makes the overhead for privileges grant independent of data size and significantly improves the efficiency of privilege revocation by applying lazy revocation to certain groups of revocation requests, respectively. We also analyze the overhead for authorization showing that our approach is able to efficiently manage frequent policy updates.

Keywords: Access control policy · Over-encryption · Batch revocation

1 Introduction

Cloud storage has certain advantages, such as paying for only what is used, being quick to deploy, offering easy adjustment of capacity and built-in disaster recovery. Therefore, individuals and companies are resorting more to cloud providers for storing their data and sharing them with collaborators. However, cloud providers are generally considered as "Honest-but-Curious", which means that the cloud will execute some functions honestly, but might pry into the sensitive data led by business interest or curiosity. To secure sensitive data and prevent illegal visitors (including cloud providers) from unauthorized access, a straightforward solution is to apply cryptographic techniques, so that data are encrypted at the user end before being outsourced to the cloud. In this case, only the data owner and authorized collaborators with knowledge of the key will be able to access the data. Therefore, access control policies are enforced through assigning proper cryptographic keys among collaborators.

© Institute for Computer Sciences, Social Informatics and Telecommunications Engineering 2015
J. Tian et al. (Eds.): SecureComm 2014, Part II, LNICST 153, pp. 341–356, 2015.
DOI: 10.1007/978-3-319-23802-9_26

However, when the access control policy needs to be updated (e.g. new collaborators join or some collaborators leave), it can be very costly for data owners to re-encrypt the data with a new key in order to satisfy the new policy. As the computation overhead for re-encryption(encryption/decryption) and transmission overhead for downloading are proportional to the size of data [1], policy updates may not propagate in real time, especially for large amounts of data. Therefore, it is not advisable for data owners with limited ability to take the heavy burden. An alternative solution is applying proxy re-encryption [2,3] which migrates the burden for re-encryption from data owners to the proxy. However, the adoption of public key cryptography impedes the wide usage of proxy re-encryption algorithms, because of the computation overhead. Over-encryption proposed in [1,4] is a practical symmetric encryption solution for delegating keys' update and re-encryption to cloud servers. Nevertheless, in the "pay-as-you-go" model of cloud computing, it is still costly for data owners to pay the cloud for the cipher operations. Furthermore, the delay for re-encryption cannot be ignored, especially in presence of multiple access control policy updates of large data with replicas across multiple cloud servers.

Our approach is based on over-encryption [1,4], which implements the update of access control policy by enforcing two layer encryption. In over-encryption, data resources are doubly encrypted at base encryption layer (BEL) by data owners and at the surface encryption layer (SEL) by the cloud. When access control updates, the data just needs to invoke the cloud to update the encryption policy at SEL. However, both granting and revoking authorizations need the cloud to encrypt over the pre-encrypted data, which brings much overhead for re-encryption computation and has an influence on the performance when large amounts of updating operations of access control policy concurrently happen. In order to implement an efficient update of access control policy in cryptographic cloud storage, this paper presents a dual-header structure for eliminating the need of re-encrypting related data resources when new authorizations are granted, and proposes batch revocation for reducing the overhead for re-encryption when revocations happen.

In our dual-header structure, data are encrypted by data owners at the base encryption layer and then over-encrypted by cloud servers at the surface encryption layer. Each data resource is divided into the data content in the body and the cryptographic keys of data content in the header. Before being outsourced to the cloud, both the body and the header of data resources are pre-encrypted by data owners. After data are uploaded to the cloud, the cloud server will first encapsulate the header by encryption. Therefore, the header of all the resources is initialized by a two layer encryption and always has a relatively small size. When granting new privileges, cloud servers only need to update the small header, instead of the body. Our dual-header structure has the following characteristics:

- High security. The dual-header structure prevents unauthorized visitors from accessing the sensitive data. Even if the cloud server suffers attacks, the sensitive data will not be divulged to unauthorized visitors.

– Low overhead. The dual-header structure makes the overhead for granting privileges independent of data size. With the dual-header structure, there is no re-encryption of any data content (possibly of large size), so it offers significant benefits in reducing the overhead when new privileges are granted.

In order to prevent the revoked user from accessing future versions of the data with the key they possess, the overhead for re-encryption brought by revocation operations cannot be avoided. Our batch revocation mechanism, combining lazy revocation to a certain group of revocation requests, provides a considerable improvement of over-encryption systems, by reducing the number of operations on large amounts of data.

The rest of the paper is organized as follows. Section 2 introduces a basic scheme and discusses its weaknesses. Section 3 presents our main scheme, and Sect. 4 describes an efficient access control policy update with low overhead. Section 5 illustrates performance analysis and security analysis. Then related work is given in Sect. 6, and finally we conclude this paper and give our future work in Sect. 7.

2 Preliminaries

Cryptographic cloud storage [5] is proposed to securely outsource sensitive data resource to the "Honest-but-Curious" cloud. It can protect sensitive data against both the cloud provider and illegal visitors, by encrypting data at the client side before outsourcing. The security lies in appropriate key distribution to users (collaborators) based on the access control policy for sharing data among collaborators. Keeping cryptographic keys secret from the cloud provider is essential for those data owners with high security requirement. However, it makes it difficult for data owners to resort to the cloud provider for updating the access control policy when the cooperative relationship changes. Additionally, data with different access control policies should be encrypted with different keys when fine-grained data access control is desired. This could upset the users, as they would be required to maintain multiple keys for different data resources.

Our work is based on the over-encryption approach [1,4], which was proposed to avoid the need for shipping resources back to the owner for re-encryption after a change in the access control policy. On the premise of implementing fine-grained access control, over-encryption also forces a user to keep one or two private keys to access all the authorized resources, by subtly constructing a key derivation structure. In over-encryption, data resources are doubly encrypted at the base encryption layer (BEL) and the surface encryption layer (SEL). At BEL, data are encrypted by data owners at client side and data owners are responsible for distributing the decryption keys to users. After data are outsourced to the cloud, the encrypted data are over-encrypted by the cloud at SEL, for updating access control policies. Only those with keys of the two encryption layers can decrypt the data, so the cloud provider offers additional protection to prevent those who can obtain the keys of the base encryption layer from accessing the data.

When the cooperative relationship or the access control requirements of data owners change, the access control policy should be updated as well. In over-encryption, the data owner only needs to call the cloud servers to re-encrypt the data at the surface encryption layer. However, re-encrypting large amounts of data and transmitting requests across multiple servers with replicas are also costly for the cloud when multiple access control policy updates happen. One potential limitation of over-encryption is that the cloud might need to re-encrypt the content of related data resources when new privileges are granted. Another improvable point is that immediate revocation could increase the overhead for repetitive cipher operations, when revoking privileges towards the same resources frequently happens.

2.1 Over-Encryption

In over-encryption, if a set of data resources can be accessed by the same access user set, they will be encrypted with the same key at the base encryption layer, or else they will be encrypted with different keys. A user just needs to maintain one or two private keys to access all the resources that are authorized to him. Over-encryption is implemented by constructing a key derivation structure, where one key can be derived from another key through public tokens.

The key derivation structure of over-encryption is based on the access control list (ACL) of data resources. In which over-encryption divides all the users into different access user sets and each access user set is associated with a key. Data resources with the same access user set are encrypted with the same key. The associated key of the access user set, can be derived by the associated key of any subset of the access user set. It is implemented by publishing public tokens and labels on each derivation path. For example, there are three data resources r_1, r_2 and r_3: the access user set of r_1 is {A,B} with associated key K_{AB}; r_2 and r_3 with the same access user set {A,B,C} are encrypted with the key K_{ABC}; by publishing token $t_{AB,ABC} = K_{ABC} \oplus h_a(K_{AB}, l_{ABC})$, the user who possesses K_{AB} can derive K_{ABC} by computing $K_{ABC} = t_{AB,ABC} \oplus h_a(K_{AB}, l_{ABC})$, where l_{ABC} is a publicly available label associated with K_{ABC}, $\oplus$ is the bita-bit xor operator and h_a is a secure hash function.

We express the key derivation structure through a graph, having the vertex v_U associated with a group of resources and keys to encrypt the resources. If U_i is a subset of U_j and a token $t_{i,j}$ is published, then there exists an edge connecting two vertices (v_{U_i}, v_{U_j}). For instance, Table 1 represents an example of access control policy, where h_d and h_a is a secure hash function, then a key derivation structure shown in Fig. 1 is constructed.

2.2 Limitations

In the key derivation structure, data resources with the same access user set are encrypted with the same key in a vertex. It reduces the number of keys and significantly simplifies key management for users. However, it might result in re-encrypting the other data resources in the same vertex of the granted data

Table 1. An example of the implementation of access control policy

(a) Secret Keys

Resources	Access User Sets	Encryption Keys
r_1, r_9, r_{10}	A,B	$h_d(K_{AB})$
r_3, r_4, r_5	A,B,C	$h_d(K_{ABC})$
r_2, r_6	C	$h_d(K_C)$
r_7, r_8	D	$h_d(K_D)$

(b) Public Tokens

Labels	Tokens
l_{AB}	$t_{A,AB} = K_{AB} \oplus h_a(K_A, l_{AB})$
l_{AB}	$t_{B,AB} = K_{AB} \oplus h_a(K_B, l_{AB})$
l_{ABC}	$t_{AB,ABC} = K_{ABC} \oplus h_a(K_{AB}, l_{ABC})$
l_{ABC}	$t_{C,ABC} = K_{ABC} \oplus h_a(K_C, l_{ABC})$

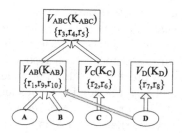

Fig. 1. Key derivation structure

resource when new privileges are granted. In the example showed by Fig. 1, if the data owner grants user D the privilege of accessing the data resource r_1, the data owner needs to provide D with the decryption key $h_d(K_{AB})$ instead of the derivation key K_{AB}, which might be used to derive the key of resources (e.g. r_3, r_4, r_5) in other vertices. However, it cannot prevent unauthorized D from decrypting r_9 and r_{10}. Therefore, the cloud provider should over-encrypt r_9 and r_{10} at the surface encryption layer instead of shipping them back to the data owner. In fact, re-encrypting data resources in the same vertex when granting privileges should be avoided.

Another improvable point of over-encryption lies in revocation. In order to prevent the revoked users from accessing future versions of the data resource with the key they possess, the cloud should re-encrypt it at the surface layer encryption. However, the costly re-encryption operations might affect the performance of the cloud storage service when multiple revocations happen. Moreover, as a data resource might be accessed by a set of users, immediately revoking the access to a certain resource will produce repetitive re-encryption operations, and may result in a long delay when revoking the privileges on large data.

3   Main Scheme

We construct a dual-header structure based on over-encryption and propose batch revocation to implement an efficient update of the access control policy in cryptographic cloud storage. In order to implement fast encryption, we adopt symmetric ciphers in our proposed scheme. Data are firstly encrypted at base encryption layer by data owners. When the access control policy changes, data owners will not re-encrypt the encrypted data any more. All of the cipher operations for matching the new access control policy are executed by the cloud. The dual-header structure makes the overhead for granting privileges independent of data size. Therefore, the cloud just needs to update a small header of the granted resource, instead of the large content of other resources encrypted with the same key of the granted resource.

3.1 Dual-Header Structure

We divide each data resource into two parts: keys in the header and the data content in the body. At the initialization phase (before uploading), the data content in the body is encrypted with the key in the header by the data owner at the base encryption layer. In our scheme, each resource uses a different key to encrypt its content. In order to prevent the cloud provider and unauthorized visitors from obtaining the secret key, the key in the header at the base encryption layer is encrypted by the data owner. When data resources in header/body form are uploaded to the cloud servers, the cloud needs to over-encrypt the header at the surface encryption layer. Therefore, the two layer encryption is imposed on the header of all the resources and we call it dual-header structure.

There are four types of keys in our dual-header structure.

– Data Content Key: dek. This is a symmetric key used in the base encryption layer to encrypt the data content in the body. It is generated and encrypted by the data owner and stays invariant in the header in the cloud. Each data resource has a different data content key. This key is stored in the header in encrypted form and requires no distribution.
– Surface Content Key: sek. This is a symmetric key used in the surface encryption layer to encrypt the already encrypted data content in the body. At the initialization phase, it is null. When the revocation of the data resource happens, the cloud will set a new surface content key and encrypt the pre-encrypted data content with it in the body. The keys of separate data resources are also different and will be changed when revocations happen. This key is stored in the header in encrypted form and requires no distribution.
– Base Head Key: BK_U. This symmetric key is used to encrypt the data content key in the header. The data owner also generates it before uploading the header to the cloud and it will also stay invariant in the cloud. It might be used to encrypt a set of resources with the same access control policy. This key is distributed to all the authorized users of set U, by constructing derivation paths from their private keys to BK_U.
– Surface Head Key: SK_U. This symmetric key is used in the surface encryption layer to encrypt the pre-encrypted data content key and surface content key in the header. The cloud generates it and it will change when the access control policy updates. Data resources with the same access control policy share the same surface head key. This key is also distributed to the authorized users of set U, by constructing derivation paths from their private keys to SK_U.

We use the four types of symmetric keys at the two encryption layer to protect the outsourced data. As the access control policy might update, the status of the data stored in the cloud is not immutable. After the data resource is uploaded to the cloud at the initialization phase, the data resource is in the initial status expressed in Table 2. When the access control policy of the data resource updates, the status of the data will change into the common status showed in Table 3.

Table 2. Initial status of data resource

Id	Header	Body
$Id(r)$	$E_{SK_{U_i}}(E_{BK_{U_i}}(dek), null)$	$E_{dek}(data)$

Table 3. Common status of data resource

Id	Header	Body
$Id(r)$	$E_{SK_{U_j}}(E_{BK_{U_i}}(dek), sek)$	$E_{sek}(E_{dek}(data))$

At the initialization phase, the data owner first encrypts the data resource with data content key dek and generates the body $E_{dek}(data)$, then encrypts dek with the base head key BK_{U_i} and achieves the header $E_{BK_{U_i}}(dek)$, and finally uploads $Id(r)$ (the identifier of the data resource r), $E_{dek}(data)$ and $E_{BK_{U_i}}(dek)$ to the cloud. After the cloud receives the data, the cloud first encrypts $E_{BK_{U_i}}(dek)$ in the header with the surface head key SK_{U_i}, and gets $E_{SK_{U_i}}(E_{BK_{U_i}}(dek), null)$ (*null* means that the cloud has not over-encrypted $E_{dek}(data)$). Then the data resource is stored in the initial status.

When the access control policy changes, the data owner should prevent the users who own dek from accessing the data. If data owners are unwilling to download the data resource and re-encrypt it by themselves, they can invoke the cloud to over-encrypt it. If the data resource is still in the initial status, the cloud needs to generate a surface content key sek and a new surface head key SK_{U_j}, then over-encrypt $E_{dek}(data)$ with sek and re-encrypt $(E_{BK_{U_i}}(dek), null)$ with the new SK_{U_j}. Then the status of the data will change into the common status. If the data resource is in the common status, the cloud will decrypt $E_{sek}(E_{dek}(data))$ with the old sek and re-encrypt it with a new sek.

Our work assumes that each data resource has an access control list ACL. In order to enforce fine-grained access control through reasonably assigning keys, we define the key derivation function $KeyDerivation(U)$ to generate encryption keys, distribute keys to shared users and publish tokens to derive keys for authorized users. For the detailed algorithm code of $KeyDerivation(U)$ refers to [4].

Definition $KeyDerivation(U) \longrightarrow (K, T, L)$:

- Access User Sets U: U is the family of subsets of all the users which derives from the access control lists of all the data resources. For instance, if the access control list of data resource r_i regulates that users $\{A, B, C\}$ can read it, then $U_i = \{A, B, C\}(U_i \in U)$ is the access user set of r_i.

- Keys K: K can be the set of all the keys used to derive the keys of the header (base head key BK_{U_i} or surface head key SK_{U_i}). At the base encryption layer at the initialization phase, $\forall U_i \in U, \exists K_{U_i}$ associated with the access user set U_i, where $BK_{U_i} = h_d(K_{U_i})$. At the surface encryption layer, $\forall U_i \in U, \exists SK_{U_i}$ associated with the access user set U_i.
- Public tokens T and labels L: T is the set of all the public tokens which are used to derive keys for the users. L is the set of all the labels which are used to mark access user sets. If $\exists U_j \in U$ and U_i is the largest subset of U_j among U, then it must exist a token $t_{U_i,U_j} = K_{U_j} \oplus h_a(K_{U_i}, l_{U_j})$ (l_{U_j}) is the label of access user set U_j.

3.2 Batch Revocation

There are two revocation approaches in cryptographic cloud storage, depending on when the re-encryption operations are executed. In an active revocation approach, the revoked data resource is immediately re-encrypted with a new key after a revocation takes place. This is costly and might cause disruptions in the normal operation of cloud storage. In the alternative approach of lazy revocation [6], re-encryption happens only when the data resource is modified for the first time after a revocation.

We propose batch revocation combining lazy revocation to achieve better user experience and reduce the overhead for revocation. In the general scheme, when data owners need to prevent revoked users from accessing their resources, they can invoke the cloud provider to re-encrypt data after a revocation. In this case, revocation operations must involve reading data from the disk, decrypting them and re-encrypting them, so the overhead for revocation cannot be ignored, especially for the data of large size. In our scheme, the cloud can delay the revocations to the time when the predefined conditions are satisfied. The predefined conditions and the final time of revocation can be set by data owners according to their requirements. For example, the cloud can select to delay the revocations on the data of large size to the next read access, which are not frequently accessed. As the base head key is not updated when the data resource is modified, the data owner will use a new data content key to encrypt the content when the data owner modifies it, and the cloud just needs to re-encrypt the header without encrypting the content in the body (the data resource is stored in the initial status). In this case, the cloud can delay the revocations to the next write access in the scenario where multiple revocation operations frequently happen.

4 Access Control Policy Updates

There are two types of access control policy update operations in most storage systems: (1) Grant new privileges to users and (2) Revoke privileges. The privileges can be referred to as read privilege or write privilege. Our target is to protect the sensitive data from being disclosed to unauthorized visitors, and we restrict ourselves to the consideration of read privileges in this paper.

Policy update operations are often executed in most network applications or systems. For instance, according to the data given in [7], there are 29,203 individual revocations of users from 2,916 different access control lists extracted from seven months of AFS protection server logs. If the updating of access control policies requires heavy overhead, it will have a negative influence on the performance. In over-encryption, both granting and revoking involve reading data from the disk, encrypting data resource and decrypting data resource, so it results in large transmission overhead and computation overhead. Our dual-header structure can efficiently reduce the overhead when new privileges are granted, by operating on the small header of the granted resource, instead of the data content with large size. As for revocation, our scheme applies batch revocation to reduce the overhead for repetitive re-encryption operations.

4.1   Granting Privileges

We define the function $Grant(u, r)$ to authorize a user u to access the data resource r in cryptographic cloud storage systems. Privileges grant in our scheme is implemented by assigning the related keys to the authorized users. In the previous work of over-encryption, grant in both Full Sel and Delta Sel [4] methods involves encryption and decryption operations on the data resource content and other related resources encrypted with the same keys of r. However, we require no re-encryption of the content and just require the cloud to re-encrypt the header of r.

When executing $Grant(u, r)$, the data owner firstly updates the access user set $r.USet$ of r, then gets the derivation key K according to $r.USet$ and computes the base head key $r.BK$ of r by hashing K. As resources with the same privileges at the initialization phase are encrypted with the same base head key, which is not changed with the access control policy, $r.BK$ may be derived from the private key K_u of u. If the base head key of r is not included in the set of keys $KSet$ which can be derived by u, the data owner has to add token from K_u to $r.BK$, in order to ensure that u can derive $r.BK$. Then the data owner invokes the cloud to over encrypt the header of r to make sure that only the new access user set $r.USet$ can decrypt the header of r. When the cloud receives the request, the cloud needs to decrypt the header of r with the old surface head key, re-encrypt the header and add tokens to ensure that all the authorized users in the access user set of U can decrypt the header at the surface encryption layer, which is implemented by calling the function $ReEncryptHeader(header, U)$. The detailed steps can be seen in Fig. 2.

For the sake of simplicity, we assume that the function $Grant(u, r)$ is referred to a single user u and a single resource r. The extension to sets of users and resources is easy to implement. The main overhead of $Grant(u, r)$ lies in decrypting and re-encrypting the small header of r: $DecryptHeader(r, r.SK)$ and $ReEncryptHeader(r.Header, U_{new})$ in Fig. 2.

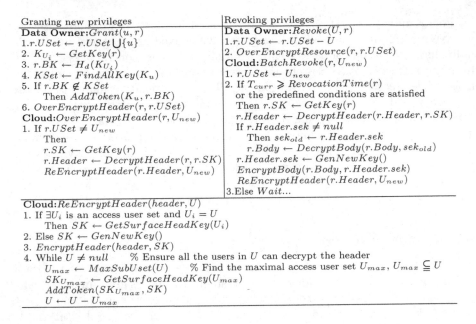

Granting new privileges	Revoking privileges
Data Owner:$Grant(u, r)$	**Data Owner:**$Revoke(U, r)$
1.$r.USet \leftarrow r.USet \bigcup \{u\}$	1.$r.USet \leftarrow r.USet - U$
2. $K_{U_i} \leftarrow GetKey(r)$	2. $OverEncryptResource(r, r.USet)$
3. $r.BK \leftarrow H_d(K_{U_i})$	**Cloud:**$BatchRevoke(r, U_{new})$
4. $KSet \leftarrow FindAllKey(K_u)$	1. $r.USet \leftarrow U_{new}$
5. If $r.BK \notin KSet$	2. If $T_{curr} \geqslant RevocationTime(r)$
$\quad$ Then $AddToken(K_u, r.BK)$	$\quad$ or the predefined conditions are satisfied
6. $OverEncryptHeader(r, r.USet)$	$\quad$ Then $r.SK \leftarrow GetKey(r)$
Cloud:$OverEncryptHeader(r, U_{new})$	$\quad$ $r.Header \leftarrow DecryptHeader(r.Header, r.SK)$
1. If $r.USet \neq U_{new}$	$\quad$ If $r.Header.sek \neq null$
$\quad$ Then	$\quad\quad$ Then $sek_{old} \leftarrow r.Header.sek$
$\quad\quad$ $r.SK \leftarrow GetKey(r)$	$\quad\quad$ $r.Body \leftarrow DecryptBody(r.Body, sek_{old})$
$\quad\quad$ $r.Header \leftarrow DecryptHeader(r, r.SK)$	$\quad$ $r.Header.sek \leftarrow GenNewKey()$
$\quad\quad$ $ReEncryptHeader(r.Header, U_{new})$	$\quad$ $EncryptBody(r.Body, r.Header.sek)$
	$\quad$ $ReEncryptHeader(r.Header, U_{new})$
	3.Else $Wait...$

Cloud:$ReEncryptHeader(header, U)$
1. If $\exists U_i$ is an access user set and $U_i = U$
$\quad$ Then $SK \leftarrow GetSurfaceHeadKey(U_i)$
2. Else $SK \leftarrow GenNewKey()$
3. $EncryptHeader(header, SK)$
4. While $U \neq null$ $\quad$ % Ensure all the users in U can decrypt the header
$\quad$ $U_{max} \leftarrow MaxSubUset(U)$ $\quad$ % Find the maximal access user set U_{max}, $U_{max} \subseteq U$
$\quad$ $SK_{U_{max}} \leftarrow GetSurfaceHeadKey(U_{max})$
$\quad$ $AddToken(SK_{U_{max}}, SK)$
$\quad$ $U \leftarrow U - U_{max}$

Fig. 2. Algorithms for granting and revoking authorizations

4.2   Revoking Privileges

Revocation in our scheme is implemented by updating the keys and re-encrypting the resource at the surface encryption layer. Users whose privileges will be revoked, might preserve the keys of the related resources locally, therefore the revoked resource should be re-encrypted with new keys. As the cloud could not change the base layer encryption data, we need the cloud to re-encrypt the resource at the surface encryption layer.

We define the function $Revoke(r, U)$ at the client side to revoke a set of users $U(|U| >= 1)$ the access to a resource r. At the cloud side, we define the function $BatchRevoke(r, U_{new})$ to revoke a set of users not in U_{new} on r. When executing $Revoke(r, U)$, the data owner updates the access user set $r.USet$ of r by deleting the revoked users U from $r.USet$, invokes the cloud to over-encrypt r and requires the cloud to ensure that only users in $r.USet$ can access the new decryption keys by executing $OverEncryptResource(r, r.USet)$. When receives the request, the cloud will record the freshest access user set of r and wait for the revocation time to execute the function $BatchRevoke(r, U)$. The data owner can define a time period for resources to execute revocations, then the cloud must execute revocations when the final time arrives. The data owner can also predefine conditions to require the cloud execute re-encryption. When the cloud needs to execute re-encryption for revoked resource r, it has to decrypt the header of r and extract the surface content key sek_{old} of r. If sek_{old} is $null$, it means that the body of r has not been over-encrypted by the cloud. Or the cloud should decrypt the body of r with sek_{old}. Finally, the cloud should encrypt the body of r with a new surface content key and re-encrypt the header to ensure only the authorized users in the access user set U_{new} can decrypt the header of r. The details are given in Fig. 2.

The main overhead for revocations lies in the two functions $DecryptBody$ and $EncryptBody$. For the data resources of large size, the overhead cannot be ignored. However, batch revocation can reduce the number of cipher operations on the resource, which will be illustrated in Sect. 5.1.

5   Analysis

5.1   Performance Analysis

In cryptographic cloud storage systems, the keys to encrypt data resources need to be updated and re-encryption might be required in order to match the new access control policy. However, the overhead for re-encryption could not be ignored, especially for large amounts of data resources in the cloud. For example, encrypting data with the size of 1 GB will consume 7.15 s by applying OpenSSL 0.9.8 k with a block size of 8 KB (AES-256, encoding rate: 143.30 MB/s) [8]. Therefore, our scheme targets at reducing the overhead for re-encryption after the access control policy changes.

The overhead for privileges grant. The overhead for privileges grant in our dual-header structure, always involves token retrieval and key derivation, reading data from the disk and encryption/decryption. At the client side, the dominant computation overhead is the retrieval of tokens and key derivation to distribute keys to the new authorized users when new privileges are granted. At the cloud side, the cloud servers have to find the key of related resources by retrieving tokens and deriving keys, read the related resources from the disk and re-encrypt them.

According to the performance evaluations of over-encryption in the extension work [1], the time for retrieving tokens, independent of resource size, is much lower than that for downloading and decrypting large data resources. However, the time required to transfer and decrypt the resource in [1], dominates in the overhead for authorization on resources of size larger than 1 MB in its local network configuration. The time also grows linearly with the increase in the resource size. Although the cloud does not transfer data resources back to the client, the cloud is required to read the resource from the disk, re-encrypt it and sometimes might transfer re-encryption request among different cloud servers with replicas. Therefore, reading data from the disk, decrypting and encrypting data dominate in the overhead for access control policy updates. As the time for reading data from the disk, decrypting and encrypting data is proportional to the size of data resources, our approach that operating on small (about KB level) header rather than operating on data content (perhaps MB/GB/TB level), has significant benefits in reducing the overhead.

The overhead for revocation. We find that the number of operations of cloud servers on data resources is different between revoking a group of users

Table 4. Comparison of the number of operations on data resource content

Example–Access policy updates :{A,B,C,D,E,F} can read r $\longrightarrow$ {A, E, F} can read r
Re-encrypt the header or the body of r with a new surface key: K_U, U is the access user set of r

Function		Main operations
Revoking one by one	$Revoke(B, r)$	$Read(r)$
		$Decrypt(r, K_{ABCDEF})$
		$Encrypt(r, K_{ACDEF})$
	$Revoke(C, r)$	$Read(r)$
		$Decrypt(r, K_{ACDEF})$
		$Encrypt(r, K_{ADEF})$
	$Revoke(D, r)$	$Read(r)$
		$Decrypt(r, K_{ADEF})$
		$Encrypt(r, K_{AEF})$
Batch revocation	$Revoke(\{B, C, D\}, r)$	$Read(r)$
		$Decrypt(r, K_{ABCDEF})$
		$Encrypt(r, K_{AEF})$

on a resource one by one and batching the revocations of the group of users on the resource. This is due to data resources with the same ACL encrypted with the same keys. We assume the header or the body of a data resource r is encrypted with a key K_{ABCDEF} at the surface encryption layer by the cloud, which means it can be read by a set of users {A,B,C,D,E,F} and now r just can be accessed by {A,E,F} after a series of revocations. We give a comparison between revoking {B,C,D} one by one and batching these revocations in Table 4. We can see that a reduction in the number of repetitive operations on the data resource by applying batch revocations. It can significantly lower much overhead for transmission and cipher operations, especially for the data resource of large size when re-encrypting the content in the body.

5.2   Security Analysis

Access control of sensitive data in our scheme is implemented by reasonably distributing keys of the two encryption layer (BEL and SEL). In the "Honest-but-Curious" model, protecting sensitive data against both unauthorized visitors and the cloud is difficult to implement when re-encryption for the update of access control policy relies on the cloud. Therefore, the security of our scheme lies in the distribution of the cryptographic keys over the two levels, which is executed by the data owner and the cloud provider by appropriately publishing public tokens to construct derivation paths.

In order to prevent sensitive data from unauthorized access, data resources are firstly encrypted with the data content key at the base encryption layer enforced by data owners. Adversaries must obtain the keys (data content key and base head key) of the base encryption layer in order to obtain the plaintext of the data resource. As the data content key in the header is encrypted with the base head key, only with the base head key can the adversary decrypt the data content in the base encryption layer. In fact, the base head key in our approach is equal to the key at the BEL of over-encryption.

We adopt the cloud to protect the base head key of the header at the surface encryption layer. In fact, unauthorized users might obtain the base head key in our scheme. For example, a revoked user might locally maintain the base head key of the revoked resource; a newly granted user might acquire the base head key of the resource r_i unintendedly, when the user is authorized to access the resource r_j, which is encrypted with the same base head key of r_i. However, unauthorized users who have got the base head key cannot decrypt the data content because the cloud consolidates the defensive barrier. For those with just the base head key, the cloud encrypts the pre-encrypted data content key in the header with the surface head key. Adversaries cannot get the data content key without the surface head key generated by the cloud. For those who have got both the base head key and the data content key generated by the data owner (revoked users), the cloud encapsulates the data content by encrypting it with surface content key, and the surface content key is also protected by the surface head key. Adversaries cannot decrypt the data content without the surface head key. The surface head key is equal to the key to over-encrypt the pre-encrypted data content in the SEL of over-encryption.

Therefore, the security of our scheme lies in protecting the surface head key and the base head key, which equals to protecting keys at both the BEL and the SEL of over-encryption. The analysis of the related collusion attack by the cloud and the unauthorized users who have obtained the keys of the base encryption layer can be referred to over-encryption [4].

6   Related Work

In order to protect shared sensitive data from unauthorized access in incompletely trusted servers, shared cryptographic file systems which implement access control have obtained considerable development. SiRiUS [9] and Plutus [7] are earlier file systems, which adopt cryptographic techniques to implement access control. SiRiUS encrypts each data file and divides each file into a meta data file and an encrypted data content file, but the size of meta data file is proportional to the number of authorized users. Plutus groups different files and divides each file into multiple file blocks. Each file group uses a file lock box key and each file block is encrypted with a unique key. However, as different file groups attach different file lock box keys, maintaining multiple keys for a user is inadvisable.

Attribute-based encryption (ABE) which was first proposed in [10], is another branch to share sensitive data in the cloud environment without maintaining keys for each file or each file group. ABE is now widely researched in cloud computing to protect sensitive data [11–13]. Shucheng Yu presents a fine-grained data access control scheme in cloud computing [11], which combines ABE, proxy re-encryption [14,15] and lazy encryption. It supports policy update. However, it cannot update a user' s privilege on a certain specific file, and revoking of users requires updating all the associated attributes and notifying the users who also maintain keys of the related attributes. Our approach just updates the key of the revoked resource.

Over-encryption [1,4] protects the shared sensitive data in "Honest-but-Curious" cloud and implements access control policy updates. Its architecture of access control is based on a key-derivation structure in [16], which is also adopted by [17–19]. In the key-derivation structure, a user just needs to maintain private keys to derive all the keys of the authorized resources. In the previous work of over-encryption, both granting and revoking need encrypt the related resources. This consumes a lot of resources and time, especially for those data of GB/TB/PB size.

To reduce the overhead of revocations, lazy revocation proposed in Cepheus [20] is widely adopted by existing cryptographic file systems [21]. Lazy re-encryption at the price of slightly lowered security [22] delays required re-encryptions until the next write access. Because it brings in much overhead for revocations (reading disc, decrypting data and encrypting data), we apply batch revocation combining lazy revocation, which reduces the overhead and improves the performance of the cloud storage service.

7   Conclusions

With the explosive growth of data, the outsourced data scale in the cloud will increase and be enlarged. However, security is the main obstacle in the way of outsourcing data to "Honest-but-Curious" cloud. Encrypting the outsourced data before uploading them to the cloud is a widely researched solution, but it brings new challenges to update the access control policy in order to share data. On the premise of implementing fine-grained access control, our scheme can achieve efficient updating of the access control policy in cryptographic cloud storage. The performance analysis shows that the proposed dual-header structure and batch revocation can significantly minimize the overhead for authorization. However, the collusion attack, launched by the cloud and the unauthorized users who have obtained keys of the base encryption layer, still cannot be solved in this paper. In order to alleviate the possibility of this collusion attack, dispersing data resources among multiple clouds and applying secret sharing techniques might be a selectable solution, which might be our next work. As the re-encryption on revoked resources is inevitable in almost all the cryptographic storage systems, efficient re-encryption on large data resource is also our next research direction.

Acknowledgment. This work is supported by by National 973 Program of China under award No. 2014CB340603.

References

1. De Capitani di Vimercati, S., Foresti, S., Jajodia, S., Paraboschi, S., Samarati, P.: Encryption policies for regulating access to outsourced data. ACM Trans. Database Syst. (TODS) **35**, 12:1–12:46 (2010)
2. Liu, Q., Wang, G., Wu, J.: Time-based proxy re-encryption scheme for secure data sharing in a cloud environment. Information Sciences (2012)
3. Hohenberger, S.R., Fu, K., Ateniese, G., Green, M., et al.: Unidirectional proxy re-encryption. US Patent 8,094,810, 10 January 2012
4. Di Vimercati, S.D.C., Foresti, S., Jajodia, S., Paraboschi, S., Samarati, P.: Over-encryption: management of access control evolution on outsourced data. In: Proceedings of the 33rd International Conference on Very Large Data Bases, pp. 123–134, VLDB endowment (2007)
5. Kamara, S., Lauter, K.: Cryptographic cloud storage. In: Sion, R., Curtmola, R., Dietrich, S., Kiayias, A., Miret, J.M., Sako, K., Sebé, F. (eds.) RLCPS, WECSR, and WLC 2010. LNCS, vol. 6054, pp. 136–149. Springer, Heidelberg (2010)
6. Backes, M., Cachin, C., Oprea, A.: Lazy revocation in cryptographic file systems. In: Proceedings of IEEE Security in Storage Workshop (SISW 2005), pp. 1–11. IEEE (2005)
7. Kallahalla, M., Riedel, E., Swaminathan, R., Wang, Q., Fu, K.: Plutus: scalable secure file sharing on untrusted storage. In: Proceedings of the 2nd USENIX Conference on File and Storage Technologies, vol. 42, pp. 29–42 (2003)
8. Resch, J.K., Plank, J.S.: AONT-RS: blending security and performance in dispersed storage systems. In: 9th Usenix Conference on File and Storage Technologies, FAST-2011 (2011)
9. Goh, E.-J., Shacham, H., Modadugu, N., Boneh, D.: SIRIUS: Securing remote untrusted storage. In: Proceedings NDSS, vol. 3 (2003)
10. Sahai, A., Waters, B.: Fuzzy identity-based encryption. In: Cramer, R. (ed.) EUROCRYPT 2005. LNCS, vol. 3494, pp. 457–473. Springer, Heidelberg (2005)
11. Yu, S., Wang, C., Ren, K., Lou, W.: Achieving secure, scalable, and fine-grained data access control in cloud computing. In: INFOCOM, 2010 Proceedings IEEE, pp. 1–9. IEEE (2010)
12. Li, M., Yu, S., Ren, K., Lou, W.: Securing personal health records in cloud computing: patient-centric and fine-grained data access control in multi-owner settings. In: Jajodia, S., Zhou, J. (eds.) SecureComm 2010. LNICST, vol. 50, pp. 89–106. Springer, Heidelberg (2010)
13. Wang, G., Liu, Q., Wu, J.: Hierarchical attribute-based encryption for fine-grained access control in cloud storage services. In: Proceedings of the 17th ACM Conference on Computer and Communications Security, pp. 735–737. ACM (2010)
14. Ivan, A., Dodis, Y.: Proxy cryptography revisited. In: Proceedings of the Network and Distributed System Security Symposium (NDSS) (2003)
15. Ateniese, G., Fu, K., Green, M., Hohenberger, S.: Improved proxy re-encryption schemes with applications to secure distributed storage. ACM Trans. Inf. Syst. Secur. (TISSEC) **9**(1), 1–30 (2006)
16. De Capitani di Vimercati, S.D.C., Foresti, S., Jajodia, S., Paraboschi, S., Samarati, P.: A data outsourcing architecture combining cryptography and access control. In: Proceedings of the 2007 ACM Workshop on Computer Security Architecture, pp. 63–69. ACM (2007)
17. Raykova, M., Zhao, H., Bellovin, S.M.: Privacy enhanced access control for outsourced data sharing. In: Keromytis, A.D. (ed.) FC 2012. LNCS, vol. 7397, pp. 223–238. Springer, Springer (2012)

18. De Capitani di Vimercati, S., Foresti, S., Jajodia, S., Paraboschi, S., Samarati, P.: Support for write privileges on outsourced data. In: Gritzalis, D., Furnell, S., Theoharidou, M. (eds.) SEC 2012. IFIP AICT, vol. 376, pp. 199–210. Springer, Heidelberg (2012)
19. De Capitani di Vimercati, S., Foresti, S., Jajodia, S., Livraga, G., Paraboschi, S., Samarati, P.: Enforcing dynamic write privileges in data outsourcing. Comput. Secur. **39**, 47–63 (2013)
20. Fu, K.E..: Group sharing and random access in cryptographic storage file systems. Ph.D. thesis, Massachusetts Institute of Technology (1999)
21. Zarandioon, S., Yao, D.D., Ganapathy, V.: K2C: cryptographic cloud storage with lazy revocation and anonymous access. In: Rajarajan, M., Piper, F., Wang, H., Kesidis, G. (eds.) SecureComm 2011. LNICST, vol. 96, pp. 59–76. Springer, Heidelberg (2012)
22. Grolimund, D., Meisser, L., Schmid, S., Wattenhofer, R.: Cryptree: A folder tree structure for cryptographic file systems. In: 25th IEEE Symposium on Reliable Distributed Systems, SRDS 2006, pp. 189–198. IEEE (2006)

International Workshop on System Level Security of Smartphones

Uncovering the Dilemmas on Antivirus Software Design in Modern Mobile Platforms

Heqing Huang[1(✉)], Kai Chen[1,2], Peng Liu[1], Sencun Zhu[1], and Dinghao Wu[1]

[1] The Pennsylvania State University, State College, USA
{hhuang,szhu}@cse.psu.edu, chenkai010@gmail.com,
{pliu,dwu}@ist.psu.edu
[2] Institute of Information Engineering, Chinese Academy of Sciences, Beijing, China

Abstract. With the rapid increase in Android device popularity, a new evolving arms-race is happening between the malware writers and AntiVirus Detectors (AVDs) on the popular mobile system. In its latest comparison of AVDs, independent test lab AV-TEST reported that AVDs have around 95 % malware recognition rate. However, as mobile systems are specially designed, we consider that the power of AVDs' should also be evaluated based on their runtime malware detection capabilities. In this work, we performed a comprehensive study on ten popular Android AVDs to evaluate the effectiveness of their scanning operations. During our analysis, we identified the design dilemmas related to two types of malware scanning operations, namely *local* malware scan and *cloud-based* malware scan. Our work opens a new research direction in designing more effective and efficient malware scan mechanisms for current antivirus software on mobile devices.

Keywords: Android · Antivirus · Malware · Mobile attacks

1 Introduction

The increasingly popularity of mobile computing devices (e.g., smartphones and tablets) attracts both normal users and malware writers. Among the popular mobile platforms, Android has not only conquered a lion's share of the market, but also gained the 98.1 % share of detected mobile malware in 2013 [3]. Therefore, being aware of the notorious fact of mobile malware shares, many reputable companies on PC security as well as new startups have turned their attention to mobile-platform security and released their antivirus detectors (AVDs) particularly for Android [1]. Here, an AVD generically refers to the signature-based antivirus detector that is deployed on mobile devices.

For AVDs on desktop and server systems, earlier work has studied the impact of polymorphic attacks [16] or file format confusion based attacks [15] on the malware scanning operation. Recently, the real world polymorphic attacks have also been reported [4] and further studied [22] for Android AVD evasion. In the era of mobile computing, a new evolving arms-race is going on between the malware writers and the AVDs. The AVD based on dynamic behavior or

© Institute for Computer Sciences, Social Informatics and Telecommunications Engineering 2015
J. Tian et al. (Eds.): SecureComm 2014, Part II, LNICST 153, pp. 359–366, 2015.
DOI: 10.1007/978-3-319-23802-9_27

other dynamic heuristics are comparatively hard to be deployed on the battery constrained mobile devices. Also, because of the centralized software distribution on Google Play, static signature based malware fingerprinting scheme gains great values, since the potential malware spreading sources are very limited (users are not suggested to install apps from untrusted sources).

Every three months, the independent AVD test lab AV-TEST generates a report [2], comparing the detection rate and usability of Android AVDs. The latest report indicates that the popular AVDs under test achieve an average detection rate of around 95 % for known malicious app samples. However, since apps are allowed to dynamically load code from external sources at runtime [21], when combined with repackaging techniques [7,14,29], malware writers demonstrates [31,32] that more advanced malware can be easily created to perform targeted attacks. Therefore, the success of the AVD's malware scan should also be measured based on its real-time detection of advanced malware.

Hence, we conduct an empirical study of ten Android AVDs on two types of malware scan operations, namely the *Local-malScan* and the *Cloud-malScan*. Our analysis result indicates that both *malScan* operations have fundamental design deficiencies. Therefore, AVD vendors should consider the design of malware scanner on Android more thoroughly.

2   Antivirus Detectors on Android Platform

In this section, we first briefly introduce some necessary background on Android Antivirus Detectors (AVDs), and then explain how we conduct the empirical study towards further understanding of the design characteristics of the current AVDs. Our analysis, particularly focuses on the real-time detection capability of the AVDs deployed on Android. More comprehensive discussions on Android security mechanisms can be found in Yan and Yin [26] and Enck et al. [11].

Table 1. Popular Antivirus Detectors (AVDs) in Our Study

ID	Vendor	AVD package name & version #	Downloads #
1	Avast	com.avast.android.........3.0.6915	50M-100M
2	AVG	com.antivirus.........................3.6	100M-150M
3	Avira	com.avira.android...................3.1	1M-5M
4	Bitdefender	com.bitdefender.security.2.8.217	1M-5M
5	Kaspersky	com.kms (premium)..........11.2.3	5M-10M
6	ESET	com.eset.ems2.gp............2.0.843	1M-5M
7	Dr. Web	com.drweb.pro.................7.00.11	10M-50M
8	Lookout	com.lookout...........8.28-879ce69	50M-100M
9	McAfee	com.wsandroid.suite.....4.0.0.143	5M-10M
10	Norton	com.symantec.mbsec.....3.8.0.12	10M-50M

Android is an operating system based on the Linux Kernel, with new features such as the Binder IPC mechanism, Power Manager and Ashmem mechanism and etc. On top of the Linux kernel, Android is loaded with four software layers, namely System Libraries, Android Runtime, Application Framework and Application. In addition to the native Linux basic discretionary access control mechanism and the SEAndroid [24] mechanism based on Linux Security Module, Android provides a fine-grained permission mechanism for all the apps running on the Application layer, including all the AVDs from third party vendors. Table 1 lists ten popular AVDs in Google Play as of Feb. 2014. The popularity of these AVDs is reflected by their overall protection rankings, according to AV Test Reports [2] for the period of Sept. 2013–Jan. 2014.

Table 2. Intents Registered and Permissions Asked by AVDs

Intents Registered	#	Permissions Requested	#
intent.action.MEDIA_REMOVED	1	android.permission.SUPERUSER	2
intent.action.MEDIA_CHECKING	3	android.permission.BATTERY_STATS	3
intent.action.PWR_DISCONNECTED	3	android.permission.google.c2dm.RECEIVE	3
intent.action.WIFI_STATE_CHANGED	4	android.permission.KILL_PROCESSES	4
intent.action.DATE_CHANGED	4	android.permission.COARSE_LOCATION	4
intent.action.SERVICE_STATE	4	android.permission.ALERT_WINDOW	5
intent.action.DIAL	5	android.permission.WRITE_BOOKMARKS	5
intent.action.MEDIA_UNMOUNTED	6	android.permission.GET_ACCOUNTS	6
intent.action.POWER_CONNECTED	6	android.permission.READ_SMS	7
intent.action.net.wifi.STATE_CHANGE	7	android.permission.READ_BOOKMARKS	7
intent.action.MEDIA_EJECT	7	android.permission.READ_CONTACTS	8
intent.action.USER_PRESENT	7	android.permission.RECEIVE_SMS	8
intent.action.ACTION_SHUTDOWN	7	android.permission.SEND_SMS	8
intent.action.NEW_OUTGOING_CALL	9	android.permission.READ_LOGS	9
intent.action.PHONE_STATE	10	android.permission.GET_TASKS	10
intent.action.PACKAGE_REPLACED	10	android.permission.WAKE_LOCK	10
intent.action.PACKAGE_REMOVED	10	android.permission.EXTERNAL_STORAGE	10
intent.action.PACKAGE_ADDED	10	android.permission.READ_PHONE_STATE	10
intent.action.BOOT_COMPLETED	10	android.permission.BOOT_COMPLETED	10

Generally, Android uses a standard template process called Zygote, which is the parent process for all the Android DVM processes, including all the AVDs' main processes. Each AVD is assigned its own unique user ID (UID) at the install time, and the access control bits for the relevant files and folders in the file system are then set accordingly by the system. The dedicated group ID (GID) numbers are assigned based on the requested permissions for the Android system resources. Also, various system daemons and apps are classified into different access control domains in the SEAndroid policy rules, in order to provide better isolation and security.

An AVD registers itself to specific broadcast intents by programmatically registering a broadcast receiver in the code or claiming the relevant receivers in the file AndroidManifest.xml. For example, an AVD may register for the system generated intents BOOT_COMPLETED, which is fired by the system once the boot process is completed. This enables the AVD to keep track of some system events of interest that are happening and then take appropriate actions.

In Table 2, the left two columns list the types of Intent actions and how frequently they are registered by the ten AVDs in our study, and the right two columns list the types of permissions and how frequently they are requested by these AVDs. From the table, it seems that the current AVDs can provide a very good real-time protection. For instance, all these AVDs listen to BOOT_COMPLETED system event to provide complete protection after the system boots up and obtain the WAKE_LOCK permission to periodically wake up the CPU to keep monitoring the system status. Also, events like PACKAGE_ADDED and PACKAGE_REMOVED are mostly registered to help monitor the newly installed or updated Android application package (APK) files.

3 Dilemmas for Malware Scan Design

3.1 Local Malware Scan Dilemma

Scan the Archived Files or Not? Our study shows that current Android AVDs have designed a comprehensive local malware scan (local-malScan), which is a thorough scan carried out on the pre-selected (sub)directories, which usually includes operations like file preprocessing and malware signature fingerprinting. Due to the power or other resource constraints, the local-malScan usually does not perform thorough file preprocessing on the files with specific formats (e.g., the archived files). Therefore, the malicious payload can be simply zipped and dropped on the file system without being identified. While some AVDs perform comprehensive scan by uncompressing the archived format files, we discover that one can construct a multi-layered archive file to conduct denial of service attacks and drain the device battery, since the scanner will keep unzipping every inner zip file in the multi-layered archive file diligently. As such, whether to preprocess or scan the special formatted files is a dilemma on current resource restricted AVD on mobile platforms.

Update the Virus Definition File or Not? During our comprehensive analysis, we discover an interesting *probing channel*. Almost all the AVDs will have the VDF file and other permanent data or cached files stored in the subdirectory at /data/[AVD_package]/*. These files are set to be "world unreadable" and enforced by Linux kernel in Android using access control policies. We find that this solid design of app data privacy protection is not enough for AVD deployment, since an adversary only needs to know the file sizes or other meta-data information of relevant files (e.g., creation and update time) in the subdirectory to infer the updating status of these files. During our analysis, we discover that by using the /system/bin/ls program, or writing a dynamic library which calls the stat() system call, one can directly probe the meta-data information of all these "world unreadable" files in an AVD's data folder. This design deficiency can potentially be leveraged to design on-demand malware polymorphism. Basically, whenever the anti-AVD app detects a VDF-update, which might contain the signature to fingerprint its current malicious payloads, it can update its payloads using a new polymorphic strategy. Therefore, the adversary will enjoy this on-demand VDF-update feature and is always one-step ahead of the AVD's static fingerprinting. Hence, whether to perform the VDF update is another dilemma for current AVD Local-malScan.

3.2   Cloud Malware Scan Dilemma

To Offload or Not to Offload? Due to the limitation of the on the Local-malScan, we sense a trend of adding the cloud-based scanning strategy for mobile platform during our analysis. Cloud-based scan (Cloud-malScan) is generally believed to be suitable for resource limited mobile devices, as it can offload the heavy computation to a remote server by sending out the collected information, including the file hashing value, the meta-data of a file etc. However, since the per UID network usage statistics can also be probed in "/proc/uid_stat/[AVD_uid]/snd(rcv)" an adversary can plan evasions against AVDs by identifying the network sending and receiving statistic pattern of Cloud-malScan. So we find that the implicit dilemma in the Cloud-malScan is whether to send enough file information to the remote server for further signature mapping and scanning. If the Cloud-malScan on the local device tries to collect less information to send out (e.g., only the file hash value or the file meta-data), then the malware scan/detection performed on the server can merely based on simple signature fingerprinting. However, if the Cloud-malScan collects more information (e.g., execution traces) to offload to remote server for deep (behavior based) analysis, its network statistics become more identifiable and is vulnerable to targeted evasions (e.g., the malicious payload will be loaded only after the Cloud-malScan performed on the device).

4   Related Work

Antivirus evasion techniques [5,15,16] have been studied previously. Oberheide et al. [17] has also generally discussed challenges in deploying antivirus detectors (AVDs) on mobile platforms. Android Dalvik Bytecode polymorphic transformation attacks have been presented by Rastogi et al. [22]. Our new evasion techniques exploit the cloud-based malware scanning behavior of the AVDs, and they are complementary to obfuscation-based or other evasion techniques, which are similar to the other attacks discussed in [12].

Malware and intrusion analysis techniques [10,11,13,26] have been designed and applied for offline analysis. Also, various interesting anti-analysis technique have been discussed [9,19] for malware on both mobile and PC. Our anti-AVD app design is conceptually similar to anti-analysis techniques, but we emphasize more on the evasion of AVD's online protection mechanism. Zhou et al. [32] provide a survey of Android malware, and similarly, the discovered design dilemmas in this paper are based on a systematic survey of ten popular Android AVDs.

Side/timing channel issue [8,18,23,25,30] is also an active research aspect in both mobile and PC era. The network based probing and fingerprinting based attacks for the AVD deployed on the mail server side have been explored by Oberheide et al. [18], also including the reconnaissance and action phases. Information hiding techniques have been discussed by Petitcolas et al. [20]. Side channel/timing channel preventions have been discussed in several papers [6,27,28]. Generally, it is one of the toughest challenges in computer security. Zhang et al. [28] provides the language-based control and mitigation for the timing channels.

5 Conclusion

Through an empirical study of ten top AVDs on the current Android platform, we identified several design dilemmas in the malware scan operations, including the local malware scan and the cloud-based malware scan. These dilemmas are related to the malware scan of the archived or other special formatted file, the virus definition file update, and the offloading file sizes of the cloud-based malware scan, and pose challenges in antivirus software design in the current Android platform. Through this study, we open a new research topic on how to improve the effectiveness and efficiency of current malware scan and detection on current mobile platforms.

References

1. Android antivirus companies. Technical report. http://www.zdnet.com/android-antivirus-comparison-review-malware-symantec-mcafee-kaspersky-sophos-norton-7000019189/
2. AV TEST report, January 2014. http://www.av-test.org/en/tests/mobile-devices/android/jan-2014/
3. Kaspersky Lab Reports Mobile Malware in 2013. http://usa.kaspersky.com/about-us/press-center/press-releases/kaspersky-lab-reports-mobile-malware-2013-more-doubles-previous
4. Server-side Polymorphic Android Applications. http://www.symantec.com/connect/blogs/server-side-polymorphic-android-applications
5. Al-Saleh, M.I., Crandall, J.R.: Application-level reconnaissance: timing channel attacks against antivirus software. In: 4th USENIX Workshop on LEET 2011 (2011)
6. Askarov, A., Zhang, D., Myers, A.C.: Predictive black-box mitigation of timing channels. In: ACM CCS 2010 (2010)
7. Chen, K., Liu, P., Zhang, Y.: Achieving accuracy and scalability simultaneously in detecting application clones on android markets. In: ICSE, pp. 175–186 (2014)
8. Chen, S., Wang, R., Wang, X., Zhang, K.: Side-channel leaks in web applications: a reality today, a challenge tomorrow. In: S&P 2010 (2010)

9. Chen, X., Andersen, J., Mao, Z.M., Bailey, M., Nazario, J.: Towards an understanding of anti-virtualization and anti-debugging behavior in modern malware. In: DSN 2008 (2008)
10. Christodorescu, M., Jha, S., Seshia, S.A., Song, D., Bryant, R.E.: Semantics-aware malware detection. In: 2005 IEEE Symposium on Security and Privacy. IEEE (2005)
11. Enck, W., Gilbert, P., Chun, B.-G., Cox, L.P., Jung, J., McDaniel, P., Sheth, A.: TaintDroid: an information-flow tracking system for realtime privacy monitoring on smartphones. In: OSDI, vol. 10, pp. 1–6 (2010)
12. Huang, H., Chen, K., Ren, C., Liu, P., Zhu, S., Wu, D.: Towards discovering and understanding unexpected hazards in tailoring antivirus software for android. In: Proceedings of the 10th ACM Symposium on Information, Computer and Communications Security, ASIA CCS 2015 (2015)
13. Huang, H., Zhang, S., Ou, X., Prakash, A., Sakallah, K.: Distilling critical attack graph surface iteratively through minimum-cost sat solving. In: Proceedings of the 27th Annual Computer Security Applications Conference, pp. 31–40. ACM (2011)
14. Huang, H., Zhu, S., Liu, P., Wu, D.: A framework for evaluating mobile App repackaging detection algorithms. In: Huth, M., Asokan, N., Čapkun, S., Flechais, I., Coles-Kemp, L. (eds.) TRUST 2013. LNCS, vol. 7904, pp. 169–186. Springer, Heidelberg (2013)
15. Jana, S., Shmatikov, V.: Abusing file processing in malware detectors for fun and profit. In: 2012 IEEE Symposium on Security and Privacy (SP), pp. 80–94. IEEE (2012)
16. Oberheide, J., Bailey, M., Jahanian, F.: PolyPack: an automated online packing service for optimal antivirus evasion. In: 3rd USENIX on Offensive Technologies
17. Oberheide, J., Jahanian, F.: When mobile is harder than fixed (andvice versa): demystifying security challenges in mobile environments. In: HotMobile 2010. ACM (2010)
18. Oberheide, J., Jahanian, F.: Remote fingerprinting and exploitation of mail server antivirus engines (2009)
19. Pék, G., Bencsáth, B., Buttyán, L.: nEther: in-guest detection of out-of-the-guest malware analyzers. In: Proceedings of the Fourth European Workshop on System Security, EUROSEC 2011. ACM (2011)
20. Petitcolas, F.A., Anderson, R.J., Kuhn, M.G.: Information hiding-a survey. In: Proceedings of the IEEE (1999)
21. Poeplau, S., Fratantonio, Y., Bianchi, A., Kruegel, C., Vigna, G.: Execute this! analyzing unsafe and malicious dynamic code loading in android applications (2014)
22. Rastogi, V., Chen, Y., Jiang, X.: Droidchameleon: evaluatingandroid anti-malware against transformation attacks. In: asiaCCS. ACM (2013)
23. Schlegel, R., Zhang, K., Zhou, X.-Y., Intwala, M., Kapadia, A., Wang, X.: Soundcomber: a stealthy and context-aware sound trojan for smartphones. In: NDSS (2011)
24. Smalley, S., Craig, R.: Security enhanced (se) android: bringing flexible mac to android. In: NDSS (2013)
25. Studer, A., Passaro, T., Bauer, L.: Don't bump, shake on it: the exploitation of a popular accelerometer-based smart phone exchange and its secure replacement. In: ACSAC 2011 (2011)
26. Yan, L.K., Yin, H.: Droidscope: seamlessly reconstructing the os and dalvik semantic views for dynamic android malware analysis. In: USENIX rSecurity 2012 (2012)
27. Zhang, D., Askarov, A., Myers, A.C.: Predictive mitigation of timing channels in interactive systems. In: ACM CCS, pp. 563–574. ACM (2011)

28. Zhang, D., Askarov, A., Myers, A.C.: Language-based control and mitigation of timing channels. In: ACM SIGPLAN Notices, vol. 47, pp. 99–110. ACM (2012)
29. Zhang, F., Huang, H., Zhu, S., Wu, D., Liu, P.: View-droid: towards obfuscation-resilient mobile application repackaging detection. In: Proceedings of the 7th ACM Conference on Security and Privacy in Wireless and Mobile Networks (2014)
30. Zhou, X., Demetriou, S., He, D., Naveed, M., Pan, X., Wang, X., Gunter, C.A., Nahrstedt, K.: Identity, location, disease and more: inferring your secrets from android public resources. In: ACM CCS. ACM (2013)
31. Zhou, Y., Jiang, X.: An analysis of the anserverbot trojan. http://www.csc.ncsu.edu/faculty/jiang/pubs/AnserverBotAnalysis.pdf
32. Zhou, Y., Jiang, X.: Dissecting android malware: characterizationand evolution. In: SP 2012. IEEE (2012)

Transplantation Attack: Analysis and Prediction

Zhongwen Zhang[1,2,3], Ji Xiang[1,2]([✉]), Lei Wang[1,2], and Lingguang Lei[1,2]

[1] Data Assurance and Communication Security Research Center, Beijing, China
[2] Institute of Information Engineering, CAS, Beijing, China
[3] University of Chinese Academy of Sciences, Beijing, China
{zwzhang,jixiang,lwang,lglei}@lois.cn

Abstract. Correspondingly, Android also becomes a common attack target. Till now, many attacks have been detected out, such as confused deputy attack, collusion attack, and root exploits attack. In this paper, we present a novel attack, denoted as transplantation attack. Transplantation attack, when being applied to spy on user, can make the malicious behavior more stealthy. The attack can evade permission check, evade device administration, and even evade API auditing. The premise of carrying out Transplantation attack is that malware is able to access resources or gain access capability. By fulfilling the premise, we do a case study about Camera device. The result indicates that Transplantation attack indeed exists. Based on these observations, we predict the kind of system resources that may suffer transplantation attack. Defence discussion are also presented.

Keywords: Android · Transplantation Attack · Prediction

1 Introduction

Nowadays, Android becomes the most wide spread mobile platform. In the mean while, it also becomes a common attack target. Many kinds of attacks towards Android system have been detected out, e.g., confused deputy attack [5,8,9,12], collusion attack [4], and root exploits attack [17,24]. In this paper, we will present a novel kind of attack, and we name it as transplantation attack.

To explain what is transplantation attack, we should mention the resource accessing procedure first. In Android system, most system resources (e.g., GPS, camera) are accessed by system services (e.g., LocationManager Service, Camera Service). Applications (apps), if want to access these resources, should send request to system services via IPC (Inter-Process Communication). Then, system services will call several system libraries (.so libraries) to talk with resource driver and collect data and return data back to apps. When resources are accessed, two

This work is supported by National Natural Science Foundation of China grant 70890084/G021102 and 61003274, Strategy Pilot Project of Chinese Academy of Sciences sub-project XDA06010702, and National High Technology Research and Development Program of China (863 Program, No. 2013AA01A214 and 2012AA013104).

© Institute for Computer Sciences, Social Informatics and Telecommunications Engineering 2015
J. Tian et al. (Eds.): SecureComm 2014, Part II, LNICST 153, pp. 367–374, 2015.
DOI: 10.1007/978-3-319-23802-9_28

processes are involved, an application's (client) process and a system service's (server) process. In this case, system *.so* libraries run in system services' address space.

However, what if malware transplant system *.so* libraries from system services' address space to their own address space, and use these libraries to talk with driver to collect data by their own? In this case, system *.so* libraries will run in malware's address space, which will lead to several security issues; and it should be considered as an attack. We call this attack as **Transplantation Attack**.

Transplantation attack enables malware accessing resources without involving IPC with system services. In transplantation attack, when resources are accessed, only one process (app's process) is involved, and there is nothing to do with system services' process. Therefore, a lot of security enforcements implemented in system services can be evaded.

By starting a transplantation attack, malware can evade permission check. In Android system, before system services respond to resource accessing request of an app, they will check the app's permissions first. If the app does not have the required permission, system services will not provide service. In transplantation attack, malware do not depend on system services to get data, instead, they collect data by their own. Therefore, the permission check process initiated by system services can be evaded in transplantation attack.

By starting a transplantation attack, malware can evade device administration. Android framework provides several special Android APIs, which are called Device Administration APIs. They could be used by device admin apps to configure a phone. Device administration is usually enforced in enterprises, in which phones are used to do business. Usually, enterprise administrators install device admin apps on these phones to protect commercial benefit. Transplantation attack will make these admin apps fail to be effective. That is because, the device administration is also implemented in system services which are not called in transplantation attack.

By starting a transplantation attack, malware can evade API auditing. Android API auditing is important to both enterprise environments and individual users. In enterprise environments, deploying API auditing on employee phones helps to decrease security risk. For individual users, API auditing helps to detect spyware. API auditing can be done when permissions are checked. Since there is no permission check step in transplantation attack, malware can evade API auditing as well.

As a result, transplantation attack, when being applied to spy on user, can make malicious behavior much more stealthy and much more difficult to detect. We have searched the CVE (Common Vulnerabilities and Exposures) list [1]. Among the 448 CVE entries that match the keyword *Android*, we find there was no such kind of attack happened before.

In this paper, we will give an overview about transplantation attack. First we will describe the premise to start transplantation attack. Then, by fulfilling the premise, we carry out a transplantation attack towards Camera device as a case study. The case study verifies that transplantation attack indeed exists, and cannot be detected out by Antivirus. Base on these observations, we predict that other resources may also suffer transplantation attack. Moreover, we discuss potential solutions against this attack.

2   The Premise of Transplantation Attack

Transplantation attack is to transplant system libraries from system services' address space to malware's address space, and then malware can collect data in its own address space.

A big premise for the transplantation attack to be carried out is that the system libraries are designed to be called by everyone. However, that malware can call system libraries does not mean the malware can successfully access resources (e.g., hardware drivers, database files). Another premise of transplantation attack is that the malware itself should be able to access resources or can gain access capability.

System resources can be divided into two types: hardware resources and software resources. The way to achieve the premise of the attack towards the two kind resources is different.

Hardware Resources. To access hardware resources, e.g., GPS, Camera, malware should be able to access hardware drivers. Hardware drivers subject to Linux file system access control. To access a hardware driver, a user (app) should be the owner or be a member of the hardware's group. In Android system, an app could be a member of a hardware's group, aka., the app could be assigned with the hardware's group id (GID).

Apps could become a group member of some hardware through obtaining a certain permission. That is because, Android has bound some permissions with some groups, which are recorded in a metadata file (*platform.xml*). If a permission has been bound to a group, then once this permission is granted to an app, the app will be automatically set as a member of the group. By applying a permission, an app can gain the corresponding GID. After gaining the GID, an app could access the corresponding hardware driver. Once an app could directly access a hardware driver, it can start transplantation attack.

Software Resources. Most software resources, e.g., SMS, Contact, social network data, exist in the form of database files or in shared memories, which are files, too. These files are owned by system apps (e.g., SMS app, Contact app) or third party apps. To access these files, malware should become a shared user with the owner of these files, aka, the malware should share UID with the owner.

Sharing UID with a system app cannot be achieved except exploiting system vulnerabilities. Nowadays, two vulnerabilities towards signature verification have been detected out in Android system [18,21]. Exploiting them, malware is able to share UID with a system app, or a third party app. To share UID with a third party app, collusion attack also is an optional way. Once an app becomes a shared user of the file owner, it can access the file. As long as malware can access resource files, it can start transplantation attack.

Others. In one case that malware neither need to become a group member nor need to become a shared user. That is, a file, either a device file or a regular file, is publicly accessed. For example, the file's access rule is set as 666 (rw-rw-rw-) or 777 (rwxrwxrwx).

An advantage of attacks towards software resources is that malware does not need to apply any permission for any reason. On the contrary, attacks towards hardware resources should apply permissions to get GIDs. Therefore, transplantation attacks towards software resources are much more stealthy and much more hard to detect than attacks towards hardware resources.

3   Case Study

To verify the feasibility of transplantation attack, we have done a case study towards Camera device. We use a malicious app to carry out a transplantation attack.

As described before, the attack just transplants necessary *.so* libraries from Camera Service's address space to the malicious app's address space, and calls picture taking function provided by these *.so* libraries to take a picture. To make the malicious app be able to access camera driver, we should put the app into *camera* group. It can be achieved by applying CAMERA permission, because Android has bound CAMERA permission with *camera* group.

After going through a lot of failures, we successfully conduct a way of picture taking inside the malicious app's address space. Also, the malicious app is successfully executed on Nexus S with Android version 4.0.4 and Sony LT29i with Android version 4.1.2.

We also tested whether the malicious app can evade detection of Antivirus and can evade enterprise device administration. The test result shows both of them can be evaded.

4   Prediction of Transplantation Attack

The case study about Camera device indicates that transplantation attack indeed exists. In this section, we will predict where transplantation attack may happen.

4.1   Attack Towards Hardware Resources

As described before, malware should be able to access a hardware before starting transplantation attack. This can happens in two situations. One situation is that the malware is able to gain the GID of a hardware. The publicly available GIDs are recorded in the *platform.xml* file. The other situation is that a hardware is publicly accessed. For example, a hardware's access rule is 666. Hardware covered by the two ways are vulnerable to suffer transplantation attack.

Take the *platform.xml* file on Galaxy Nexus of version 4.1.2 as an example, available GIDs are *net_bt_admin, net_bt, inet, camera, log, sdcard_r, sdcard_rw, media_rw, mtp, net_admin, cache, input, diag, net_bw_stats, net_bw_acct*; and 15 of them in total. Hardwares involved in these GIDs are vulnerable to suffer transplantation attack, such as Bluetooth (GID: *net_bt_admin, net_bt*), Internet (GID: *inet*), Camera (GID: *camera*). The GPS' group id is not publicly available, so GPS does not suffer this attack.

Taking advantage of the transplantation attack, malware could enjoy Bluetooth stealthily. Nowadays, Bluetooth is commonly used in e-health area such as blood pressure monitor, glucometer, and wearable devices such as watches, glasses. Malware may steal this kind of high sensitive data without leaving any record.

Sometimes, vendors mistakenly configure a phone [23]. For example, on Samsung GT-I9300 phone, the GID *radio* is recorded in the *platform.xml* file as well. By gaining the GID *inet* and *radio*, malware may be able to use Internet without being detected. Attacks towards Internet will lead to users' financial lose.

Besides hardware whose GID can be applied may suffer the attack, mistakenly configured hardware may suffer the attack, too. According to [23], vendors set access rules of some hardware drivers on some phones as 666, which means all users can read and write these drivers. On these phones, malware can directly access those mistakenly configured hardware drivers without gaining their GID, aka, without applying any permission.

4.2 Attack Towards Software Resources

Software resources like private database files or shared memories are owned by apps. The GID of these files are not bound with permissions. Therefore, unless these files can be publicly accessed, malware should become a shared user to initiate attacks on them. It is designed that shared users can access each other's data, and, if desired, run in the same process. So, once malware becomes a shared user, it seems that it is not necessary to do transplantation attack.

However, regular access way may leave auditing record. For example, database files are regularly accessed via Content Provider, which can be used to do API auditing. Moreover, other shared users may do extra access control or do auditing inside their execution flows, too. These obstacles may become a motivation of carrying out a transplantation attack towards software resources.

In case of malware sharing UID with other apps contain private data, we predicate that transplantation attack may happen.

5 Defence Discussion

There may be several ways to defend the transplantation attack, but some of them may not work out. For example, forbidding the usage of system libraries may sound a good idea to defend the attack. However, as apps can ship their own copy of the required system library, this way may not work out. Here, we discuss two possible ways as follows.

5.1   Breaking the Binding Between Permission and Group ID

The transplantation attack should get the capability of accessing a hardware device. To gain this capability, the malicious app should be assigned with the hardware's group ID by applying corresponding permission. Noticing this, a defence is that we could break the binding between permission strings and group ids. Taking Camera device as an example, breaking the binding between camera permission and camera group id will not affect the normal apps to take pictures. That is because Camera device has a daemon process (*mediaserver* process, in which Camera Service runs) in charge of taking pictures. Apps just need to send request to the daemon process, and the process will handle the picture taking. One weakness of this defence is that when the hardware has zero daemon process (e.g., Sdcard) or more than one daemon processes, it is possible to result in denying of services.

5.2   Using SEAndroid Policy

SEAndroid enforces mandatory access control to every process (user) under a fine-grained access control policy. Every process belongs to a domain (type). Here, third-party apps are classified into the *untrusted_app* domain, which will be blocked when directly access protected files (device files, regular files).

Although SEAndroid can block the access to protected files, it has a rather limited enforcement range. SEAndroid [20] is merged into AOSP since version 4.3 and enforced since version 4.4. According to Google's survey [14], the phones shipped with version 4.3 and 4.4 each accounts for 8.5 % of the total at the beginning of May, 2014. That a phone shipped with 4.3 version of Android does not mean that the SEAndroid is enforced. So, nearly 90 % of the Android phones in the wild are however not protected by SEAndroid. Among the phones used by our labmates, 93 % of them without SEAndroid. It may take a long period of time before SEAndroid can be widely deployed in the wild. During this period of time, many users may suffer from the spy-on-user attack.

Besides the distribution range limitation, SEAndroid has weakness as well. Pau Oliva shows three weaknesses of SEAndroid and gives out four ways to bypass SEAndroid [22]. We did an experiment, in which we change SEAndroid from enforce mode to permissive mode via PC terminals. The same principle could be applied to apps. The experiment shows that SEAndroid can indeed be bypassed.

6   Related Work

Confused Deputy Attacks. Confused deputy attack means a malicious app without permission P exploits the unprotected interfaces of other apps with permission P to perform a privileged task for itself. To detect whether an app has unprotected interfaces, a number of detection tools have been proposed [2,6,11,13]. These static analysis tools are likely to be incomplete, as they cannot completely predict the actual confused deputy attack occurring at runtime.

To address this issue, some framework extension solutions [9, 12] have been proposed.

Collusion Attacks. Different from the confused deputy attacks, the collusion attacks concern malicious apps that collude to combine their permissions. So, one malicious app does not need to apply all permissions, which can evade the detection of Kirin [10]. To address the collusion problems, [3, 4, 15] are proposed. These solutions can confront both the deputy attacks and the collusion attacks.

Root Exploits Attacks. According to [24], attacks exploiting root privilege play a significant role in compromising Android security. Among the root exploiting malware, the *DroidKungFu* [17] is a typical example. Attacks exploiting root privilege could break the boundary of Android sandbox and could access resources without applying permissions. The root exploits attacks could be blocked by SEAndroid [20]. By introducing SEAndroid, processes even running with root privilege cannot access the protected files and devices.

Security Enhancements. Some framework security extension solutions [7, 16, 19, 25] enforce runtime permission control to restrict apps' permissions at runtime. These solutions aim at providing a fine-grained access control for IPC. The novel transplantation attack does not call Android APIs or does not involve IPC. Therefore, these solutions cannot block the transplantation attack.

7 Conclusion

In this paper, we give an overview about the transplantation attack, which can make malicious behavior much more stealthy when being applied to spy on user. We first describe the premise of the attack, then we do a case study on Camera device, which verifies the attack indeed exists. Based on the premise and case study result, we predict that there are other resources may suffer transplantation attack. At last, we discuss potential defences towards the attack.

References

1. CVE: Common vulnerabilities and exposures. http://cve.mitre.org/
2. Au, K.W.Y., Zhou, Y.F., Huang, Z., Lie, D.: Pscout: analyzing the android permission specification. In: ACM CCS (2012)
3. Bugiel, S., Davi, L., Dmitrienko, A., Fischer, T., Sadeghi, A.R.: XMandroid: a new android evolution to mitigate privilege escalation attacks. Technische Universität Darmstadt, Technical Report TR-2011-04
4. Bugiel, S., Davi, L., Dmitrienko, A., Fischer, T., Sadeghi, A.R., Shastry, B.: Towards taming privilege- escalation attacks on android. In: 19th NDSS 2012 (2012)
5. Chan, P.P., Hui, L.C., Yiu, S.: A privilege escalation vulnerability checking system for android applications. In: 2011 IEEE 13th International Conference on Communication Technology (ICCT), pp. 681–686. IEEE (2011)
6. Chin, E., Felt, A.P., Greenwood, K., Wagner, D.: Analyzing inter-application communication in android. In: 9th MobiSys 2011 (2011)

7. Conti, M., Nguyen, V.T.N., Crispo, B.: Crepe: context-related policy enforcement for android. In: Information Security (2011)
8. Davi, L., Dmitrienko, A., Sadeghi, A.R., Winandy, M.: Privilege escalation attacks on android. In: Burmester, M., Tsudik, G., Magliveras, S., Ilić, I. (eds.) Information Security. Lecture Notes in Computer Science, vol. 6531, pp. 346–360. Springer, Heidelberg (2011)
9. Dietz, M., Shekhar, S., Pisetsky, Y., Shu, A., Wallach, D.S.: Quire: lightweight provenance for smart phone operating systems. In: USENIX Security (2011)
10. Enck, W., Ongtang, M., McDaniel, P.: On lightweight mobile phone application certification. In: 16th ACM CCS, pp. 235–245. ACM (2009)
11. Felt, A.P., Chin, E., Hanna, S., Song, D., Wagner, D.: Android permissions demystified. In: 18th ACM CCS, pp. 627–638. ACM (2011)
12. Felt, A.P., Wang, H.J., Moshchuk, A., Hanna, S., Chin, E.: Permission re-delegation: attacks and defenses. In: USENIX Security Symposium (2011)
13. Fuchs, A.P., Chaudhuri, A., Foster, J.S.: Scandroid: automated security certification of android applications. University of Maryland, Manuscript (2009)
14. Google: Dashboard, March 2014. http://developer.android.com/about/dashboards/index.html?utm_source=ausdroid.net#Platform
15. Grace, M., Zhou, Y., Wang, Z., Jiang, X.: Systematic detection of capability leaks in stock android smartphones. In: 19th NDSS (2012)
16. Nauman, M., Khan, S., Zhang, X.: Apex: extending android permission model and enforcement with user-defined runtime constraints. In: 5th ACM CCS (2010)
17. NC State University: security alert: New sophisticated android malware droid-kungfu found in alternative chinese app markets (2011). http://www.csc.ncsu.edu/faculty/jiang/DroidKungFu.html
18. NIST: Cve-2013-4787 (2013). http://web.nvd.nist.gov/view/vuln/detail?vulnId=CVE-2013-4787
19. Ongtang, M., McLaughlin, S., Enck, W., McDaniel, P.: Semantically rich application-centric security in android. Secur. Commun. Netw. 5(6), 658–673 (2012)
20. Smalley, S., Craig, R.: Security enhanced (se) android: bringing flexible MAC to android. In: NDSS (2013)
21. Squad, A.S.: Bug 9695860 (2013). http://blog.sina.com.cn/s/blog_be6dacae0101bksm.html
22. viaForensics: Defeating SEAndroid C DEFCON 21 Presentation. https://viaforensics.com/mobile-security/implementing-seandroid-defcon-21-presentation.html. Accessed August 3, 2013
23. Xiaoyong, Z., Yeonjoon, L., Nan, Z., Muhammad, N., XiaoFeng, W.: The peril of fragmentation: security hazards in android device driver customizations. In: 35th IEEE Security and Privacy, pp. 1–18. IEEE (2014)
24. Zhou, Y., Jiang, X.: Dissecting android malware: characterization and evolution. In: Security and Privacy (SP), pp. 95–109. IEEE (2012)
25. Zhou, Y., Zhang, X., Jiang, X., Freeh, V.W.: Taming information-stealing smartphone applications (on android). In: McCune, J.M., Balacheff, B., Perrig, A., Sadeghi, A.-R., Sasse, A., Beres, Y. (eds.) Trust 2011. LNCS, vol. 6740, pp. 93–107. Springer, Heidelberg (2011)

Timing-Based Clone Detection on Android Markets

Yingjun Zhang[1(✉)], Kezhen Huang[1], Yuling Liu[1], Kai Chen[2],
Liang Huang[1], and Yifeng Lian[1]

[1] Trusted Computing and Information Assurance Laboratory, Institute of Software,
Chinese Academy of Sciences, Beijing, People's Republic of China
yjzhang@tca.iscas.ac.cn
[2] State Key Laboratory of Information Security, Institute of Information Engineering,
Chinese Academy of Sciences, Beijing, People's Republic of China

Abstract. With the growth of smartphone users, mobile phone applications increase exponentially. But a lot of apps are cloned. We design a timing-based clone detection method. By choosing several lists of inputs, we can get the corresponding CPU time usage, which composes a CPU time usage tuple. After comparing these tuples, we can find the clone apps. At last, we do some experiments to verify our methods.

Keywords: Clone detection · CPU time usage · Smartphone security

1 Introduction

With the growth of smartphone users, mobile phone applications increase exponentially. However, according to [1], they find 44,268 cloned apps from 265,359 free Android apps in 17 Android markets. Moreover, malicious users use these cloned apps to gain economic benefits by adding some advertisement or malicious code. So clone detection is important for users and legitimate developers.

Clone [2] means large-scale computer program is duplicated code. Current clone detection techniques mostly analyze the program execution, including control flow and/ or data flow. They are mostly based on graph [3, 4], AST [1], token [5] and so on [6]. These techniques are not robust to code obfuscation [7]. In addition, some work focus on analyze binary code instead of source code [8]. Clone detection methods are mostly inefficient.

Birthmarks [9, 10], is an effective way to identify programs and prove ownership, which is a characteristic of an app for clone detection. However, static birthmark can be easily identified by attackers and removed. Researchers designed some methods [11], especially dynamic birthmarks [12], to protect the birthmarks. However, some kinds of the birthmark are overwhelming and easily changed, which make the cloned apps difficult to be detected. Our approach is a kind of dynamic birthmark. Different from previous birthmarks, our birthmark is not running statuses of program variables. In this way, attackers cannot change the birthmarks by obfuscating the exact variables that we use as birthmarks.

J. Tian et al. (Eds.): SecureComm 2014, Part II, LNICST 153, pp. 375–381, 2015.
DOI: 10.1007/978-3-319-23802-9_29

We designed a new kind of clone detection method based on CPU time usage. After giving each app several lists of inputs, we could get the CPU time usage tuple. Then we compare the tuples. If they are similar, the two apps may be clones at high possibility. At last, we do some experiments to verify it.

In sum, we made several contributions as follows.

- We use CPU time usage as a kind of dynamic birthmark on Android apps, which could be used to detect app clones on Android markets.
- We made several evaluations to verity the effectiveness of this timing-based birthmark. The results show that this kind of watermark is good to detect similar apps.

The rest paper is organized as follows. In Sect. 2, we introduce the motivation and overview of our system. Next, we will introduce our approach and implementation in detail. In Sect. 4, we give some evaluations. Then, we will discuss some problems further. The last section is our conclusion.

2   Motivation and Overview

2.1   Motivation

As we known, each application (app for short) has its own functionalities. Different apps have different functionalities. Different functionalities will use different numbers of CPU circles with high possibilities. CPU circles are represented as CPU time usages. Thus, we could use the CPU time usage to stand for an app and compare different apps.

With this idea, we made two experiments. We feed the same inputs to two cloned apps (Fig. 1) and two different apps (Fig. 2). The results are:

(1)   For the cloned apps, the CPU time usages are almost the same if the inputs are the same (Fig. 1).
(2)   For different apps, the CPU time usages are different with high possibility (Fig. 2).

For cloned apps, attackers would not like to change the original functionalities much. They want the cloned to run as stable as possible for long-term revenue. For example, based on previous work [13, 14], attackers only replace some variable names or change the order of statements. So the cloned apps have almost the same functionalities as the original one. That is to say the cloned apps may have almost the same CPU time usage if the inputs are same. Then we want to use CPU status to do our clone detection.

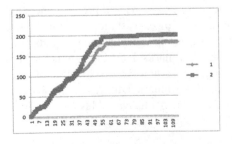

Fig. 1.   The same app using the same inputs

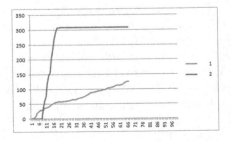

Fig. 2.   Two apps using the same inputs

One problem in using CPU time usage is that different apps (especially the apps with simple functionalities) may have very similar CPU time usage when feed with the same inputs. To solve this problem, we do not use a single list of inputs. Instead, we use several lists of inputs. Each list includes several inputs. We have the following overview in design.

2.2 Overview

We design a system that is based on CPU time to do clone detection. It consists of three main steps as Fig. 3.

- Step 1: For app A:
  First, we use one list of inputs, like Inputs 1, and get the CPU time usage CPU1. In order to monitor the changes, we choose appropriate time interval and record the status of CPU time usage. Then, we choose the appropriate part to analyze. We express it as a vector CPU1 = <c1, c2, ..., cn> , the element "ci" ($1 \leq i \leq n$) is the status of the i-th CPU time usage status.
  Second, we use several other lists of inputs, like Inputs 2...Inputs n, to get the corresponding CPU time usage. As above, we choose the appropriate parts of CPU status for each lists of inputs, which avoid unchangeable CPU status, and express them as a tuple UC = <CPU1, CPU2, ..., CPU n>.
- Step 2: For app B or other apps:
  For each app to be analyzed, we do the same thing as those in "For app A". Note that the lists of inputs should be the same as "For app A", and the initial state of the apps should be the same for each testing.
- Step 3: Compare the lists for the two apps.
  After getting the CPU time usage of several apps, we just compare the UC tuples to do clone detection. We mainly do similarity comparison between two UC tuples. By designing a judge algorithm, we get the distance, and then use a threshold to judge whether two apps are cloned or not.

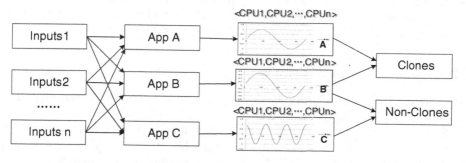

Fig. 3. The overview of our approach

We will talk about these steps in detail in the next section.

3   Our Approach and Implementation

Based on the overview, we give our detailed design and implementation.

3.1   Get the CPU Time Usage

In order to get the correct CPU usage, we have to make sure some pre-conditions as follows are satisfied.

- We need to keep the initial running status as the same for each run. For example, after doing some operations in a testing app, the status of the app is different from the status when the app starts. To make sure the initial statuses are the same, we shut down the app, and open it again. Otherwise, the CPU time usage may be impacted.
- We have to generate the same lists of inputs. Moreover, the inputs should better trigger some complex operations with various types. To generate such inputs, we use the Monkey [15], which is a tool for testing. By emulating a normal user, it generates different kinds of events such as clicks and swipes. In addition, if the seed to the Monkey is the same, the generated inputs are also the same.
- We need to choose the appropriate time interval. With regard to the CPU time usage, if the time interval is long, it may lose some details about CPU changes. If it is short, we have to compare a lot of useless data. To meet this condition, we try to generate different numbers of inputs for each app. For example, the long inputs will trigger more events and make the time interval longer. So we could have different lengths of time intervals.

After we meet the conditions, we could get the CPU time usage. To get the usage, we do not want to insert any code into the apps. If we do so, attackers could find the code and remove all the code, which will effectively undermine our approach. This will also further expose our birthmark.

So we want to get the CPU usage without changing the original apps. As we know, in Linux system, each process has a status file in the system. That is the "/proc/[pid]/stat". In the status, there is a number which indicates the usage of CPU. The number changes when the CPU usage is changed. To read the stat file, we first need to get the pid of the target app. Then we read the stat file every 100 ms.

3.2   How to Compare Different Lists

After getting the CPU time usage tuples, we design an algorithm to compare them. The result shows their similarity.

Suppose there are two apps App1 and App2. Using the same lists of inputs, we get the CPU time usage (i.e., birthmark) $UC1 = <CPU1, CPU2, ..., CPUn>$ for App1 and $UC2 = <CPU1', CPU2', ..., CPUn'>$. We define the distance between the two apps using following equations.

$$Distance = (\sum_i (|CPUi - CPUi'|) / (CPUi + CPUi'))/n.$$

After observing the CPU time usage of apps, we find that it increased with time. So we use the CPU time usage after a list of inputs is fully executed by an app. We use a threshold to judge whether two apps are similar or not.

4   Evaluation

We do some experiments about clone detection. We first use two cloned apps ("com.gamelin.gjump" and "com.ladty.gjump") to test. The result is as Fig. 4. We can see that the results of CPU time usage of cloned apps are almost the same. And the Distance = ((|40−41|)/(40 + 41) + (|19−09|)/(19 + 20) + (|33−31|)/(33 + 31) + (| 18−18|)/(18 + 18) + (|25−24|)/(25 + 24))/5 = 0.018.

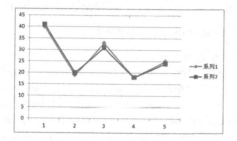

Fig. 4. The CPU time usage of two Cloned apps

Then we do experiments on two apps (com.android.calculator2 and com.android.browser). The result is as Fig. 5. We find that the distance is as follows:

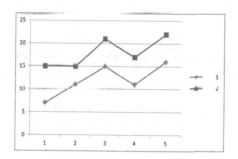

Fig. 5. The CPU time usage of two apps not cloned

Distance = ((|7−15|)/(7 + 15) + (|11−15|)/(11 + 15) + (|11−17|)/(11 + 17) + (| 16−22|)/(16 + 22) + (|15−21|)/(15 + 21))/5 = 0.211. So we can choose the threshold as 0.1 and find the cloned ones. In future, we will do more experiments and get a proper threshold.

5 Discussion

(1) How to remove the impact of Internet?

In android applications, some operations may be closed related with Internet, which may change the CPU time. For example, users have to submit some personal information when register most of applications. In addition, some apps inclusion of ads may also use Internet without notice. But the speed of Internet is impacted by several factors, like Internet speed, operation performance and so on. And our testing result may change a lot in different places.

In order to remove the impact of Internet, we try to choose some inputs, which can avoid operations using Internet. Moreover, we can add some codes to bypass or block internet connections when testing. We will do it in the future.

(2) How to avoid the impact of obfuscation?

Attackers often use some obfuscation methods to avoid similarity detection. They can add some useless code, change the execution sequence and so on. These modifications all impact the CPU time usage, which is the basis in our method.

In order to avoid the impact of obfuscation, our inputs lists should cover most of the functions, and avoid repetition. So if some parts are changed, the overall result will be influence little. In addition, if the attackers modify most parts of the apps, the tuple will change a lot. For example, supposing the original vector is CPU = $<c1,c2,...,cn>$, if attackers add some junk code everywhere in the app, the vector will be CPU' = $v * CPU$. That means it increase every element of CPU in a linear way. And we will pay more effort on this issue in future.

6 Conclusion

In this paper, we design a timing-based clone detection method. First, we have to choose some suitable lists of inputs. Secondly, by using these inputs, we get the corresponding CPU time usage as a tuple. Then, we compare tuples from different apps using the same lists of inputs. From the comparative result, we can find out the cloned apps. Finally, we do some experiments, and the results show the effectiveness of our method.

Acknowlegements. The authors would like to thank the anonymous reviewers for their constructive feedback. This material is based upon work supported in part by the National Natural Science Foundation of China under grant no. 61100226 and 61303248, the National High Technology Research and Development Program (863 Program) of China under grant no. SQ2013GX02D01211, and the Natural Science Foundation of Beijing under grant no. 4122085 and 4144089.

References

1. Gibler, C., Stevens, R., Crussell, J., Chen, H., Zang, H., Choi, H.: Adrob: examining the landscape and impact of android application plagiarism. In: Proceedings of 11th International Conference on Mobile Systems, Applications and Services (2013)
2. Baxter, I., Yahin, A., Moura, L., Anna, M., Bier, L.: Clone Detection using abstract syntax trees. In: Proceedings of International conference on Software Maintenance (1998)
3. Pham, N.H., Nguyen, H.A., Nguyen, T.T.: Complete and accurate clone detection in graph-based methods. In: Proceedings of the 31st International Conference on Software Engineering, pp. 276–286 (2009)
4. Krinke, J.: Identifying similar code with program dependence graphs. In: Proceedings of Eighth Working Conference on Reverse Engineering (2001)
5. Kamiya, T., Kusumoto, S., Inoue, K.: CCFinder: a multilinguistic token-based code clone detection system for large scale source code. IEEE Trans. Software Eng. 28(7), 654–670 (2002)
6. Chen, K., Liu, P., Zhang, Y.: Achieving accuracy and scalability simultaneously in detecting application clones on android markets. In: ICSE (2014)
7. Wang, X., Jhi, Y., Zhu, S., Liu, P.: Behavior based software theft detection. In: CCS (2009)
8. Sæbjørnsen, A., Willcock, J., Panas, T.: Detecting code clones in binary executables. In: ISSTA (2009)
9. Schuler, D., Dallmeier, V., Lindig, C.: A dynamic birthmark for java. In: Proceedings of the Twenty-Second IEEE/ACM International Conference on Automated Software Engineering, pp. 274–283 (2009)
10. Wang, X., Jhi, Y.C., Zhu, S., Liu, P.: Detecting software theft via system call based birthmarks. In: ACSAC, pp. 149–158 (2009)
11. Choi, S., Park, H., Lim, H., Han, T.: A static birthmark of binary executables based on API call structure. In: ASIAN, pp. 2–16 (2007)
12. Chan, P.P.F., Hui, L.C.K., Yiu, S.M.: JSBiRTH: dynamic JavaScript birthmark based on the run-time heap. In: IEEE 35th Annual Computer Software and Applications Conference (COMPSAC), pp. 407–412 (2011)
13. Crussell, J., Gibler, C., Chen, H.: Attack of the clones: detecting cloned applications on android markets. In: Foresti, S., Yung, M., Martinelli, F. (eds.) ESORICS 2012. LNCS, vol. 7459, pp. 37–54. Springer, Heidelberg (2012)
14. Zhou, W., Zhou, Y., Jiang, X., Ning, P.: Detecting repackaged smartphone applications in third-party android marketplaces. In: CODASPY, pp. 317–326. ACM (2012)
15. Nyman, N.: Using monkey test tools. Softw. Test. Qual. Eng. (2000)

A New Trust Chain Security Evaluation Model and Tool

Wei Hu, Dongyao Ji$^{(\boxtimes)}$, Ting Wang, and Gang Yao

State Key Laboratory of Information Security, Institute of Information Engineering,
Chinese Academy of Sciences, Beijing, China
jidongyao@is.ac.cn

Abstract. We've build a model of trust chain, and developed TCSE, a tool for estimating the security properties of the trust chain. The highlight of TCSE is that it can generate a probabilistic finite state automaton and verify or calculate four security properties of a trust chain following our algorithms. These properties are: credibility, usability, restorability and conformity. With these four values of a trust chain, we can estimate the security of a trusted computer (a computer with a trusted computing module). Using this tool, an ordinary user with the help of the Common Vulnerability Scoring System (CVSS) from which one can easily get the needed parameters can figure out these four properties quickly. This tool can be used in the area where the security of trusted computers are needed to be precisely quantized.

Keywords: Trusted computing · Trust chain · Model checking · Probabilistic finite state automaton · Probabilistic computation tree logic

1 Introduction

Trusted computing is a trend of information security technology and it has been used on a large scale at present. One key aspect of trusted platform is its ability to record the trust relationship among components that make-up the trusted platform. Trust is the expectation that a device will behave in a particular manner for a specific purpose. When one trusted component measures the trustworthiness of a second component, trust is transferred transitively from the first component to the second. That's the principle of the trust chain and an example is showed in Fig. 1. The implementation of the trust chain is up to its vendors, so it's possible that the implementation of it doesn't conform to its specifications and may lead to some security problems. The key technology of trust chain testing is the conformance testing. Xu [1] focused on the behavior characters of specifications of trust chain, and proposed a conformance testing framework for it based on labeled transition system. Fu [2] built a formal model of trust chain specifications based on finite state machines and analyzed the test sequence generation procedure with unique input/output sequence. Zhan [3] gave a conformance testing model of TPM based on state machine model. But there is no model that based

© Institute for Computer Sciences, Social Informatics and Telecommunications Engineering 2015
J. Tian et al. (Eds.): SecureComm 2014, Part II, LNICST 153, pp. 382–391, 2015.
DOI: 10.1007/978-3-319-23802-9_30

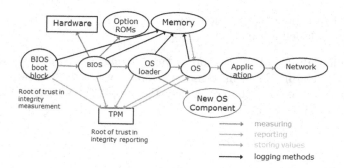

Fig. 1. Example of trust chain emanating from the trust root

on probabilistic finite state automaton to describe trust chain, and there is no tool that can calculate the values of the security properties of the trust chain.

We build a model of a trust chain with PFSA (probabilistic finite state automaton) and give four security properties in the form of PCTL (probabilistic computation tree logic), and present TCSE, a tool for estimating the trust chains on trusted computers. We analyse four characteristics of the trust chain: credibility, usability, restorability, conformity and invoke PRISM [4] (Probabilistic Symbolic Model Checker) to calculate the values of them. The reason why we choose these four properties to be verified and calculated is that they play the most important roles in the security of the trust chain. This paper describes the complete tool features and the implementation details of TCSE developed by us.

2   Formal Model of Trust Chain

2.1   Probabilistic Finite State Automaton

Markov chains [5] is a kind of probabilistic finite state automaton, it behaves as transition systems with the only difference that nondeterministic choices among successor states are replaced by probabilistic ones. That is to say, the successor state of state s, say, is chosen according to a probability distribution. This probability distribution only depends on the current state s, and not on, e.g., the path fragment that led to state s from some initial state. Accordingly, the system evolution does not depend on the history (i.e., the path fragment that has been executed so far), but only on the current state s. This is known as the memoryless property. A (discrete-time) Markov chain is a tuple $M = (S, P, l_{init}, AP, L)$ where:

- S is a countable, nonempty set of states,
- P: $S \times S \rightarrow [0, 1]$ is the transition probability function such that for all states
  s': $\sum_{s' \subset S} P(s, s') = 1$,
- l_{init}: $S \rightarrow [0,1]$ is the initial distribution, such that $\sum_{s \subset S} l_{init}(s) = 1$, and

– AP is a set of atomic propositions and
– L: $S \rightarrow 2^{AP}$ a labeling function.

Markov chains' ability of expression is very strong, so we use Markov chains to model trust chain, Fig. 2 is a markov model we built for the trust chain. Considering many aspects that can affect the properties we considered, we use variables to describe the probabilities.

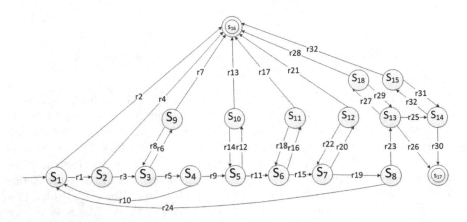

Fig. 2. The PFSM of a trust chain

In Fig. 2 showed above, there are 17 states in it. These states are described below. S_1:system boot, S_2:CRTM power-on self-test, S_3:BIOS measurement, S_4:BIOS user authentication, S_5:key component and configuration measured by BIOS, S_6:measurement of MBR and OS Loader, S_7:measurement of OS kernel and drivers and system files, S_8:OS user authentication, S_9:BIOS recovery, S_{10}:core component and configuration recovery, S_{11}:recovery of MBR and OSLoader, S_{12}:recovery of OS kernel and drivers, S_{13}:static integrity measurement of applications, S_{14}:dynamic integrity measurement of applications, S_{15}:dynamic recovery of applications, S_{16}:untrusted state, S_{17}:trusted state, S_{18}:static recovery of applications. We can get the state transition probabilities of the model from CVSS, since the semantics of these transitions are very clear. CVSS is is a vulnerability scoring system designed to provide an open and standardized method for rating IT vulnerabilities. With the help of it, we can achieve the values from r1 to r32. With these parameters, we can figure out some security property values.

2.2   Trust Chain Probabilistic Model Checking

CTL is an important branching temporal logic that is sufficiently expressive for the formulation of an important set of system properties. It was originally used by Clarke and Emerson and (in a slightly different form) by Queille and Sifakis

[6] for model checking. More importantly, it is a logic for which efficient and as we will see rather simple model-checking algorithms do exist. It has a two-stage syntax where formulae in CTL are classified into state and path formulae. The former are assertions about the atomic propositions in the states and their branching structure, while path formulae express temporal properties of paths. Compared to LTL formulae, path formulae in CTL are simpler: as in LTL they are built by the next-step and until operators, but they must not be combined with Boolean connectives and no nesting of temporal modalities is allowed.

Probabilistic computation tree logic (PCTL, for short) is a branching-time temporal logic, based on the logic CTL. A PCTL formula formulates conditions on a state of a Markov chain. The interpretation is Boolean, i.e., a state either satisfies or violates a PCTL formula. The logic PCTL is defined like CTL with one major difference. Instead of universal and existential path quantification, PCTL incorporates, besides the standard propositional logic operators, the probabilistic operator $P_J(\varphi)$ where φ is a path formula and J is an interval of $[0, 1]$. The path formula φ imposes a condition on the set of paths, whereas J indicates a lower bound and/or upper bound on the probability. The intuitive meaning of the formula $P_J(\varphi)$ in state s is: the probability for the set of paths satisfying φ and starting in s meets the bounds given by J. The probabilistic operator can be considered as the quantitative counterpart to the CTL path quantifiers $\exists$ and $\forall$. The CTL formulae $\exists\varphi$ and $\forall\varphi$ assert the existence of certain paths and the absence of paths where a certain condition does not hold respectively. They, however, do not impose any constraints on the likelihood of the paths that satisfy the condition ϕ. Later on in this section, the relationship between the operator $P_J(\varphi)$ and universal and existential path quantification is elaborated in detail.

PCTL state formulae over the setAP of atomic propositions are formed according to the following grammar:

$$\phi :: = true|a|\neg\phi|\phi_1 \wedge \phi_2|P_{\lhd p}(\varphi)$$

where a $\in$ AP, φ is a path formula and J $\subseteq$ $[0, 1]$ is an interval with rational bounds. PCTL path formulae are formed according to the following grammar:

$$\varphi :: = \bigcirc\phi|\phi_1 \bigcup \phi_2$$

Let a $\in$ AP be an atomic proposition, M=(S, P, l_{init}, AP, L) be a Markov chain, state s $\in$ S, Φ, Ψ be PCTL state formulae, and φ be a PCTL path formula. The satisfaction relation $\models$ is defined for state formulae by

$$
\begin{aligned}
s &\models a & &\text{iff } a \in L(s) \\
s &\models \neg\phi & &\text{iff } not(s \models \phi) \\
s &\models \phi \wedge \psi & &\text{iff } s \models \phi \text{ and } s \models \psi \\
s &\models P_{\lhd p}(\varphi) & &\text{iff } Prob(s \models \varphi) \lhd p
\end{aligned}
$$

With PCTL we can describe the four security properties. The formulas used below are based on: $Prob(s \models \varphi) = Pr\{\pi \in Paths(s)|\pi \models \varphi\}$, Paths(s) stands for paths which use state s as the initial state. We provide four formulas and use PRISM to calculate these security property values.

2.3   The Computational Formulas of the Four Security Properties

Credibility. In the calculation of credibility, we need to use cylinder set. Let $\pi' = s_0 \cdot s_1 \cdots \cdot s_n \in Paths_{fin}(M)$ the cylinder set of π' is defined as:

$$Cyl(\pi') = \{\pi \in Paths(M)|\pi' \in pref(\pi)\}$$

The cylinder set spanned by the finite path π' thus consists of all infinite paths that start with π'. the probabilities for the cylinder sets $Pr(Cyl(s_0 \cdot s_1 \cdots \cdot s_n)) = P(s_0 \cdot s_1 \cdots \cdot s_n)$, where $P(s_0 \cdot s_1 \cdots \cdot s_n) = \prod_{0 \leq i < n} P(s_i, s_{i+1})$.

According to Fig. 2 state s_{17} is the final trusted state. So the credibility of the trust chain can be described as $Pr(\diamond s_{17})$. The following formula is used to calculate credibility. We use $Pr(\diamond B)$ to stand for credibility of the trust chain and B stands for the final state that we expect the system to reach.

$$Pr(\diamond B) = \sum_{s_0 \cdots s_n \in Paths_{fin}(M) \cap (S \backslash B)^* B} Pr(Cyl(s_0 \cdots s_n))$$
$$= \sum_{s_0 \cdots s_n \in Paths_{fin}(M) \cap (S \backslash B)^* B} P(s_0 \cdots s_n)$$

In the formula above, we use $s_0...s_n$ to stand for paths in M (our trust chain model) and $s_0...s_{n-1} \notin B, s_n \in B$. So these paths can be expressed as:

$$Paths_{fin}(M) \cap (S \backslash B)^* B.$$

$Cyl(s_0...s_n)$ is the cylinder set [6] of finite path $s_0...s_n$. According to the definition of cylinder set, we have $Cyl(s_0...s_n) = \{\pi \in Paths(M)|s_0...s_{(n)} \in pref(\pi)\}$. According to this formula we can calculate the value of credibility.

Usability. Some kinds of attacks can make the trust chain lose its function. For example, in TOCTOU [8] (Time Of Check to Time Of Use) attack, an adversary can exploit the time difference between when software is measured and when it is actually used, to induce run-time vulnerabilities. We notice that the current TCG architecture only provides load-time guarantees. Integrity measurements are taken just before the software is loaded into memory, and it is assumed that the loaded in-memory software remains unchanged. However, this is not necessarily true. Another attack called the Cuckoo attack [9] happens when malware on the local machine may forward the user's messages to a remote TPM that the adversary physically controls. Thus, the user cannot safely trust the TPM's state, and hence can't trust the computer in front of him. Both of these attacks can make some measurements through the trust chain bypassed. Specific to these attacks, we build a new model that can take these situations into count. Then we can handle this probabilistic automation and figure out the usability.

Restorability. In the TCG specification, a trusted computer should provide a component to help it recover from bad states. For example, an OS Loader's backups can help it recover from damages. But in practice many manufacturers omit these components for the sake of cost reduction. So we figure out the final reliability differentials between the model in specification and the model of the user to gain the restorability value.

Conformity. In a complete trust chain, there are a lot of components to be measured, for example, CRTM, BIOS, OS Loader and so on. But some trusted computers may leave out some of these components and we don't know how much it influences our computers' security. So we use PPTL [10,11] (Propositional Projection Temporal Logic) to calculate this value. Let Prop be a countable set of atomic propositions. The formula P of PPTL is given by the following grammar:

$$P ::= p \mid \bigcirc P \mid \neg P \mid P_1 \bigvee P_2 \mid (P_1, ..., P_m)prjP$$

where $p \in$ Prop, $P_1,..., P_m$ and P are all well-formed PPTL formulas, $\bigcirc$(next) and prj (projection) are basic temporal operators. The abbreviations true, false, $\land$, $\rightarrow$ and $\leftrightarrow$ are defined as usual. In particular, true $\stackrel{def}{=}$ P$\lor\neg$P and false $\stackrel{def}{=}$ P$\land\neg$P for any formula P. Also we have the following derived formulas:

$$\varepsilon \stackrel{def}{=} \neg \bigcirc true \qquad\qquad more \stackrel{def}{=} \neg\varepsilon$$
$$\bigcirc^0 P \stackrel{def}{=} P \qquad\qquad \bigcirc^n P \stackrel{def}{=} \bigcirc(\bigcirc^{n-1}P)$$
$$len\, n \stackrel{def}{=} \bigcirc^n \varepsilon \qquad\qquad skip \stackrel{def}{=} len\, 1$$
$$\odot P \stackrel{def}{=} \varepsilon \lor \bigcirc P \qquad\qquad P; Q \stackrel{def}{=} (P, Q)prj\, \varepsilon$$
$$\diamond P \stackrel{def}{=} true; P \qquad\qquad \Box P \stackrel{def}{=} \neg\diamond\neg P$$
$$halt(P) \stackrel{def}{=} \Box(\varepsilon \leftrightarrow P) \qquad fin(P) \stackrel{def}{=} \Box(\epsilon \leftrightarrow P)$$
$$keep(P) \stackrel{def}{=} \Box(\neg\varepsilon \rightarrow P)$$

where $\odot$(weak next), $\Box$(always), $\diamond$(sometimes), and ;(chop) are derived temporal operators; ε(empty) denotes an interval with zero length, and $\bar\varepsilon$(more) means the current state is not the final one over an interval. Prj projection operation allows the characterization of different time granularity calculation process. To explain $(P_1, ..., P_m)$ prj Q, requires two different time granularity state sequence: one is executed $P_1, ..., P_m$ of the local sequence, and the other is the Q of the overall sequence of parallel execution. Visually speaking, Q and P_1, ..., P_m parallel execution on an interval and the interval Q state is only P_1, ..., P_m each interval the initial state and final state, as shown in Fig. 3, projection operation Allow Q, P_1, ..., P_m each independently, have the right to define its execution interval.

In order to figure out this value, we should first transform PPTL's properties into NF (Normal Form), and then make out the NFG (Normal Form Graph). If the NFG is an NFA (Nondeterministic Finite Automaton), we should transform

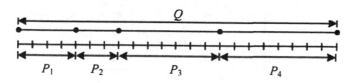

Fig. 3. Semantics of (P_1, P_2, P_3, P_4) prj Q

it into a DFA (Deterministic Finite Automaton). Then we can calculate the conformity with the inputs which should be the product of the model and its property which is the product of a Markov chain and a DFA..

The product of Markov chain and DFA is showed as follows:

Suppose $M = (S, P, s_0, AP, L)$ is a Markov chain, $A = (Q, 2^{AP}, \delta, q_0, F)$ is a DFA, so the product of M and A $M \otimes A$ is a Markov chain: $M \otimes A = (S \times Q, P', s_0', \{accept\}, L')$ and in it:

$$L'(\langle s,q \rangle) = \begin{cases} \{accept\}, if\ q \in F \\ \emptyset,\ else \end{cases}$$

$$s_0' = \begin{cases} \langle s_0,q \rangle, if\ q = \delta(q_0, L(s_0)) \\ 0,\ else \end{cases}$$

$$P'(\langle s,q \rangle, \langle s',q' \rangle) = \begin{cases} P\langle s,s' \rangle, if\ q' = \delta(q, L(s')) \\ 0,\ else \end{cases}$$

The path of $M \otimes A$: $\pi = < s_0, q_1 >< s_1, q_2 > \ldots$ is the combination between path of M: $s_0 s_1 \ldots$ and the path of A: $q_1 q_2 \ldots$ In order to calculate the probabilistic of the path in the Markov chain M that satisfy the property of Q, which is $Pr^M(s_0 \vDash Q)$, the property Q of PPTL should be changed into NF(Normal Form), then the NFG(Normal Form Graph) can be drawn. Since the NFG is not a NFA, so it should be changed into a DFA. In order to calculate $Pr^M(s_0 \vDash Q)$, we can get the product of M and A, which is $M \otimes A$. Then we can get the final formula as: $Pr^M(s_0 \vDash Q) = Pr^{M \otimes A}(s_0' \diamond accept)$

3   Main Features and Implementation of TCSE

Figure 4 illustrate the architecture and the components of TCSE, the core features of it will be described detailedly below.

The Graphical User Interface (GUI). The GUI of TCSE provides users with functions to calculate their trusted computers' security properties. Users can refer to the CVSS [7] to ascertain the values of the parameters which are shown on the interface of TCSE. The GUI is designed with VC++6.0, and we

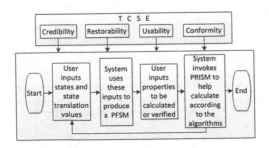

Fig. 4. The architecture of TCSE

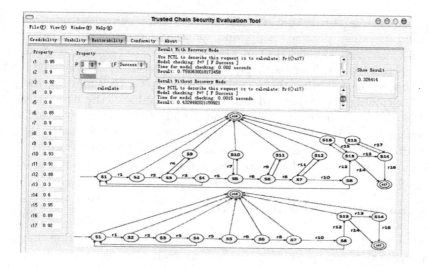

Fig. 5. The property of credibility

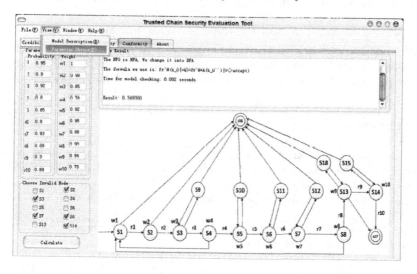

Fig. 6. The property of conformity

use a skin library to make the interface more artistic. We give a standard model of a trust chain provided in the TCG (Trusted Computing Group) specification with all sides considered. So users can compare their trust chains with this model and then get the parameters from the CVSS, these parameters are used to make up the PFSM (Probability Finite State Machines). After these parameters are given, users can verify or calculate any expressions in the form of PCTL.

Implementation of TCSE. We use four classes derived from class CPropertyPage in MFC (Microsoft Foundation Class) to deal with each property. Each property page (is also a kind of dialog box in MFC) provides interface with users and users can get the results and some detailed calculation information from the interface. The system can also produce state translation graphs and some explanations to describe them, so that users can understand the models established by us following the specifications of TCG. By supplying the parameters (including the states and state transition values), the new trust chain model is then established and that's the model of the user's own computer's trust chain. Our calculation and analysis are based on the new model. We make use of PRISM to make our algorithms and realization simple. An overview of the standard perspective of the tool can be seen in Figs. 5 and 6 as follows.

4   Conclusion and Future Work

The security of trust chain is very important in trusted computing, but there are no tools that can quantify it. Formal methods of modeling the trust chain and verifying its security properties have been put forward by many scholars, but these methods are hard to put into practice. We develop this tool to help users to figure out some security parameters, so as to get a clear understanding of the security situation of their trusted computers. For future work, we plan to integrate our recent work on trust chain security properties measurement, and composite our results to evaluate the security of trust chain, and we are also interested in extending our trust chain model to expand its applicability.

References

1. Xu, M., Zhang, H., Yan, F.: Testing on trust chain of trusted coputing platform based on labeled transition system. Chin. J. Comput. **32**(4), 635–645 (2009)
2. Fu, L., Wang, D., Kuang, J.: Conformance testing for trust chain of trusted computing platform based on finite state machine. J. Comput. Inf. Syst. **7**(8), 2717–2724 (2011)
3. Zhan, J., Zhang, H.: Automated testing of the trusted platform module. J. Comput. Res. Dev. **46**(11), 1839–1846 (2009)
4. Kwiatkowska, M., Norman, G., Parker, D.: PRISM: probabilistic symbolic model checker. In: Field, T., Harrison, P.G., Bradley, J., Harder, U. (eds.) TOOLS 2002. LNCS, vol. 2324, pp. 200–204. Springer, Heidelberg (2002)
5. Ching, W.-K., Huang, X., Ng, M.K., Siu, Tk: Markov Chains: Models, Algorithms and Applications, vol. 189. Springer, Heidelberg (2013)
6. Christel, B., Joost, P.K.: Principles of Model Checking, pp. 757–765. The MIT Press, Cambridge (2008)
7. CVSS. http://www.first.org/cvss
8. Bratus, S., D'Cunha, N., Sparks, E., Smith, S.W.: TOCTOU, traps, and trusted computing. In: Lipp, P., Sadeghi, A.-R., Koch, K.-M. (eds.) Trust 2008. LNCS, vol. 4968, pp. 14–32. Springer, Heidelberg (2008)
9. Bryan, J.P.: Trust extension as a mechanism for secure code execution on commodity computers. Ph.D.thesis, School of Electrical and Computer Engineering Carnegie Mellon University, April 2010

10. Zhen, H.D., Cong, T., Li, Z.: A decision procedure for propositional projection temporal logic with infinite models. Acta Informatica **45**(1), 43–78 (2008)
11. Tian, C., Duan, Z.: Model checking propositional projection temporal logic based on SPIN. In: Butler, M., Hinchey, M.G., Larrondo-Petrie, M.M. (eds.) ICFEM 2007. LNCS, vol. 4789, pp. 246–265. Springer, Heidelberg (2007)

A System for Privacy Information Analysis and Safety Assessment of iOS Applications

Bin Li[1,2(✉)] and Zhijie Feng[1,2]

[1] Data Assurance and Communication Security Research Center,
Beijing, China
libin@iie.ac.cn
[2] State Key Laboratory of Information Security,
Institute of Information Engineering, CAS,
Beijing, China

Abstract. As the intelligent mobile phone stores more and more users' privacy information, the privacy information security in mobile terminal has become more and more important to mobile users. So how to protect the sensitive information of mobile phone users has become the focus of research in recent years. This paper analyzed the security mechanism of iOS platform and security status and development of iOS Apps, and then proposed a scheme–iOS software sensitive information analysis and security assessment system, for detection of iOS analysis software of leaking sensitive information. The system is used to detect whether APPs in iOS platform is revealing user privacy data, and make evaluation of safety grade according to the severity of privacy disclosure of APPs. We give an evaluation algorithm about security level for evaluating the severity of APPs. This system is the overall solution of the iOS application software acquisition, privacy leak detection and security assessment.

Keywords: iOS · Privacy leak · Dynamic analysis · Security level

1 Introduction

With the popularization of mobile intelligent devices, and continues to increase of hardware performance, the intelligent mobile terminal are increasingly used to deal with all kinds of important data. While currently the most intelligent terminal operating system are focus on iOS and Android. With the popularity of iPhone mobile phone and iPhone "legalization of jail break" means, iPhone mobile phone security issues are also increasingly prominent. A recent research report said that 96 % of iOS apps have the ability to access sensitive information (contact information, calendar details, or location) from the device [1]. And many of them have privacy leaking or other security problems. In order to ensure safety of user information, iOS designed its own set of security mechanism:

Trust Boot. The system boots from the boot program, loading the firmware, and the firmware starts the system. The firmware via the RSA signature, only through the verification can get to the next step, and then to the firmware verification. In this way, the system establishes a trust chain at the root of bootstrap program.

© Institute for Computer Sciences, Social Informatics and Telecommunications Engineering 2015
J. Tian et al. (Eds.): SecureComm 2014, Part II, LNICST 153, pp. 392–398, 2015.
DOI: 10.1007/978-3-319-23802-9_31

Program Signature. The file format of iOS APPs is Mach-O format file [2]. This file format supports encryption and signature, and the directory structure is stored in memory through the SHA-1 hash. Both directory and software must be digitally signed.

SandBox. The application sandboxing has been defined by Apple as a set of fine-grained control that limits the application access to the file system, network and hardware [3]. Apple uses SandBox to isolate applications and limit the access of each process to the file system. Each application has its own memory space, and IOS applications can only read the file which is created for the program while other applications cannot access. Thus, all the application requests must be through the authority detection.

Address space layout randomization (ASLR) is one of the security protection technology and ASLR makes address predicting more difficult by randomizing the location of objects in memory. In iOS, the location of the binary, libraries, dynamic linker, stack, and heap memory addresses are all randomized [4].

Key chain and data protection. Password, certificate, keys are stored in Sqlite database, and data is encrypted in the database which has the strict access control.

While the mobile operating system need to protect information such as the mobile phone number, mail list, SMS, account passwords and other private information, so it's needed to be more careful in guarding privacy protection. However, Apple Corp does not pay much attention on the privacy protection. Although the Apple will ask users if they agree APPs to access their mail list, tracking the location information, and even the use of camera in iOS6 and future version [5], the user privacy security is likely to remain unresolved. Because you cannot determine whether these data acquired by APPs is stored encrypted or transmission. In the application software, the Apple Corp mainly relies on their own software review mechanism to guarantee the security of iOS software, and the application can be published to the App Store only by approval, so strict inspection prevents malicious programs to the system. However, millions of jail-break mobile phone users download APPs not only from App Store, but also from non-official app stores that almost never do any strict and meticulous examination of their applications. Even some companies steal user privacy information for their personal intention. Thus, privacy leak has become a universal phenomenon in mobile applications, a serious threat to the security of user data. Therefore, we need to design a set of detection system of sensitive information for iOS platform, automatic detect on the application of APPs in the market stores, determine the privacy problems of each APPs, in order to ensure the security of user information.

2   Privacy Information Analysis and Safety Evaluation System

In this paper we design and implement a system that makes a set of automatic detection to apps for sensitive/privacy information on the iOS platform. The system can provide awareness of potential user privacy leaks, such as contact information, phone numbers, text message, user account, password, etc. and prompted user the potential risk of software. And then we store and analyze the results, define the security level according to a specific algorithm of software security ranking for each app. The system is mainly divided into three parts: app acquisition platform, app analysis platform and information management platform.

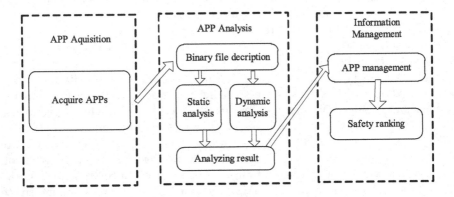

Fig. 1. System composition

As is shown in Fig. 1, app acquisition platform is responsible for collecting apps from the app store and store markets. The apps analysis platform is mainly for app decryption and analysis. Because all the apps that stored in app store have been certified with signature authentication and their code section are encrypted. So we need binary decryption of apps before analysis. App analysis includes dynamic and static analysis. The system checks all the APIs that may result in user privacy leak, and transfer analyzing results to the information management platform. Information management platform store security information of the apps, and calculate safety score by privacy scoring algorithm.

2.1 Binary File Decryption

Since the code segment of the apps have been encrypted by Apple, we cannot view the assembly code and call stack through the disassembly tool directly. We need to make decryption operations to apps. The executable file of iOS apps are Mach-O file, which copyrighted content with DRM [6], so the key is to decrypt the encrypted part of Mach-O file. When the program runs in the mobile phone, program is in decrypted state in memory. We must determine the position where the encryption code section locates in memory. We can use otool to see the FAT of the binary file. We need three parameters: cryptid, cryptoffset, cryptsize. cryptid is encryption state, 0 represents no encryption, 1 represents encrypted; cryptoffset represents offset of encrypting section; cryptsize means size of encrypting section in bytes. After located encrypted code section, we export it through gdb tools, and replace the code section. Finally, we finish the decryption by recomposing the binary.

2.2   Static Analysis

After we decrypted the binary file of the app, we step into static analysis. Static analysis subsystem first disassembled the decrypted app, to get the APIs and selector references of the app, and by comparing the APIs in the app and in "local privacy API repository" (we need to create it in advance), the subsystem tells that whether the app binary contains privacy APIs. And we can make a conclusion that one app is safety if it does not contains any privacy APIs. The flow of static analysis is as the following chart.

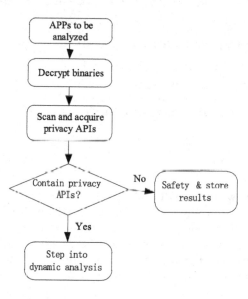

Fig. 2. Static analysis

2.3   Dynamic Analysis

In the dynamic analysis, we mainly use the behavior analyzing technique. We analyze the apps' behavior in the running process including when and how to evoke these privacy APIs. Dynamic analysis system detects APPs running on iOS devices and tracks the program running behavior real-time. It implements the real-time tracking of privacy APIs using MobileSubstrate/CydiaSubstrate framework. Cydia Substrate (formerly called MobileSubstrate) is the de facto framework that allows 3rd-party developers to provide run-time patches to system functions [7]. We can write hook function within the framework, and we add tracking detection in the hook function by implementing MSHookMessageEx/MSHookFunction. MSHookMessage() will replace the implementation of the Objective-C message -[class selector] by replacement, and return the original implementation, while MSHookFunction()is like MSHookMessage() but is for C/C++ functions. When these hook functions are added into Dynamic libraries of iOS devices, the framework will invoke the Dynamic libraries automatically to implement the tracking procedure. The hook function is implemented by Mobile-Loader in MobileSubstrate framework. MobileLoader loads 3rd-party patching code into the running application [7]. An example will show the following substitution:

```
static CFArrayRef (*original_ABAddressBookCopyArrayOfAllPeople) (ABAddressBookRef addressBook);
CFArrayRef replaced_ABAddressBookCopyArrayOfAllPeople (ABAddressBookRef addressBook)
{
    printf("function: ABAddressBookCopyArrayOfAllPeople called!!\n");
    original_ABAddressBookCopyArrayOfAllPeople (addressBook);

}
MSHookFunction (ABAddressBookCopyArrayOfAllPeople,
            replaced_ABAddressBookCopyArrayOfAllPeople,
            &original_ABAddressBookCopyArrayOfAllPeople);
```

Fig. 3. API subtitution

In above example we track API of AddressBook achieving. When the app has invoked this API while running in the iphone, the API will be recorded. Thus, we need to build a repository for storing all possible privacy APIs and networking interfaces, and tag them in hook function; the MobileSubstrate framework to replace the memory code, the privacy information of the API will be recorded into a file for further analysis.

2.4 Security Level Scoring Algorithm

We use the Security level scoring algorithm for computing the security level of target apps. According to importance of privacy information in mobile phone we define the corresponding values for each privacy API. When the application leaks privacy data, the corresponding values will be recorded. Finally, we add up all the values and get a total score. We judge the security level according to the total score. We define the Security level scoring algorithm:

$$\sum_{i=0}^{n=item.length} score = factor1 * weight1 + factor2 * weight2 + ... \qquad (1)$$

$$+ factorn * weightn + ScoreInternet$$

ScoreInternet means the app invokes the Internet interface to exchange data. At this point, we need to analyze the content of data packets. We think that one operation is risk when the data packets contains call records, contact records, phone number and other sensitive/privacy information. Calculating scores of this part as follows:

$$ScoreInternet = (10 + factori + factorj) * Maxi, j(weight) \qquad (2)$$

If the app does not send any data through network, the ScoreInternet = 0. The following table lists the contents of sensitive information and the corresponding score:

Sensitive information	Value	Weight	Remarks
phoneRecord	15	3	Call records
Contactbook	15	4	Contact book
smsRecord	20	4	SMS
Location	5	2	Location information
IMEI	5	2	Mobile phone device code
Calendar	5	1	Calendar
IMSI	5	2	International mobile station identity
Phone number	10	3	Phone number
Takepicure	15	2	Photographs
Mediarecord	15	1	Media data
Internet	$15 + x$	$max(y_i, y_j, \ldots, y_k)$	x: score that sensitive information represents; y: maximum weight in all kinds of sensitive information

We set the scoring range of apps:

$$1 \quad safe: \quad 0 < score <= 25 \qquad (3)$$

$$2 \quad low\ risk: 25 < score <= 80 \qquad (4)$$

$$3 \quad medium\ risk: 80 < score <= 125 \qquad (5)$$

$$4 \quad high\ risk: score > 125 \qquad (6)$$

For example, App A obtained the location position, the phone numbers of user, and also invoked network interface:

NSURL Connection::send Synchronous Request:returning Response, and data packets contains location and phone number, so the score of A is:

$$\sum_{i=1}^{n=3} score = factor1 * weight1 + factor2 * weight2 + \ldots \qquad (7)$$

$$+ factorn * weightn + ScoreInternet$$
$$= 5 * 2 + 10 * 3 + (5 + 5 + 10) * 3$$
$$= 100$$

Thus, the security level of A is medium risk.

References

1. Al-Hadadi, M., Al Shidhani, A.: Smartphone security awareness: Time to act. In: Current Trends in Information Technology (CTIT) (2013)
2. http://www.rdacorp.com/2012/08/mobile-application-developmentsecurity/
3. Li, Q., Clark, G.: Mobile security: A look ahead, security & privacy. IEEE **11**(1), 78–81 (2013)
4. Ahmad, N., Musa, M.S.: Comparison between android and ios operating system in terms of security
5. Charlie, M., Dion, B., Stefan, E., Vincenzo, I., Ralf-Philip, W.: iOS Hacker's Handbook
6. http://www.apple.com/iphone/
7. saurik: http://iphonedevwiki.net/index.php/mobilesubstrate

How We Found These Vulnerabilities
in Android Applications

Bin Ma[✉]

State Key Laboratory of Information Security, Institute of Information Engineering,
Chinese Academy of Sciences, Beijing, People's Republic of China
mabin@iie.ac.cn

Abstract. With the rapid growth of application markets, many developers now spend their time and money to develop new smartphone applications, bringing ever more intelligent applications to smartphone users. However, the rapid development process of applications without full testing made them neglect the security of the applications. In this paper, I took UC Browser and Mobile QQ as examples to show some vulnerabilities.

Keywords: Vulnerabilities · UC browser · Mobile QQ · Smartphone security

1 Introduction

The technology of mobile phones has developed dramatically over the last decade. Many developers now spend their time and money to invent new smartphone applications, bringing ever more intelligent applications (apps for short) to smartphone users. People can finish most of the demands for daily through these diversiform apps such as reading, chatting, consuming, etc. Apps on mobile platform have brought great convenience to ordinary people and improved their standard of living [1].

To grab chances in these fast growing smartphone application markets, most of the developers usually promote their products online when finishing the basic function demand, while ignoring the potential security problem existed in their apps. These security issues are usually caused by some logic problems or check mechanisms, which can't be protected by the operating system. Once these vulnerabilities are exploited by hackers, the app may be under great threat, the accounts or information of users may be in danger.

In this paper, we seek to show the risk of these vulnerabilities in some common apps on Android platform. Section 2 describes a high risk information leakage problem existed in UC Browser, which looks like a Google Hacking [2] problem but appears on mobile platform. Section 3 shows a high risk logic flaw existed in Mobile QQ, which can be exploited to spread malicious information in the QQ group. In addition, we revealed the process of finding these vulnerabilities and demonstrated the seriousness of them. After reporting them to the corresponding company, the level of vulnerability is evaluated as high risk, and we also received a big reward for the report.

© Institute for Computer Sciences, Social Informatics and Telecommunications Engineering 2015
J. Tian et al. (Eds.): SecureComm 2014, Part II, LNICST 153, pp. 399–406, 2015.
DOI: 10.1007/978-3-319-23802-9_32

2   Information Leakage in UC Browser

2.1   Background

UC Browser [3] is a leading mobile internet browser with more than 500 million users across more than 150 countries and regions, which derives from benefit of its large user base in China (34.83 %) and their rapidly growing Indian market. The majority of smartphone users access the web through UC Browser, which means that once the vulnerability occurred, the influence is enormous.

The vulnerability existed in the search engine of UC called Shenma (sm.cn), which is developed by UCWeb Inc and Alibaba Inc in July 2013 [4]. Shortly after the release, we found the vulnerability and reported it to UCWeb Inc.

Mobile search is an evolving branch of information retrieval services that is centered on the convergence of mobile platforms and mobile phones. With the rapid development of mobile internet, a search engine for mobile platform is urgent for the great demand of smartphone users. Web search engine ability in a mobile form allows users to find mobile contents on websites which are available to mobile devices on mobile networks [5].

Web search engines use Web crawling or spider software to update their web content or indexes of others sites' web content [6]. Web crawlers can copy all the pages they visit for later processing by a search engine that indexes the downloaded pages so that users can search them much more quickly.

However, the crawler on mobile platform is very sensitive. Because the input method through mobile is difficult for its limited screen and small keyboard, programmers adopt some easy methods to remember the users' login data, such as a unique string called SID (Security Identifiers) which is invisible to users and attached in the link of the login page. When users open the links, the remote server will make a check automatically to finish a login process. But once these links are grabbed by the mobile search engine especially for a new mobile search engine without any filtration mechanism, users' accounts will be in great danger.

As we know, Google hacking is a computer hacking technique that uses Google Search and other Google applications to find security holes in the configuration and computer code that websites use [7]. While that can happen on mobile platform with mobile search engine. The following shows the risk of a new search engine.

2.2   A Description of Finding the Vulnerability

UC Browser takes Shenma as its default search engine. The crawler of Shenma grabbed sensitive links (for example, private links to maintain the login-in state) and saved them and the corresponding contents in its database without any information filtering. For this, we only need to search some related keywords of the login page, the search engine will fetch the corresponding contents from its database, which means that anyone can get these sensitive links just by some simple search to enter a certain user's main page. In addition, the browser supports advanced search like "site:[website][keywords]", which reduces the difficulty of search and increases the risk of user's personal account.

Here we take Renren as an example, a Chinese social networking site which has been called the Facebook of China [8]. We entered a search string like "site:3g.renren.com [keywords]", ("3g.renren.com" is a website designed for the smartphone users of Renren, and the keywords are some symbolic words when users finish a login and back to the main page, using these keywords, we found many other information leakages problems in UC Browser) the search results were so amazing (Fig. 1 shows the results). We got plenty of entries to different Renren users' main pages. When clicking these results, we can enter the main pages of different users without any login process or password, we also got the permissions like a normal user, and we can update or delete the user data, send a message, upload or download a picture etc. In a word, we can operate a Renren account at will and without any password just like the actual user.

(a) The search results when seraching the keywords in UC Browser

(b) Entering the main page of different users when clicking the results

Fig. 1. Screenshots of the example of Renren.

After further studying, we found that the crawler of UC Browser grabbed the links with a SID (Security Identifier) which is a unique string to mark the user who has finished a login process. For example, when a Renren user finished a login process, a new SID will be generated (e.g., the SID is "CEKfLCa0n8obv_QmTVh7am"), which means that the user can enter his or her main page without inputting the password and only by accessing "3g.renren.com/home.do?&sid=CEKfLCa0n8obv_QmTVh7am" next time. Unfortunately, the links with SID was grabbed by Shenma and stored in its database. When searching some keywords, these entry web addresses with SID will be shown in the browser. For other mobile websites, they take a similar approach to keep users in the login-in state. According to this, hackers can control someone's account only by searching the corresponding SID.

2.3   Threats of This Kind of Vulnerability

This kind of information leakage may cause great damage. When we first find the vulnerability of Renren, we thought it may be the problem of Renren. After further researching, we located the problem of UC Browser, and a series of information leakage occurred except for Renren. Users who have this kind of information leakage are generally because they used UC Browser to finish a login process before, and their entry web addresses were captured by its search engine.

We found that most of the famous Chinese mobile websites like Tecent, Sina Weibo all have this problem. For example, we can search the keywords like "site:ish.z.qq.com [keywords in the main page of Qzone]" to find a great information leakage in Qzone. In a similar format, we can find the problem of Sina Weibo by search "Site:weibo.cn [keywords]". All of the search results can be exploited to control the corresponding accounts. Figure 2 shows the results.

We also researched the SID of several large mobile websites of China. (Figure 3). Based on the table, we can see that the SID is widely used in most mobile websites, once a smartphone user finished a login process through UC Browser, his SID may be grabbed

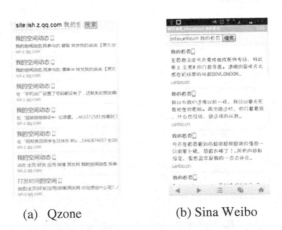

(a) Qzone   (b) Sina Weibo

Fig. 2. Information leakage of Qzone and Sina Weibo.

	Tencent Weibo	QQ Zone	Netease Weibo	Renren Mobile	Sina Weibo
Keep user logging in with SID	✓	✓	✕	✓	✓
Log in with old SID	✕	✓	✕	✓	✓
Dead time of SID	Session Time	Session Time	✕	30 days	30 days

Fig. 3. The SID of several large mobile websites of China.

by the crawler, and his entry web address of main page may be searched by others easily, his personal information may be exposed in public. That's really dangerous.

2.4 Bug Reporting and Fixing

After finding the vulnerability, we reported it to the UCWeb Inc and shared the details and our analyses with them. They realized the seriousness of the problem and deleted the sensitive links in a short time. And they gave us a rank of 20 about the vulnerability (the highest rank) and sent us a reward [9].

3 Logic Flaw in Mobile QQ

3.1 Background

For most online apps, there are some web interfaces for apps to communicate with the remote servers to update data. These interfaces are usually invisible to the app for the decompilation protection mechanism, and the remote server are generally designed for the specific app, which means we can't access the interfaces through a browser or other methods. Because of this, finding the vulnerabilities in apps becomes difficult.

Some people are trying to analyze the source code or decompilation code of Android apk file to mine vulnerabilities [10]. In theory, this mining techniques can find more bugs and have higher efficiency. But the method may not work sometime for the decompilation protection mechanism in apps. In addition, a decompilation of apk file may take a lot of effort to find a logic flaw.

In this section, we use an agent tool called Burp Suite [11] to capture the packets between app and remote server to get the interface. In this way, we can get the request or post data sent to the server, by changing the post parameters and replaying the packet, we can find some vulnerabilities easily, especially for some logic flaws. According to this, we can also achieve a common tool for automatic detection, which may have higher efficiency and lower cost.

3.2   A Description of Finding the Vulnerability

As mentioned above, we decide to capture the packets between app and remote server to find vulnerabilities. We use a tool called Burp Suite to act as an internet agent between the local app and remote server, which means that all the http packets between them will be captured by the agent. In addition, Burp Suite can modify the parameters of the packets and drop certain packets or replay certain packets. So we can find some vulnerabilities by this way.

There is a new functionality called QQ Notice in the mobile client of QQ, which means that users can add a reminder and edit the contents of reminder in a QQ group at a future moment. When the time is up, group users on mobile platform will receive a notice message, and group users of PC (personal computer for short) will receive a notice at the bottom right corner of the screen. Figure 4 shows the notice in mobile client and PC client.

(a) Mobile client   (b) PC Client

Fig. 4. The notice in Mobile client and PC client.

To check if there are any bugs, we captured the post data when creating a reminder. Figure 5a shows the packet and parameters. We can see that there is a parameter called "tu", which is short for "to user" and represents the QQ Group number we want to send a notice. We tried to modify the parameter to any other Group number, and replay the post packet, finally we received a 200 OK response.

To confirm the findings, we conducted a simple experiment. We registered two users named A and B, user A created a QQ group which only have one member namely A itself, user B replay a packet whose group number was modified to the group that user A created just like the way we mentioned above. Finally we received the notice sent from user B in user A's group, but B is not the member of the group. Figure 5b shows our results.

3.3   Threats of the Vulnerability

The vulnerability can be described as sending a notice to any QQ Group without becoming a member of the group. Because the content of the notice can be edit casually,

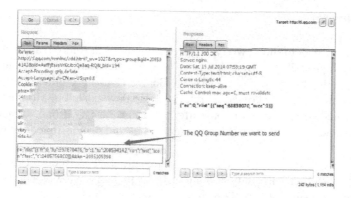

(a) The packet and parameters when creating a reminder

(b) There is only one member in the group, namely user A, but A received the
notice sent from B who are not in the group.

Fig. 5. Screenshots of our experiment.

hackers can exploit the bug to send any message to any QQ Group, such as advertisements, malicious links, illegal information etc. Thus a vulnerability of notice become a
huge bug of spreading all kinds of spam information.

For instance, we can use a crawler to get all of the existed QQ Group numbers and
names, and simulate a mobile login process on the computer, then we can send the notice
packet to specific QQ Group. In this way, hackers can carry out a precision message
sending.

3.4   Bug Reporting and Fixing

We reported the vulnerability to TSRC (Tencent Security Response Center) [12] and
shared the exploit methods with them. After a short while, they realized the seriousness
and froze the notice functionality. Three days later, they fixed the vulnerability and set
the risk level as 7 (The highest is 10) for the vulnerability [13]. To express their gratitude,
they gave us a reward which is worth more than 800 Yuan.

4   Conclusion

In this paper, we seek to show two types of vulnerabilities in Android applications, both of which are high-risk. We first described a high risk information leakage problem existed in UC Browser, which looks like a Google Hacking problem but appears on mobile platform. Then we showed a high risk logic flaw existed in Mobile QQ, which can be exploited to spread malicious information in the QQ group. In addition, we revealed the process of findings these vulnerabilities and demonstrated the seriousness of them.

In future, we will devote to finding an automatic method to detect these types of vulnerabilities, and we will study continuously for finding out the other vulnerabilities of generic apps on smartphone platform.

References

1. Young, J.R.: Top smartphone apps to improve teaching, research, and your life. Educ. Dig. Essent. Read. Condens. Quick Rev. **76**, 12–15 (2011)
2. Google hacking. http://en.wikipedia.org/wiki/Google_hacking
3. UC Browser. http://en.wikipedia.org/wiki/UC_Browser
4. Search engine of Shenma. http://baike.baidu.com/view/13036750.htm
5. Lagerspetz, E., Tarkoma, S.: Mobile search and the cloud: the benefits of offloading. In: 2011 IEEE International Conference on Pervasive Computing and Communications Workshops (PERCOM Workshops), pp. 117–122. IEEE (2011)
6. Olston, C., Najork, M.: Web crawling. Found. Trends Inf. Retrieval **4**, 175–246 (2010)
7. Billig, J., Danilchenko, Y., Frank, C.E.: Evaluation of google hacking. In: Proceedings of the 5th Annual Conference on Information Security Curriculum Development. ACM (2008)
8. Renren Inc. http://en.wikipedia.org/wiki/Renren
9. Report of vulnerability in UC Browser (2013). http://wooyun.org/bugs/wooyun-2014-060257
10. Zhang, W, Cao, C., Liu, W., et al.: Vulnerability mining techniques in android platform (2013)
11. Burp suite. http://en.wikipedia.org/wiki/Burp_suite
12. Tencent security response center. http://security.tencent.com/
13. Report of Mobile QQ (2014). http://security.tencent.com/index.php/report/detail/11857

Author Index

Printed in the United States
By Bookmasters